Contents

Preface

This book is intended primarily for students preparing for GCE Ordinary level History, or equivalent examinations. It may also be helpful as an introduction for students on more advanced courses and as a guide for any who wish to begin to know about the century in which they live. The present edition is a totally revised version of a book which first appeared some ten years ago. It now starts at the end of the First World War and covers the most important features of world history from then until the present day. Emphasis is given in this edition to contemporary source material such as photographs, posters, cartoons and documents. While it is hoped that most benefit will be achieved by a study of the entire book, it should also be possible for a teacher to direct students to the particular areas which are to be covered in the course that is being taught.

Each chapter is followed by three questions of the standard and style found at Ordinary level. One of these questions is based on visual or documentary material found in the chapter. Within questions of this type the various sub-questions are followed by a suggested mark allocation in brackets. Though all of the questions relate principally to the content of the chapter with which they are linked, material in other chapters will often be essential in the achievement of a good answer. In working on the questions, students should be prepared to use the index.

I am indebted to many people for their assistance in my work on this new edition. George Bartle, Head of the History department at the West London Institute of Higher Education, has throughout given the fullest encouragement and guidance. Sean Garrett, who read most of the final typescript, made characteristically thought-provoking and constructive comments which were of great help to me. Flavio Andreis, Anthony Barnes, David Cross, Richard Harrison, Dr Mark Glasswell, Marie-Louise Martell, Peter Prior, Ed Rayner, Ron Stapley, Gerard de Vries, and Brian York have all, in different ways and from different points of view, contributed helpful advice. These debts of gratitude having been paid, I hasten to add that the responsibility for what follows rests with me alone.

August 1979   John Martell

The Twentieth-Century World (third edition)

by

John Martell, M.A.,

Senior Lecturer in History, West London Institute of Higher Education

Acknowledgments

Illustrations

Associated Press, p. 282; BBC Hulton Picture Library, pp. 6, 13, 17, 27, 101, 102, 110, 186, 262, 287, 310; BPC/Picturepoint, p. 72; Brown Brothers, p. 35; Camera Press, pp. 118, 144, 163, 171, 203, 280, 283, 308, 326; Conservative Research Department, p. 98; European Community Information Service, p. 211; Foreign and Commonwealth Office Library, p. 301; Fox Photos, pp. 60, 132, 176, 219; Franklin D. Roosevelt Library, p. 39; Gernsheim Collection, University of Texas, p. 11; Illustrated London News, pp. 168, 320; International Institute of Social History, Amsterdam, pp. 59, 76, 82, 88, 269; John Hillelson Agency, p. 155; Keystone, pp. 136, 138, 142, 149, 152, 180, 183, 225, 231, 266, 315, 338; Library of Congress, U.S., p. 41; Low/London Express, pp. 20, 190, 340; Macdonald and Co. Ltd., pp. 45, 48; Magnum/Burt Glinn, p. 251; Mansell, pp. 49, 66, 216; Musée Royale de l'Armée, Brussels, p. 123; National archives, U.S.A., p. 131; Popperfoto, pp. 97, 111, 133, 134, 161, 193, 244, 248, 249, 254, 295, 319; Punch, pp. 213, 333; Roger Viollet, pp. 69, 84; Gerald Scarfe, p. 313; SCR photo Library, p. 78. Mary Evans Picture Library, pp. 62, 199; Burt Glinn/Magnum, p. 293.

First published in Great Britain 1980
by HARRAP LIMITED
19-23 Ludgate Hill, London EC4M 7PD

Reprinted 1981; 1982

ISBN 0 245-53578-0

Typset by Santype International Ltd, Salisbury, Wilts
Printed in Great Britain by
J. W. Arrowsmith Ltd, Bristol

1

The Russian Revolution

As we look back over the twentieth century, the revolutions which occurred in the lands of the old Russian Empire during the year 1917 stand out sharply as among the most significant events of the entire century. From its persecuted origins, the minute Bolshevik party struggled with skill, determination and a good measure of luck to establish Communism in place of one of the most unrepresentative and despotic of the régimes of the old world. By our own time this development of Communism, and its spread to widely different areas of the world's surface, has helped to make the world in the last years of the twentieth century very different from the first. Before 1917 the old world was still recognizable: after 1917 its collapse had begun. The Russian Revolution thus forms a suitable starting point for our study of the twentieth-century world.

The Russian tsarist system

The last tsar of the House of Romanov, Nicholas II (1894–1917), believed inflexibly in the traditional system of government practised by his predecessors. In this system, the tsar stood in a position of supreme authority. The government, the civil service and the church all came under his imperial control. The ministers of the central government and the governors of the provinces were appointed directly by him. In most other European countries there was a cabinet system of government, which enabled ministers to consult together, but no such system existed in Russia. Nor was there any parliamentary system, which might have compelled ministers to accept a responsibility as the elected representatives of the people. Instead there was a direct personal link between each minister and the tsar: the ministers organized their departments and reported individually to the tsar, who alone had the power to issue the decrees by which changes were made.

The main work of the administration was in the hands of the vast, uniformed civil service, within which promotion depended solely on the effectiveness of each minister in carrying out the administration of the Russian Empire, and not at all on individual initiative. Little change could therefore be expected from the civil service. The Orthodox church gave forceful spiritual support to the whole tsarist system: in return it was protected by the tsar, and minority religious denominations were persecuted.

The Russian Empire controlled territories of varied climate, landscape and race: in extent it covered one sixth of the world's surface. The lands it held had been conquered by the tsars over the centuries, and had little in common. The various nationalities within Russia each possessed a distinct identity, fostering its religion, literature and customs. The policy of the tsarist system towards the different nationalities had always been one of *Russification*, of removing national differences and instilling a sense of loyalty to the tsar. Nicholas II's government pursued this policy as vigorously as had previous governments. The crushing of a sense of national identity led to constant opposition: it is significant that among the opponents of tsarism, many were from the national minorities.

This despotic system existed for the advantage of the wealthy. It did not see as part of its responsibility the care of ordinary people, who had either to accept their inferior status or to suffer persecution if they tried

In the prewar Russian Empire, Tsar Nicholas II and the Tsarina Alexandra are greeted respectfully by their people. Their young son was often carried in this way, as—due to his illness—a fall could prove fatal.

in any way to change it. For the majority of the peoples of the Empire, life held the near-certain prospects of poverty and oppression.

Industrial change came much later to Russia than to other European countries. At the turn of the century a serious start was made to the exploitation of the Empire's vast natural resources. Finance Minister Sergei Witte's creation of a policy of *economic protection* (charging high taxes on imported goods so that their high cost encouraged the purchase of the home-produced goods) was one way by which he encouraged the development of industry. Capital from western Europe financed much of this industrial development: to many west European financiers, Russia appeared to offer complete safety for investment and vast potential for profit. There was a noticeable growth in the size of towns to accommodate the new industries and their workers, who were attracted by the prospects of employment. But for these new town workers conditions were poor. They were accommodated in crude, insanitary and overcrowded barracks, often sleeping in bunks vacated by other workers who were working a different shift. Trade unions and strikes were prohibited. When a strike did occur it was an illegal act, and usually developed into a desperate and futile local revolution. Although efforts were made by some employers to look after workers' interests, their general standard of living was miserable.

In the countryside the peasantry were by law no longer serfs, as serfdom had been abolished in 1861. Although some peasants prospered, most found life a bitter struggle for survival. Foremost among their demands was securing their own land and freedom from the landowners, whose control over the lives of many peasants was serfdom in all but name. Life in Russian villages was in reality little more than a struggle for survival against both natural and man-made obstacles.

In these deprived urban and rural conditions, many workers looked hopefully to the tsar for help. The civil servants, they felt, came between them and the tsar and prevented the tsar from assisting them. They held to this belief in the tsar whom they considered the 'little father' of his people. But some were losing their faith in the tsarist system, and were beginning to look for more fundamental change.

Opposition to the tsarist government

By the early part of the twentieth century there were three main opposition groups to the tsarist government. The Russian Liberals had little disciplined party organization, and consisted of different groups which pressed for reform of the tsarist system rather than its replacement. Their political activity was rooted in the local councils or *zemstva* which had been created as a part of earlier reforms. The Socialist Revolutionaries followed an old Russian tradition of violent opposition to authority, especially that represented by landowners. They looked to the peasantry as the class around whom the revolution would take place. Their plans for the future of the country once tsarism had been defeated were unclear, and, like the Liberals, they lacked disciplined organization. Nevertheless, they developed a strong following in the Russian countryside.

The Social Democratic party was a smaller organization than either the Liberals or the Socialist Revolutionaries. The party was inspired by the ideas of the nineteenth-century German political thinker Karl Marx, who had worked out a definite course for the historical development of society. Marx saw two main stages in the history of society in Europe: the decay of feudalism, which had been based on the ownership of land by the aristocracy, and the development of capitalism, which was based on the exploitation by successful business of both natural resources and the lives of workers. He saw that just as in his time feudalism was giving way to capitalism, so in its turn capitalism would give way to communism. As a result of the suffering of the workers under capitalism these workers would take part in the revolution of the proletariat (the workers). After their triumph in that revolution the proletariat would transform society totally, so that it reflected the interests of the new dominant class. In seeking a revolution manned by the new industrial workers of the towns, the Social Democrats encouraged the industrialization of Russia, as with this development came capitalism, and from capitalism would eventually emerge the triumph of the proletariat.

From its foundation in 1898, the Russian Social Democratic Workers party was dominated by the personality of Vladimir Lenin. Born in 1870 into a comfortable, middle class and politically liberal family, Lenin as a young man studied law and became committed to the ideas of Marx. An important factor in making him a revolutionary may well have been the emotional effect on him, when he was 17 years old, of the execution of his elder brother for plotting to assassinate the tsar. Lenin applied the ideas of Marx to the Russian situation and produced the political theory known as Marxist-Leninism. Acknowledging that most of the workers of Russia merely looked for an improvement in their conditions and had no real wish for revolutionary changes, Lenin urged the creation of a powerful inner circle of revolutionary leaders to bring about the revolution. But many party members were unwilling to give the complete obedience which Lenin expected. At a party meeting in 1903 held outside Russia, it split into the Bolshevik (majority) section, which accepted Lenin's ideas, and the Menshevik (minority) section, which wanted a softer approach and a looser party organization.

The revolutions of 1905 and tsarist concessions

In 1905 the immediate event which brought the smouldering dissatisfaction within Russia to the surface was the defeat of the Russian army and navy by Japan, which was regarded at that time as a comparatively minor power. As a result the tsarist system was discredited, and revolutions of widely differing kinds occurred throughout the Russian Empire.

Two other events in 1905 which were particularly important in stimulating revolution were the massacre of Bloody Sunday and the mutiny on the *Potemkin*. The Bloody Sunday massacre took place in January 1905 when, under the leadership of a priest from St Petersburg, Father Gapon, the people went to the tsar's palace to seek improvement in their living and working conditions. Their protest was made in a spirit of humble request rather than revolution, but the tsar's guards became anxious and charged into the petitioners, killing hundreds of them. News of this cruel action spread throughout Russia, and strikes occurred in many different places to show sympathy with the victims of St Petersburg. The mutiny on the battleship *Potemkin* took place on the Black Sea during June 1905, when the sailors refused to tolerate the miserable conditions, the rotten food and the brutal treatment they suffered at the hands of a set of arrogant officers. Though eventually the mutiny was defeated, for some months the *Potemkin* sailed around the Black Sea, giving encouragement to rebels on the land and diminishing Russia's standing in the eyes of foreign powers.

The opponents of the tsar attempted in their different ways to take advantage of these events. Strikes, the seizure of land, assassinations, demonstrations all took place, but a unified lead was lacking. This fundamentally disunited approach helped the tsarist authorities to reassert control. Further, the authorities were prepared to make a few changes so that the revolutionaries would feel that they had produced results by their activities. On the advice of Witte, the tsar issued the October Manifesto, which made various concessions such as freedom of speech, freedom of association, and curbing the arbitrary powers of the police. While the October Manifesto did not create the widely desired constituent assembly to which the tsar's government would be responsible and which would be elected by universal suffrage, it did create a *duma*, an assembly with strictly limited powers and elected on a limited suffrage.

Four dumas were held in the years after 1905. As the first two, in 1906 and 1907, showed opposition to the tsar, they lasted only a matter of months. Because the two later dumas from 1907 to 1912 and from 1912 to 1917 were more cooperative, they lasted longer, but played no significant part in the government of the Empire.

The tsar's chief minister, from 1906 until his assassination in 1911, was Stolypin. He had risen to prominence as a governor of a central Russian province. As chief minister to Nicholas II he showed a determination to maintain the tsarist system, but also to take steps to reform it. He gave much attention to the encouragement of reform in the rural areas. Stolypin's assassination in 1911 and the opening of the First World War in 1914 both held back these reforms, which represented bold but belated attempts to solve some of the fundamental problems in rural Russia.

The First World War and the Revolution of February 1917

The Russian Empire entered into the First World War in August 1914 as an ally of Britain and France and as an enemy of Austria-Hungary. Just as the small Russo-Japanese war had led to the unsuccessful 1905 revolutions, so the First World War led to the successful 1917 revolutions. The war intensified Russia's problems. Though, as in all European countries, it began with displays of patriotism and loyalty, and though in the early stages the Russians were encouraged by some military successes, by 1915 the Russian armies were in retreat. A spirit of defeatism steadily gripped the millions of Russian soldiers for whom, as the war dragged on, the fighting became little more than systematic slaughter. Russia was fighting a modern, mechanized war by old-fashioned methods. She did not yet have the industrial capacity to produce arms and equipment in sufficient quantities, nor an adequate communications system to transport troops and raw materials.

The economy was dislocated by the absence of many men in the army. From 1916, as a result partly of poor productivity but mainly of inefficient distribution, food shortages were felt throughout Russia, creating a desperate situation, especially for the town-dwellers. In these years government changes and government incompetence were widely attributed to the activities of Gregory Rasputin. This Siberian peasant had a great deal of influence at the tsar's court on account of his skill in treating the tsar's son for the hereditary disease, haemophilia. Rasputin's influence on government policies may not have been particularly great but his drunken and disorderly life, together with the rumours of the extent of his power and his relationship with the German-born tsarina, Alexandra, further tarnished the image of the tsar's government.

Nicholas II, never a particularly competent administrator, made the unwise decision in the summer of 1915 to take command of the Russian armies in the battlefield. Russia's lack of military success thus became attributed directly to him. Much of the administration at home was left in the hands of the Tsarina Alexandra, whose control of internal affairs showed poor judgment, and who was extremely unpopular, partly because of her German connections. The régime, oppressed by so many problems, was ill prepared for the revolution that broke in the early months of 1917.

Two revolutions occurred in 1917: the first, in February, led to the establishment of a Provisional government; and the second, in October, led to the establishment of a Bolshevik government. The revolutions are often dated March and November, but until 1918 Russia followed the Julian calendar, which was 13 days behind the more commonly-used Gregorian calendar. The revolution in February developed from a riot by the inhabitants of Petrograd (as St Petersburg had been renamed during the war) who, reduced to starvation by a serious food shortage, were demanding merely their daily bread. There was nothing new or surprising about a food riot during the First World War, and so the authorities took little action against it. But on this occasion the riot got totally out of control. The soldiers who were sent to suppress it joined the rebels, and within a matter of days the riot had developed into a full-scale revolution.

Power in Petrograd was seized by two very different bodies. The duma developed as the Provisional government of Russia and took on the usual functions of government. The Petrograd soviet (council) of the deputies of workers and soldiers was formed by left-wing politicians: it represented the interests of the revolutionaries more closely, and had control of much of the day-to-day administration in Petrograd. From the start the relationship between the Provisional government and the Petrograd soviet was uneasy. It took Nicholas II some days to realize that these events had removed for ever the basis of Romanov power in Russia. After attempting unsuccessfully to secure the accession of his son and then of his brother, he abdicated and was exiled to his estates in Russia, where he was initially treated with modest respect.

The Provisional government lasted for little more than seven months. At first it was led

These three cartoons look at the events from February to October 1917 from the point of view of the Bolsheviks.

9

by a liberal aristocrat, Prince Lvov, and from July by Alexander Kerensky, who was the only member of the Provisional government also to be a member of the Petrograd soviet. Its aim throughout these months was to establish for Russia a form of constitutional government similar to that found in other parts of Europe: it abolished much of the repression of tsarist times, it declared freedom of speech, of the press and of the right to strike, and it promised that a constituent assembly would meet to decide the permanent future form of the government of Russia.

But the Provisional government failed to tackle decisively enough some of Russia's fundamental problems. In order to maintain good relations with Russia's Western allies, it continued Russia's involvement in the First World War, in spite of the war's bitter unpopularity. Meanwhile the Petrograd soviet had established soviets of soldiers in the battle areas, and had abolished capital punishment for desertion. All this made the war effort even more ineffective. Brusilov's offensive against the Germans and Austrians in the summer of 1917 produced negligible results. Nor was the land problem within Russia adequately tackled; a final decision on this problem was to await the formation of the constituent assembly, though meanwhile, government requisitioning of land provoked widespread hostility from the peasants.

After the failure of his campaign, Brusilov was replaced as commander-in-chief by General Kornilov. This forceful soldier, originally from Asiatic Russia, had a hatred of the revolution and all that it stood for. Towards the end of August 1917, in order, so he asserted, to forestall a German attack on Petrograd and to re-establish proper authority throughout Russia, Kornilov attempted a coup which would, he hoped, lead to a military dictatorship under his control. But the lack of support from his own troops and acts of sabotage by political opponents combined to bring about the collapse of this right-wing attempt to overthrow the Provisional government. Foremost among the opponents of Kornilov was the Bolshevik party, which was much stronger at this time.

The Bolshevik party and the Revolution of October 1917

The strength of the Bolshevik party had been growing steadily since the February Revolution. When that first revolution occurred Lenin was in Switzerland, having been exiled by the tsar. The Provisional government's early moves towards greater freedom made it possible for Lenin to return to Russia. The Germans cooperated in his return, as they knew Lenin to be opposed to the war, and they hoped that his influence might lead to a Russian withdrawal. Back in Russia, Lenin once again took control of the Bolshevik party.

Lenin saw the various soviets throughout Russia as the bases for the revolution by the proletariat. His main policy throughout 1917 was to encourage their support under the slogan 'All Power to the Soviets', even though in the months just after the first revolution the Bolsheviks did not have majorities on the soviets. Meanwhile, through another slogan, 'Bread, Peace and Freedom', the Bolsheviks told the masses that they would end food shortages and the useless war, and would ensure liberty. In view of the failure of the Provisional government in all of these areas, the Bolshevik message had a strong appeal.

Leon Trotsky, a recent convert to Bolshevism, was organizing the Red Guards, members of the Bolshevik party who would take the lead when the revolution came. By the autumn the time seemed right for a Bolshevik revolution. By then Bolshevik power in the soviets was growing, though they were aware that they might not secure a majority in the constituent assembly, the elections for which were imminent. During the night of 24–25 October 1917, with comparatively little bloodshed, Red Guards took over all the major buildings in Petrograd, imprisoned the ministers of the Provisional government and established a Council of People's Commissars (ministers) in which Lenin was Prime Minister, Trotsky was Commissar for Foreign Affairs and Stalin was Commissar for Nationalities. Decrees were at once issued to proclaim withdrawal from the war and to give approval to land seizure by the peasants. A week later a similar revolution occurred in Moscow, though it was accompanied by more violence than in Petrograd.

Although the revolution of the proletariat had not quite followed the text-book pattern of Marxist-Leninism, it had nevertheless been achieved, and Lenin was at once concerned to preserve and to develop it. To do this, the new Bolshevik government adopted from the start, policies of force. A major constitutional threat was the long-awaited constituent assembly. Before they came into power the Bolsheviks had pressed so strongly for this that now it would have been difficult and unwise to prevent it. The elections which

took place gave the Socialist Revolutionaries a large majority, and the Bolsheviks only a quarter of the seats. The constituent assembly duly met in January 1918, but for only one day, during which the Socialist Revolutionaries bravely put forward their policies. On the second day Red Guards were sent to disband the assembly, thus removing this awkward obstacle to Bolshevik rule.

The elections to the constituent assembly had shown that there was considerable political opposition to the Bolsheviks. To root out this opposition the Bolsheviks created an effective police force, the Cheka. Its victims in the years just after the revolution were not just political opponents, but often people

The storming of the winter palace in Petrograd in October 1917 was one of the most dramatic and decisive events in the success of the Bolsheviks.

whose middle class origins, business associations or religious opinions made them suspect. Though police activity of this kind has varied in intensity throughout Russian history, it has rarely been entirely absent.

Negotiations for a peace treaty with Germany were begun in December 1917, at the Polish town of Brest-Litovsk. From the start, the Germans made far-reaching demands from their defeated enemies. The treaty which was eventually signed at Brest-Litovsk in March 1918 was certainly harsh. The Russian parts of Poland and the three Baltic states of Estonia, Latvia and Lithuania were to become German possessions; Finland, Georgia and the Ukraine were each to become independent of Russian control; by a special trade arrangement, the Ukraine was to provide Germany with wheat; finally, a vast payment of 6,000 million marks was to be paid by Russia as reparations to Germany. The economic effects of the treaty were severe, as the lands which Russia lost were highly populated and were rich in industrial and agricultural resources. Germany was stripped of these gains after her later defeat by the West. But Russia was not involved in the closing stages of the First World War, so she was naturally not a participant at the Paris peace conference of 1919, and was unable to press her case against the defeated Germany at that time. Thus Russia did not receive back all her lost possessions, most of which had, in any case, a reasonable claim to independence. Poland, Estonia, Latvia, Lithuania and Finland all secured their independence as a result of the later treaty, though Russia was able to resecure control of the Ukraine and Georgia and the German reparation demands against Russia collapsed.

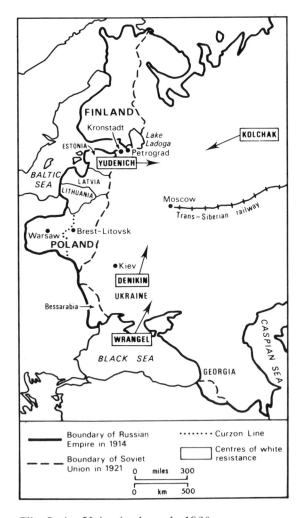

The Soviet Union in the early 1920s

The Civil War and the Russo-Polish War

During 1918 opposition to Bolshevik rule developed into a state of confused civil war. The opponents of the 'Reds' (the Bolsheviks) were collectively known as the 'Whites'. The political standpoint of these opponents was generally right-wing, though a few of them went so far as to support a return to tsarist rule. The power of the Whites was concentrated in particular areas and around individual leaders. Admiral Kolchak ruled tyrannically parts of Siberia; General Yudenich, with some Western aid, maintained a government in the north; Generals Denikin and later Wrangel established for a while the Don Republic in the south; along stretches of the Trans-Siberian railway, territories were in the hands of Czechoslovak prisoners of war.

In the closing stages of the First World War some British, French and American troops were sent to Russia as a precaution against possible German seizure of arms sent earlier to Russia by the allies, especially in the north and in the oil-fields of the south. Some Western politicians were eager to extend their commitment to the right-wing by giving military aid to the White forces against the Bolsheviks. They had some reason for wishing to do this: the Bolshevik government had deserted the Russian alliance with the West and had nationalized Western-owned business interests in Russia, quite apart from setting up a revolutionary form of government which Western governments viewed with grave suspicion. But the Western governments were unwilling, after four years of bitter warfare, to commit their troops to fight alongside the Whites. Though some Western troops remained until 1920, their involvement in the actual fighting was minimal. Nevertheless, military supplies were given to the White armies. However limited this involvement was, the Bolshevik government was aware of it as an act of distinct hostility at the very time they were seeking to establish their rule: it was a factor which caused suspicion between the Bolshevik government and the Western powers for many years to come.

Certain clear advantages lay with the Bolsheviks in this struggle. The Red Army was under the brilliant command of Trotsky. Advantage was taken of the military experience of tsarist officers, while their political reliability and that of the rest of the army was ensured by the propaganda work of political commissars. An overriding strategic advantage was the Red Army's possession of Moscow, Petrograd and the central regions of Russia. The efforts of the Whites were dispersed, and their armies were poorly co-ordinated. Despite the divisions of the country, the Red Army increasingly secured the patriotic support of the people as the force

Lenin addresses a crowd during the revolutionary events of 1917. Few men have had such influence in the twentieth century on the course of Russian history, or on the course of world history.

which stood for Russian interests against the Whites, who had Western support.

Neighbouring Poland had little reason to show sympathy towards the new government in Russia. For more than a century most of Poland had been ruled by Russia: only in 1919, as a direct result of the Paris peace conference, was an independent Poland re-created. But by the terms of the treaty the eastern boundary of Poland was marked by the Curzon Line, allowing Russia to keep substantial territories which the Poles felt should be theirs. The Russian civil war provided for Poland the perfect opportunity to secure these territories. In May 1920 the Polish army made a swift and successful invasion as far as the Ukrainian capital of Kiev. Russians and Ukrainians were equally roused by a sense of injured patriotism, and a successful counter-attack was launched against the invading Polish army, which was chased back into Poland itself. Lenin now sought to establish a Communist government in Poland, which could form a valuable link with Germany, which Lenin considered to be on the verge of a Communist revolution. But the plan failed. Although the Red Army reached Warsaw and besieged it, Poland secured military aid from France, its traditional ally, and at the battle of the river Vistula Lenin's invading forces were defeated. By the terms of the treaty of Riga, March 1921, Poland secured the coveted territories east of the Curzon Line.

The economy and society under Lenin

Marxist-Leninism envisaged the economy functioning for the benefit of the proletariat. To function in this way, it was thought that the economy would have to be controlled by the state. Lenin had hoped that this state take-over of the economy would be orderly, with an initial period of cooperation with capitalists. But many industries, at the time of the revolution, were taken over by workers, independent of government direction. By the time of the decree on nationalization, in June 1918, by which all large-scale businesses were taken over, the process of nationalization

was already well advanced. In the countryside land had been taken over by the peasantry at the time of the October Revolution, but the circumstances of war and food shortages in the towns forced the government to requisition all grain. This appeared to the more wealthy and more successful peasantry as a direct threat to their livelihood, and as a protest many reduced their output of grain. The combination of these sudden policies of state take-over in both industry and agriculture, together with the inevitable chaos of the civil war period, resulted in economic disaster. Peasant produce diminished, starvation in the towns increased and the inflation rate rose rapidly. Industrial output declined, so that by 1921 it was less than a quarter that of 1914. Drought in the Volga region in 1921 contributed to overall bankruptcy during these years of what was termed *war communism*.

This situation of serious economic decline was an obvious breeding ground of dissatisfaction with Lenin's government. In March 1921 opposition showed itself dramatically at the northern port of Kronstadt. Sailors in this formerly loyal Bolshevik stronghold put forward a series of demands for greater freedom. When these were not met the sailors launched an open rebellion which, in bitter weather conditions, was defeated by Trotsky. But Lenin interpreted the Kronstadt uprising as a warning that war communism was not working, and that the economy needed to be directed in a quite different way.

The solution provided by Lenin was the New Economic Policy, the fundamental idea of which was that the government would make some concessions to capitalism in order to encourage a more successful development of the economy. Requisitioning of grain was replaced by a standard rate of taxation on it. This move encouraged the peasantry to grow more, as they could profit from the sale of the grain which was surplus to taxation requirements. As a result of these changes the wealthier peasants, known as the *kulaks*, flourished. The development of a market economy remained a feature of Soviet life throughout the 1920s. Change also took place in industry, where the government retained control of the major industries, but allowed the smaller ones to return to private enterprise. Other modifications of the economy were also made, such as the employment of foreign aid in industry and the stabilization of a new rouble. Many Marxist-Leninist principles were overthrown in implementing the New Economic Policy, but it did work to the economic advantage of Russia, and by 1926 the economy had regained its pre-war stability.

Throughout the difficulties during the years after the October Revolution, the new government sought to create a coherent constitutional framework for the development of Communism within the lands of the former Russian Empire. A preliminary constitution was worked out in 1918, and a further one was composed during Lenin's last years, and formally accepted in 1924. The Union of Soviet Socialist Republics (USSR) was created as a result of this second constitution, in an endeavour to stress the identity of the individual nationalities, under ultimate Soviet control. Each of the republics was controlled by a Soviet government, and each was represented at Moscow in the Soviet of Nationalities. Also at Moscow was the Soviet of the Union. Both these Moscow soviets were elected, the former to represent the views of the different republics and the latter to represent the views of the Soviet Union as a whole. The inner government was in the hands of the Politbureau.

Since the only candidates for election were Communists, the whole structure of the Soviet Union was dominated by the Communist party, membership of which was regarded as essential by those who wished for success in politics or business. All appointments were made by it and its leading post of General Secretary became one of great power and prestige. During the last two years of his life, Lenin was a sick man, but he became profoundly suspicious of the new General Secretary of the Communist party, Josef Stalin. However, when the founder of the Soviet Union eventually died in January 1924, at the age of 53, it was Stalin who very soon held the reins of power.

Questions

1. Study the three Soviet cartoons on page 9 and then answer questions (a) to (c) which follow.

   (a) In the case of the first cartoon:
      (i) Identify the ruler who is being overthrown, and
      (ii) explain the events of 1917 which led to his overthrow.
      (1+4)

   (b) In the case of the second cartoon:
      (i) Give the names of two of the leaders of this new government.
      (ii) What does the cartoonist suggest to be the main work of this new government?
      (iii) Comment on the accuracy or otherwise of the cartoonist's view of Russia during this period, so far as the organization of government and involvement in the First World War are concerned.
      (1+1+4)

   (c) In the case of the third cartoon:
      (i) Name the political party whose action is shown here, and name the leader of that party.
      Why is the party shown in the cartoon as a fist?
      (ii) Explain the events which brought about the action shown in this cartoon.
      (iii) In what ways did the new government during the next four years continue the work begun here?
      (2+3+4)

2. How do you account for the collapse of (a) the tsar's government and (b) the Provisional government in 1917?

3. Show the importance of the work of Lenin in (a) bringing about the Bolshevik Revolution and (b) consolidating the hold of the Bolsheviks in Russia.

2

The Peace settlement

At eleven o'clock on the morning of 11 November 1918, after more than four years of fighting, the armistice agreement ending the First World War came into effect. Throughout the 1920s and 1930s the generation that had suffered the war's physical and emotional ravages referred to it variously as the 'Great War', the 'War to end all Wars' or 'Armageddon', the last battle of all, foretold in the Book of Revelation. For more than four years the forces of the central powers, the German Empire, Austria-Hungary, Bulgaria and the Ottoman (Turkish) Empire, had battled against the allied powers: Britain, France and the Russian Empire initially, joined by Italy in 1915 and by the United States in 1917. The fighting had been bitter, characterized throughout by the unthinking employment of the policy of 'attrition', of wearing down the other side by constant attack, which through the supremacy of defensive weapons resulted in the death of millions of soldiers. Eventually, in the autumn of 1918, the allied forces had been able to advance sufficiently to persuade Germany and the other central powers to seek an armistice.

The conflicting aims of the peace makers

From January to June 1919 the allied leaders met in conference at Paris to work out a peace settlement. Although the conference was divided into committees and councils, and was assisted by a host of civil servants, the major decisions were taken by the three most important leaders: president Woodrow Wilson of the United States, prime minister Lloyd George of Great Britain and

prime minister Georges Clemenceau of France, who were collectively known as the 'Big Three'. Each of these men went to Paris with different ideas on how best to deal with their enemies and ensure the future peace of the world.

Woodrow Wilson was the most idealistic. Unhappy boyhood memories of the American Civil War helped to make him a man of peace, and it had only been with extreme reluctance that he had finally asked Congress to declare war on Germany in 1917. In January 1918 he had issued his Fourteen Points for creating a lasting peace when the war eventually ended. Of these, points 1 to 5 were general, applicable both to the victorious powers and to the defeated, and designed to ensure that the circumstances which encouraged the outbreak of the First World War should not occur again. Diplomacy was to be open, navigation of the seas was to be free, barriers to trade to be abolished as far as possible, armament levels were to be reduced and colonial claims were to be adjusted. Points 6 to 13 were concerned with practical ways in which effect could be given to Wilson's principle of *self-determination*, according to which national groups, which had increasingly asserted their importance during the last century, were to be allowed to decide the nature of their own government. In these central points he pledged his support for French re-acquisition of Alsace-Lorraine, the fulfilment of Italy's boundary claims, the evacuation of Belgium, freedom for the Russians to decide their future form of government, the recreation of Poland and self-determination for the subject races of Austria-Hungary and the Ottoman Empire. Point 14 was the creation of the League of Nations, an assembly for settling international disputes and thus preserving peace. Serious problems prevented Wilson from fully achieving the aims of the Fourteen Points. The American people gave them only half-hearted support. Wilson was unwise in not including in his delegation to Paris some representatives of the opposition Republican party, which totally opposed them, and which, in the autumn of 1918, had secured a majority in Congress.

No other major leader stated in such clear and idealistic terms the bases on which peace was to be built. Clemenceau took a sterner and more practical view. Almost 80 years old, he also had been much influenced by a previous war: the Franco-German War of 1870–71, in which France had been defeated by Germany and had been compelled to accept the loss of Alsace-Lorraine. The damage inflicted by the German army in north-east France during the First World War had sharpened Clemenceau's deep hatred of Germany, a feeling which, at that time, many French people shared. Clemenceau had a twofold aim at the peace negotiations: to ensure that France was protected from the threat of any future invasion, and to ensure that Germany was punished.

Lloyd George adopted an attitude of compromise towards Germany: he held that the future prosperity and peace of Europe depended upon Germany accepting a reasonable peace settlement. This was sensible and far-sighted, though it did not reflect the popular view in Britain, which was hostile towards Germany and insisted that Germany should pay for the damage done during the war. Lloyd George therefore occupied a position of moderation, between Wilson's idealism and Clemenceau's vengeance.

It is impossible to say which of these men had most influence in the Paris negotiations, as the eventual treaty terms reflected in various ways the aims of each of them. Other leading statesmen counted for comparatively little in the negotiations. The Italian prime minister, Orlando, was so dissatisfied at the manner in which the Big Three disregarded some of Italy's claims to territories that he temporarily left the conference. Japan took part, but she too believed she had gained too little by the terms of the treaty.

The peace settlement consisted of several treaties, each of which dealt with a separate defeated power.

Date	Treaty	Power
June 1919	Versailles	Germany
September 1919	St. Germain	Austria
November 1919	Neuilly	Bulgaria
June 1920	Trianon	Hungary
August 1920	Sèvres	Turkey
July 1923	Lausanne	Turkey

The Treaty of Versailles

Only after the clauses of the treaty had been agreed by the Big Three were they shown to a German delegation which, though appalled at so gross a humiliation for Germany, had no choice but to accept them. So, on 28 June 1919 in the Grand Hall

A break in the discussions for the statesmen who bore most responsibility for the decisions at Versailles. From left to right: Lloyd George, Orlando, Clemenceau, Wilson.

of Mirrors at the Palace of Versailles, the same hall in which half a century previously the German Empire had been proclaimed after the French defeat in the 1870–71 war, the representatives of Germany publicly accepted their country's humiliation. They resignedly signed the treaty. It was a massive document. The first part contained the Covenant of the League of Nations, considered in more detail in the following chapter. Its position at the start of each of the peace treaties signed at Paris emphasized the fundamental importance of this new attempt to preserve peace for the future.

Fundamental to the whole treaty was Article 231 which compelled Germany to accept the responsibility for starting the First World War.

> The Allied and Associated governments affirm, and Germany accepts, the responsibility of Germany and her allies for causing all the loss and damage to which the Allied and Associated governments and their nationals have been subjected as a consequence of the war imposed upon them by the aggression of Germany and her allies.

Looking back, there is no doubt that this enforced admission of German guilt for the war was unjust. There is no easy answer to the question of who caused the First World War, but no historian of today would suggest that Germany alone was responsible. But in 1919 the Allied leaders, including Wilson, considered that Germany's responsibility was beyond dispute. This accusation against Germany should be seen as the foundation of the treaty, the harsh terms of which are then more readily understood.

The extensive changes made to the boundaries of Germany at Versailles were based partly on the self-determination of certain regions, and partly on the economic and strategic needs of neighbouring states. The most important adjustments were in the favour of Germany's western neighbour, France, and her new eastern neighbour, Poland. Extensive iron-ore made Alsace-Lorraine an area of considerable value. For half a century it had been in German hands and

Germany after the Treaty of Versailles

it was now restored to France, though many of its inhabitants were German-speaking and were displeased by the transfer. France also made strong claims to the important coal-mining region of the Saar, because of the German destruction of the coal mines in north-east France. But the population of the Saar was predominantly German-speaking, and a compromise arrangement was agreed. For 15 years the Saar would be under the control of the League of Nations, but the Saar coal mines would be under the control of France: at the end of the 15-year period a referendum would decide the future of the area. French concern with the defence of her eastern boundaries led to her demand that the Rhineland should either be transferred to France, or should be created as an independent state. The eventual agreement was that the Rhineland (defined as all territory to the west of the Rhine and a strip 50 kilometres wide to the east) was to remain German territory but was to be permanently demilitarized: it was therefore a forbidden area for Germany's troops and fortifications. For a limited period an Allied army of occupation was to be stationed there. Though all of these clauses concerning Franco-German border areas were viewed by Germany as unjust, they were also viewed by France as an inadequate defence against possible German aggression in the future, and a less than adequate recompense for the previous German aggression. Clemenceau believed that Lloyd George had had too strong a hand in these territorial changes, and the two wartime allies began to show signs of basic disagreement. This did not bode well for the future enforcement of the treaty.

Germany felt more bitter about the treatment of the eastern boundaries. The recreation of Poland meant that the successors to the old Empires of Germany, Austria-Hungary and Russia, all of which had absorbed parts of the area of the former Poland, would be compelled to give territory to the resurrected country. The territories lost to Poland were not only the largest losses that Germany suffered but they also divided East Prussia, still German territory, from the rest of the country. The Polish Corridor provided Poland with an essential means of access to the sea at the port of Danzig. As this city was predominantly German in population and yet was essential to Poland's economy, it was placed under the administration of the League of Nations. Throughout all of these areas lost to Poland there were German-speaking minorities, but if the economy of the new Poland was to succeed it was essential that these areas were secured. Upper Silesia, in the south-east corner of Germany, was an area of vital economic importance and of mixed Polish-German nationality. Decision on its future was postponed until the early 1920s, when the League of Nations supervised a referendum in the area.

Germany was forbidden to unite in any way with the new republic of Austria. This was to prevent a revival of German power. Other small border changes were uncontroversial. The areas of Eupen and Malmédy were acquired by Belgium. A referendum in German-held Schleswig showed that southern Schleswig wished to remain German while northern Schleswig wished to be incorporated into Denmark: this was carried out. The area of Memel was acquired by Lithuania.

The German Empire overseas was totally broken up, though the former German colonies were not given outright to the victorious powers. They were instead placed in their trust as mandates, to be administered by them on behalf of the League of Nations, a system described more fully in the following chapter. Most German colonies were in Africa. German East Africa, renamed Tanganyika, became Britain's responsibility. German South West Africa became the responsibility of the Union of South Africa. Responsibility for the German Cameroons and German Togoland was divided between Britain and France. The other German colonies were in the Pacific area: responsibility was taken for the Samoan Islands by New Zealand, and for New Guinea and the Bismarck archipelago by Australia, while the Marshall Islands and some of Germany's former Chinese possessions were given as mandates to Japan.

These territorial losses in Europe and overseas seriously weakened Germany's power, and strict clauses compelling Germany to disarm went further in the same direction. The demilitarization of the Rhineland, already noted, was one aspect of this. In addition, the German army was to be limited to 100,000 men; there was to be no German air force and no German submarine force; the German navy was limited to six battleships, six light cruisers and a few smaller craft. It was hoped that German military power, the country's pride in pre-war years, would be crippled by these clauses. It was also hoped that German disarmament would be a preliminary step towards a general disarmament throughout the world. Both these hopes remained unfulfilled. As will be shown later, Germany evaded strict fulfilment of the disarmament clauses, and attempts at general world disarmament made no real progress.

The Allies agreed at Versailles on the principle of the payment of reparations by Germany, though no conclusions were reached about their amount. Though payment was meant to begin at once, for the next three years a Reparations Commission discussed the full details of the payments. By 1920 they had agreed the proportions that each victor power was to receive: France was to receive half, Britain a fifth, Italy a tenth, with the remainder divided between the other powers. By the spring of 1921 the Reparations Commission announced the total due from Germany to be the approximate currency equivalent of six thousand, six hundred million pounds, payment of which was to be made partly in currency and partly in goods. The German government considered this figure monstrously high; much popular opinion outside Germany held it to be far too low. Reparations payments as such had been seriously questioned by the economist J. M. Keynes in his important study entitled *The Economic Consequences of the Peace*: he argued that to demand payment from a country which had lost territory, resources and markets would inevitably lead to general economic chaos. Many thoughtful politicians agreed with this view, and in the summer of 1921 the total sum demanded was reduced by more than half. Even so, until their final abandonment in the summer of 1931, the issue of reparations seriously troubled international relations.

On reparations, as on other matters regarding Germany, the Allies failed to agree on a policy. The terms of the peace treaties left some of the Allies feeling extremely unhappy, thinking the terms too weak or, conversely, too harsh. Obviously Germany thought that they were far too harsh, and it was not too long before she realized that she could use the differences in policy of the Allied powers to her own advantage.

This cartoon of the late 1920s illustrates the unrealistic nature of German reparations payments. The loans Germany received during the 1920s were scarcely adequate to support the weight of debt that she is carrying.

The treaties of St Germain and Trianon

The Imperial government of Austria-Hungary had collapsed in the closing stages of the First World War, and a reorganization of the territories of the former Empire was a priority at Paris, once the settlement of Germany had been agreed. The intention had been to deal with the whole of Austria-Hungary in one peace treaty, but within Hungary a Communist régime established itself briefly in 1919 and the consequent upheavals led to delay in signing the Hungarian treaty: hence the gap between the signing of the treaty of St Germain with Austria in September 1919 and the treaty of Trianon with Hungary in June 1920.

Together, these two treaties confirmed the complete destruction of the old Austria-Hungary. Austria was confirmed as a republic encompassing within its now considerably reduced boundaries only German-speaking people. Though the majority of people now separated from Austria's rule were not German-speaking, there were substantial German minorities in the new Czechoslovakia and in the areas acquired by Italy. Many people in this weaker Austria favoured union with Germany, but such a union was strictly forbidden. In Hungary's case also boundaries were considerably reduced. They excluded the Hungarians in the new Czechoslovakia, and in the territories acquired by Romania. Both countries suffered economic disadvantage by being made totally landlocked. Technically, both were also made subject to reparation payments, though in practice their resources were so slender that these payments were never made.

The lost territories were taken over by neighbouring or new countries. Italy secured the areas of Trentino and South Tyrol, bordering on to the new Austria; Trieste and the area of Istria, bordering mainly on to the new Yugoslavia: all these areas contained Italian majorities. The southern part of the new Poland was formed from Austria-Hungary's north-eastern province of Galicia, populated predominantly by Poles. Romania, a comparatively new country,

created only in the middle of the previous century, secured large areas of Transylvania from the south-east of Austria-Hungary. This generous addition to Romania's territories was a reward for Romanian intervention on the allied side in the First World War, but the territory it secured contained Hungarian minorities.

Two new countries, Czechoslovakia and Yugoslavia, benefited even more directly. The creation of the new Czechoslovakia marked the successful achievement of many decades of struggle by the Czechs, in the western part of the country, and the Slovaks, in the centre. The new country had useful economic resources and a president, Thomas Masaryk, who was devoted to its well-being. Unfortunately, it suffered from nationality problems. Though both the Czechs and the

Austria-Hungary after the treaties of St Germain and Trianon

Slovaks had wanted independence, neither had wanted to be united with the other. The minority Slovaks came increasingly to feel that the country was too strongly dominated by the Czechs. Czechoslovakia contained other minorities who shared the Slovak dislike of Czech dominance: Ruthenians in the east, Hungarians along the border region with Hungary in the south, some Poles in the area of Teschen and a large minority of over three million Germans in the Sudetenland mountains which formed the western boundary of the new country.

Yugoslavia (also spelt Jugoslavia) was created by linking the Austro-Hungarian provinces of Slovenia, Croatia, Bosnia and Dalmatia with the adjacent lands of Serbia and Montenegro. The uniting of all these territories brought the *Yugoslavs* (southern Slavs) together into one country, and thus realized an ambition for which many of them had striven for decades. The Serbian monarchy now ruled Yugoslavia, and though this new country was not much troubled by separatist national groups, many Yugoslavs were conscious that their government especially under the first prime minister, Nikola Pasic represented Serbian rather than Yugoslavian interests.

Though many of the changes brought about by the treaties of St Germain and Trianon were undoubtedly a source of strength to the new countries, they were also open to criticism. In order to determine the wishes of the populations, a referendum was to be held in some disputed areas, but no referendum was permitted among the German-speaking people of South Tyrol, nor the Sudetenland, nor among the people of Austria on the issue of union with Germany. One of the few advantages of the old Austria-Hungary was that it had formed an economic unit, within which free trade had developed successfully. In spite of Wilson's ideal of removing barriers to trade, the division of the territories of the old Empire in practice created new ones.

The treaty of Sèvres and the treaty of Lausanne

The First World War dealt the final death blow to the Ottoman Empire, which for centuries had been in a state of decline. Though the Empire's territorial losses under the treaty of Sèvres appeared extensive, many of these territories had in practice been independent for some time. This was particularly true of the Middle Eastern possessions of the Ottoman Empire, where Saudi Arabia was to become independent, and where mandates were created for France in Syria and Lebanon, and for Britain in Palestine, Transjordan and Iraq, all considered in their Middle Eastern setting at the start of chapter 22. The Middle Eastern losses, together with recognition of earlier losses in north Africa, were accepted by the Ottoman Empire with little protest. But the territorial changes in Anatolia and in Europe were less welcome to the Turkish people who were angry at the ease with which the Ottoman government accepted the loss of territories to their traditional enemies, the Greeks. The area around Smyrna (now Izmir), some Aegean islands, and East Thrace were to be transferred to Greece. Italy secured the Dodecanese islands and some portions of southern Anatolia. Plans were suggested for the independence of the eastern part of Anatolia, but little progress was made towards their implementation.

The arrival of Greek forces in Ottoman territory even before the details of the treaty had been agreed, aroused strong feelings of resentment among the Turks. They rallied enthusiastically under the leadership of Mustafa Kemal, a Turkish officer who had secured a widespread following both before and during the First World War. Basing himself upon the Anatolian town of Ankara, Kemal conducted a vigorous campaign against the Greeks in Ottoman territory and against the British and French forces which came to their assistance. Kemal was assisted by Russian military aid and by a French withdrawal from opposition. By August 1922 the Greeks were totally expelled from the area around Smyrna. Kemal now turned his attention to the expulsion of the Greeks from East Thrace. In the autumn of 1922 at Chanak, Kemal faced determined opposition from British forces, intent upon preventing any further erosion of the terms of the treaty of Sèvres. Conflict at Chanak was prevented by the initiative of the British military authorities there, who made an agreement with Kemal, conceding East Thrace to him in return for his guarantee for the permanent neutrality of the Dardanelles Straits. Kemal received wide acclaim from the Turks for these successes, and he felt confident enough after the episode at Chanak to advance on the capital city of Constantinople (now Istanbul) where, with minimum violence, he overthrew the Sultan of the Ottoman Empire and established himself as President of the new republic of Turkey.

After these important changes in the territory and the government of Turkey, a further conference was summoned to reconsider the country's treatment. Discussion took place in Switzerland, at Lausanne, throughout the first half of 1923 and a treaty was signed there in July. The restoration of Smyrna, East Thrace and some Aegean islands to Turkey was confirmed; Greeks in Turkish territory were to be returned to Greece and Turks in Greek territory were to be returned to Turkey. The loss of the Dodecanese to Italy was accepted, as was the loss of the former Middle Eastern parts of the old Ottoman Empire. The new republic also kept to its part of the Chanak bargain by guaranteeing the neutrality of the Dardanelles Straits. Alone of all the treaties considered so far in this chapter, the treaty of Lausanne was a properly negotiated treaty in which the power concerned was allowed to contribute equally to the discussions on the treaty's terms. After Lausanne, Turkey had no important grievances against other powers, and under Kemal's leadership throughout most of the interwar years was able to undertake much needed internal reforms.

Revision of the treaty of Brest-Litovsk

No Russian representatives were permitted at the Paris peace conference, as Russia had withdrawn from the First World War after the Bolshevik revolution and had been compelled to accept, in March 1918, the severities of the treaty of Brest-Litovsk, considered in the previous chapter. After Germany's defeat there was no prospect of these territories remaining German possessions, but on the principle of self-determination there was no prospect, either, of them being restored to Russia. In any case, the Western powers viewed Russia with general dislike, on account both of her withdrawal from the war and the nature of her new government.

The three Baltic states of Estonia, Latvia and Lithuania, which had long sought independence from the Russian Empire, threw off the German rule imposed at Brest-Litovsk and declared themselves independent republics. The allies at Paris viewed favourably this assertion of self-determination, though it was only in the early 1920s that full recognition of their independence was made. Finland's independence had been guaranteed at Brest-Litovsk, and was generally accepted, though border areas with Russia continued to be disputed for some years. Poland was the most controversial issue in this area during the postwar years. Russia had been compelled to abandon her part of what had once been Poland, at Brest-Litovsk. At Paris this large loss was confirmed, but the conflicting views on Russo-Polish relations led to war between 1920 and 1921, at the conclusion of which the treaty of Riga made less generous provision for Russia in relation to Poland than had the allies at Paris. Romania profited from the general dislocation of these years by seizing Bessarabia from Russia, an action which did not provoke protest from the peace-making powers.

International relations in the early 1920s

In spite of the hopes and efforts that went

into framing the Paris peace settlement, and in spite of some of its solid achievements, it was surrounded by a general sense of disappointment. Many major powers were unhappy about its provisions. The United States, in circumstances more fully described in chapter 4, refused to sign any of the peace treaties or to belong to the League of Nations: the absence of this major power, whose president had played such an important rôle in creating the settlement, was a serious blow to its chances. The Germans viewed the treaty of Versailles as a humiliation which was virtually forced upon them: under the circumstances, Germany was unlikely to cooperate whole-heartedly in fulfilling the treaty's terms. The powers outside Europe and the United States took the view that the whole settlement was too much concerned with European interests.

Many of the outbreaks of violence in Europe immediately after the war are attributable to the clauses of the Paris peace treaties. Most of these are considered in more detail in other parts of the book. Looked at collectively they are:

> Graeco-Turkish War, 1919–22, see pages 22–23
> Russo-Polish War, 1920–21, see page 14
> The Fiume episode, 1919–22, see page 45
> The French occupation of the Ruhr, 1923, see page 56

A significant development in these years was the drawing together of the 'outcast' nations of the peace settlement. In April 1922 Russia and Germany concluded the treaty of Rapallo by which Germany recognized the Soviet government of Russia, and by which the economies of the two countries came closer.

In the autumn of 1925 the foreign ministers of the major powers gathered at the Swiss lakeside resort of Locarno. Here discussions were held in a relaxed and friendly atmosphere, leading to the signature of the Locarno treaties, which were greeted as a constructive step on the road to permanent international peace. The treaties consisted of a series of agreements between different European states, the most significant of which were those whereby Germany undertook to regard her western boundaries as permanent and to accept the demilitarized status of the Rhineland. More significant, on Germany's part, was what the treaty omitted: there was no German guarantee that her eastern boundaries were to be regarded in the same way. This omission led to a promise by France to assist both Poland and Czechoslovakia in the event of attack. But the overall purpose of Locarno was to reconcile Germany with the rest of Europe, and as a further step in that direction negotiations were begun on the German entry into the League of Nations, which took place in the following year.

Questions

4. Study the map of Germany below, on which the heavy lines show the country's boundaries in 1914, and then answer questions (a) to (d) which follow.

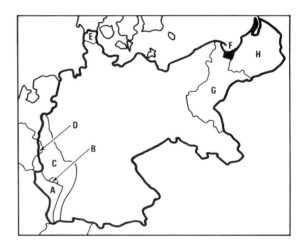

(a) (i) Name areas A, D, E, G and H, and also the country to which each of them was assigned by the Versailles treaty.

   (ii) With reference to *two* of these areas, explain the reasons why they were designated as they were by the terms of the Versailles treaty.

(5+3)

(b) (i) Name area B and city F.
 (ii) Describe the arrangements made at Versailles for the administration of B and F, and explain why these particular arrangements were made.

(1+3)

(c) (i) Name area C.
 (ii) Describe how and explain why area C was subject to particular limitations by the terms of the Versailles treaty.

(1+2)

(d) Describe how and explain why Germany was compelled by the terms of the Versailles treaty to
 (i) abandon her colonies, and
 (ii) pay reparations.

(5)

5. Examine (a) the differing attitudes of the 'Big Three' towards Germany at the 1919 peace negotiations and (b) the way in which Germany was eventually treated by the terms of the Versailles treaty.

6. What do you understand by the term *self-determination*? Show to what extent this principle was put into effect by the terms of the Paris peace treaties of 1919–20.

3

The League of Nations

After each of the two world wars, world-wide desire to establish organizations that would preserve peace and advance human welfare, resulted in the creation of the League of Nations in 1920 and the United Nations Organization in 1945. They responded very differently to the situations they encountered. In many respects the United Nations has proved the more successful of the two, and has been able to profit from the shortcomings of the League.

The origins and organization of the League of Nations

In the half-century before 1914 international cooperation on a number of world issues had developed significantly. The International Telegraphic Union, the Universal Postal Union, the International Institute of Agriculture and the International Health Office had all been established with the intention of fostering cooperation. There had been a tendency for governments to seek consultation on issues that might lead to conflict, such as the partitioning of Africa into colonies, and the decline of the Ottoman Empire. Nations were more ready to take disputes to international arbitration than they had once been. Particularly important international meetings had taken place, on the initiative of Tsar Nicholas II, at The Hague in 1899 and 1907 to seek ways of limiting armaments and maintaining international peace.

President Wilson's fourteenth point recommended:

A general association of nations must be formed under specific covenants for the purpose of affording mutual guarantees of political independence and territorial integrity to great and small states alike.

Wilson pursued this point vigorously in the peace negotiations of Paris while a number of world leaders among whom were Pope Benedict XV and the Prime Minister of South Africa, General Smuts, gave support to the idea and made practical suggestions for its organizational structure. All the Paris peace treaties signed later in 1919 and 1920 accepted the principles on which the League was based.

The document in which the principles and organization of the League of Nations were put forward was known as the *Covenant*. Its opening clauses were concerned with the League's aims and purposes: maintaining international peace, respect for international law, and open negotiations between governments. The League Assembly consisted of representatives of each member nation, meeting together in the autumn of each year. The Council, a smaller and more effective body, consisted of representatives of each of the major victor powers of the First World War: Britain, France, Italy and Japan, together with four other powers, represented in rotation. One highly controversial requirement was that both in the Assembly and in the Council, all decisions had to be unanimous; consequently comparatively minor powers were able to place a veto on the proposed action of the League. A Secretariat under the control of a Secretary General was established, to oversee administrative work. The first Secretary General was Sir Eric Drummond, formerly a member of the British Foreign Office, and a man dedicated to the ideals for which the League stood. He took steps to ensure that the Secretariat was fully international in its composition:

Representatives at the Assembly of the League of Nations in the early 1920s. The enthusiastic hopes that were then placed in the League as a means of keeping world peace had been destroyed by the late 1930s.

it thus formed the early beginnings of an international civil service that was to develop considerably in later institutions of the twentieth century. A Permanent Court of International Justice was established and its judges, chosen from all the member nations, were to have responsibility for making decisions on legal disputes, between them. The Assembly, Council and Secretariat were all eventually housed in the specially-constructed Palace of the Nations in Geneva; the Permanent Court was at The Hague.

Some articles from the Covenant of the League of Nations

Article 2. The action of the League under this Covenant shall be effected through the instrumentality of an Assembly and of a Council, with a permanent Secretariat.

Article 11. Any war or threat of war, whether immediately affecting any of the members of the League or not, is hereby declared a matter of concern to the whole League, and the League shall take any action that may be deemed wise and effectual to safeguard the peace of nations.
Article 22. A permanent Commission shall be constituted to receive and examine the annual reports of the mandatories and to advise the Council on all matters relating to the observance of the mandates.

As is suggested by Article 11 above, the Covenant laid down procedures for the preservation of peace, and using the Permanent Court was one way in which peace could be maintained. Countries submitting a dispute to the Permanent Court were pledged to accept any decision which the Permanent Court gave. It was hoped that the Assembly or Council would reach unanimous decision in condemning an aggressor and in dissuading him from military action. But in the event of a lack of unanimity, the aggressor was expected to delay some months before war was actually commenced. Provided the Assembly or Council gave a unanimous lead against an aggressor, they would call upon the member nations to apply economic sanctions by cutting trade and financial relations with the aggressor. In practice, that marked the limit of the League's actions. There was provision for member nations to give military assistance to the League, but this provision was never put into effect. Obviously the League would only be effective in preserving peace if all its members felt that peace was important.

The Mandates Commission had oversight of the administration by the victorious powers of the former German colonies and former parts of the Ottoman Empire. The areas administered in this way were known as *mandates* and the countries which administered them were *mandatories*. Category 'A' mandates were the former possessions of the Ottoman Empire which were almost ready for independence; categories 'B' mandates and 'C' mandates were the former colonial possessions in Africa and the Pacific, and for them independence was considered to be a long way off. But with all categories of mandate the eventual aim was independence. In the meantime, the protection and the well-being of their populations were to form the essential responsibilities of the mandatories. The mandatory was not to consider the mandate as a useful addition to its colonial empire: to emphasize the overall responsibilities that the system involved the mandatory was required to submit an annual report of its work to the League of Nations Mandates Commission.

The work of a number of the previously existing international organizations was encouraged by the League. From the discussions of a number of trade unionists and civil servants, the International Labour Organization (ILO) was created to generally oversee living and working conditions within the countries of the League members.

In these different ways, the League made provision for advancing the interests of human welfare throughout the world. But in this connection also, the League Covenant was insufficiently thorough as it never went so far as did the later United Nations Charter in acknowledging the equality of all human beings. The proposed inclusion of a statement to this effect was not accepted, as such a statement at that time would have troubled the confident imperial position of many of the great powers.

Membership of the League of Nations

When formally inaugurated in January 1920, 42 nations belonged to the League. Many of these were small, but among them were almost all the major victor powers of the First World War. The United States was not a member, as the Senate had exercised its right under the American constitution to reject the Paris peace treaties: by rejecting these treaties they rejected the Covenant of the League which formed a part of them. The creation of the League owed much to President Wilson's idealism: the absence of his own country from it owed much to his political obstinacy. In November 1918, in the mid-term elections, the opposition Republican party gained a majority in the Senate. Opposition to any continued American involvement in world affairs developed under the leadership of Senator Lodge, assisted by many immigrant groups who were opposed to the adverse effects that some of the terms had on their fellow-countrymen in Europe. Wilson was unwise not to take firmer steps to pacify this potentially dangerous opposition. He had refused to permit Republicans to be represented at the Paris negotiations, and by the time he did embark upon efforts to accommodate this opposition, it had taken too firm a grip. The Senate's rejection of the peace treaties was never reversed. By its action the League's prospects for success were seriously harmed. The United States was to have been one of five great powers permanently represented on the Council, the importance of which consequently declined. Opposition to the League in many member countries tended to be encouraged by the example of the United States: throughout the League's existence a total of 17 countries withdrew, though 20 new states joined.

Among the countries which joined the League were Germany and the Soviet Union. Many of Germany's wartime allies joined in the early 1920s and Germany became a member in 1926, just after the signing of the Locarno treaties. No longer was it possible to suggest that the League consisted only of the war's victors. Germany was in fact honoured with a permanent membership of the Council, an honour which implied recognition of Germany as a great power. To try to satisfy those countries which became angry at this privilege, the total number of non-permanent members was increased from six to nine. But the German membership was short-lived and Hitler withdrew his country from membership in October 1933, when Germany's plea for equal treatment regarding armaments was rejected. The Soviet Union had not participated in the creation of the League and the general atmosphere of hostility which it encountered kept it outside until September 1934 when Stalin, anxious to seek allies against possible German aggression, sought entry. Soviet membership was also short-lived. In December 1939 the Soviet Union was declared no longer a member as a consequence of the Soviet invasion of Poland and the Baltic States in the opening months of the Second World War.

Two other important founder members left in the 1930s, after the League had condemned their aggressive policies: Japan in March 1933 and Italy in December 1937. The circumstances that led to the withdrawal of these two countries are considered in chapters 7 and 5 respectively.

The League's work in attempting to solve disputes in the 1920s

Throughout the 1920s a number of comparatively minor disputes were successfully resolved by the League and were seen as encouraging signs that this new attempt to control international relations was in fact working. In 1921 the League ruled in favour of Finland continuing to hold the Aaland islands in the Baltic Sea, thus upholding its sovereignty granted by earlier international treaties. This early issue was a comparatively minor one, but it showed a willingness on the part of Finland and the Aaland islanders to accept the League's judgment in the interests of peace and harmony in the Baltic. The League was required to take another decision on territorial possession in 1921, on the issue of the division of Upper Silesia between Poland and Germany. The majority of the population had, in a referendum, expressed a clear desire to remain under German rule, yet the new Poland needed the support of this economically valuable area. The League's task was therefore a delicate one. The division which it proposed satisfied neither side, though the League's decision was, under strong protest, formally accepted by both in May 1922.

In October 1925 the League took direct action to preserve peace when an invasion of Bulgaria was launched by the forces of Greece, at that time under a military dictatorship which appeared to be following the recent example of the Italian attacks on Greece in order to secure territory which it claimed. The Council met and successfully insisted on a Greek withdrawal and on the payment by Greece of compensation to Bulgaria. As this resolution of the Graeco-Bulgarian conflict came just after the successful Locarno conference, and as it followed to the letter the procedure laid down for such crises by the League Covenant, it was hailed with great enthusiasm as evidence of the successful working of the League. But it must be remembered that the dispute was a straightforward one and the two powers involved were small, and would have found it impossible to resist the combined weight of the great powers represented on the Council.

Other minor instances of successful work along these lines can be found throughout the 1920s. But there were disputes during that decade in which the League's intervention was far from successful. The area around the town of Vilna, considered by the people of newly created Lithuania to be essentially Lithuanian territory, was coveted by the neighbouring country of Poland. Taking advantage of the circumstances of the Russo-Polish war of 1920–21 Poland had seized Vilna, whose status was being discussed by the League at that time. Opposition within both Lithuania and Poland to this attempt made by the League to resolve the problem led to the matter being referred to a Conference of Ambassadors which, on doubtful legal grounds but perhaps with an eye to immediate realities, declared Vilna to be a part of Poland. Over Vilna the League certainly failed: the solution reached by the Conference of Ambassadors was unjust and disputes over Vilna embittered relations between Poland and Lithuania throughout the interwar years.

A similar instance of aggression going unchecked by the League is the case of the Italian attack on Corfu in 1923. In response to the murder of some Italian officers who were surveying the boundary between Greece and Albania, the Italian dictator Mussolini presented a list of outrageously arrogant demands to Greece, in whose territory the murder had taken place. In consequence of the Greek government's expected rejection of them, Mussolini bombarded and occupied the Greek island of Corfu off the west coast of mainland Greece, to which Italy had some rather shadowy historical claim. The Council side-stepped its responsibilities over Corfu by handing the matter over to the Conference of Ambassadors, largely on the grounds that it was to that Conference that the murdered Italian officers had been responsible. The Conference dealt more leniently with the situation and persuaded the Greek government to make a satisfactory financial settlement to Italy, in return for which the Italian forces withdrew from the island. The Council failed to act very decisively on this issue, which is generally regarded as one of the League's failures. Nevertheless, it was from the League, and particularly from the Assembly, that strong opposition to Italian aggression had been voiced. The Corfu incident had shown

Poland's gains agreed by the League of Nations

that aggression would not pass without some reaction from the League.

Attempts at closer international cooperation

At the meeting of the Assembly in the autumn of 1924 attempts were made, largely as a result of the work of the British Prime Minister, Ramsay MacDonald, to improve the methods by which the League could fulfil its role as peacemaker. The results of these attempts were contained in a document known as the *Geneva Protocol*, under which arbitration was to be compulsory in disputes which might lead to war. If this work of arbitration was ignored, League members were to provide armed forces to compel the aggressor country to make peace. Though the governments of most League members accepted the Protocol willingly, the British government, fearing that its own freedom of action would be limited by the Protocol and that it might be drawn into disputes that were of little relevance to Britain, refused to do so. This British refusal influenced other League members and led to the collapse of the Protocol. A number of League members had made their own acceptance of the Protocol conditional on the British acceptance: furthermore, the Commonwealth countries shared their mother-country's reservations.

The collapse of the Protocol was an unfortunate, but not a fatal, setback in the development of the League. Its immediate effect was softened by the general sense of European peace and stability achieved at Locarno in the following year. Many League members were anxious to develop the League along the lines suggested by the Protocol and to strengthen the Covenant. Much attention was given at Geneva to these issues but little progress was made.

The 1928 Kellogg-Briand pact was an attempt made outside the League of Nations to strengthen international cooperation. The work of Frank Kellogg, American Secretary of State, and of Aristide Briand, Foreign Minister of France, led to the signature of this pact in August 1928 and to its acceptance by 65 countries. Its main provisions were simply the renunciation of war as an instrument of policy and the settlement of disputes by peaceful means.

The main articles of the Kellogg-Briand pact
Article 1. The High Contracting Parties solemnly declare in the names of their respective peoples that they condemn recourse to war for the solution of international controversies, and renounce it as an instrument of national policy in their relations with one another.
Article 2. The High Contracting Parties agree that the settlement or solution of all disputes or conflicts of whatever nature or of whatever origin they may be, which may arise among them, shall never be sought except by pacific means.

Though the creation of the pact was not the work of the League, these provisions were fully acceptable to League members: indeed few countries would wish to disagree with provisions of this kind publicly. A particularly important aspect of the pact was that its main origins and its main support came from the most significant absentee from the League, the United States, where public opinion was strong in its support. The Soviet Union also agreed to it. Hopes were expressed that the pact might symbolize fuller American involvement in world affairs and possibly even American membership of the League of Nations. But such hopes came to nothing.

Fundamentally, the pact was a weak document. It made no provision for imposing sanctions on countries which ignored its terms. Its weakness was well illustrated three years later, in October 1931, when Japan, one of its signatories, totally ignored the restrictions of the pact when it launched its invasion of Chinese-held Manchuria.

The Manchurian crisis signalled much more than the collapse of the Kellogg-Briand pact. It also showed starkly the weakness of the League of Nations in tackling aggression. The League's later inability to prevent the aggression of totalitarian powers in Abyssinia, Spain and central Europe in the mid and late 1930s confirmed the weakness that was made apparent in Manchuria. The League's role in the 1930s was slight and ineffective; the crises of those years are more appropriately considered later, in chapters 5, 9 and 11.

The League's work for human welfare and disarmament

The League's efforts to improve economic and social conditions throughout the world met with a good measure of success in the interwar years. International organizations under the direction of the League increased in number and in scope. The International Labour Organization was one of the most significant. It was under the leadership of Albert Thomas, a forceful and dedicated French Socialist, and it drew much of its support from trade unionists in member countries. Whilst always forming a part of the League of Nations, it tended to develop along semi-independent lines, as it continued to pursue its work of seeking improvement in labour conditions and in the general lives of workers throughout the world. In the 1930s the United States, while keeping to its non-membership of the League, actually became a member of the International Labour Organization. In many respects it was the most successful part of the League and was later incorporated into the United Nations.

In the early years the Communication and Transit Organization was particularly effective. Valuable work was done on the international coordination of different transport systems. The simplification of passport and visa regulations, the creation of standard forms of radio communication and of regulation for the new forms of communication by air, were all among the important practical work necessary in a world in which communication was of increasing importance. The Health Organization was another successful part of the League. Valuable research work into diseases was undertaken and much practical medical aid to under-developed countries was arranged, particularly in curbing epidemics. These two organizations were in many respects the ones whose world influence was the most significant. The work of the Mandates Commission represented the most important innovation. European governments had not previously held responsibility for colonies from an international body and had generally not previously placed much emphasis on the eventual achievement of independence by the colonial lands. One enlightened statesman who had envisaged eventual independence and who had worked for many years as a British colonial governor in West Africa was Lord Lugard, who became a dominant influence in the Mandates Commission. The accountability of the mandatories to the Mandates Commission created some elements of irritation on the part of the mandatories, but it was generally agreed that it worked well.

The clauses of the treaty of Versailles requiring the disarmament of Germany were intended to be the first steps in a general world disarmament. One of the main tasks of the League was the exacting one of attempting to organize this general disarmament. But in spite of much effort throughout the interwar years it failed to bring about any significant reductions in armament levels.

Organization of disarmament got off to a slow start mainly because international tensions remained high for some years after the end of the war. Even then, the great powers which would have been required to reduce their arms levels were still very nervous. Only after the 1925 Locarno conference had produced a more peaceful atmosphere, in Europe especially, was it possible for constructive work in disarmament to go forward. A Disarmament Conference was to be held, but discussion about its composition and function continued for so long that it was not until February 1932 that it met at Geneva. A scheme under which members were to allow a proportion of their armed forces to come under the direct control of the League had been prepared in advance and was expected to be the main focus of the discussions. But in the event more attention was given to the German claim for equality of treatment with other nations over armaments, and to the fears of other nations, especially France, that this request caused. After considerable debate had taken place and after generous suggestions had been made on this issue, Germany, at Hitler's request, withdrew from the Disarmament Conference and from the League in October 1933. This withdrawal signified the end of the Disarmament Conference.

Not all of the efforts to achieve disarmament took place under the direction of the League. The Washington agreements of 1921 and 1930, by which the comparative size of navies was regulated, and the Kellogg-Briand pact of 1928, were all concerned with disarmament and were undertaken by direct governmental exchanges outside the League. Neither these nor the limited work of the League itself were able to produce firm results. Undoubtedly one of the main reasons for this lack of success was the absence of a common policy between the victorious Allied powers, especially in their attitude towards the defeated powers. This was the same problem that had hampered the Paris peace conference. The defeated powers, particularly Germany, were not slow to notice and use these divisions to their own advantage.

Questions

7. Study the articles from the Covenant of the League of Nations on page 27 and then answer questions (a) to (d) which follow.
   (a) Describe the composition and work of *each* of the three parts of the League of Nations mentioned in Article 2.

(6)

   (b) With reference to Article 11, examine
      (i) *one* example of the successful working of this article during the 1920s, and
      (ii) *one* example of the unsuccessful working of this article during the 1930s.

(6)

   (c) With reference to Article 22,
      (i) name one *mandatory*, and
      (ii) name one *mandate* to which it was linked.
      (iii) Apart from those mentioned in article 22, describe the responsibilities of a mandatory for its mandate.

(1+1+2)

   (d) Outline the main humanitarian work of the League of Nations during the interwar years.

(4)

8. Describe the attempts made by the League of Nations during the interwar years to preserve world peace. How do you account for the general failure of this work by the 1930s?

9. Examine the attempts that were made during the interwar years to (a) improve the efficiency of the peacekeeping work of the League of Nations and (b) reduce the armaments held by the major powers.

4

Normalcy and the New Deal

During the decade after the First World War, the American people sought to isolate themselves from the rest of the world. They wished to revive within the United States the traditional American values which had brought them wealth and happiness in their earlier pioneering history, when the struggle had been to establish the nation and to exploit its resources. The Republican party's promise to reassert these values enabled it to maintain political leadership of the country throughout the decade. American society, the Republicans suggested, was threatened by new developments since the turn of the century. The increase in the size and number of towns threatened the long-standing importance of the countryside; immigrants from the poorer parts of Europe and Latin America threatened the social position of the descendants of the earlier, English settlers; the growth of Communism, fired by its success in Russia in 1917, appeared to some to be a threat to the two-party system of government and even to the American constitution itself. At the close of the First World War, President Wilson's attempts to involve the United States in the League of Nations and in a more active world role, already noted in the previous two chapters, was seen as the most serious threat of all: a threat to the American isolationist tradition, already sorely battered by direct American involvement in the European fighting during the closing stages of the war. The Republican presidents of the 1920s sought to return their disturbed land to what they termed 'rugged individualism', the 'normalcy' of earlier times.

The Republican presidents of the 1920s

Warren Harding (1921–23), Calvin Coolidge (1923–29) and Herbert Hoover (1929–33) were the men who presided over a period of economic boom which ended after 1929 in economic disaster. Though in November 1920 Harding was elected by a landslide Republican vote and though throughout his presidency he managed to maintain his image as a popular and kind-hearted president, there have been in fact few presidents less suited to the office. His earlier experience of political life had been confined to the state politics of his native Ohio and as president he floundered hopelessly out of his depth. A keen card player, he did little to enhance the dignity of the presidential office by inviting visiting diplomats to all-night poker sessions in the White House. More serious were the corrupt activities of the 'Ohio gang' of politicians brought into office by Harding, a group whose members used their ministerial positions to make substantial profits. As Harding died in office in August 1923 he was able to avoid facing the consequences of scandals in which he was implicated and which could have caused him difficulties similar to those faced over the Watergate scandals by Richard Nixon a half-century later.

The vice president, Calvin Coolidge, succeeded automatically in 1923 and was elected to the presidency in 1924. A silent, withdrawn politician, holding firmly to the belief that the foundations of America's greatness were to be found in the application of hard work and the acceptance of fundamental Christianity, Coolidge presided quietly over the greatest boom the American people had ever seen. 'The business of America is business' said Coolidge, and the successful encouragement of American business activity remained his main aim.

When Herbert Hoover campaigned successfully in 1928, he was able to capitalize on this economic boom and to assert that America was 'nearer to the final triumph over poverty than ever before in the history of any land'. Hoover had entered political life only recently, and was widely admired for his relief work among refugees during the First World War. He inherited a prosperous legacy and was certainly a more able and a more energetic president than either Harding or Coolidge.

The substantial advances made by American industry in the 1920s cannot be attributed directly to government policy. It was Republican policy to help create a situation in which business could flourish without

Gasoline (petrol) stations such as this were a novelty in the United States in the 1920s. The smart new cars and the widely varying advertisements give further evidence of the affluence within the country during these years.

government interference. Harding said that while he wanted to see 'more business in government' he also wanted to see 'less government in business' and his successors followed the same policy. Coolidge even maintained that, 'if the Federal government should go out of existence, the common run of people would not detect the difference in the affairs of their daily life for a considerable length of time'. Government policy was directed towards the support of those who controlled big business. Herbert Hoover, secretary of commerce until his appointment as president, was concerned by needless internal competition between firms engaged in similar work, and encouraged amalgamations between firms: small firms and small shops were the victims of this policy, while the large firms and chain stores consolidated their importance in the American economy. Andrew Mellon, an elderly and successful businessman, who was secretary of the treasury throughout the 1920s, moved in a similar direction with his policy of drastic tax cuts that benefited substantially the wealthy business class. Mellon's justification for these tax cuts was that they made available more cash for investment by the wealthy and that the American economy therefore benefited through higher wages and higher employment. But this was of little comfort to many less wealthy Americans who paid a high proportion of their own income in tax.

American industry was highly protected throughout the years dominated by the Republican party. The Fordney-Mc-Cumber Act, 1922, raised import taxes on foreign goods to a level that compensated for cheaper production in foreign countries. As with Mellon's tax cuts, this and similar acts brought little benefit to many Americans, for whom its main effect was to increase prices. Once again, American financial policy was geared to the requirements of those who controlled big business. Apart from these government measures, industry was also assisted throughout the 1920s by the increasing use of electricity and by the application of new stream-lined methods, such as the assembly line production techniques at the new Ford car factories.

Immigration, prejudice and prohibition

The pattern of immigration into the United States changed significantly in the quarter-century before the First World War. Not only were the immigration figures for these years substantially higher than before, but whereas most of the earlier immigrants had arrived from western Europe, a majority of the prewar immigrants were from the poorer lands of southern and eastern Europe. These immigrants grouped together in the American cities where they found employment as unskilled labourers but where their living and working conditions often continued to be desperately poor.

The continuing entry of such immigrants attracted hostile criticism from many Americans. After asserting much pressure, the opponents of immigration had been able to secure an obligatory literacy test in 1917, which discriminated against the poorer immigrants, who were often unable to read. Harding's Republican government was unlikely to have much sympathy with the plight of poor immigrants. The Immigration Act of 1921 introduced the principle of the *quota*, by which the number of new immigrants from a country was limited to a quota of three per cent of the number from that country already living in the United States in 1910. As in that year the number of immigrants from southern and eastern Europe was slight, the principle of the *quota* was much to their disadvantage. Later Immigration Acts of 1924 and 1929 reduced the percentage of the quota still further.

The prosperity of the 1920s linked to the desire for a return to 'normalcy' tended to encourage strong prejudice against minority nationalities and new ideas. The 'white, Anglo-Saxon Protestant' (WASP) was portrayed as the type of American on whom the country's greatness had been constructed and whose status the Republican government sought to defend. The impact of prejudice was felt by blacks, Jews, Roman Catholics, poorer immigrants and those who supported political innovations of the left, such as Socialism, trade unionism and Communism, all of which were considered to impede America's path to political and economic greatness. Forceful expression of these various prejudices was given by the Ku Klux Klan, a theatrical but sinister organization founded during the Civil War and revived during the First World War. By the mid-1920s it had increased its membership to four-and-a-half million. It found support in the rural areas of the southern states and its campaigns of hostility against blacks, immigrants and Socialists often led to violence and lynchings.

Trade unions were also suspect. The Republican government itself showed opposition to trade unionism and was supported by widespread popular opposition, stimulated especially by a series of postwar strikes. No legislation directly opposed to the trade unions was introduced: instead the government and the major companies introduced the more subtle policy of undermining trade unionism by making government provision for many of the welfare needs of the workers. In many industries, however, conditions continued to be poor and trade union activity continued to be discouraged. The courts played an important part in these anti-union moves, by giving legal judgments in support of action taken by companies against trade unions, in particular by supporting 'yellow dog' contracts, in which workers agreed not to involve themselves in union affairs.

Prohibition had been introduced by the Volstead Act of 1919, by which the sale and manufacture of alcoholic drinks throughout the country was prohibited. Prohibition was now written into the American constitution as the eighteenth amendment, marking the triumph of the pressure asserted by the powerful temperance movements. But it proved impossible to enforce. Liquor was illegally manufactured and imported and was drunk in the intimate 'speakeasies': the outlawing of drink merely boosted its popularity.

The clearly unjust nature of prohibition led many Americans to take advantage of the black market in liquor, and to have less respect for the law. Gangsters made fortunes by successfully organizing the production and importation of liquor: prohibition agents were often bribed. The more powerful gangsters involved themselves in other illegal activities, such as assisting illegal immigrants; warfare between rival gangs became a serious problem. The most notorious of the gangsters, Chicago's Al Capone, pursued a profitable and blood-stained career throughout the 1920s, to be eventually arrested and imprisoned in 1932 on the comparatively unimportant charge of tax evasion.

The Wall Street crash and the Depression

In October 1929 the prosperity of the Republican era came suddenly and unexpectedly to an end, when there was a fall of 40 per cent in the value of shares on the Wall Street stock market in New York. The wealthy minority of stock market investors suffered immediate financial loss. Subsequent lack of investment led to an industrial decline which left few Americans unharmed by its effects. The effects of the crash were felt increasingly outside the United States during the following years of the Depression.

The crash revealed the insecure foundations on which American prosperity had been constructed during the 1920s. Bank managers and stockbrokers had been lending money readily for their clients to invest in the stock market, thus encouraging the progress of share values to unrealistically high levels. The world of the stock market had become so separated from industry that the workers' wages showed none of the benefits which the increased share values suggested. As a consequence, people could not afford to buy goods, and towards the end of the 1920s a number of American industries found that they were unable to sell their products. American agriculture had never shared in the boom conditions of the 1920s and it also was producing more than it could sell. Protectionist policies had led to a decline in American overseas trade, so there was no hope of selling abroad.

President Hoover considered the financial panic of October 1929 to be unwarranted. The economy, so he assured the American people, was fundamentally sound and was merely passing through a period of minor crisis, a 'healthy shakeout' as he described it. His well-publicized meetings in the autumn of 1929 with prominent businessmen and trade union leaders helped to create a more stable atmosphere but could do nothing to stem what was the most serious financial crisis that America had ever faced.

The only workable solution was for the government itself to make substantial investment in American industry and agriculture and to give relief to the unemployed. But both these ideas were contrary to the Republican policies of private initiative which had appeared to work so successfully before the crash. Hoover did make some moves in the direction of government assistance: private industry received credit, public works schemes were encouraged, tax rates for the lower paid were reduced, and excess farm produce was purchased by the government. But, although his grant of over 400 million dollars for public works was generously high, this overall policy of government assistance was only pursued weakly. Other government policies ran counter to it. Hoover's insistence that budgets should remain balanced led to the curbing of government expenditure, whilst his agreement to increase import taxes led to a further decline in foreign trade.

In the autumn of 1930, the Democrats won narrow control of Congress. Their pressure for fuller governmental involvement in solving the crisis could now be more effective, while mounting unemployment and continuing financial uncertainty gave edge to their demands for action. Hoover responded in December 1931 with an imaginative programme of aid, the most important feature of which was the creation of a Reconstruction Finance Corporation with the task of loaning government money to ailing industry. Other features of the programme involved reform of the banking and mortgage systems. Democrats criticized the scope of this programme, saying that it was inadequate; many Republicans considered it to have gone too far. Its effects were limited, though the Reconstruction Finance Corporation played a useful role and continued to function significantly in American finance throughout the 1930s. Even at this stage, some few years after the crash, Hoover refused to allow direct federal relief for the unemployed: when the Democrats passed legislation to provide for this, Hoover took advantage of his presidential powers to veto it. In his view, relief for the unemployed remained the responsibility of local and voluntary organizations.

On this matter, Hoover's policies were unrealistic. By 1932 the number of unemployed was thirteen million, a figure that represented a quarter of the available work force of the United States. To provide voluntary relief for this vast number was a total impossibility. Consequently the unemployed suffered cruelly, with the black and immigrant unemployed suffering most. These years meant for those without work, lack of food, lack of clothing, and the near impossibility of finding a job. Many lived in unhygienic shanty towns, derisively known as 'hoovervilles'. In the summer of 1932 the President's apparent disregard for the desperate plight of the American unemployed was illustrated on the outskirts of Washington. The United States Army was called upon to demolish a large 'hooverville' inhabited by ex-servicemen who were demanding immediate payment of a government bonus, as a means of relief in their unemployment. This action further weakened any belief in Hoover as a president sympathetic to the needs of ordinary Americans in the era of the Depression.

Franklin Roosevelt's New Deal

It was no surprise that the Republicans were defeated in the presidential election of November 1932 and that the Democratic candidate for the presidency, Franklin Roosevelt, was successful. Roosevelt has been widely regarded as one of the greatest of all American presidents. His popular support at the time is illustrated by his election to the presidency on four occasions, in 1932, 1936, 1940 and 1944; he died in 1945 during his fourth term of office. Subsequent legislation prevented the election of the same person to the presidency for more than two terms of office.

Franklin Roosevelt came from a well-established American family of Dutch origin. He was distantly related to Theodore Roosevelt who had been American president between 1902 and 1909 and his wife, Eleanor, was a niece of this earlier president. Woodrow Wilson was the president whom Roosevelt most admired and he had served in his government. In 1920 he had stood as the vice-presidential candidate for the Democratic party and continued his close involvement in Democratic politics throughout the 1920s in spite of the fact that a polio attack in 1921 left him partially crippled. In 1928 he was elected Governor of New York state and held that position during the Depression years of the early 1930s. His positive concern for the plight of the unemployed was shown when in September 1931 New York state became the first to provide for their relief.

Roosevelt was a skilful and flexible politician and a man of great personal charm. These qualities he used to maximum effect during the presidential election campaigns of 1932. His promise of a 'New Deal' for the American people, though its nature and its implications were not clearly thought out, won the support of a majority of Americans, disillusioned by the apparent inability of the Republicans to resolve the problems which the Depression had brought.

Roosevelt's inaugural speech in March 1933 came as a clarion call to a distressed and confused nation:

> First of all let me assert my firm belief that the only thing we have to fear is fear itself – nameless, unreasoning, unjustified terror which paralyzes needed efforts to convert retreat into advance.
>
> Our greatest primary task is to put people to work. This is no unsolveable problem if we face it wisely and courageously. It can be accomplished in part by direct recruiting by the government itself, treating the task as we would treat the emergency of a war, but at the same time, through this employment, accomplishing greatly needed projects to stimulate and reorganize the use of our natural resources.

President Franklin Roosevelt with his wife Eleanor greeting the crowds in Washington at the time of his third inauguration as President. Elected to the presidency on four occasions, Roosevelt is still widely regarded as one of the greatest of American presidents.

> Hand in hand with this, we must frankly recognize the overbalance of population in our industrial centres and, by engaging on a national scale in the redistribution, endeavour to provide a better use of the land for those best fitted for the land.
>
> I shall ask the Congress for the one remaining instrument to meet the crisis – broad executive power to wage a war against the emergency as great as the power that would be given me if we were in fact invaded by a foreign foe.

The action which he promised followed swiftly and effectively. So sudden and so strong were the measures he took during the first hundred days of his presidency that the period has been regarded as the nearest the United States has approached towards dictatorship. The Democratic majority in Congress, conscious that the times demanded firm leadership, placed no obstacles in his employment of full presidential powers.

His first concern was the restoration of confidence in the country's financial structure. Two days after his inauguration he issued a proclamation which temporarily closed all banks and prohibited the export of gold. This was followed by the Emergency Banking Act which strengthened reliable banks and forced unreliable banks out of business. This was a conservative start to the New Deal, but Americans could now have full confidence in the banking system, and the economy of the United States benefited by renewed investment in banks. Roosevelt followed this move by an Economy Act, which reduced government salaries and government pensions by up to 15 per cent. By the creation of the Federal Emergency Relief Administration he took immediate steps to ensure that the federal government contributed directly to the relief of the unemployed. Harry Hopkins, who was placed in charge of the administration of this relief, held to the view that, though in the short term direct financial relief for the unemployed was essential, in the long term the government should seek to provide the unemployed with work. During the first hundred days work began on many bills designed to bring this about.

The New Deal: economic and social change

Most of the New Deal's early legislation was directed in one way or another at providing employment. Roosevelt continued to support the Reconstruction Finance Corporation which the Republicans had created, but broadened its loan-making activities by encouraging assistance to small businesses. The Civilian Conservation Corps was established to help preserve natural resources, such as forests. Its members were mainly young, unemployed men: by the late 1930s its membership was about half a million.

The National Recovery Administration (NRA), under the direction of General Hugh Johnson, had wider scope and made greater impact. Labour conditions were to be improved and supervized by the NRA: as a result of its work a minimum wage of 40 cents an hour and a maximum working week of 40 hours, and the abolition of child labour, were achieved. The symbol of the blue eagle was adopted to show that a firm accepted NRA standards. The Public Works Administration, a section of the NRA, was concerned with the organization of state-financed projects. Although much success was achieved by the NRA it was mainly the large businesses that benefited from it.

Of the public works schemes encouraged by Roosevelt, by far the most important was the Tennessee Valley Authority (TVA). This scheme was the idea of Senator Norris and was designed both to prevent the widespread flooding of the Tennessee Valley and to provide hydro-electric power in the area. A number of existing dams were improved and new dams were constructed; the transportation of goods along lengthy stretches of the river and its tributaries was made possible. The results were wholly beneficial: industry was attracted to the area, farming was improved and during the Second World War the area became essential for the production of armaments. The most novel feature about the organization of the TVA was that, as a government enterprise, it covered a number of states, and thus conflicted with the traditional American view of state rights.

Conditions in the rural parts of the United States in the early 1930s are movingly portrayed in John Steinbeck's novel, *The Grapes of Wrath*. Agriculture had been in a depressed state for many years before the Wall Street crash, and many farmers were now reduced to poverty and desperation. The essential problem which Roosevelt sought to correct was the high output, for which farmers were unable to find a market. The Agricultural Adjustment Act was a bold attempt to solve this problem. It made provision for federal subsidies to agriculture in return for reducing agricultural output. An unfortunate immediate consequence of the Act was the destruction of crops and livestock in order to reach the lower output targets. Reduced output also caused many poorer farmers to be evicted from the lands which they cultivated. Despite these unhappy consequences, the Agricultural Adjustment Act worked. Output became better aligned with market requirements, prices improved and despair lifted. A new Agricultural Adjustment Act of 1938 created a Surplus Marketing Administration to prevent the wholesale wastages of the earlier years and schemes for soil conservation, export subsidies and crop loans were also brought into effect.

The early legislation of the New Deal therefore emphasized the revival of the American economy. From 1935, a period sometimes known as the 'second' New Deal, the emphasis shifted to the reform of American society. The Social Security Act, the work of Frances Perkins, the first woman member in the American cabinet, was a revo-

lutionary piece of legislation in this connection. The Act broke with the long-established American tradition of allowing the sick, the aged and the unemployed to fend for themselves as best they could, assisted only by family and voluntary aid, and by strictly limited local aid. By this Act, federal aid was to be made available for pensions for the elderly, relief for certain categories of disabled unemployed, and assistance for families. Although the immediate effects of the Act were limited, the scope of its provisions increased throughout the 1930s. Also in 1935 a new direction was given to the type of relief given by the Works Progress Administration (a new name for the earlier Public Works Administration) which, under the supervision of another dedicated New Dealer, Harry Hopkins, provided relief for the unem-

An Arkansas family stop on their journey westwards to change a tyre on the van which contains all of their possessions. During the Depression years the search for employment frequently led American families to undertaking gruelling, humiliating journeys such as this.

41

ployed in the form of work rather than money payments. In the late 1930s as many as two million people were employed through the Works Progress Administration, in jobs ranging from the construction of buildings and streets to the writing of music and books. A real effort was made to achieve practical and humane solutions to the continuing problem of unemployment.

The difficulties of the American trade unions had, to an extent, been relieved just before the commencement of the New Deal. The Anti-Injunction Act of 1932 protected the trade unions by making unenforceable the 'yellow dog' contracts that many employers had imposed on their workers. Union activity began to flourish and in 1935 the Labour Relations Act, often known by the name of its sponsor in Congress as the Wagner Act, provided for full recognition of trade unions and their rights in collective bargaining. As the economy revived in the late 1930s, industrial relations declined. There were many serious conflicts between the unions and the management of large firms, sometimes resulting in violence between police and strikers.

Opposition to the New Deal

The 1936 presidential election resulted in a landslide victory for Roosevelt and enabled him to continue the New Deal policies, assured of substantial American support. But there were strong elements which opposed him. Many Americans still favoured a minimal role for government in the United States, and preferred the 'rugged individualism' favoured by the Republican party in the 1920s. To these opponents the New Deal suggested far too much government action: 'big government' and 'creeping socialism' were the slogans flung at many of the New Deal agencies. Other Americans criticized the New Deal for not going far enough in its aid and not distributing the aid fairly enough. Senator Huey Long of Louisiana, employing the slogan 'share the wealth', put this viewpoint very strongly, although he never developed as a really ser-

ious challenge to Roosevelt and he was assassinated in 1935. As for the leadership of the opposition Republican party, it recognized that by the mid-1930s the New Deal was producing results and could not be completely reversed. It pledged itself to continue the New Deal, but to reorganize its administration.

Opposition to the New Deal was not, however, merely a matter for electoral politics. A particularly serious source of opposition was the United States Supreme Court, which had ruled as unconstitutional some of the legislation of the New Deal. In particular the smooth working of the Social Security Act, the National Recovery Administration and the Agricultural Adjustment Act had been seriously hampered by Supreme Court rulings. At his second inauguration, in January 1937, Roosevelt assured the American people that he would overcome this opposition. To do so would involve altering the law of the United States and, at a time when many of the dictatorships of Europe were ominously consolidating their power, this could have invited accusations of dictatorship. But Roosevelt pursued his policy, and in February 1937 announced his intention to appoint new judges to replace the elderly judges who had so seriously undermined his work. Thus threatened, the Supreme Court adopted a less unhelpful attitude towards New Deal legislation and the new appointments were in the event not necessary.

American isolationism in the 1920s and 1930s

The isolationist feeling that had reasserted itself at the time of the Paris peace conference continued to grip the United States throughout the next two decades. The American absence from the League of Nations, the imposition of high import taxes, the insistence on the repayment of loans from wartime allies and the restrictions on immigration all suggest that the United States was engaged in a whole-hearted pursuit of isolationism. Only with the American entry into the Second

World War in December 1941 was this isolationism finally broken.

Nevertheless, even under the Republicans in the 1920s, America did show some involvement with the rest of the world. Successful American businessmen found it difficult to resist the opportunity of investing money abroad: the spread abroad of the chain stores of Woolworths and the mass-production car factories of Fords were direct ways in which the United States, through its thriving economy in the 1920s, became involved elsewhere. Direct government aid was given to Germany in 1924 under the Dawes plan and in 1929 under the Young plan. Concern for the achievement of world disarmament and the maintenance of world peace was shown by the leading participation of the United States in the Washington Naval Conference of 1921, which agreed proportions of naval strength to be 5:5:3 for the United States, Britain and Japan. It also played a large part in the 1928 Kellogg-Briand pact which outlawed war.

Throughout the 1930s Congress continued to support isolationism. This was especially shown by the passing of a series of Neutrality Acts in 1935, 1936 and 1937, prohibiting American loans and aid to countries engaged in war. During these years the United States firmly refused to involve itself in the conflicts within Abyssinia, Spain and China. But Roosevelt became increasingly concerned by the aggressive policies of Germany in central Europe and of Japan in the Pacific area. He warned his fellow-countrymen that, in spite of isolationism, these policies could well involve the United States in war: he urged Congress to abandon the Neutrality Acts and to show American support for countries threatened by aggression. But Congress refused to change its isolationist stand. Even after the Second World War began in Europe in September 1939, isolationist feeling remained strong, though United States sympathies lay with the allied side, as is shown at the start of chapter 13. Only in December 1941, with the shock of the Japanese attack on Pearl Harbor, did the United States enter the Second World War.

Questions

10. Study the extracts on page 39 from President Roosevelt's speech when he was sworn in for the first time as President of the United States, and then answer questions (a) to (e) which follow.
    (a) Give
        (i) the year in which this speech was delivered,
        (ii) the party to which Roosevelt belonged,
        (iii) the name of the outgoing President, and
        (iv) the number of times on which Roosevelt was elected President of the United States.
        (4)
    (b) Describe the features of American life to which Roosevelt is referring in the first paragraph.
        (4)
    (c) Describe the steps which Roosevelt took to fulfil his *primary task* (lines 6–7), showing in what specific ways he employed the methods he outlines in the second paragraph.
        (5)
    (d) Describe the policies pursued by Roosevelt to achieve the aims outlined in the third paragraph.
        (3)
    (e) (i) What do you understand by the term *broad executive power* as used in the final paragraph?
        (ii) Show how the President encountered opposition in his use of such power and how he overcame this opposition.
        (1+3)

11. How do you account for the prosperity of many people within the United States throughout the 1920s? Show for what reasons and in what ways this prosperity had come to an end by the early 1930s.

12. Examine the reasons that led to Roosevelt's success in the presidential election of 1932. How far, during his first two terms of office, did Roosevelt justify the confidence that the majority of Americans placed in him?

5

Fascist Italy

Unification of Italy had been achieved in the second half of the nineteenth century, so by the end of the First World War, Italy was still a new country and was still experiencing difficulty of adjustment. The war, though victorious for Italy, had added to the country's problems, and in the years immediately after 1918 there were disturbances in the political life of the country, problems in its economic and social life and humiliations in its foreign relations.

Italy's postwar problems

Although the Savoy monarchy of Victor Emanuel III (1900 to 1946) provided some degree of stability within the country, its political life became confused after 1918, and coalition governments succeeded each other so rapidly that good government became impossible. Two parties made particular impact in these years: the Socialist party and the Popular party. The Socialist party, despite the split of the extreme left-wing in 1921 to form the Italian Communist party, more than doubled its prewar support. The growth of the new Popular party, founded in 1918 by a Sicilian priest, Don Luigi Sturzo, showed that the Roman Catholic church was prepared again to involve itself in the politics of the state.

The successful development of these two parties threatened the continued hold on government power which the Italian Liberal party and its political allies had maintained in the years before and during the First World War. The general election of November 1918 showed clearly that the days of Liberal political supremacy were over.

Italian general election: November 1918	
Liberal party and allies	252
Socialist party	156
Popular party	100

Many of the Socialist and Popular deputies were completely new to parliamentary practice and their parties were only weakly united. The Popular party gave its support to the Liberals and therefore Liberal ministries continued to be formed, though none of the Liberal prime ministers of these years seemed able adequately to control parliament or solve the country's many other problems.

Fundamental to these other problems was the collapse of the Italian economy. Compared with other West European countries, Italy has few natural resources; before 1918 industrial development in the south had been negligible and in the north only slight. After the war economic problems increased. The balance of payments had seriously worsened and consequently the country's meagre financial resources were being drained in payment for imports. Recent legislation in the United States cutting down on immigrants had severe effects on Italy and contributed to the mounting number of the country's unemployed. The countries allied to Italy during the war were no longer prepared to continue their earlier loans and financial support.

These economic problems made the years 1919, 1920 and 1921 ones of severe social unrest. Trade union membership increased tenfold during these years. In the towns there were strikes and factory occupations. In the countryside there were demonstrations and land occupations, showing that the peasantry were no longer prepared to suffer as silently as they had done in the prewar years. Although Anarchist and Communist elements were present in all these disturbances, no real leader of the working classes emerged; Italy in these years lacked a Lenin.

The middle classes also suffered. Inflation meant that their investments in war loans were almost worthless. They were hard hit by taxation, and those who owned property were forbidden to increase the rents that they charged. Many of this class were outraged by the violence and disturbances that plagued their country during these years.

The bait that had tempted Italy to enter the First World War in 1915 was the treaty of London signed by Italy with France and Britain. By this treaty the areas of Trentino, South Tyrol and parts of Dalmatia were to be acquired by Italy at the successful conclusion of the war; Italy would also be allowed a share in the German colonies. But at the peace treaties of 1919, Italy was denied many of the possessions that she expected in Dalmatia and, unlike her wartime allies, she received none of the German colonies. Her acquisition of Trentino, South Tyrol and the Istrian Peninsula were not enough to satisfy her. Prime Minister Orlando left the Paris peace conference angered by the Allies' refusal to allow Italy the territory to which he felt Italy had a just claim: a strong sense of outrage gripped the country.

This feeling was expressed by the dramatic exploits of Gabrielle D'Annunzio. This romantic writer and pioneer airman led an army group to seize the disputed city of Fiume (today, Rijeka), on the border with the newly created Yugoslavia. For more than a year D'Annunzio and his forces held the city and attracted much support in Italy for a stand which appeared to be more purposeful and practical than the weak uncertainties of the Italian government on foreign issues. Though in January 1921 he was eventually compelled to leave, partly as a result of the increasing unpopularity in Fiume of his right-wing régime, he had nevertheless dramatically attracted attention to Italy's grievances and to her government's inadequate treatment of them. He had also demonstrated that force could get results.

Benito Mussolini and the Fascist seizure of power

Before the First World War, Benito Mussolini, born in the rebellious Romagna province of north-east Italy, had been an active Socialist engaged among other things in the production of the Socialist paper, *Avanti* (Forward). His political views changed after the Italian defeat by the Austrians at the battle of Caporetto in 1917: the effect of that traumatic defeat led him to support national ambitions and to abandon Socialism.

After the war the Fascist movement was founded by Mussolini in the industrial northern Italian town of Milan in March 1919. From its origins the movement stressed the need for authority in all aspects of Italian life. In place of political confusion and the

Benito Mussolini enjoyed situations such as this, when he could pose as the idolized leader of the Italians. In reality, his relations with his fellow-countrymen became increasingly less harmonious.

45

weakness of the Italian liberal tradition, Fascism promised political stability and strength. In place of economic dislocation, Fascism would create a strengthened economy based partly on the Socialist ideals to which Mussolini in the early stages of Fascism still showed some attachment. In place of foreign humiliations, Fascism promised an Italy that would fully assert itself in relations with foreign powers. By means of propaganda and effective organization, the movement spread throughout Italy. Many members grouped themselves into *squadre* (teams) for action in support of Fascism, adopting the Fascist uniform of the black shirt and employing as their symbol the *fascio* of ancient Rome, a bundle of rods and an axe strapped together, an appropriate representation of the discipline and force which the movement felt to be the answer to Italy's ills.

It was not until 1921 that Fascism received any significant increase in support. By then, much of the violence from the left, the industrial disorders and take-overs of farmland by the peasants, had virtually ceased. But the Italian middle classes were still gripped by a fear of Communism and of revolution. Fascism played strongly on these fears in its appeal. By 1921 Fascism had also become more attractive to the middle classes in other ways: no longer did Fascism press for changes in the direction of Socialism nor for any changes in Italy from monarchy to a republic, nor for any lessening in the power of the church. This more moderate appeal of Fascism tended to persuade leading liberal politicians, such as the highly-respected Giolitti, and leading churchmen, such as the newly elected Pope Pius XI, that Fascism could be a useful means of restoring order in Italy. At the same time, they felt sure that, by virtue of their experience, they would be able to maintain control of the new movement.

By 1922 the political situation had declined seriously. Prime Minister Giolitti had retired in June 1921. His immediate successors headed coalition governments which were unable to bring any improvement. In the face of social disruption coalition government was clearly not working.

In August 1922 the Fascists took over, by force, the administration of a number of important cities in northern and central Italy and the success achieved in this way attracted more recruits to their cause; in many areas local trade unions became Fascist. The Socialists and Communists proved incapable of responding adequately to these threats and were racked by internal differences. Pius XI's support of Fascism was a serious blow to the new Popular party. King Victor Emanuel III was inclined to consider Fascism the best answer for Italy.

By the late autumn circumstances in Italy seemed to favour a take-over by force. A large congress of Fascists meeting in Naples in late October voted overwhelmingly and enthusiastically for a march on Rome, in order to overthrow the government by a show of force. To oppose this threat, the King was persuaded to declare martial law, but later changed his mind. No stand was therefore made against the threatened Fascist take-over. The King had no choice but to ask Mussolini to form a government. It was therefore the threat of violence that permitted Mussolini to secure power, as few Fascists had in fact entered Rome at the time of his appointment as Prime Minister. Only later was Rome reached by the Fascist marching columns, bedraggled and muddy from the torrential rain that fell throughout Italy during these days of crisis.

The development of the Fascist state

The government that Mussolini formed in October 1922 was in fact itself another coalition and in the first months of his premiership he showed few signs of establishing a dictatorship. But in July 1923, parliament was presented with the Acerbo electoral bill which provided that the party securing a majority of at least a quarter of the votes in the election should receive two-thirds of the seats in parliament. Mussolini threatened that if this bill was not passed, he would resign and thus plunge Italy once again into disorder. His threat was sufficient to secure the passage of the bill by a parliament in which the Fascists were still a minority. In April 1924 the first elections under the Acerbo Law were held and resulted in an overwhelming Fascist victory.

This Fascist victory was attributed partly to their thorough organization and partly to the many divisions among their opponents. It was also attributable to the violent tactics of the Fascists during the elections: meetings of opposition parties were abandoned after Fascist disruption, leading members of opposition parties were physically assaulted, and Fascist *squadre* asserted pressure even at the polling booths. Nevertheless, slightly less than a third of the deputies were opponents of Fascism and, in a speech in the Chamber, Giacomo Matteotti, a forthright Socialist, roundly condemned the behaviour of the Fascists during the election. Matteotti paid a bitter price for his bravery. In early June he disappeared and two months later his body was discovered on the outskirts of Rome.

The disappearance and murder of Matteotti aroused a storm of protest throughout Italy. The whole issue became one of the severest challenges ever faced by Mussolini during his rule. The opposition deputies showed their contempt by walking out of parliament and forming their own parliament in the Aventine area of Rome. The crisis continued throughout the second half of 1924. To resolve this crisis Mussolini decided to take a great risk by stating in parliament in January 1925 that he alone took 'the political, moral and historical responsibility for all that has happened'. This policy of frankness worked. However much he was criticized, Mussolini was still regarded as the only man who could maintain stability in Italy, as *duce*, or leader. The controversy surrounding the Matteotti murder subsided, and from this point of strength Mussolini began, in his own words, 'to make the nation Fascist'.

Mussolini took immediate steps to amass considerable control in his own hands and was empowered to rule by decree, regardless of the opinions of parliament. The Fascist Grand Council took on an important role as the inner group that advised Mussolini

on policy. As for parliament, it began to count for little: the Aventine group, having decided to return to parliament, was refused readmission: throughout the country opposition parties and the press were suppressed. The same occurred in local government, where elected councils were abolished and Fascist ones appointed from Rome. Judges also came to be spokesmen of Fascism, and a secret political police was created. Italians who were brave enough to show opposition were imprisoned or banished to remote islands and villages in the south. Among many who suffered banishment under the Fascists was Carlo Levi who has left a vivid picture of his sun-baked village exile and its poverty-stricken inhabitants in his book, *Christ Stopped at Eboli*. In the course of 1925 and 1926 Mussolini had created the firm basis of a totalitarian system within Italy.

From this firm basis, Mussolini developed his totalitarian rule still further. By a law of April 1926, the corporative system was created, as a revival of a medieval system of trade organization similar to the medieval guild system in England. Different corporations were created for the different trades and professions. They were bodies on which both the employers and the employed were represented and were dominated by the Fascist Ministry of Corporations. By their nature they were unlikely to represent adequately the interests of the workers, and they became a useful means by which the Fascist state was able to control the workers, who were virtually compelled to join a corporation, as employment was very difficult to find without a corporation membership card. The Italian trade unions were totally overtaken by this new system.

By a second electoral law in May 1928, the corporations were given the task of naming the majority of the candidates for the Chamber. They were to present their list of names to the Fascist Grand Council for a final selection. The electorate merely had the right to accept or to reject the carefully selected Fascists who were presented to them. The Chamber thus became a mere rubber stamp for the decisions of the Fascist government. In 1934 the corporative system was further reorganized into 22 corporations; in 1939 a Chamber of Fasces and Corporations replaced parliament, thus marking the complete triumph of the Fascist corporative system over the Italian political system.

The Fascist economy

Apart from the control exercised through the corporations, the Fascist government had no clear ideas about the economy. In its early years of power, Fascism followed liberal economic policies, involving minimal state interference in the economy of the country and, by tax concessions, giving encouragement to investment. These policies were modelled virtually on the policies then being pursued with apparent success by the government of the United States. In the mid-1920s these policies produced favourable results: production rose, unemployment declined and the Italian economy seemed at last to be adjusting itself satisfactorily.

But the effects both of the Wall Street crash of October 1929 and the abandonment of reparations payments in July 1931 were felt strongly in Italy. By this time also, the effects of the limitations imposed on immigration by the United States in 1921 were beginning to be felt widely throughout the Italian peninsula. The decline of the economy led to an increase in unemployment to well over a million in the early 1930s.

The government intervened increasingly in the country's economy. The Battle for Wheat was a government-directed programme to increase Italian wheat production. Public works schemes were important in both agriculture and industry. To aid agriculture the government undertook schemes for draining land, the reafforestation of mountainous areas and the construction of irrigation systems. By succeeding in draining the Pontine marshes, Mussolini's government achieved more than any previous administration in Italy: critics suggested that it was mainly for show and was given particular attention due to its proximity to Rome, but nevertheless new towns were built on the drained areas and the disease of malaria,

A new town constructed by the Fascist government on the drained Pontine marshes. Notice the severely functional form of the architecture, the grid pattern of the streets and the church in the right foreground.

which had haunted these marshy areas for centuries, was eliminated in that part of Italy. Similarly the construction of the Aqueduct of Apulia brought irrigation and improved agricultural output to the drought-ridden heel of Italy. To aid industry, attention was given to the improvement of communications, by the development of the railway system and the construction of motorways. The extensive building programmes displayed the distinctive features of Fascist architecture in which the use of large columns, impressive entrances, high façades and mural and mosaic decorations suggested the grandeur of the Fascist régime. The substantial rebuilding of the city of Rome was designed as a showpiece for Fascism.

A major criticism of all these economic policies was that they were designed more to display the superficial grandeur of Fascism than to tackle the real problems of the country. Together with Fascist colonial and foreign policies, they also suggested that Italy was being put on a war footing. Both these criticisms could be applied to the Battle for the Births, a Fascist campaign designed to increase the Italian population by allowing tax concessions to large families and by suggesting through propaganda that the pro-creation of children was a patriotic duty. In the circumstances of increasing unemployment in the early 1930s, the Battle for the Births was particularly foolish, though in fact it had little impact on population figures.

Government intervention in the economy was deepened in the mid-1930s, mainly as a direct consequence of the difficulties experienced in Italy after the government's invasion of Abyssinia, considered later. The policy pursued at this time is known as *autarky*: the creation of complete economic self-sufficiency within the country. Importation of goods was now severely restricted: exportation of Italian goods was encouraged. Such a policy compelled the government to make thorough efforts to utilize fully the basic economic potential within Italy: agricultural production and land reclamation schemes were more vigorously pursued, the use of oil, coal and other minerals was more fully developed, and efforts were made to manufacture synthetic products rather than to rely on foreign imports. But the policy of autarky failed to work, as it involved the virtual economic isolation of Italy. The countries whose trade in Italy had been cut off were unlikely to buy Italian goods in return. Furthermore, the advantages from autarky tended to be offset by the increasing emphasis on preparation for war.

The Lateran treaties

In the second half of the nineteenth century the Roman Catholic church had lost its extensive central Italian territories, forcibly taken from the church by the state, when Italy was unified. For more than half a century these losses embittered church-state relations, as successive popes denounced the Italian Liberal state and refused to recognize its existence. Relations softened in the early twentieth century with the creation of the Popular party, the Roman Catholic-based party which actively involved itself in the politics of the state. In the 1920s Pius XI also showed a willingness to reach agreement with the state, and Mussolini was conscious of the value to his régime of a successful solution of this long-standing Italian problem. Negotiations began in 1926 and were concluded with the signature of the Lateran treaties and concordat in February 1929.

The most important agreement reached in 1929 was the recognition by the church of the state: in return, the church accepted considerable financial compensation for the territories lost to the state in the previous century. The pope was allowed sovereign power over the Vatican city, where he and his predecessors had lived since the unification. The status and practice of the Roman Catholic religion was guaranteed throughout Italy. The agreements had not really been very difficult to reach: there had been strong desire on both sides to bring about a solution to this problem. Although thereafter church-state relations were not always in perfect harmony, Mussolini nevertheless received much credit for the concordat, which still regulates church-state relations in Italy, even though some aspects of it are subject to criticism by many Italians.

Prime Minister Mussolini looks on as Cardinal Gasparri, representing Pope Pius XI, signs the concordat in the Lateran Palace at Rome, in February 1929, thus ending more than half a century of church-state hostility. Mussolini secured much support from the improved relations with the church.

The imperial expansion of Fascist Italy

Fascism, while posing as the solution to Italy's problems in the twentieth century, also looked back to Italy's greatness in classical and medieval times. Italy had been left behind other major European powers in the scramble for colonies in the late nineteenth century and had secured only Libya in northern Africa, Somaliland and Eritrea in the Horn of Africa and the Dodecanese islands in the Mediterranean.

From the start the Fascist government was intent on developing the colonies already subject to Rome, and on advancing Italian power into other areas. The Italian people were told that the development of colonies would bring increased economic advantage to Italy and would provide lands where Italians could settle. But throughout the Fascist era, nothing came of these alleged advantages: in fact the Italian government subsidized all its colonial possessions and the numbers of Italians who settled in the colonies was extremely small. Prestige and the desire to make up for lost opportunities in earlier decades were the real motives behind Fascist colonial policies.

The Italian invasion of Abyssinia was an act of blatant aggression and was irrelevant to Italy's immediate needs. Fifty years earlier, in the 1880s, such campaigns were fairly typical of European powers, but by the 1930s they were badly out of date. Abyssinia was an independent African state with a long and distinguished history of its own and a solid tradition of independence. Italy had nurtured ambitions against Abyssinia for some decades and already had colonial territories in neighbouring Somaliland and Eritrea. In 1896 an Italian attempt to seize Abyssinia had been defeated at the battle of Adowa. The Fascist government developed close commercial relations with Abyssinia by a treaty of friendship in 1928, but in the late 1920s and early 1930s Italian troops made surreptitious advances across the ill-defined borders with Eritrea and Somaliland. By the mid-1930s Italy believed that other countries would take over her trade with

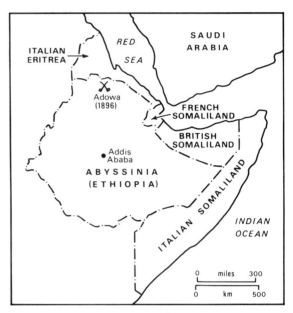

Fascist Italy's African Empire

Abyssinia unless the Fascist government controlled Abyssinia completely.

In October 1935 Italian forces, which had increased in the neighbouring colonies to more than half a million troops within a few months, invaded Abyssinia. Advances were comparatively slight until Badoglio took command of the war in December. Encouraged and virtually directed by Mussolini himself, Badoglio employed terror tactics such as the use of poisonous gas and extensive aerial bombardments. In May 1936 the Italian army entered the Abyssinian capital of Addis Ababa and Abyssinia was proclaimed a part of the Italian Empire, though there were still substantial areas of Abyssinia which were not under Italian control. To coerce these territories, further methods of terror were employed in subsequent months.

The British and French governments responded weakly to Italy's aggression: in December 1935 their foreign ministers worked out what became known as the Hoare-Laval plan by which they agreed to allow Italy control of parts of Abyssinia. Public opinion in both Britain and France was outraged at this proposed concession to the Italian dictator's aggression. The two foreign ministers resigned and the plan was dropped. The League of Nations had shown a more vigorous response. Even at the outbreak of this war, it had condemned the invasion as aggressive, and had called upon its member nations to impose economic sanctions against Italy. It was this action by the League of Nations which rallied the Italian people to support the Abyssinia war, which was then seen not just as an offensive war against Abyssinia, but as a defensive war against the League of Nations. Futhermore, as the economic sanctions did not include oil, the Italian economy was not too seriously affected by them, though their imposition further encouraged the development of the economic policy of autarky.

Fascist Italy's Mediterranean neighbours

Foreign relations of Fascist Italy

Once in power, Mussolini's main aim was the fulfilment of his earlier promise to reassert Italy's national greatness after the postwar humiliations. But in seeking its achievement, Mussolini's policies too often suggested the arrogant bullying of small powers or the thoughtless commitment of Italian troops to foreign adventures in which they could not hope, in the long run, to succeed. Evidence of both of these tendencies has already been seen in Italy's colonial policy: it was to be much the same in foreign policy.

In attempting to advance national greatness in foreign affairs, Mussolini emphasized especially the role of Italy in the Mediterranean. One of the many Fascist slogans asserted that 'if for others, the Mediterranean was merely a road, for us Italians it is life itself'. In the 1920s Mussolini was much concerned to emphasize this particular role. In 1923 some Italian officers were murdered on the boundary between Greece and Albania. After the Greek government had refused to accept the stringent terms which Italy had demanded because of this incident, Italian forces bombarded the Greek island of Corfu. As we have seen, in chapter 3, the intervention of the League of Nations was ignored in this matter. In 1924 the status of the city of Fiume, a matter of controversy since the D'Annunzio episode between 1919 and 1921, was resolved between Italy and Yugoslavia, allowing Italy to secure control of most of the city. This partially satisfied Italian claims against Yugoslavia, but Yugoslavia had absorbed the lands promised to Italy by the treaty of London, and relations with this eastern neighbour were generally poor: the separatist tendencies of parts of Yugoslavia were given active encouragement by Italy. Partly because of its nearness to Yugoslavia and partly as a means of securing Italian control over entry into the Adriatic Sea, Italy showed an increasing interest in Albania. After early moves to increase Italian investment there and to support the struggle for power of the Fascist-inclined Albanian chieftain, Ahmed Zog, Mussolini signed a treaty with Albania in 1926 which made the country an Italian satellite. In the spring of 1939 Italian troops invaded the country and took complete control of it. As with other colonial acquisitions, it is doubtful whether Italy derived any benefit from the seizure of Albania.

In the mid-1930s Mussolini began what was to prove ultimately the most disastrous of his foreign policies: alliance with Nazi Germany. The mutual concern of the two countries for a Nationalist victory in the Spanish Civil War is shown in chapter 9, and the progress of German–Italian relations after the conclusion of their axis agreement is considered in chapter 11, which deals with the causes of the Second World War, among which German–Italian relations play an important part. Italy's war effort and the events that led to the unseating of Mussolini in July 1943, and to his death at the hands of Italian partisans in April 1945 follow in Chapters 12 and 13.

Questions

13. Study the three photographs in this chapter and then answer questions (a) to (d) which follow.
    (a) (i) Name the Italian Prime Minister who is shown in the centre of the photograph on page 45 and watching the signing of the document on page 49,
        (ii) give the year in which he was appointed Prime Minister, and
        (iii) outline the events in Italy which led to this appointment. (1+1+4)
    (b) (i) For what purposes were photographs of the type shown on page 45 taken?
        (ii) To what extent did the actions of this Prime Minister justify the type of greeting that he is receiving from Italians of this particular age range? (3)
    (c) By reference to the evidence shown

in the photograph on page 48 and to the other work of the Prime Minister, examine the extent to which the Italian economy benefited from his policies.

(5)

(d) (i) Give the year in which the signing ceremony shown in the photograph on page 49 took place,

(ii) name the agreement that is being signed,

(iii) describe the problems which it was hoped to solve by the agreement being signed, and

(iv) describe the main ways in which the agreement attempted to solve these problems.

$(1+1+2+2)$

14. Explain why Mussolini managed to secure power in Italy in 1922. Show how he subsequently developed a dictatorship in Italy. To what extent did the Italian people benefit from his internal policies?

15. To what extent do you agree that Mussolini's foreign and imperial policies between 1922 and 1945 reveal nothing more than 'showmanship'?

6
Weimar and Nazi Germany

Germany did not expect defeat in the First World War. In the autumn of 1917 the Russian withdrawal from the war had led to German victory in the east, and in the spring of 1918 there was a sense of optimism as the military offensive of General Ludendorff in the west brought substantial gains for Germany. But in the summer and autumn of 1918 the German people received no news of the successful allied counter-offensives, so that the reasons for the German government's request for an armistice in November 1918 was not easily understood by many Germans, who felt it to be unnecessary. The myth developed that the 'November criminals' of the German government had delivered a 'stab in the back' to the army.

The creation of the Weimar republic

The new German republic thus began at a very heavy disadvantage. It had been established only a few days before the armistice, as a result of uprisings throughout Germany in early November. These uprisings had begun at North Sea ports where sailors, tired both of the war and of their officers, mutinied when commanded to set out on a dangerous and purposeless expedition into the English Channel. As in Russia in February 1917, the revolution spread rapidly, but it was not generally violent. In Berlin, pressure from the Socialists within the government and demonstrations by workers throughout the city combined to persuade Kaiser Wilhelm II that his only course was abdication: he left at once for exile in Holland, and so the ruling house of Hohenzollern, around which German unity in the previous century had been built, ended.

Karl Ebert, the leader of the Socialists, took control in Berlin and a republic was proclaimed. Ebert took care to ensure that his new republican government was moderate and broadly based, but in achieving this moderation he failed to satisfy either the extreme right or the extreme left. The most dangerous opposition came in January 1919 from the Berlin Communists, known as the Spartacists, who abandoned what little faith they had put in the new republic and, inspired by the example and encouragement of Russian Communists, organized an uprising in Berlin. The Freikorps, groups of loyal but brutal ex-soldiers, were employed by the Ebert government to suppress the rising, in the course of which the main Spartacist leaders, Karl Liebnecht and Rosa Luxemburg, were murdered at the hands of Freikorps. Amidst this background of disorder at home, and overhung by the sense of failure in the war, attempts were made to establish firmly the proclaimed republic. The election for a constituent assembly, in January 1919, produced the following results:

Majority Socialist party	163
Independent Socialist party	22
Centre party	91
Democratic party	75
Nationalist party	44
Populist party	19

The Majority Socialists were the moderate wing of the Socialist party and were able to form a coalition government with the support of two other moderate parties, the Centre party, representing Roman Catholic interests, and the Democratic party, representing liberal interests. The more extreme Independent Socialists, who had links with the Spartacists, refused to cooperate with the new government, and further opposition came from the more extreme right-wing parties, the Nationalists and the Populists who, while outwardly giving support to the new republic, in fact disliked the changes that Germany was experiencing.

The Assembly met in the town of Weimar to frame a new constitution. The choice of Weimar was largely in order to escape the confusion and violence of Berlin and to emphasize that the new Germany did not need to be dominated by Prussian interests, as the Kaiser's Empire had been. In the new constitution certain traditional political features of Germany were combined with completely new, liberal ideas: the new constitution was intended to mark a break with the old Germany of the Kaiser and of Bismarck. But in spite of these good intentions and in spite of sensible features which the constitution contained, it produced many problems.

The President was to be elected every seven years. His powers were extensive and included the command of the armed forces and the appointment of the German Chancellor. Provision was made for the President to rule by decree in certain circumstances. This provision was designed to enhance the status of the presidency, but unfortunately it contributed to a dangerous increase in presidential power in the early 1930s.

The legislature consisted of two houses, the Reichstag, elected every four years and representative of all the people of Germany, and the Reichsrat, a less important second chamber, consisting of the delegates of the state governments throughout Germany. Elections to the Reichstag were by proportional representation. An unfortunate result of the use of this system was the development of numerous small parties which made for political instability. The governments of the 11 states of Germany still held considerable power, though less than before. Their functions were largely confined to the supervision of the administration of justice, education and other local matters.

Fundamental to the whole constitution was an emphasis on democracy. For the first time in German history, women were permitted to vote and all elections were on the basis of universal suffrage. Provision was made for the holding of a referendum on important issues. Special emphasis was given to the right to work and to the provision of workers' councils in factories, so that matters concerning conditions of work could be resolved in a democratic way.

The Weimar republic: the early years

The Assembly at Weimar could also resolve matters concerning foreign affairs. When the terms of the Versailles treaty were made known to the new government there was an immediate sense of outrage both within the government and throughout the country. It had been thought in Germany that the replacement of the Kaiser's government by the new republic would soften the treatment of Germany by the Allies, as the government which had asked for peace in 1918 was a different type of government to that which had declared and fought the war in the years after 1914. The possibility of Germany refusing to sign the treaty was discussed, but the only alternative to such a refusal was a renewal of the fighting, a prospect which no-one in Germany could seriously face. Though the government of the day resigned in protest at the treaty's terms, the terms nevertheless were accepted. Another government resignation followed the announcement of the final figure of reparations in April 1921, but Germany again had no alternative but to accept this further humiliation imposed by the Allies.

The new Chancellor in 1921 was Josef Wirth, a member of the Centre party. He no longer continued the attitude of total opposition to the demands by the Allies, but instead developed a more cooperative policy of *fulfilment* of the requirements of the Versailles treaty and of the demands for reparations. He thought that Germany's attempted fulfilment of the terms would show the Allies how unjust these terms were, and in this way there might be some modification of them. Within two years, the policy of fulfilment received a severe set-back. Throughout 1922 Germany experienced genuine difficulty in maintaining the agreed level of reparation payments. The French Prime Minister, Raymond Poincaré, cast grave suspicions on German intentions and persuaded the Belgians to join with France in an invasion of the industrial district of the Ruhr, in Germany, in order to secure the payments that were due. No action by the Allies caused so much opposition within Germany as did this invasion. The workers of the area adopted passive resistance towards the occupying forces; extremists conducted acts of sabotage. The Ruhr occupation wrought havoc with the already fragile German economy. The comparatively modest inflation rate during the First World War had held some advantages in providing cheap money, thereby assisting industry and exports. But during the Ruhr occupation, when the government was committed to further expense in supporting the passive resistance campaign, inflation reached astronomical proportions. As the situation went badly out of control, the life savings of many Germans were totally lost, and prices vastly outpaced wages.

Value of German currency in relation to the dollar	
1914:	4.2
1919:	14.0
1921:	76.7
August 1923:	4,620,455.0
November 1923:	4,200,000,000,000.0

A new coalition cabinet was formed in August 1923 under the chancellorship of Gustav Stresemann, founder and leader of the Populist party, who held the posts of Chancellor and Foreign Minister in the 1920s, and who was one of the most able of the German leaders of the interwar years. Though his government in 1923 lasted for only three months, it was he who was able to bring Germany out of its financial crisis.

In the first instance he gave way to Poincaré by calling off the policy of passive resistance, which was clearly making worse an already difficult situation. He then established a new German currency, the *rentenmark*, to take the place of the earlier and now worthless currency. The success of the rentenmark was much encouraged internally by severe restraint in government expenditure, and externally by the beginning of the American Dawes plan in the summer of 1924, which provided for a more relaxed system of reparations payments, based on Germany's ability to pay. This interest on the part of the United States was prompted by concern for American commercial interests that appeared to be threatened by the German inflation. Acceptance of the Dawes plan by France and Britain was easier in 1924 when left-wing governments, generally sympathetic towards the rehabilitation of Germany, came to power in both countries.

Many Germans saw the Weimar republic as the product of military defeat, and thus a symbol of their country's humiliation. They despised the new republic for its humiliating origins and for the disasters which befell Germany during its early years: the revolutionary activities of the left, the occupation of the Ruhr and the ravages of inflation. Altogether, the republic appeared a poor successor to the Kaiser's Germany. But in many ways German life was untouched by the change of régime; many long-established German institutions continued to function as they had under the Kaiser, and made little secret of their contempt for the republic.

In the schools, few serious attempts were made to educate Germany's young people in the values of democracy, though attention was given to German greatness in the past and to the humiliation of having lost an empire. The judiciary revealed a lack of regard for the republic by its tendency to deal leniently with right-wingers who agitated against the republic, and severely with left-wing agitators.

The German army gave even fuller evidence of these reactionary views. Under the overall command of Hans von Seeckt, a soldier who made no secret of his dislike for the republic, the army continued its traditionally important role in German society. As for the restrictions on its size, laid down by the Versailles treaty, it was common knowledge within Germany that these restrictions were largely ignored, so that the army was able to lay the foundations of the remarkably rapid German expansion in the early stages of the Second World War. Some German politicians of the left were critical of the secret rearmament that was taking place, but most Germans, and some foreign observers, felt that the disarmament clauses of the Versailles treaty were so unjust that Germany had every right to attempt evasion of them.

The Weimar republic: the years of revival and the years of the Depression

The seven-yearly elections for the presidency took place in 1925. The Socialist Ebert was replaced by General von Hindenburg, a famous military leader of the First World War. Hindenburg represented the old Germany and the German people's choice of him in preference to a more moderate candidate is further evidence of the way in which they were looking back to their former greatness. As President, Hindenburg naturally supported the republic. But his policies and the manner in which he carried them out showed a preference for the strong, autocratic government that had typified the Kaiser's Germany.

If in these ways Germany tended to look to the past and to despise the present, she nevertheless, by the mid-1920s, showed increasing confidence and prosperity. German industries amalgamated with larger and more powerful organizations, among the most important of which was the chemical firm, Farben, which attracted foreign investments and produced increasing revenue in exports. Much new building and reconstruction took place in these years: the influence of the German Bauhaus School of Art and Architecture, typified by bold, simple designs, was to be found in this new work.

Its influence became extensive throughout all Europe.

The sense of recovery from the War increased in a number of ways in the mid and late 1920s, mainly as a result of Stresemann's policies. Germany's standing among the nations of the world was significantly improved by her signature of the 1925 Locarno treaties in which Germany participated on an equal footing with the other powers: Germany was also able by these agreements to keep open the possibility of adjustment of her eastern and south-eastern frontiers, while giving assurances of no desire for frontier adjustments in the west. Locarno opened the way for another improvement in Germany's position, membership of the League of Nations, to which Germany was admitted in September 1926. This membership enabled German politicians to put forward more openly the grievances that Germany felt as a consequence of the Versailles treaty, especially the continuing problem of reparations and the existence of German minorities in neighbouring countries. As for reparations, in 1929 the Young plan, once again American-inspired, eased the payment of reparations considerably, reducing the overall sum to less than a third of the 1921 figure; the manner in which the payments were made was also improved by the creation of the Bank of International Settlement at Basle. In 1929 agreement was reached for the withdrawal of French and British troops from the occupied Rhineland area in the following year, even though the Versailles treaty had stipulated 1935 as the year of withdrawal.

No European country was as seriously affected by the financial collapse of the American stock market in October 1929 as Germany, partly because no other European country had received, throughout the 1920s, such large American investments. With the Wall Street crash, these investments ceased, and American loans were gradually withdrawn. Germany's exports could no longer be sold, as her overseas markets were also affected by the Depression and could no longer afford to purchase goods. The German banking system was endangered, though the worst effects on banking were felt later, in 1931, after the collapse of the Austrian Kreditanstalt bank. As the manufacturing industries decreased, unemployment in Germany increased. For the second time since 1923 economic disaster faced the Weimar republic. The unemployment problem in the early 1930s, though different from the inflation problem of the early 1920s, was no less serious in its consequences for millions of Germans. By 1932 as many as six million Germans were unemployed.

Government became increasingly totalitarian during these years of economic difficulty. In October 1929 Stresemann died. In March 1930 Heinrich Brüning, leader of the Centre party, was appointed Chancellor, and for the next two years adopted the unpopular policy of restraint on government expenditure and heavier taxation, as the best means of preventing further economic disasters. In the long term, his policies were successful, but results showed only after 1933, and it was to be the new Chancellor, Adolf Hitler, who received unjustified credit for these improvements. Brüning was responsible for the end of reparations, a move from which the German economy benefited, though once again these benefits were felt during the Hitler years. Opposition to Brüning's measures within the Reichstag was strongly expressed, and from July 1930 the government had therefore to rely on the use of the presidential powers to rule by decree in times of emergency, powers which Hindenburg readily employed.

National Socialism

Against this background of a disintegrating economy, governmental restraint, and increasingly dictatorial rule, support for extremist parties increased. In the general election of September 1930, on the extreme left the Communist party secured 77 seats and on the extreme right the comparatively new National Socialist party secured 107 seats.

The National Socialist German Workers party, usually called the Nazi party (from the first four letters of the German word *Nazional*), was one of a number of right-wing groups which came into being during the revolutionary times at the end of the First World War. Adolf Hitler joined the party in 1920 and quickly became its leader. His life until that time had been unsuccessful and frustrated. Born in 1889 into an Austrian family, he had spent his youth in Vienna and in Munich, unable to realize in either city his ambition of becoming an architect, and subsisting in conditions that bordered on poverty. He fought in the First World War, achieved the rank of corporal, and displayed distinct qualities of bravery. The German defeat in 1918 he blamed on the 'November criminals' of the new republic, an institution which he totally despised.

Like a number of other right-wing groups, the National Socialist party had a semimilitary formation attached to it, the SA or brown-shirts, controlled by Ernst Röhm. This body gave support at Nazi meetings and created an image of strength. In November 1923, taking advantage of the disillusion throughout Germany caused by the Ruhr occupation and the opposition towards Berlin that was strongly felt throughout Bavaria, Hitler, together with the distinguished soldier General Ludendorff, led a movement of revolt. Hitler's Munich Putsch bore resemblance to Mussolini's March on Rome of the previous autumn, but Hitler's attempt failed. In a Munich beerhall Hitler delivered an emotional speech to an audience that gave its support to his call for a national revolution and the removal of the Berlin government. But on the following day, the army in Bavaria showed loyalty to the republic by preventing Hitler's forces from marching through Munich: an exchange of shots occurred in a narrow street near the city centre, 16 Nazis were killed and the Nazi attempt to overthrow the government disintegrated.

Those who participated in the Munich Putsch were put on trial, but none of them received severe punishments. Hitler was sentenced to imprisonment for five years, but served less than one year of the sentence. Although the Munich Putsch had been a failure, Hitler and his movement nevertheless benefited from it. The main lesson that Hitler learnt was that revolutionary action of the type that helped Mussolini to power in Italy was unlikely to succeed in Germany: in the future his path to power was by means of elections and political campaigns. Both through his rôle in the Putsch and through his defence in the well publicized trial, Hitler became known among a wider circle of Germans as a potential leader, dedicated to restoring German pride.

During his imprisonment, Hitler wrote his autobiography, *Mein Kampf* (My Struggle). There is, in fact, little autobiography to it, as the book dwells mainly on Hitler's thoughts, expressed poorly and chaotically. Few people in Germany or elsewhere read it: had they done so, they may well have been more uncertain of Hitler's aims. Nevertheless, by the mid-1920s certain features did characterize National Socialism. The key feature is found in the two words of its name. *Nationalism* was the basis of the party and in this respect the Nazis sought both to put right the 1919 humiliations and to continue earlier German policies of increasing German power in Europe and in the world: underlying the Nazi emphasis on Nationalism was the stress on German racial superiority. The appeal to *Socialism* was less well defined and was little more than a bid for the support of the German working classes, though the strongly working-class SA particularly stressed the Socialist appeal.

A feature which strongly contrasted the National Socialist party with other parties was its appeal to idealism: the dramatic rallies with their employment of uniformed personnel, boldly designed *swastikas* and military-style parades allied with the patriotic appeals for struggle and sacrifice in the cause of Germany suggested that National Socialism stood for much that was missing in the Weimar republic.

Useful work was done in the organization of the party during the late 1920s, when its public support was not particularly strong. Many party branches were established in different parts of Germany, the work of the brothers Gregor and Otto Strasser being im-

'Our last hope: Hitler'. In his bid for power in the early 1930s, Hitler made strong appeal to Germany's six million unemployed, as this poster of the time suggests.

portant in this connection. In 1925 the SS, or black-shirts, were established under the control of Heinrich Himmler: at first occupying an inferior position to the SA this other semi-military body, with its elitist approach, came eventually to dominate over the SA. Thus by the time Germany was plunged into the economic and political confusion of the Depression, the National Socialist party was strong enough to be able to put itself forward as the country's salvation in its time of distress.

Hitler secures and consolidates power

Success in the 1930 election naturally gave the Nazis much encouragement. The SA grew, business firms were by this time giving generously to the party, and Hitler's own popularity went from strength to strength. In the summer of 1932, when the time came for another presidential election, Hitler stood as a candidate and had the support both of the Nazi party and of the Nationalist party. Though he failed to secure the presidency and though Hindenburg was once again elected, Hitler's defeat was comparatively narrow. Shortly after this, at the end of May 1932, Franz von Papen replaced Brüning as Chancellor, and followed up his appointment with an election in July. This election brought increased support for the Nazi party, making it the largest single party in the Reichstag, though not providing it with an overall majority.

Hitler now had a clear right to expect appointment as Chancellor. Hindenburg, however, continued to support von Papen as Chancellor and Hitler refused all offers of minor office, stressing that he intended to be Chancellor or nothing. Even more political confusion followed in the Reichstag, compelling von Papen to call a second election in 1932, in November, in which the Nazis, though gaining rather fewer seats than in July, were still the largest single party. Kurt von Schleicher became Chancellor in December but, like his predecessor, was unable to assert political control over the Reichstag.

Meantime von Papen still had much influence with Hindenburg and persuaded him that if Hitler were appointed Chancellor it should be possible to control both the Reichstag and Hitler, as any government which he headed must be a coalition government. Hindenburg was persuaded by these arguments and at the end of January 1933 he at last overcame his opposition to Hitler and appointed the one-time corporal of the imperial German army as Chancellor of the German republic.

Once in power, albeit as Chancellor of a coalition government, Hitler strove to consolidate his position. Elections in March 1933 had been preceded by a purge of the Communists after they were accused by the government of the responsibility for burning down the Reichstag building in February. The elections themselves were held in an atmosphere of violence and forceful Nazi propaganda, particularly in those states whose local governments were already under Nazi control. Even so the Nazis obtained less than half of the seats in the Reichstag, which they were able to dominate only with the support of their Nationalist allies.

Hitler now set out on a policy of ruthless suppression of opposition groups. Later in March 1933 he managed to persuade the

Adolf Hitler had an unerring ability in securing rapturous support during his public appearances. Though scenes like this were common in Germany during prewar years, during the war itself Hitler became increasingly remote from the German people.

Reichstag to agree to the Enabling Act, allowing the government emergency powers for a four-year period, and granting extensive authority to the chancellor. This Act was to be the basis of Hitler's power as *Führer* (leader) of what was now styled Germany's *Third Reich* (Empire). By skilful political management he guided the act through the Reichstag, which now met in the Berlin opera house instead of the gutted Reichstag building. Only the Majority Socialists opposed the passage of this Act: all other parties had been won over, at least temporarily, to Hitler's support.

Hitler's control of Germany now made rapid progress. In May the trade unions were abolished, in July the Nazi party was declared the only legal party, in November elections were held and the Reichstag became totally packed with Nazi deputies. By mid-1934 the SA had become too powerful. So in June Hitler directed an SS purge of them, in the course of which Röhm and hundreds of other SA leaders were murdered. In August, on President Hindenburg's death, the powers of President as well as Chancellor went to Hitler.

Life in Hitler's Germany: the economy

The Nazis had no well-defined plans for the improvement of the German economy. In any case, the improvements which did take place during the years after 1933 cannot be attributed directly to Nazi economic policies: much was the result of general improvements throughout the world, and of the earlier policies of Brüning. The idea was put forward by Hitler that the German economy should be the servant of the Nazi state, but this was a vague idea, typical in many respects of National Socialist policy statements on internal German affairs.

Overall charge of the economy was given to Schacht, an experienced and agile economist, and an earlier supporter of the Nationalist party. His objective was *autarky*, economic self-sufficiency for his country. This objective was a fairly common one in most European countries in the 1930s, but the Nazis under Schacht's direction pursued it with greater vigour than most. Goods were sold abroad at less than their real value in order to obtain foreign currency; special agreements were made with foreign countries for obtaining raw materials at favourable prices; attention was given within Germany to the production of synthetic products. In 1936 a four-year plan was begun under the direction of Goering. It was designed to speed up the achievement of autarky and also to prepare the German economy for a future war. A more rigorous economic policy was undertaken and much attention was given to the manufacture of synthetic products, particularly steel, at the newly established Hermann Goering Steel Works at Salzgitter, where inferior grade German ores were used instead of better grade Swedish ores.

The directors of big business, such as Thyssen and Krupp, found their businesses greatly aided by Nazi policies. Proprietors of small businesses fared less well and were discouraged; this hostile attitude culminated in a law of October 1937 which forcibly dissolved about a fifth of the small businesses of Germany. Some small businesses were encouraged to amalgamate with bigger firms. But for those businessmen who survived these difficulties, profits under the Third Reich were good.

One important reason for good profits in German business was the total absence of strikes, and the discipline which the Third Reich imposed upon the German workers. In October 1934 the Labour Front was created to take the place of the trade unions. Under the control of Robert Ley, the Labour Front jointly represented the interests of employers and workers: its officials were all members of the Nazi party. The major objective of the Labour Front was the advancement of the best interests of German industry generally, regardless of the interests of the workers. Overall the economic condition and status of the workers deteriorated: net wages declined, taxation and state contributions increased, workers freedom of movement was increasingly curtailed. There were nevertheless ways in which the workers could benefit. The *Strength through Joy* organization made provision for sport, cultural activity and very cheap holidays for German workers on a scale not equalled in other countries. But above all else, the Third Reich had provided full employment for the German workers and full security of jobs. In this all important respect its record contrasted most favourably with that of the republic and this overriding benefit encouraged workers to accept many of the régime's disadvantages and restrictions.

Life in Hitler's Germany: society

With the sole exception of his history teacher, who taught a strongly nationalistic type of German history, Hitler hated the teachers of his boyhood, and he maintained this hatred of teachers and of education throughout his life. His Nazi movement had little respect for the values of education in the development of a human being, and in the advancement of knowledge, but the movement did have a keen awareness of the importance of a young person's formative years in the making of a loyal Nazi. Hence from the start, the Nazi government ensured that their ideas were taught in schools and that all teachers were loyal to these ideas. Special provision was also made for the activities of young people out of school. In 1933, Baldur von Schirach, a man then only in his mid-twenties, was given control of the development of the Hitler Youth organization for young people between 14 and 18. Before the age of 14 they could enter a junior branch of the Hitler Youth and after 18 they entered labour service or were conscripted into the army. The Hitler Youth was run along lines similar to the SA, with emphasis on military activity and with indoctrination of Nazi ideas, but it again had its positive side in affording opportunity for sport and recreation, similar to those provided by the *Strength through Joy* organization for adults. There was pressure placed on young people to join the Hitler Youth, though membership did not become compulsory until March 1939.

Though Hitler himself had no real belief

A Hitler Youth camp in the 1930s. Though Hitler's government was intent on instilling Nazi ideas among the young, it made better provision than most countries did at that time for their health and recreation.

in the Christian religion, it was important for him, as leader of Germany, to secure some kind of cooperation with the Lutheran church and the Roman Catholic church, both of which had much influence among the German people. But he was not totally successful in getting the support of both these churches for his policies. Quite early in his chancellorship, Hitler signed a concordat with the Roman Catholic church in Germany, then represented by Cardinal Pacelli, the future Pope Pius XII. It provided for reasonable church-state relations in Germany and it added to Hitler's prestige at the time. But his failure to keep to its terms caused Pius XI in 1937 to issue an encyclical, in

German, entitled *Mit Brennender Sorge* (With burning sorrow) in which the Pope was critical not only of the failure by the Nazis to keep to the concordat, but also of the dangers he saw in Germany at that time. The German Lutheran church came more effectively into harmony with National Socialism. Through the cooperation of Pastor Müller, whom he created Reich Bishop, Hitler ensured the loyalty of much of the Lutheran church. But a section under Pastor Niemöller refused to accept the close links between their church and the new state. Both Lutherans and Roman Catholics who showed their opposition were detained in the concentration camps that were set up for those Germans who opposed their new government.

It did not take long for the National Socialist hatred of the Jews to be put into effect. Persecution of the Jews began within a few months of Hitler's appointment as Chancellor, when encouragement was given to the boycotting of Jewish shops, and the dismissal of Jewish state officials. In September and November 1935 a more forceful Nazi approach to anti-semitism was given effect by the Nuremberg laws, passed by the Reichstag during the holding of the annual party rally at Nuremberg. The following extracts from the laws show their most important features:

> A citizen of the Reich may be only that subject who is of German or kindred blood, and who, through his behaviour, shows that he is both desirous and personally fit to serve loyally the German people and the Reich.
> A Jew cannot be a citizen of the Reich. He cannot exercise the right to vote; he cannot occupy public office.
> Any marriages between Jews and citizens of German or kindred blood are herewith forbidden.

The effects of these laws were considerable. No longer was it possible for a Jew to be regarded as a German citizen, nor was it possible for Jews to marry non-Jews. Persecution of Jews was now more widespread. In November 1938, after a Nazi official had been murdered by a Jew in Paris, a wave of anti-semitic violence spread throughout Germany.

Some Jews decided that, as they were made so unwelcome in their own country, their best course during these years was to leave. But others preferred to remain where they had grown up, and suffer the persecutions as best they could. It was not until January 1942, well into the Second World War, that the *Final Solution* for the extermination of the Jews was approved by the Nazi government. The effects of this barbarous policy are considered in Chapter 12.

It was Hitler's aim to dominate all aspects of life in Germany. So forcefully were the policies applied that by the late 1930s Hitler's dominance of Germany was complete. Increasingly, as is shown in chapter 11, he sought to build up Germany's importance in Europe. In working towards this goal, he was ready to risk war for his country, for Europe and for much of the world.

Questions

16. Study the poster on page 59 and then answer questions (a) to (d) which follow.
    (a) (i) Give the full title of the political party led by the politician named in the poster, and
        (ii) outline the development of that political party during the 1920s.
        (1+3)
    (b) How do you account for the fact that by the early 1930s a large number of German people found themselves in the economic condition shown in this poster?
        (4)
    (c) (i) Apart from the situation shown in the poster, what other grievances among the German people led in the early 1930s to the increasing support of the politician named in the poster?
        (ii) Outline the stages by which this politician secured and consolidated his power in Germany between 1932 and 1934.
        (3+5)

(d) Show in what ways the situation shown in the poster improved under the government of this politician.

(4)

17. Outline the main provisions of the Weimar constitution of 1919 and show the importance of the work done by the governments of the Weimar republic in home and foreign affairs during the 1920s.

18. Trace and explain the rise to power of Hitler between 1929 and 1934. To what extent did the German people benefit by his domestic policies during the following five years?

7
China and Japan between the wars

The early years of the twentieth century were the last years of the rule of the Manchu dynasty over the vast land mass of Imperial China. The system of government in China at this time was highly autocratic. The Emperor was served by an extensive and efficient civil service, and supported by a body of complex and archaic laws and customs. The main religions of China, Confucianism, Buddhism and Taoism all tended to encourage the Chinese to respect authority, whether that of the far-off Emperor, the local landowner or the family.

Contacts between this vast, archaic empire and the Western powers was developed only in the nineteenth century and then on a comparatively limited scale. As the result of a series of mid-nineteenth-century wars and what the Chinese call the 'unequal' treaties which followed them, Western powers such as Britain, France, Germany and Portugal were able to establish control of a number of China's coastal towns, which they used as bases for successful commercial dealings with China.

The 1911 Revolution

In the early years of the twentieth century the developing revolutionary groups found a leader in Sun Yat-sen, a Chinese doctor who had travelled extensively in the United States and western Europe and who was convinced of the need for China to adopt Western ideas of progress in place of the stifling imperial system. He put forward a moderate policy of reform, based on the *Three People's Principles* of Nationalism, Democracy and Socialism: independence for China from the Western dominance allowed by the unequal treaties,

establishment of a republic in place of the imperial system and, by the application of Socialist principles, improvement in the lives of the Chinese. Sun's movement was, however, small and poorly-organized. Its financing came largely from overseas Chinese communities, who were perhaps more conscious of the need for change than were many who lived within China itself.

The efficiency of the Manchu secret police resulted in the failure of a number of revolutionary attempts against the Manchu dynasty. But in October 1911 an uprising successfully secured control of the city of Wuchang. Within days, similar uprisings took place in other Chinese cities and the rebels proclaimed Sun Yat-sen as president of the new republic of China. But the Manchu dynasty had not yet fallen. The northern areas of China did not involve themselves so fully in the revolution as did the southern areas, and the Manchu government felt it might yet survive if Yuan Shih-kai, a retired military commander, could be persuaded to come to its defence and thereby ensure the loyalty of the army to the dynasty. Yuan played a shifty role in the winter of 1911 to 1912. He was a man who respected the traditional heritage of China and who approved of autocratic government, yet he was realistic enough to see that the revolutionary forces were becoming firmly established and that the Manchu dynasty was unlikely to survive long even if he were to give it his support. He therefore negotiated with the rebels, who were well aware that, as an enemy, Yuan would be capable of crushing their movement. The rebels offered the presidency of the republic to Yuan in return for his abandonment of the Manchu dynasty, whose fate was sealed when Yuan

Two important civil servants of the Chinese Empire join a train under escort during the revolutionary turmoils of 1911. Their style of dress, traditional in China for many centuries, was abandoned by the new rulers.

decided to accept the offer. In February 1912 the last Manchu Emperor, a mere five-year-old boy, abdicated. Sun resigned from the presidency which he had briefly occupied and Yuan entered into full power.

Until his death in June 1916, Yuan ruled China in a manner similar to that of the emperors before him. No real progress was made in implementing the Three People's Principles of Sun Yat-sen. Though a parliament was established, it was a mere façade for the tyrannical rule of Yuan, characterized by disregard for the law, corruption among his supporters, and a heavy reliance on the powers of the army. For those who had worked for the Revolution of 1911, this turn of events was a bitter disappointment.

The Nationalist (Kuomintang) party developed in these years as the main force opposing this new tyranny, and its members inherited the ideals for which Sun, now exiled in Japan, had earlier striven. The Kuomintang party's main aim was to secure true parliamentary government for China. In order to pursue this important goal more effectively, other more controversial matters were excluded from their programme.

Warlord tyranny and early Japanese hostility

No leader within China was sufficiently strong to take over the presidency when Yuan Shih-kai died in 1916. For approximately ten years after his death, though a form of government continued in the capital, Peking, and was recognized by foreign powers as the government of China, real power was held between hundreds of *warlords* scattered throughout the country. The warlords were men of differing origins, some were from the Chinese aristocracy and others were self-made men who came from poor and insignificant families. They all relied on their own armed forces to give effect to their rule over a particular region. During these years the frequent clashes between warlords intensified the division of China and cruelly affected the life of the peasantry. Apart from often being compelled to fight in the armed forces of the local warlord, the peasants were also subject to his excessive taxation and the general tyranny of his rule. Under the warlords, sufferings increased vastly: the Revolution of 1911 appeared to have led now to a deterioration rather than an improvement of peasant conditions.

These appalling internal conditions were not the only problems then confronting China: Japan also posed an increasing threat. Japan was more industrialized, and more effectively united than China: she took advantage of the circumstances of the First World War and of the rule of the warlords to present to China the *Twenty-one Demands* in January 1915. These collectively consisted of an assertion of Japanese rights in China, especially over areas along the coast which were then held by Germany, against whom Japan was then fighting. Later in the year, after some attempts at resistance to the demands by diplomatic means, China accepted them. To strengthen her international position, China entered the war against Germany in 1917: this brought China into alliance with Japan's own Western allies who, China hoped, would assist China against excessive Japanese demands in the peace settlement. But this hope came to nothing, as in the Versailles treaty Germany's possessions along the Chinese shores at Kiaochow and in the Shantung peninsula were awarded to Japan and not to China. This was a hard blow for the Chinese, who had a particular claim to the Shantung peninsula as the birthplace of Confucius, the Chinese philosopher and religious leader. Traditional Sino-Japanese (Chinese-Japanese) hostility was sharpened by this Japanese presence along China's shores.

The Nationalists and the Communists

The ease with which the Chinese negotiators had given way at Paris to the international pressure for these Japanese gains caused widespread anger among many Chinese. Expression was given to this anger in the *May Fourth movement*. On that day in 1919, and for some time thereafter, students demonstrated in Peking. Never before, not even in the 1911 Revolution, had there been so spontaneous a demonstration of Chinese nationalism and of dissatisfaction with the weak Chinese government. These revolutionary events were suppressed, but they left behind strong feelings of grievance and of desire to work for a changed situation, which in the following years benefited the reviving Nationalist party and the new Communist party.

For most of the years during which the warlords ruled, the Nationalists were centred on the southern city of Canton, where Sun Yat-sen attempted to spread the Three People's Principles to which he and the Nationalist party were pledged. After the 1917 revolution in Russia the Nationalists received useful aid from the new Bolshevik government, which saw possibilities of the Nationalists developing as a fully revolutionary party. Among the Russians whose influence was important in these years was Michael Borodin, famed for his work in encouraging revolution in many countries of the world. Under Borodin's influence and the now highly revered leadership of Sun Yat-sen, the Nationalists revived and were able to put themselves forward as a real alternative to the anarchy which the warlords had created.

The example of Communist success in Russia and of Communist aid in China led to the formation in 1912 of the Chinese Communist party. Prominent in the party in these early years was its future Chairman, Mao Tse-tung, then a library assistant in Peking. Though it had few members – even in 1923 there were less than 500 of them – it nevertheless made an impact in China in these years, by taking up the cause of working people in town and country and by organizing strikes. Even from its birth the Chinese Communist party, unlike Communist parties in Russia and elsewhere, looked to the peasantry as the basis on which its support was to be built. Partly as a result of Borodin's influence, the relationship between the Communist party and the Nationalist party was a harmonious one in these early years when they were united together in the struggle against warlord tyranny.

But this harmony did not long survive the death in March 1925 of Sun Yat-sen. Once his stabilizing influence had gone, political differences developed within the Nationalist party between those wanting development on more fully Socialist lines and those wanting more moderate development and a break with the Communists. In practice, these political developments counted for comparatively little at that time as power was increasingly held by General Chiang Kai-shek. This Commander of the Military Academy, where officers of the Nationalist Army were trained, had developed a loyal following among his military students, and his power increased markedly after Sun's death. In the summer of 1926 Chiang's forces set off on the Northern Expedition against those warlords who still clung to power: the efficiency of Chiang's forces combined with useful propaganda work of the Communists resulted in spectacular victories for Chiang, thus further consolidating his prestige. With the Nationalists now under his dictatorial control, and with the warlords virtually defeated, Chiang Kai-shek was ready to break the alliance with the Communists, now his only main rivals for complete power in China.

The success of the Nationalist party

Shanghai was the city in which Chiang's break with the Communists took place. In these years Shanghai was a thriving commercial centre, though appalling conditions of poverty and ill-treatment existed among its millions of workers. The city's wealthy business community was concerned by the in-

fluence of Communism among the Shanghai workers, and readily supported Chiang's actions against the Communist party. In April 1927 a purge was ruthlessly carried out: starting in Shanghai and spreading to other major cities, Chiang's forces murdered leading Communists and completely suppressed the trade unions.

Those Communists who survived retreated to the provinces of Hunan and Kiangsi: Chiang felt that in these southern interior provinces they were no longer an immediate menace and he could devote his attention to the defeat of the official government of China. In 1928 he undertook a second Northern Expedition against the remaining warlords and on the successful completion of this expedition he entered Peking and with little opposition overthrew the official government. He then established his own government based in the southern city of Nanking.

Chiang's climb to power in the late 1920s had at least ended the internal chaos suffered by China since the death of Yuan Shih-kai more than 12 years earlier. The Nationalists had triumphed over their enemies, but in the process they had lost the early idealism of Sun Yat-sen and his Three People's Principles. China under Chiang Kai-shek was dominated by the Nationalist party and took on the characteristics of a military dictatorship. Though Chiang promised reforms for the Chinese, little progress was made towards achieving them. This lack of progress may have been due partly to further challenges to his rule in the 1930s, and partly to the threatening presence of the Chinese Communists and the steady advance of the Japanese invaders.

The Long March to Yenan

In the remote southern provinces of Hunan and Kiangsi, Communist support among the peasantry continued to grow as the peasantry became convinced that Communism alone would help them. The besieged conditions in which the Communists found themselves encouraged the formation of the Red Army under the command of Chu Teh, a former

Nationalist forces during the fight against the Communists in the early 1930s. Their lack of skill in guerrilla warfare meant they were ill-matched with their opponents.

Chinese aristocrat, now converted to Communism. The army became skilled in methods of guerrilla warfare, their major strategy being the negative one of avoiding open combat: 'When the enemy advances we retreat, when he retreats we advance; when he stops we harrass him, when he is tired we attack him' was the manner in which Mao described it. In the early 1930s with peasant support continuing to increase, and with 300,000 soldiers enrolled in the Red Army, the Communists were a dangerous menace to the Nationalist government.

The Nationalists responded to this situation by increasing their attacks on the Communist-held regions. By 1934, in spite of their strength, the Communists felt sufficiently

threatened to decide on withdrawal from Hunan and Kiangsi. In October 1934 under Mao's leadership, 100,000 Communists set off on the lengthy journey to the northern province of Shensi. Their journey through these remote parts of China was difficult: many died as a direct result of the cold, hunger and exhaustion on the journey, and many were killed by the attacks of the Nationalist forces. Only 30,000 arrived at their destination in October 1935. The Long March, as the journey became known, is now regarded by the Chinese Communists as a heroic adventure, though at the time it was regarded as a desperate retreat: not only was there the suffering of the march itself, but the area of Shensi was one of the most poverty-stricken of all China. Yet by travelling so extensively through China the Communists were able to spread their beliefs among more of the peasantry, who came to know and respect Communism as a movement which was genuinely concerned with their grievances. Further, Mao consolidated his leadership of Chinese Communism during the course of the March: once they had arrived in Shensi province, the Communists looked to no-one else for leadership.

The city of Yenan within the Shensi province now became the centre of Communist power in China. There Mao and his followers were able to develop and put into practice their own particular style of Communism, free from the Nationalist attacks which had troubled them in the south. They were also prepared to learn from the mistakes they

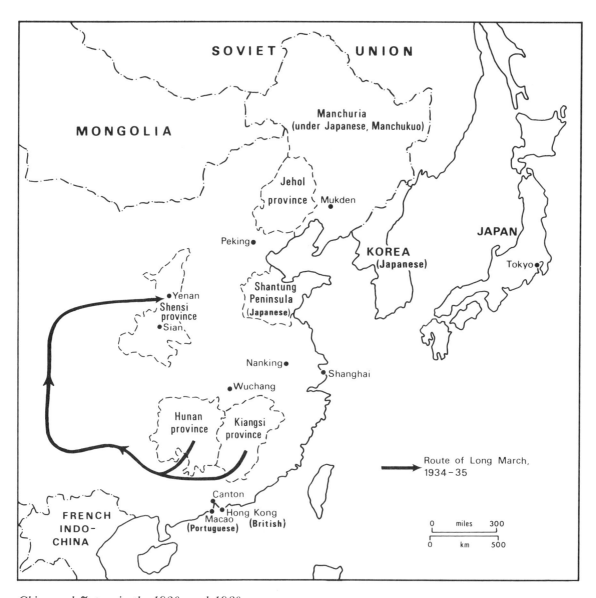

China and Japan in the 1920s and 1930s

had made earlier. It is during the time at Yenan that Chinese Communism adopted the policies which, after its ultimate success in 1949, it was to impose on all China. Reforms from which the peasantry would benefit were given most attention: the abolition of the landlord class, the distribution of land among the peasants and the curbing of excessive taxation demands. A system of soviets (workers' councils) came into being, and in these also, peasant influence predominated. Most remarkable was the purposeful, communal spirit which developed among the Communists in Yenan. In 1940 one of Mao's most important works, *The New Democracy*, was published, in which he outlined the policies of Chinese Communism and showed how Marxist-Leninism was to be applied, in a practical way, to the Chinese situation. Yenan provided the vital experience which strengthened the Chinese Communist party for the struggle for supremacy in China. In these years, however, Japanese hostility towards China grew more menacing. The struggle to impose Communism on China would have to be postponed until this aggression from outside had been repelled.

Japan after the First World War

By the early twentieth century Japan was seeking to develop the economic and social life of the country along the lines already found in western Europe and the United States: it was becoming a *westernized* country. In this respect Japan contrasted significantly with China, its traditional enemy for many centuries. In August 1914 Japan entered on the side of the Allies in the First World War, during which it conquered the German possessions in China and gained them by the terms of the Versailles treaty. Though this upset China, the Japanese also had reason to feel dissatisfied at the attitude towards their country by the Allies: the exclusion of a statement in the Covenant of the League of Nations acknowledging racial equality was interpreted as an insult to the Japanese and at the Washington Naval Conference in 1922, the agreement that the size of the Japanese

navy could equal no more than 60 per cent the size of the British or the American navies suggested again that the great powers did not regard Japan as an equal. Another naval agreement in 1930 treated Japan in a similar way.

There was little stability in Japan's economic and political life in these years. The changed pattern of international markets after the war had helped the already well-established Japanese industry to advance into areas which had earlier been closed to them; export of Japanese textiles flourished especially in these years. This successful economic development produced problems. Japanese workers were attracted to the towns by the prospect of work. But their conditions were generally poor, and they were particularly hit by the problem of inflation. Much of the new industry was in the hands of the *zaibatsu*, the large-scale companies whose ambitious directors adopted almost any means that came to hand to advance the interests of their companies.

The political system was a combination of elements from Japanese tradition and Western example. The country was ruled by the Emperor Hirohito (from 1926) but a two-chamber parliament existed and was elected, after 1925, on the basis of universal male suffrage. But in spite of this favourable appearance, political life lacked a solid base. Parties were poorly united and too numerous: their members showed little real loyalty. Corruption was common, and the way in which the directors of the zaibatsu sought to advance their commercial interests by bribing politicians was notorious. The modest development of trade unionism and Socialism was met with total opposition from most politicians and businessmen.

No one movement came to be of more importance than the others, as was the case with Fascism in Italy and National Socialism in Germany, but Japanese nationalism became steadily more influential and thus assisted the rising political importance of various right-wing organizations. The Japanese army was also beginning to assert stronger influence on the government: many army officers had links with the Nationalist societies and a number of them were prepared to take action on their own account, regardless of the policies of the government. It was from the army and the Nationalist societies that demands came for the creation of a *Co-prosperity Sphere* for Japan, involving the extension of Japanese control over surrounding areas and the securing of their economic resources for Japanese use. Many Japanese officers and politicians in the early 1930s were actively planning aggressive moves against neighbouring countries and were even contemplating eventual war with the United States in the event of American support for the countries that Japan attacked. At the end of 1931 Japan embarked on this expansion that led to war with the United States ten years later: a decade of aggression which the Japanese have since termed the 'dark valley' of their country's history.

The conquest of Manchuria

A part of the Japanese army was already stationed in Manchuria for the purpose of protecting Japanese property in that part of China. In September 1931 an explosion occurred at Mukden, on a part of a Japanese railway. This was not the first time that Japanese property in Manchuria had been attacked and the incident was taken by the leaders of the Japanese army as an excuse for bringing the whole of Manchuria under Japanese control, a process which they successfully completed by February 1932. Manchuria was renamed Manchukuo and absorbed into Japan's developing Co-prosperity Sphere. The Japanese government in Tokyo did not itself give orders for this military action, but the spectacular success achieved by the Japanese soldiers and the support given to them by Japanese public opinion, made the government decide that its best policy was to accept the army's action. For Japan's internal affairs, these events signified an important increase in the authority of army action over government policy.

World concern was expressed particularly at the League of Nations, which sent a com-

This portrayal of Japan as a traditional samurai warrior, victorious over all opposition, illustrates the way in which many countries, both in the Pacific and elsewhere, viewed the rising might of Japan in the 1930s and early 1940s.

mission under the chairmanship of Lord Lytton to enquire into the situation in Manchuria. The report of this commission was published a year after the invasion had begun: Japanese aggression was condemned and Japan was requested to evacuate the conquered areas. Having by then secured good control of Manchuria, the Japanese government felt confident enough to ignore this request and to withdraw from the League of Nations. Japan thus treated world opinion with sharp contempt, bringing upon Japan much hostility from the leading nations of the world. The only countries which gave recognition to Japanese Manchukuo were Germany and Italy, and as the 1930s progressed Japan's links with these countries grew increasingly close, as is shown in chapter 11.

Further Japanese conquests in China

A major objective of the Co-prosperity Sphere was securing economic resources for Japan. Having established their state of Manchukuo, the Japanese did much more than the Chinese authorities had earlier done to exploit the economic potential of the region: this successful economic development brought benefits to the Chinese of the area as well as to Japan. Attempts were made by the Japanese to gain areas near Manchukuo: in 1933 they secured control of the region of Jehol, and although an attempt in 1935 to establish Japanese control of all northern China was unsuccessful, Japanese influence in many parts was strong.

Hostilities between the Communist party and the Nationalist party in the early 1930s had weakened the Chinese resistance to these attacks, but now the two parties came together in an alliance against their common enemy. The alliance received strong encouragement from Moscow: Stalin's fear of Germany and Japan in the mid-1930s led him to encourage political alliances between Communists and other parties in an endeavour to prevent further expansion of the power of these enemies of the Soviet Union. The Chinese Communists put to the Nationalists proposals for an alliance in place of warfare, but it was an episode within the Nationalist ranks that finally led Chiang Kai-shek to form the alliance. Many of Chiang's troops, especially those which came from conquered Manchuria, were angered at being compelled to fight against fellow Chinese at a time when their country was suffering foreign invasion. In December 1936 during a mutiny of young Nationalist officers at Sian, Chiang was captured and threatened with death if he did not agree to an alliance with the Communists. The Communist-Nationalist alliance was created shortly afterwards,

and was greeted with widespread popularity throughout China.

In July 1937 at the Marco Polo bridge, just outside Peking, shots were exchanged between Chinese and Japanese troops. This comparatively minor incident was followed by substantial Japanese advances which continued until October 1938, by which time Japan occupied most of northern China and parts of southern China; the capital cities of Peking and Nanking and the vital port of Shanghai had all fallen to the invaders. Japan then proclaimed the creation of a *New Order in East Asia* (which meant virtually the same thing as the *Co-prosperity Sphere*) as an economic bloc based on Japanese control. The recently formed Communist-Nationalist alliance put up impressive resistance to the invaders, but the Chinese were unable to overcome the superior military might of their enemies.

The Sino-Japanese warfare of 1937 to 1938 also had an importance in international relations. The League of Nations was unlikely to find a solution: confidence in the League had by now been seriously undermined after failure in Manchuria in the early 1930s and Abyssinia in the mid-1930s. As is shown in chapter 11, Japan had by now become linked with Fascist Italy and Nazi Germany in the Anti Comintern pact and Japan was aided by German military supplies. China's most useful ally was the Soviet Union, with whom a non-aggression pact was signed in August 1937; Soviet military aid was given to China and Soviet aggression along their border with Manchukuo compelled the Japanese to keep much of their army in that area instead of using it against the Chinese in further advances elsewhere.

By the late 1930s the Communist-Nationalist alliance was kept going only with great difficulty and there were instances of attacks by the Nationalists on the Communists: civil war was emerging again, even while an invader held control of much of the country. The Japanese presence was so extensive and so strong that the only hope which the Chinese had of expelling them was the active involvement of the great powers on China's side. The Second World War brought a solution which eventually worked for China's benefit: as is shown in chapter 13, further Japanese aggression in the early 1940s caused the great powers to declare war on Japan and in conducting that war they necessarily came to the aid of China. After the Japanese defeat in 1945, the history of the two countries was less closely entwined. For both, the immediate postwar years were unhappy: for Japan they brought American military occupation and for China they brought renewal of the civil war between the Nationalists and the Communists.

Questions

19. Study the poster on page 72 and then answer questions (a) to (c) which follow.
    (a) (i) Name the country represented by the armed warrior,
        (ii) name its two major allies, shown by two of the three flags in the background, and
        (iii) trace the developing relations between these three countries during the late 1930s.
        $(1+1+3)$
    (b) (i) Show how during the 1930s the actions of the country represented by the warrior justified this type of portrayal.
        (ii) How do you account for the military actions of this country during the 1930s?
    (iii) Explain the steps taken by other countries during the 1930s to limit the power of the country represented by the warrior.
        $(3+3+3)$
    (c) The poster portrays an attack which took place towards the end of 1941.
        (i) Name the country against which the attack was made, and
        (ii) name the place where the attack occurred.
        (iii) What is the evidence in the poster on which you base your answer to (c) (ii)?
        (iv) Describe the events in the previous two years which led to this attack.
        $(1+1+1+3)$

20. Show the importance in the history of China of (a) the ideas of Sun Yat-sen, (b) the rule of Yuan Shih-kai, (c) the dominance of the warlords and (d) the massacres at Shanghai.

21. Describe the changing relationship between the Communists and the Nationalists in China between 1927 and 1949. How do you account for the eventual victory of the Communists over their opponents by 1949?

8
Stalin's Soviet dictatorship

Rivalries for supremacy in the mid-1920s

As a young man Josef Stalin had been destined for the priesthood of the Orthodox church. It was during his priest's training at the Tbilisi seminary that he became involved in revolutionary activity, rejected the doctrines of the church and accepted instead the doctrines of Marxism. Such attitudes naturally led to his expulsion from the seminary, after which he became closely involved with the work of the Social Democrats, abandoning his original surname of Djugashvili in favour of the name Stalin, literally meaning 'man of steel'. At the time of the February Revolution he was exiled in Siberia and at once returned to play an important, though not a leading part, in the struggles of 1917 which in October brought the Bolsheviks to power.

During Lenin's rule, Stalin had a number of major responsibilities. He became editor of the party newspaper, *Pravda* (Truth). Just after the October Revolution he was created Commissar for Nationalities and, in 1922, General Secretary of the Communist party. In this latter position he was able, by the many party appointments he made, to build up a following of men who were all dependent directly upon him for their position and status. By the time of Lenin's death, Stalin had made himself very powerful within the party.

Lenin died in January 1924: Stalin became the undisputed leader in December 1927. During that period of nearly four years, while the Soviet Union continued to be governed along the lines laid down by Lenin, an internal struggle for power took place. Its main participants were Leon Trotsky and Josef Stalin. Trotsky had developed a popular following as a result of his leadership of the Red Army in the civil war, and he had been favourably regarded by Lenin, and came near to him as an intellectual equal. Like Lenin, he wanted to encourage the spread of Communism to other countries as well as its development within the Soviet Union. Stalin, in no way the intellectual equal of Lenin, did not give so much importance, as Lenin, to the spread of Communism to other countries: instead he wished to see Communism develop satisfactorily inside Russia alone. Towards the end of his life, Lenin had regarded Stalin with strong suspicion. In terms of slogans, the difference was between 'Permanent Revolution' advocated by Trotsky, and 'Socialism in one country' advocated by Stalin.

At the time of Lenin's death, the Soviet Union was controlled by a group of three men: Kamenev, Zinoviev and Stalin. Trotsky was at that time Commissar for War and his criticism of this group of men led to his dismissal. Subsequently Kamenev and Zinoviev split from Stalin and in 1926 allied themselves politically with Trotsky. This new group of Kamenev, Zinoviev and Trotsky launched a series of political attacks against Stalin in 1926 and 1927, criticising him for a slack application of Communist ideals inside Russia, and of weak support of Communism in foreign countries, especially China, where, in 1927, the Communists were massacred. In late 1926 and 1927 Stalin succeeded in securing the dismissal of these enemies and their followers, first from the Politbureau, and then from the party. At the meeting of the Fifteenth Party Congress in December 1927, shortly after having secured these expulsions, Stalin was greeted by tumultuous applause from the delegates. From that time, he was accepted as the country's undisputed leader, and his dictatorship was secure.

After public acknowledgement of their 'errors', Kamenev and Zinoviev were re-admitted to the party. But Trotsky refused to acknowledge any errors. In 1928 he was exiled to Siberia, and in 1929 expelled from the Soviet Union. But these moves did not silence Trotsky who, throughout the 1930s, from exile abroad, continued to criticize Stalin and develop ideas for his country's future. He still had a following inside the Soviet Union and this following was troublesome to Stalin. Only the murder of Trotsky in Mexico in 1940 at the hands of Stalinist agents brought Stalin a real relief from the Trotskyite threat to his rule.

The Third Revolution: the planning of industry

The New Economic Policy had been acknowledged in 1921 as a temporary but necessary retreat in the development of Communism. By the late 1920s the time seemed right to abandon it and recommence more firmly and more fully the state direction of industry and agriculture. The disturbances of recent years, such as the First World War, the revolutions and the civil war, had all imposed tremendous strain on an economy which was in any case seriously underdeveloped for so vast a country. The years after 1917 had necessarily been taken up with building the foundations of a Communist society. Stalin now led the Soviet Union in a direction of more thorough exploitation of its economic potential. So thoroughly revolutionary was this new direction of the Soviet economy that it has been termed *The Third Revolution*, the first and the second having been the two revolutions of 1917.

Although there had always been state control of industrial policies during the previous ten years, it was only in the autumn of 1928 that *Gosplan* (the State Planning Commission) formulated the first five year plan, originally intended to last until the autumn

A poster urging full commitment by the people of the Soviet Union to the aims of the first five-year plan. At the top are the words of Stalin: 'The reality of our programme is living people, it is you and I.'

of 1933. What made this and later five year plans particularly important was that the whole plan became a part of Soviet law: failure to achieve the plan's targets was therefore regarded as a punishable crime. The targets themselves were ambitious: they were often revised in an upward direction or the time allowed for their achievement was shortened. Only a few of these highly ambitious targets were fully achieved, but there was nevertheless a considerable improvement in production levels in all essential industries.

The first five-year plan was intensified by the decision to complete it a year earlier than was originally intended. The main emphasis was sensibly placed on the means of production, so that foundations were laid for long-term economic development. Electricity, coal, iron and steel, all showed substantial production increases by the time the plan ended. Much of this development took place in the already established industrial areas, but a start was made on industrial development in new areas east of the Ural mountains. Emphasis was given to the production and export of grain, to pay for importing machine tools, thus again emphasizing the plan's focus on the means of production. The attention which the plan gave to grain production was a factor leading to the collectivization of agriculture, considered later.

The second five year plan was to last the complete five years from 1933 to 1937. By now, the emphasis on heavy industry and the neglect of expenditure or subsidies on housing and consumer goods had caused a decline in urban living standards: the second plan gave some attention to improvements in these respects. There was also greater attention to the education of workers in the more effective use of equipment, leading to an improvement in the quality of the material they produced. Throughout, as in the first plan, the major emphasis continued to be placed on the means of production: many projects, started in the first plan, were continued in the second. The third five-year plan was to last from 1938 to 1942 and was generally designed on similar lines to its predecessor. But the third plan came up against a number of crises: there was a shortage of fuel and labour and, even though the Soviet Union was able to benefit from her Polish and Baltic conquests in the autumn of 1939, by the early 1940s attention was diverted from the plan's original targets to the more urgent need of improved armaments production for the inevitable war with Nazi Germany.

The planned industrial economy resulted in substantial changes for the people of the Soviet Union. Many left the countryside to work in the new industries. Throughout the 1930s, they experienced increasing control over their lives by the Soviet authorities. It was made difficult to change jobs. Above all else, the worker was expected to work

hard, as the plans were arranged to produce maximum output. Wages were usually paid on a piece-work system, as such a system encouraged high output. The Stakhanovite movement, named after the miner Stakhanov who, by physical effort and skill, mined immense quantities of coal in the Donbas region, encouraged high output in industry by the award of incentives such as cash, holidays and medals to those workers who produced similarly high outputs. The system was not entirely popular among the workers as the fact that such high targets could be reached by some workers led the authorities to increase the normal output expected from all. The key administrative personnel in the fulfilment of these plans were the plan managers. Though well rewarded and promoted if the enterprise under their direction successfully achieved its targets, they were liable to imprisonment and dismissal in the event of failure. Only by ruthless administration of those under their control could they expect to fulfil their tasks adequately.

The Third Revolution: the planning of agriculture

Two major considerations brought changes in agriculture. Under the New Economic Policy the kulaks, the wealthy peasants, flourished: such a state of affairs was held by Stalin to be unacceptable in a Communist society. Under the terms of the first five year plan grain output was to be increased for the benefit of the Soviet Union as a whole, but the desired increase could not take place under the New Economic Policy, which gave freedom to peasants to develop agriculture as they wished. Prompted by both these considerations, a programme of mass collectivization was begun in December 1929.

The decision to embark on mass collectivization was announced suddenly. It was not clear what prompted it, but it may have been peasant resistance to some recent demands for food requisitioning by the state. During the bitterly cold winter months, the policy was ruthlessly implemented: the kulaks were sent to Siberia, and in a haphazard manner lands were amalgamated to form vast collective farms. Peasant resistance was strong: slaughtering livestock by the peasantry was a particularly effective way in which this resistance was shown. By March 1930, with the Russian countryside in a state of chaos, Stalin urged a less wholesale approach to collectivization, blaming his subordinates for an excess of zeal in implementing the changes. Between 1932 and 1933 famine again afflicted many rural areas and, combining with the chaotic effects of collectivization, resulted in the deaths of many millions of peasants, possibly as many as ten million. As the Soviet economy was developed during these years in almost complete isolation from the rest of the world, the plight of these starving millions was little known outside the Soviet Union.

The process of collectivization continued throughout the 1930s and by the outbreak of the Second World War, almost all Soviet farms were collectivized. A typical collective farm in the 1930s had communal control of the land and livestock, sharing out the farm implements among the members, and hiring tractors from the local machine tractor station for harvesting large fields. The farm had the appearance of being run democratically, but in practice it was largely under the direction of its chairman, who performed functions in the organization of agriculture that were similar to those of managers in industry. The main responsibility which the state placed on him and on the farm in general was the provision of the required quota of the farm's produce for use by the towns.

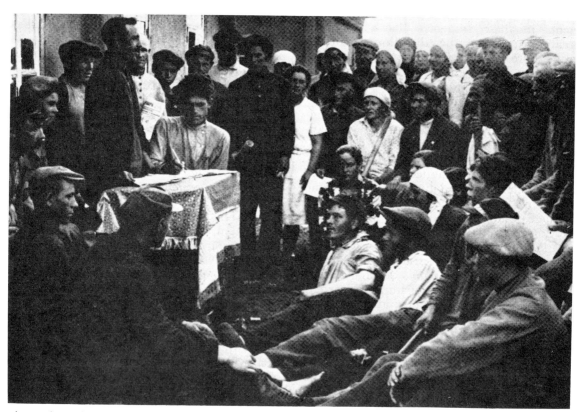

A meeting of workers on a collective farm. Though by the late 1930s the collectives were producing increased agricultural output, they did not always work with the harmony suggested by this photograph.

The main concession in the modified system of collectivization was the provision of a private allotment for each member of the collective. These allotments were small, but they provided the members with the means of supplying the needs of their own families and the possibility of producing some goods for private sale. So long as the all-important collective quota had been met, members were free to sell their goods at local town markets.

The Stalinist purges

Purges (expulsions) from the party had taken place earlier, during Lenin's rule. But Stalin's purges took place on a far wider scale than before, and were accompanied by public trials of the purged, and their execution in vast numbers.

The incident which started a great wave of purges was the murder of Kirov, the leader of the Communist party at Leningrad, in December 1934. Kirov was a rival for the leadership of the Soviet Union and it may be that his murder was arranged by Stalin as a convenient excuse to purge the party and to secure the elimination of others who were believed to be opposed to Stalin's rule. For the next three years people inside and outside the Communist party were subject to persecution. The charges against them varied enormously. In the early stages complicity in the murder of Kirov was a common accusation, but victims were also accused of being spies for foreign powers, of being in league with the exiled Trotsky, of being kulaks or 'wreckers' of the planned economy. Many early Communists, who had in many cases played a far more heroic and far more significant role in the events of 1917 than Stalin, were eliminated during these years, sometimes after carefully rehearsed show trials. Kamenev, Zinoviev and the head of the Red Army, General Tukhachevsky, were among leading Communists treated in this way.

The machinery for conducting the purges worked with great efficiency. The police organization that had major responsibility for conducting the purges in these years was the NKVD, one of the successors to Lenin's Cheka. The NKVD made arrests and subjected its victims to interrogation in which physical and mental torture were often employed. Some victims, especially the more prominent, were prepared in these ways for the show trials, usually presided over by Chief Prosecutor Vyshinsky, where they made public acknowledgement of their guilt. The total number of deaths during the purges will never be known, but it can certainly be numbered in millions.

Stalin embarked on these purges in order to protect his dictatorship. He was aware of political opposition to him and he was aware that Trotsky, in spite of his exile, still had a substantial following within the Soviet Union. By the mid-1930s he was worried by Hitler's hostility: a German invasion could create a suitable opportunity for Stalin's internal enemies to remove him from power. He also felt that he had the answer to the country's basic economic problems and was willing to use any means to achieve what he considered desirable ends. In such a vast country the idea of 'enemies within' brought about greater unity. Stalin could appear to be the saviour of the nation. That is why show trials were held. Stalin certainly got the results he wanted. The policy of terror assured him of the continuation of his rule: a few years later his leadership of the embattled Soviet Union during the Second World War consolidated his position and strengthened the links between the Soviet people and their dictator.

The Great Patriotic War

The role of the Soviet Union during the time of its alliance with Germany (1939–41) and its war with Germany (1941–45) is considered in chapters 12 and 13. For the Russians, the struggle with Germany was seen as the *Great Patriotic War*. Although the purges in the army in the late 1930s made for a lack of military preparedness, Stalin's leadership of his people in these desperate years, and his direction of the war effort, led to ultimate victory and further enhanced his position both at home and abroad.

An enthusiastic sense of patriotism gripped the Soviet Union during these years: even the Orthodox church gave Stalin support, as the old differences between Christianity and Communism were put aside. But this patriotism was not entirely spontaneous. The NKVD took on the important role of ensuring the loyalty of troops and of arresting those who showed weak commitment to the fighting. Stalin himself stated at the start of the war that any Soviet soldier who allowed himself to be captured by the enemy was a traitor to Russia. This condemnation affected many Soviet soldiers who were captured by the Germans. After enduring the miseries of German concentration camps during the war, they were handed back at the insistence of the victorious allies, only to be reimprisoned or shot on their return by their fellow-countrymen. Others who were similarly handed back in 1945 to Soviet control, generally against their will, were natives of Byelorussia, the Baltic provinces and the Ukraine who in the early stages of the war had even welcomed Hitler's forces as a possible means of liberation from Stalin's tyranny.

Enthusiasm for the war effort was therefore not entirely spontaneous nor entirely wholehearted. Nevertheless, partly because of the vastness of the country and partly because of the crucial nature of the campaigns that took place there, no country made greater sacrifices nor suffered more than the Soviet Union during the Second World War. About 15 million Soviet citizens were killed, a figure that represents approximately half the total deaths throughout the entire world during the course of the Second World War. As reward, the Soviet Union secured influence and territory in eastern Europe. Essentially, however, the fight had been a defensive one against the Nazi invaders. In spite of justifiable criticism that might be made of the Soviet authorities in these years, the term the *Great Patriotic War* is suitable, and equal to the Soviet struggles of these years.

Questions

22. Study the Soviet propaganda poster of the late 1920s on page 76 and then answer questions (a) to (d) which follow.
    (a) (i) Name the Soviet leader shown in the front foreground.
        (ii) Why does the poster show him clothed in this way?
        (iii) Trace his rise to power from the time of the revolutionary events of 1917 to the time of this poster.
        $(1+1+3)$
    (b) (i) Describe the main features of the organization of the Soviet economy during the years just before the appearance of this poster.
        (ii) Explain why the Soviet leader wished to change the organization of the Soviet economy.
        $(2+2)$
    (c) (i) What evidence does the poster contain of the particular aims of the first five-year plan?
        (ii) Describe the methods that were used to ensure that these aims were achieved during the time of both the first and the second five-year plans.
        $(2+3)$
    (d) Describe the steps taken by this leader during the middle years of the 1930s against his suspected enemies within the Soviet Union. Why did he feel it necessary to take such action?
        (6)

23. Trace and explain the rise to power of Stalin during the 1920s. To what extent does his direction of Soviet industry and Soviet agriculture before the outbreak of the Second World War deserve the description, the *Third Revolution*?

24. Outline the varying fortunes of Russian foreign policy between 1917 and 1941. Why do Russians refer to their fighting during the following four years as the *Great Patriotic War*?

9
France and Spain between the wars

France should have been a contented country in 1919: Imperial Germany had been defeated and the French Empire had been extended. With her extensive natural resources, France was now in a position to become the dominant force in Western Europe, as she had earlier been at different times in European history. But in almost all respects, the 1920s and the 1930s were years of French decline. The roots of that decline lie in the confused condition of France's political and economic life, and in the uncertain relations which France had with the rest of the world.

French politics and the French economy

The 1920s and the 1930s form the last decades in the history of the Third French Republic. Created after the German invasion of 1870, it was to be defeated after the German invasion of 1940. Though the Third Republic managed to survive longer than any other system of government in France since the Revolution, before the First World War its history had revealed serious internal divisions. After the war, the divisions continued to damage the republic and to create a fragmented political life, a process further encouraged by the system of proportional representation used in French elections.

In the immediate postwar years the political parties in France formed themselves, very approximately, into three groups: the right, the left and the centre. The right consisted of many different factions: some were old-established, representing traditional French interests, while others such as the influential *Action Française* were the forerunners of the

French Fascist leagues of the 1930s. Immediately after the war, a coalition of the right held power until 1924 though during that time, as throughout the whole of the interwar years, the composition of the government changed on a number of occasions. After 1924 power was transferred to a coalition of the left, dominated by the French Socialists. The new Prime Minister, Herriot, was unable to hold together this coalition for very long and after 1926 various right-wing governments were formed. In all of these political manoeuvres the Radical party played a crucial role: this was the party of the centre, which at times allied with the right and at times with the left. During the early 1930s, in the aftermath of the world financial crisis, French political life entered a period of serious instability which only ended when Léon Blum formed a Popular Front government in April 1936.

Much of this political instability is attributable to the condition of the French economy during the interwar years. Throughout the 1920s the French were concerned by what they considered to be their inadequate share of German reparations. The French claimed, rightly, that most of the damage of the war had been suffered by their country and though more reparations were paid to France than to any other country, they maintained that the amounts received were nowhere near adequate for the damage that Germany had done. Poincaré's drastic policy of occupation of the Ruhr in 1923, already considered in chapter 6, received widespread support in France as a stand for essential French claims against Germany. The end to reparations payments in early 1931 therefore hit France badly and at a time when the effects of the world financial crisis were also being experienced. A serious economic slump resulted, but though industrial production declined, the maximum unemployment figure of half a million was much smaller than the unemployment figures for the United States, Britain and Germany.

Apart from these financial effects of the Versailles treaty and the Wall Street crash, the highly unequal distribution of wealth in France was also a cause of instability in the country's political and social life. It was often said in these years, that France was governed not by the politicians who held office but by the 'two hundred families' who owned most of the French wealth and who, representing no interests other than their own, exercised undue influence in the government of France. Between the wealth and luxurious style of those who controlled French finance, and the poverty and hard work of the rest

of the population there was a gulf wider than that found in most other European countries in these years. The wealthy virtually blackmailed successive French governments: if their interests were not given priority, then they would withdraw their wealth from France, and invest it abroad. Governments, naturally anxious that the country's economy should flourish, therefore sought to accommodate the interests of high finance. Right-wing governments tended to accommodate these interests fairly satisfactorily, but left-wing governments which attempted to reform the injustices of French society, found that they were powerless to resist the influence of the 'two hundred families'. Many French felt that the influence of wealthy financiers was so strong that unless compliant governments of the right were in power, all hope of stability was lost.

A Communist election poster names wealthy financiers and emphasizes the strong influence they had on the government of France: 'The bank against the nation. These men do not represent creative work . . . they are just the parasites of the stock exchange, of speculation and of profit.'

The French Fascist leagues and the Stavisky affair

In the confused circumstances of the 1930s, many Frenchmen turned to Fascism as a possible solution to their country's problems. Instead of one Fascist party, there were in France a number of different Fascist leagues. *Action Française*, which hoped to recreate the greatness which France had achieved in the past, originated before the First World War and in many respects inspired the various leagues which developed during the interwar years. The leagues took on highly patriotic names and, though all were distinctly right-wing in their political outlook, they each had a particular emphasis to make. *Les Camelots du Roi* (the Agents of the King) looked to a restoration of the monarchy; *Les Jeunesses Patriotes* (The Young Patriots) sought support from the youth of the country; *Solidarité Française* (French Solidarity) imitated the example of the Italian Fascists.

The lack of unity among the leagues tended to make them less effective than similar movements in Germany and Italy. But in 1934, the Stavisky affair brought them as near to success as they ever came. Sacha Stavisky, a man of Russian origins, lived flamboyantly in French high society from the profits he made from many fraudulent dealings. The most remarkable aspect of Stavisky's career was his ability to evade trial for his numerous shady business deals. It was widely believed that if Stavisky stood trial, he would reveal the names of politicians who had been involved in his dealings in one way or another. It was similarly believed that these politicians asserted influence to prevent such a dangerous trial from taking place. Trial of Stavisky could not, however, be postponed indefinitely. But in early 1934, when it became imminent, Stavisky was discovered dead in his villa in the French Alps. Had he been murdered or had he committed suicide? The matter will probably never be satisfactorily resolved. At the time it was widely believed that his death had been arranged by those politicians who feared they might be incriminated at Stavisky's trial.

The Fascist leagues seized on Stavisky's mysterious death as evidence of government corruption. It was they who led widespread and violent protests against the government, which resulted in the resignation of the Prime Minister, Chautemps, himself widely regarded as being connected with Stavisky's dealings. The leagues continued to agitate and on 6 February 1934 they organized violent demonstrations in the centre of Paris at the Place de la Concorde, near the French parliament. The *Stavisky Riots*, as they became called, appeared therefore to be a threat to the maintenance of ordered government in France. The formation of a coalition government under Doumergue, a former well-respected French President, saved the situation for France. Though this government fell in November 1934 and was therefore as short lived as so many others, it made a spirited attempt to tackle some of France's problems, making important proposals for fundamental constitutional reform.

Léon Blum and the Popular Front

Anxiety over the growing power of totalitarian countries such as Germany, Italy and Japan, caused the government of the Soviet Union to encourage Communists in other countries to ally with other left-wing parties to form with them a *Popular Front*. Thus practical steps were taken to attempt to exclude from power parties which might be hostile to the Soviet Union. France was one of the countries in which this new Moscow policy produced results. The Communist party linked up with the Socialist party and the Radical party to form a Popular Front, an effective alternative to the threats posed by the Fascist leagues in the chaotic political circumstances of the mid 1930s. In the general election of the spring of 1936, the success of the Popular Front heralded an entirely new style of government for France.

The new Prime Minister was Léon Blum, leader of the Socialist party. Under him, the Popular Front government made brave attempts to ignore the influence of those who controlled French finance and to embark on the desperately-needed social reform. The pitifully low wages of French workers were substantially increased, the rights of trades unions in negotiations with employers were guaranteed, the school leaving age was raised to 14 and some reforms were made in the organization of industry and finance. In these ways the Popular Front government brought about some of the most important reforms in the whole history of the Third Republic.

But even sustained by his political alliances and electoral success, Blum was unable to fulfil all that he intended. The influential financiers, much opposed to his reforms, sent their money abroad, thus causing a serious weakening of the French economy. This contributed to the mounting inflation, which for many workers wiped out the gains they had secured from the Popular Front government. It was these financiers also who prevented Blum from giving whole-hearted support to the Popular Front government in neighbouring Spain when it was attacked by Nationalist forces in the Spanish Civil War after July 1936. Many on the right

in French politics hated Blum and all that he stood for so much that the expression 'Better Hitler than Blum' was often heard among them. In June 1937, Blum resigned and the Popular Front government was virtually at an end.

In April 1938, Edouard Daladier, leader of the Radical party, became Prime Minister. Foreign affairs were the dominant issue during his government, which lasted into the war itself. The French pursuit of appeasement had already been much in evidence over the issues surrounding Abyssinia and the Rhineland in the 1930s, and the eager pursuit of this policy by the Daladier government in the late 1930s is shown in chapter 11. When in 1940 the German forces made a concerted attack on France, it was not only the French armed forces which collapsed: the Third Republic was also brought down and, as is shown in chapter 12, it gave way to the collaborationist régime of Vichy.

The problem of poverty was more serious in Spain than in any other European country during the interwar years. This photograph, taken in the remote west of the country, shows the mean housing, unmade road, animal transport and the old clothing and implements.

Spain: the forces of tradition and of change

Early twentieth-century Spain was a poverty-stricken land. The majority of the population were peasants, eking out a hard and meagre existence by their work on the estates of landowners or, if they were among the fortunate minority to possess one, on their own small holdings. Illiteracy among the peasantry was high, and their agricultural methods were primitive. Lack of natural resources and lack of investment capital meant that development of industry had been slight. Those peasants who were tempted to seek further fortune in the towns often found the poverty and exploitation in new surroundings as intolerable as in the countryside.

Responsibility for these depressing conditions lies in the traditional structure of Spanish society, power being based upon the landowners, the church and the army. Throughout Spain, landowners were determined to maintain their profitable hold over the peasantry. The Spanish church held extensive possessions of its own both in land and in buildings, many of which were monastries and cathedrals of exceptional beauty. Most elementary education was in church hands and the established social order received the fullest support from the Spanish church. The army provided many young men of wealthy family with a secure and privileged career. Though the efficiency of the army was poor, its loyalty to Spain was never in question.

At the head of this traditional and archaic structure was the Spanish monarch, King Alfonso XIII (1902–31). Despite the fact that the Cortes (the Spanish parliament) was elected on a system of universal suffrage, the landowners, by skilful manipulation of the electoral system, still managed to maintain control. Only in the years immediately after the First World War did movements for change emerge forcefully enough to challenge this situation.

Two forces for change were particularly significant at that time: Socialism and Anarchism. The Spanish Socialist party aimed to develop its Socialist goals in Spain by working through both the Cortes and the trade unions: its work was usually non-violent and similar to that done by Socialist parties in other European countries. Anarchism was more distinctly Spanish. Its aim was the destruction of Spanish authority, as represented by government, landowners, church and army: only after that destruction was achieved would it be possible to construct a new and just society.

Thus in the immediate postwar years Spain showed the divisions that were to deepen in the 1920s and to lead to civil war in the 1930s: on the political right, the landowners, the church and the army; on the political left, the Socialists and the Anarchists. In addition to these problems there was also disruption caused by regional conflict and colonial defeat. The industrialization of Catalonia and the Basque provinces had sharpened their long-standing sense of discontent with the central government. Demands for regional self-government were accompanied by violence, which the Spanish army was not able entirely to contain. The army similarly failed to suppress the rising against Spanish rule in Spanish Morocco.

All these problems were reflected in rapid changes of government during the years after the war. Then in 1923 the army, with the connivance of the King, asserted its traditional role when General Miguel Primo de Rivera established a dictatorship. Until his fall from power in 1930 he asserted a control over Spain similar in some respects to that of Mussolini over Italy. The Cortes was suspended, political parties were banned and the press was censored. But his dictatorship was not particularly harsh and he had some useful achievements to his credit: the more moderate trade unions were able to cooperate with him, some important public works schemes were started, transport facilities were improved and encouragement was given to manufacturers. The rebel forces in Morocco were defeated. But as financial difficulties re-emerged in the late 1920s, de Rivera's popularity declined, and when in January 1930 he lost the vital support of the army, he fell from power.

The elections of April 1931 showed that the inhabitants of the towns favoured a republic: Alfonso XIII abdicated and at once left Spain. A republic was proclaimed, its constitution providing for a one-chamber Cortes to be elected by universal suffrage. Though the republic was greeted with enthusiasm by some Spaniards, many saw it as a threat to Spain. In practice it led to a deepening of the country's divisions.

Spain as a republic: the outbreak of civil war

As a result of the first general election for the republic, a coalition between the Socialist party, the Republican party and some members of the Radical party formed a government, under the leadership of the moderate Republican politician, Manuel Azaña. This government was distinctly left-wing and embarked on a programme of reform which appeared to threaten the established social structure in Spain. Many church privileges were attacked: the state would in future make no contribution to the payment of the clergy and a number of influential religious orders were forcibly dissolved. The size of the army was drastically reduced. Attempts to grapple with land reform were less positive: the government was divided on whether the landless peasantry should be allowed to own individual plots, or whether they should work in a collectivized system.

Though extensive, these reforms satisfied few Spaniards: for the right-wing they were too advanced and for the left-wing they were too limited. Disorder grew in the early 1930s: anarchist violence, bitter strikes and army discontent were all in evidence. The right-wing, highly alarmed by the government's policies, realized that they must respond more effectively to these challenges. Under the leadership of Gil Robles, the Catholic Association emerged as a well-financed political group which aimed to attract the political support of Roman Catholics. It achieved success in the general election of November 1933. By allying with the monarchist parties and with the Radical party,

whose early alliance with Azaña's government had been broken, Robles was able to form a government and to remain in power until February 1936.

The main efforts of the Robles government were directed towards the destruction of the work of the Azaña government. The bitterness felt by peasants and workers, as they saw themselves robbed of the limited gains secured under Azaña, led to further anarchism, more strikes and some serious armed clashes. The worst violence was in the northern Asturias region where, in 1934, the well-organized industrial workers rose in violent rebellion and established their own soviet to govern the region. In October 1934 the army, consisting mainly of troops from Morocco, undertook the task of suppression with savage brutality, resulting in death and imprisonment for thousands of the rebels. Many Spaniards were unaware of the full horror of the suppression and looked with admiration on the army which once more had shown that it could perform a decisive role in Spanish affairs. Foremost among the military leaders of the suppression was General Franco.

The third general election in the history of the republic, in February 1936, was of crucial importance. The left-wing parties united for this election in a *Popular Front* consisting of Socialists, Republicans, Communists and some members of the Radical party. The right-wing parties similarly united as a *National Front* consisting of the Catholic Association, the Monarchists, the Landowners party and a new Fascist party, known as the Falange. The result of the election was as follows:

	Popular Front	National Front
Seats in Cortes	256	143
Total votes in the country	4.1 million	3.8 million

Robles was therefore defeated and Azaña again formed a ministry. Though he was intent on re-creating his earlier reforms, he again pursued a moderate policy. But many on the left were seeking more than Azaña's moderation would allow. Peasants, discontented with the slowness of genuine land reform, were taking the law into their own hands and were seizing land themselves. The Communists, whose support even in the election of February 1936 had not been very strong, were gathering more popularity as they urged fuller policies of reform, and forecast that a Communist coup would unseat the moderate Azaña, just as the moderate Kerensky had been unseated in the 1917 Revolution in Russia.

The militancy of the left naturally aroused fears among those who had supported the National Front. Examination of the election figures above will show that the National Front had a justifiable grievance in their claim that the electoral system had worked to their disadvantage as the number of seats they had secured in the Cortes failed to reflect fairly their proportion of the total vote in the country. Just as on the left the Communist supporters increased noticeably after the election, so on the right the new Falange party grew in strength. This was led by José Antonio Primo de Rivera, son of the military dictator of the 1920s. It consciously imitated successful Fascist-style parties elsewhere in Europe, such as the Fascist party in Italy and the National Socialist party in Germany: like them it aimed to create a strong government of the right and like them it developed its own militia, which in early 1936 was recruiting many men from all the parties of the right.

In this volatile situation Azaña knew that the army was the real danger. But in spite of sensible government precautions such as the removal of untrustworthy officers, including Franco, to remote parts of the country, military leaders successfully plotted an uprising of the army. In mid-July 1936, assassination of the right-wing opposition leader Calvo Sotelo accidentally provided a suitable excuse for the uprising, and the army was ready to put their plans into action.

During the night of 17–18 July 1936 the uprising followed a traditional and well coordinated pattern throughout Spain: the army marched from local barracks, joined forces with sympathetic elements such as the local Falange militia and took over the local administration. Franco's arrival in Spanish Morocco, from his exile in the Canary Islands, had been the signal for the start of the rising, which by the end of the month had successfully secured control of about a third of Spain. The revolt had got off to a good start, aided by the government's policy of refusing to arm those who wanted to defend the republic: the government's hope was that this conciliatory move would lead to a settlement, though in practice it merely aided the success of the rebels. By late July it was clear that a civil war existed between the rebel forces of the right, the Nationalists, and the defenders of the left, the Republicans.

The undisputed leader of the Nationalists, who were based in the city of Burgos, was the 44-year-old General Francisco Franco. He had entered a Spanish Military Academy at an early age and on active service earlier in Spanish Morocco had shown himself to have qualities of bravery and efficiency, combined with ruthlessness. As a loyal army officer he supported movements of the right and had become known throughout Spain for his leading part in the suppression of the 1934 rising, in the Asturias region. But it was only in 1936 that he became actively involved politically, in plotting the overthrow of the republic. After the start of the civil war, Franco received the support of all the elements of the right: the traditional elements such as the landowners, the army and the church, together with the newer political parties such as the Catholic Association and, more significantly, the Falange. Essentially a practical man, he stood for no philosophy and for no ideal other than the restoration to Spain of the order and stability of the past which, so he held, were the foundations of Spain's greatness.

This political poster, produced by the republic during the Civil War, takes an expectedly unfavourable view of 'Los Nacionales' (The Nationalists), emphasizing that many of them represented interests from outside Spain. Notice how the Falange slogan 'Arriba España' is linked to a map of Spain hanging from a gallows.

The civil war and its international significance

The Spanish Civil War sharpened the already tense atmosphere in European relations in the mid-1930s. As Blum's government in France was the only other Popular Front government in Europe, its sympathies lay with the besieged republic. But Blum's political position was insecure: intervention on behalf of the republic would have been so controversial that it could have brought down his government. Blum wanted to be certain that if his government did not intervene on the side of the Republicans, neither should other governments intervene on the side of the Nationalists. He therefore cooperated with the British government to bring into being in September 1936 the *Non-Intervention Committee*, which met throughout the war and which became progressively more meaningless as its basic objective was flouted by three of the countries represented on it: Italy, Germany and the Soviet Union.

Italy intervened on the Nationalist side early in the war and Mussolini maintained Italian forces in Spain throughout. Italian forces were the most numerous forces of intervention, but proved the least valuable. Mussolini reckoned that a Nationalist Spain, grateful for Italian help, would be a further step towards Italian dominance of the Mediterranean area. German intervention followed Italian intervention and was at times a decisive element in Nationalist success. For Hitler, a Nationalist Spain would be a valuable counterweight in any future German offensive against France: additionally, the war provided training opportunities for his army and the chance to secure some valuable Spanish minerals. Italian and German intervention in Spain on the Nationalist side led to closer links between the two countries, as shown in Chapter 11.

The only external aid secured by the Republic from foreign governments was from the Soviet Union: in the end this aid failed to prevent the republic's collapse, though it was an important element in the republican success in a number of engagements. As Stalin had encouraged the formation of

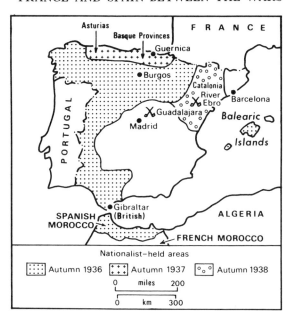

The Spanish Civil War, 1936–39

Popular Front governments in the first place, it seemed appropriate that he should give active encouragement to maintain one.

Intervention was not confined to intervention by governments. The Spanish Civil War made an appeal to the idealism of many individuals in countries pledged to neutrality: to these individuals, members of the *International Brigades*, the Spanish revolt represented the Fascist challenge that had already succeeded in other parts of Europe and which, by fighting for the republic, they intended to help defeat in Spain.

After the successful Nationalist advances in summer 1936, the position of both sides remained fairly static during the following winter. Most of the Republicans' attention was given to the successful defence of Madrid, in which Soviet assistance played a vital part. By March 1937, when the Italian besieging forces were defeated at Guadalajara, Madrid was saved, at least for the time being. In 1937 the Nationalist forces transferred their main attention to the defeat of the northern areas of the Basque and Asturias provinces. In these strongly Republican areas memories of October 1934 were still acute, and resistance was strong. But by the end of the year the Nationalist forces had secured victory there. A controversial engagement had taken place at Guernica in April 1937, when the German Condor Legion virtually razed this northern city to the ground in a devastating series of air attacks, suggestive of the tactics that might be employed in any future European war.

In the spring and summer of 1938 the Nationalists successfully advanced their control into south-eastern Spain, in the region of Catalonia: the Republican victory at the river Ebro in July failed to stem the enemy's advance for long. With the fall of Barcelona in January 1939, it was clear that the republic was doomed. Madrid, the one main centre still loyal to the republic, was now in a desperate situation, and after a successful Nationalist campaign in the spring of 1939, the capital fell in April and the war came to an end.

Why were the Republicans defeated and the Nationalists successful? The Nationalists had the support of the Spanish army (including the highly-efficient Moroccan contingent), most of the civil guards, the Falange militia and substantial foreign help from Italy and Germany. They were therefore militarily more efficient and better-organized than the Republicans, who relied on what was left of the army and civil guards, ill-disciplined militia groups, the dedicated but poorly-coordinated International Brigades, and Soviet assistance which, though valuable in the early stages, was withdrawn towards the end of 1938. The Nationalist leadership by Franco was undisputed, and obeyed throughout the Nationalist-held territories. But the Republican government changed its leadership, the Socialist leader Caballero giving way in the spring of 1937 to the Communist leader Negrin: neither was fully in control of the disruptive elements within the Republican areas. The economy in the Nationalist areas was more successfully organized, partly as a result of their good fortune in holding support in the better agricultural regions; the lack of rationing and the comparatively low taxation in these areas contrasted favourably with the situation else-

where. But Franco's military and political skill in the war could not hide the fact that his inheritance in April 1939 was still a bitterly divided land.

Questions

25. Study the political propaganda poster on page 88, produced by the Spanish government after the outbreak of the civil war, and then answer questions (a) and (e) which follow.

  (a) Name
    (i) the Spanish political leader to whom all the persons in this ship gave allegiance throughout most of the civil war, and
    (ii) the type of Spanish government which the opponents of this ship sought to defend during the civil war.

    (2)

  (b) Explain the significance of
    (i) the town named on the side of the ship, and
    (ii) the slogan shown in the centre of the ship.

    (3)

  (c) (i) Name the home area of the two soldiers shown in the background, and
    (ii) explain their significance in the civil war.

    (1+2)

  (d) (i) Name the institution represented by the man in the centre foreground,
    (ii) name the country represented by the man with the bag on the right, and
    (iii) name the country represented by the man with the cannon on the left.
    (iv) In the case of *each* of the above three, explain why they travelled in this ship, and assess the importance of their contribution towards the success of their joint cause in the civil war.

    (1+1+1+5)

(e) Apart from the opposition which they faced, what other factors contributed to the increasing weakness of the opponents of this ship?

(4)

26. Show the importance in the history of France of *each* of the following: (a) the French financiers, (b) the Fascist leagues and (c) the Popular Front government.

27. Examine the divisions which existed within Spain during the years after the First World War. Why had these divisions resulted in the outbreak of war by 1936 and why were the Nationalists victorious in that war by 1939?

10
Britain between the wars

When the armistice took effect in November 1918, signalling the end of four years of fighting and slaughter on the battlefields of Europe, great hopes were placed on the ability of the government of Britain to create 'a land fit for heroes'. Foremost was a need to improve on the injustices of the pre-war days. Only in 1918 did Britain allow votes for all men over twenty-one and votes for women over thirty. Society was still bitterly divided by class and made only slight provision for the welfare needs of its members. Though the interwar years saw efforts by different governments to construct an improved economy and a fairer society, severe crises in the economic and political life of the nation made progress towards these goals slow and uncertain. The 1920s and the 1930s were unhappy decades for most people in Britain.

Lloyd George's postwar coalition government

The leader of the Liberal party, David Lloyd George, had formed a coalition government in 1916, in which Liberal, Conservative and Labour ministers served. Having successfully led the country to victory in the war, Lloyd George sought to continue his coalition government in peacetime. The Conservative party supported him, though the Labour party felt that in peacetime they

Governments in Britain during the interwar years		
General election	*Government*	*Prime Minister*
December 1918	Coalition of Conservatives and Liberals	David Lloyd George (Andrew Bonar Law from October 1922)
November 1922	Conservative	Andrew Bonar Law (Stanley Baldwin from May 1923)
December 1923	Labour	James Ramsay MacDonald
October 1924	Conservative	Stanley Baldwin
May 1929	Labour	James Ramsay MacDonald
October 1931	National (Conservative-dominated)	James Ramsay MacDonald (Stanley Baldwin from June 1935)
October 1935	National (Conservative-dominated)	Stanley Baldwin (Neville Chamberlain from May 1937)

A coalition government of all parties was formed in May 1940 with Winston Churchill as Prime Minister. Due to wartime circumstances, no general election was held until July 1945.

should continue the political struggle outside the coalition. A general election, the first for eight years, was held in December 1918. This election is often called the *coupon election*, the coupon being the letter sent jointly by Lloyd George and the Conservative leader, Bonar Law, to those parliamentary candidates, of either the Liberal or the Conservative party, whom the leaders accepted as standing for the coalition. The election, held as it was in a mood of elation at the victory associated with Lloyd George, resulted in a substantial majority for him.

The divisions within the Liberal party were deepened as a result of that election. Before 1914 the Liberal party and the Conservative party were the major political parties within Britain. But Lloyd George's decision to create the coalition in 1916 had led to a division within the party, as a group under the leadership of Herbert Asquith had stressed the party's need to remain independent. The decision to continue the coalition in 1918 could only harden this division. The Labour party, a minority party before the war, was beginning to play a fuller part in the country's political life. At the end of the war it refused to continue to cooperate with the coalition and drew up a new constitution which stated more strongly the party commitment to nationalization of major industries and the extension of welfare aid. At the end of the war, therefore, the prospects of these two parties differed sharply: the Liberal party was divided and declining in support, while the Labour party was united and increasing in support. During the 1920s the Labour party succeeded in overtaking the Liberal party and establishing itself as one of the country's two main political parties. The Liberals virtually ceased to be an important political force.

A major responsibility of the Prime Minister in 1919 was to assist in the creation of the peace treaties at Paris; Lloyd George's work in this connection has been fully considered in chapter 2. At home, the economy demanded attention. For the previous four years it had been organized on a wartime basis which was obviously no longer appropriate. The initial effects of the end of the

war on the economy were good, as the return of peace brought an inevitable upsurge in demand for goods. But government policies did little to prevent these favourable conditions giving way to a slump between 1920 and 1921. By the end of 1921 unemployment had risen beyond two million. The main reason for this was that both the leaders of government and the directors of industry failed to realize the significance of the changes in world markets which had been produced by the war; many formerly valuable foreign purchasers, especially among the Commonwealth countries, had seen their trading with Britain disrupted by the war and were now seeking to trade with their immediate neighbours or to develop industries of their own. Nor was provision made for future development in these post-war years by effective modernization of industry.

The government was compelled to give increasing attention to the management of the economy, though its attempts in this direction created further opposition and division. A committee on government expenditure made recommendations in February 1922 for substantial cuts, recommendations usually known from the name of the committee's chairman, as the 'Geddes axe'. Education and the armed services were to feel the weight of the 'axe' in particular. Economic protection, the charging of import taxes in order to bring foreign-produced goods to the same price level as home-produced goods, had always been an idea rejected by the Liberal party in pursuit of its ideal of free trade. But some import duties imposed during wartime had not been lifted when the war ended and were, in fact, extended by the 1921 Safeguarding of Industries Act, which provided for an import duty of as much as a third of the original cost of the imported item. The act led to a deepening of the division of the Liberal party, at a time when Lloyd George no longer held the admiration he had attracted towards the end of the war.

Though the country's economy entered a decline during the years of Lloyd George's coalition, his government nevertheless produced some important domestic legislation which benefited many sections of society. Legislation in 1920 extended the benefits of the National Insurance Act of 1911 to all unemployed workers, and increased the amount of benefit that could be paid. Thus 'the dole' came into being and provided a means of living, though a sparse one, for the unemployed throughout the interwar years.

One of Lloyd George's promises in the coupon election had been the building of 'homes fit for heroes' and, to an extent, he fulfilled this promise by the Addison Housing Act of 1919. This act required local authorities to supervize the housing needs of their area and provided them with government grants to help build houses themselves. The first housing estates were constructed by local authorities in many areas as a result of this act. The designers of the estates attempted to create space between houses, or blocks of houses, to attach private gardens to them and generally to avoid the terraced arrangements which typified the homes of most workers in the prewar years.

The Fisher Education Act was passed in 1918 before the First World War had ended. Not until 1944, just before the Second World War came to an end, was there an Education Act of similar importance. The Fisher Act succeeded in raising the school leaving age to fourteen and providing fuller financial assistance for pupils at grammar schools, where fees were still charged. It failed in its aim to provide part-time education for those between fourteen and eighteen. Lack of adequate financing meant that teachers in state schools were often unable to teach their pupils as effectively as they wished. One particular problem, which remained throughout the interwar years, was the very large size of classes, many of which contained more than fifty pupils. A number of politicians

were in any case not anxious to assist education, as they viewed with concern the prospect of too many well-educated people, who might not be willing to take on essential manual work.

Political changes in the early 1920s

A declining economy and a divided party were not the only problems facing Lloyd George in 1922. In India and in Ireland, both considered separately elsewhere in this book, these were years of strong challenge to continued British rule. The solutions which Lloyd George brought to them remained controversial. Lloyd George's personal reputation declined when it became known in 1922 that money had been paid into a political fund by those anxious to obtain a title or an honour.

In October 1922 Lloyd George fell from power on an issue of foreign policy. His firm military opposition to the militant nationalist movement of Mustafa Kemal within the Ottoman Empire, considered in Chapter 2, was criticized by a number of Conservative MPs who felt that the government should be supporting Mustafa Kemal instead of opposing him. These members met at the Conservative Carlton Club where, largely at the urging of Stanley Baldwin, then President of the Board of Trade, they voted to withdraw their support from the coalition government. Lloyd George had no alternative but to resign and the King appointed in his place Bonar Law, who then held a general election in November 1922.

This was the first of three general elections that were to take place at the end of successive years. For the political development of Britain they are an important set of elections, the results of which are summarized below.

	November 1922	December 1923	October 1924
Conservative	345	258	419
Liberal	116	159	40
Labour	142	191	151

The election of November 1922 returned the Conservative party to power and confirmed Bonar Law as Prime Minister. The fortunes of the other two parties varied considerably: the badly divided Liberal party returned many fewer candidates, while the Labour party had increased its representation substantially from the 63 seats obtained in 1918. But the Prime Minister was a sick man, and in May 1923 he resigned on account of his weakening health. To the bitter disappointment of the Foreign Secretary, Lord Curzon, the prime ministership went to Baldwin, who had the advantage of House of Commons membership, which by the 1920s was considered essential for a Prime Minister. Baldwin held that the country's economic problems would only be solved by the pursuit of a full policy of economic protection. As at that time such a policy was not a part of Conservative policy, Baldwin felt it right to summon an election on the issue.

As can be seen from the figures above, in the election of December 1923 the Conservatives lost many seats. The Liberals, now more fully united in defence of free trade, improved their performance. Most significant of all was the increased success of the Labour party. By examining the figures, it can be seen that a Labour government could be formed if the Liberal MPs were willing to give support to it. Soon after the election, the MPs of these two parties voted together against the Conservative government, which then resigned. In January 1924 the King summoned Ramsay MacDonald, the leader of the Labour party, and appointed him Prime Minister.

The formation of this first Labour government, which lasted from January to October 1924, was a significant point in the history of political life in Britain. But this Labour government, like the second one between 1929 and 1931, was only a *minority government*: it depended upon the support of the Liberal MPs and if that were withdrawn, the government would fall. Consequently, the first Labour government was unable to put into effect legislation for nationalization and welfare, which were the basis of its policies, as such legislation would not be fully sup-

ported by the Liberals. These circumstances therefore removed the exaggerated fears of some that the new government would bring chaos to the country. In any case, many of the new ministers had experience of government office through membership of the wartime coalition and in Ramsay MacDonald they possessed a firm leader, who was unlikely to allow the party's extreme left-wing to direct government policy.

Accepting the limitations of its power, the government embarked on a useful programme of legislation. The Wheatley Housing Act of 1924 was one of its most noticeable achievements. It increased the subsidy which the state provided for the construction of houses to be rented from local authorities. Negotiations to increase the number of workers engaged in building and to improve working conditions were undertaken. The subsidy scheme ended in 1933, but by then over half a million houses had been built as a result of it. Cuts were made in defence expenditure, and more money was allowed to various social security schemes which had recently themselves been cut. The method of payment of financial benefit to the unemployed was improved and its amount was increased. Philip Snowden, as Chancellor of the Exchequer, pursued a free trade policy and considerably reduced taxes on many basic products.

MacDonald took on the functions of Foreign Secretary as well as Prime Minister. The League of Nations had always been more actively supported by the Labour party than by the other parties and, as has been shown in chapter 3, MacDonald was largely responsible for proposing, in the Geneva Protocol, new means of preserving the peace. Towards Germany, he adopted an easier policy than earlier governments, assisting in the establishment of financial aid through the Dawes plan and in the withdrawal of French troops from the Ruhr occupation of the previous year. But towards the Soviet Union he pursued too adventurous a course. At this time, some seven years after the Revolution, the British government had still not given recognition to the Communist government in Russia. MacDonald broke this uncertainty by giving recognition and by negotiating a trade treaty. These conciliatory moves aroused unjustified fears of Communist influence within the Labour government. These fears became enflamed when the government retreated from prosecuting the editor of the British Communist paper, the *Workers Weekly*, for its publication of a revolutionary article. The Liberal MPs combined with the Conservative MPs to bring down the government and a general election was again called.

The 'Red Scare' aroused by the government's relations with the Soviet Union dominated the election of October 1924. The publication of the Zinoviev letter a few days beforehand sharpened the unreasoning atmosphere in which the election was fought. This letter was said to have been written to the leader of the British Communist party from Zinoviev, the President of the Communist International, a body which sought to spread Communism throughout the world. The letter urged British Communists to support closer government relations with the Soviet Union and also to work for revolution within Britain. Though the Zinoviev letter has now been proved to be a forgery, at the time it was accepted as genuine and it aroused many fears.

Even without the incident of the Zinoviev letter, it is likely that the Labour party would have been defeated in the election, though the party which registered the greatest loss of seats was in fact the Liberals. The Conservatives were returned with a large overall majority, which ensured their continuation in power for almost the next five years: Baldwin became Prime Minister for the second time. Its comfortable majority assured the government that it would have little difficulty in implementing its policies in parliament. But Baldwin's government faced its most serious challenge not from within parliament, but from industrial relations, outside parliament.

The General Strike

The origins of the 1926 General Strike were in the coal-mining industry. The miners had been angered in 1921 at the government's rejection of a proposal for nationalization of the coal industry. There had almost been a general strike in that year. Though since then the mining industry had revived, it was again in difficulties by the mid-1920s, when coal exports were declining. With the ending of the Ruhr occupation, the German coal industry had revived and was providing strong competition for British coal abroad. The government's decision in 1925 to restore the gold standard, by which the international value of the pound was to be linked to the value of gold, was an unrealistic move. It made British exports more expensive for foreign purchasers, and affected coal exports in particular.

To meet these problems, the mine owners proposed a reduction in miners' wages and an increase in the length of their working day. For the miners, who were already paid badly and who worked in dangerous conditions, this was an intolerable proposal, though it was not untypical of the unthinking, domineering attitude of the mine owners at that time. If the owners imposed these conditions, the miners would strike. This threat was supported by their fellow members of the *Triple Alliance*, the railway and transport workers, and by the Trades Union Congress (TUC). Towards this threat, and towards the whole problem of a General Strike, Baldwin adopted a spirit of compromise. In 1925, to help in the short-term recovery, he gave a government subsidy to the industry and, to advise on long-term developments, he appointed a commission under Sir Herbert Samuel.

When the Samuel Commission reported in March 1926, it had something to offer both sides. It proposed nationalization and modernization of coal mines as an eventual aim, though it supported the mine owners' demand for an immediate reduction in wages. The miners became militant. 'Not a penny off the pay, not a minute on the day' was the slogan which inspired their actions in the subsequent months, as they rallied under the determined leadership of Herbert Smith and Arthur Cook. The TUC pledged its support for the miners. The government was unable to end the deadlock in the negotiations between the miners' leaders and the mine owners. At the end of April the miners struck, government negotiations came to an end, and on 3 May 1926 the TUC declared a General Strike.

The strike lasted for nine days. Its impact was reduced by the fact that it took place during good weather when the demand for coal and transport is less, but most working people throughout the country took part in strike action. Essential services were kept running largely through the work of the Organization for the Maintenance of Supplies, a voluntary body on which the government heavily relied. Many middle-class people volunteered to help the Organization for the Maintenance of Supplies and though their action had the appearance of a public-spirited gesture, it was considered by the strikers as blacklegging. Though Baldwin endeavoured to seek a compromise solution, not all members of his Cabinet were as tactful as their Prime Minister. Winston Churchill, the Chancellor of the Exchequer, spoke of the need for 'unconditional surrender' by the strikers, an attitude which he continued to press in the columns of the *British Gazette*, the government paper which he edited. To Churchill and those who thought like him, the strike was virtually a revolution by the workers against the authority of the government.

To the mass of the striking workers, these events were nothing so extreme. Although Communist elements did see in the strike the potential beginnings of a revolution, the majority of the strikers felt that their action was solely directed towards supporting the miners' struggle for justice. On their side also, the strikers were well organized and had their own newspaper, the *British Worker*. But the anxiety of the TUC leaders that the strike should not be too prolonged made them ready to accept a compromise formula worked out by Sir Herbert Samuel which, by its continued acceptance of a cut in the miners' wages, was unacceptable to them. At the same time, the confidence of the TUC was sapped by a government statement that a General Strike was illegal. In spite of the

Some assistance by the middle class is given with the milk churns in London during the General Strike. Though in many respects a public-spirited gesture, action of this kind was viewed as blacklegging by the strikers themselves.

wish of the miners to continue the struggle, the TUC ended the General Strike on 12 May.

The strike had failed in its purpose of achieving justice for miners. Embittered at what they considered to be a betrayal of their cause by the TUC, the miners continued their strike despite the lack of an adequate strike fund. By the end of the year, grinding poverty and increasing desperation drove them back to the mines and to the original terms of the mine owners. Their immense struggle had been totally in vain and they had achieved nothing. Industrial relations in other industries were disturbed by these events of 1926. Despite promises to the contrary, there was a good deal of victimization by employers when their workers returned after the strike. The government itself appeared to adopt a similar attitude in the

Trade Disputes Act of 1927, which declared that taking part in a general strike was an illegal act and that civil servants were not to be members of unions which were linked with the TUC or the Labour party. The act included an even more controversial clause which made it necessary for trade union members who wished part of their trade union subscription to go to the support of the Labour party to 'contract in' to pay this political levy. Previously it had been necessary, to 'contract out' if a member did not wish to pay the political levy. The general supposition was that under the new arrangements, the funds of the Labour party would be reduced, as many trade unionists would not bother to agree to make the extra payment. Until its reversal in 1946, the act was a constant source of grievance to the trade union movement and to the Labour party.

Conservative and Labour in the 1920s

Inevitably, the General Strike dominates any study of Baldwin's government of 1924–29. But important legislation was also produced by this government.

The most extensive piece of legislation introduced by Baldwin's government was the Local Government Act of 1929. By this act, the authority of local government was considerably increased. The Poor Law Unions and their Guardians, which had existed since Elizabethan times to provide various kinds of relief for the poor, were abolished, and their functions were transferred to counties and county boroughs. County councils received additional powers, especially in connection with roads, public health, child welfare and town and country planning. Grants of money from the central government were also to contribute further to cover the cost of organizing the additional responsibilities which the government now passed to the local authorities.

A few steps towards nationalization were taken by the Conservatives in two measures of December 1926. The Electricity Act created the Central Electricity Board to

MESSAGE FROM THE PRIME MINISTER:

Constitutional Government is being attacked.

Let all good citizens whose livelihood and labour have thus been put in peril bear with fortitude and patience the hardships with which they have been so suddenly confronted.

Stand behind the Government who are doing their part

confident that you will co-operate in the measures they have undertaken to preserve the liberties and privileges of the people of these islands.

The Laws of England are the People's birthright.

**The laws are in your keeping.
You have made Parliament their guardian
The General Strike is a challenge to Parliament and is the road to anarchy and ruin.**

STANLEY BALDWIN.

This government appeal was typical of Baldwin's approach to the problem of the General Strike.

supervize the distribution of electricity on a grid system throughout the country. Some Conservatives condemned it as being basically a Socialist move, but Labour members felt that the Central Electricity Board would not have enough power. Lovers of the countryside deplored the erection of pylons which this new distribution system made necessary. But by the arrival of the Second World War, it had proved its real value. In the same year, the British Broadcasting Corporation, which had started its existence in 1922, was given a Royal Charter. The man responsible for the BBC in its early days was John Reith, an autocratic Scotsman of high ideals, who wished the new Corporation to bring into the homes of people 'all that is best in every department of human knowledge, endeavour and achievement'.

The Conservative election slogan of 'Safety First' in the May 1929 general election, suggested that the Labour party could not be trusted again with the responsibilities of government. But the slogan and the government's record failed to persuade the electorate that under continued Conservative rule, the country could expect forthright government of the type it needed. Unemployment, now at about one million, was the most important issue. The Liberals suggested means of solving the problem and they experienced a slight revival in their fortunes. The Labour party's promise to solve this and other problems attracted the largest single group of votes and a second Labour government was formed under MacDonald. But the figures for the election show that, as earlier, the Labour party had no overall majority and continued to depend on Liberal support in the House of Commons. Once again, its initiative was limited.

General Election of May 1929	
Labour	288
Liberal	59
Conservative	260

This time the Labour party was to remain in power for two and a quarter years. A number of useful measures were introduced. The Coal Mines Act was an attempt to try to do something for the coal miners, by reducing their day from eight hours to seven and a half hours. The Housing Act dealt mainly with the question of slum clearance, by providing further government subsidies to local authorities. The Agricultural Marketing Act created marketing boards to grade and price products. Other government measures failed to get through parliament, including an attempt to repeal the hated 1927 Trade Disputes Act. A proposal to raise the school-leaving age from 14 to 15 was defeated in the House of Lords.

The crisis of 1931

Unemployment was the major difficulty of the second Labour government. J. H. Thomas had been appointed Lord Privy Seal with special responsibility for this problem. An ever-optimistic man, he spoke vaguely of future improvement, of 'the day dawning' and 'the cloud with the silver lining', but little came from his efforts. The number of unemployed gradually rose and by the end of 1930 it stood at 2,500,000. In January 1930 the Prime Minister had created an Economic Advisory Council, which included a number of men from outside politics, but its monthly meetings achieved little. In June 1930 Thomas was transferred to another department and the problem of unemployment was taken over by MacDonald, who was equally unsuccessful in solving it. The Conservatives meantime loudly advocated economic protection as the only answer to the country's problems.

By July 1931 unemployment had risen to 2,800,000. A special committee on government expenditure recommended that taxes would have to be increased and cuts made in government spending, mainly by cutting the dole given to the unemployed. Many foreign investors believed that there would be major bankruptcies in Britain as there had been in other European countries early in 1931. They therefore withdrew their deposits from England, thus worsening the situation and adding to the lack of confidence in the Labour government. The suggestion was made that the formation of a National government of all parties might be a means of restoring confidence. The Labour government was in any case severely divided on the issue of the proposed cuts in the dole since the people unemployed in 1931, for the most part, had helped vote Labour into power in 1929. The Bank of England was expecting to receive a substantial loan from the United States, but this would be forthcoming only if the government agreed to the financial cuts. These were agreed to, the loan arranged and the financial crisis over. MacDonald resigned as Labour Prime Minister.

On 24 August 1931 the formation of a National government was announced with MacDonald as Prime Minister, Baldwin as Lord President and the Liberal leader Samuel, as Home Secretary. King George V considered this to be the best solution, and urged this course on MacDonald, who had little hesitation in accepting. Many Labour party supporters were bitterly disillusioned: the cuts may have been inevitable, but MacDonald's action in continuing as Prime Minister of a government containing Conservative and Liberal ministers seemed to them inexcusable. The Labour party now came under the leadership of Arthur Henderson.

The new government decided to hold an election in October. It was a complicated election in which the Liberal and Labour parties both produced two types of candidates: those who would support the National government and those who would oppose it. The Conservative party was united in support of the National government. The election campaign was extremely confusing for the electorate, and many who voted for National government candidates may well have done so from a misplaced sense of patriotic duty in a time of crisis. The election was a resounding success for the National government, which returned 558 members, of whom 471 were Conservatives, 68 Liberals, 13 National Labour and some Independents. The opposition consisted mainly of 52 Labour members.

Economic recovery under the National government

Unemployment was the greatest problem facing the National government and its gradual reduction throughout the 1930s was the government's greatest achievement. In 1931 there were just under three million unemployed; this number reduced slowly during the early 1930s, more rapidly during the late 1930s and by the eve of the Second World War stood at just over one million. Life for the unemployed in these years was hard. The early decision to put into practice the cuts in the dole was a cause of deep-felt resentment among these unemployed workers, who experienced a further decline in their already sparse living conditions. In addition, the government imposed a means test, by which an unemployed man's benefit would be lowered if other members of his household were in employment. As the means test would result in a further reduction of the money paid in benefit the government felt justified in imposing it. But it humiliated and divided the families of the unemployed. Working-class men of the 1930s, brought up to respect the value of work and the responsibilities of a family man, hated the experience of finding the family reliant not on the father, but on the wife, sons and daughters, if they were fortunate enough to have jobs. In many cases, families split up, as in the absence of employed members of the household, the unemployed father would be able to receive unemployment benefit.

The unemployment problem was not found in all areas of Britain. It tended to concentrate especially in the north-west, the north-east, Scotland and South Wales; in the Midlands and in the south, the problem was less serious. The drabness of life in the unemployed areas, the poverty of the unemployed and the despair that overshadowed their search for work has been vividly illustrated in many books written in the 1930s, such as George Orwell's *Road to Wigan Pier* and Walter Greenwood's *Love on the Dole*. But at that time, many unemployed felt that neither the government nor the rest of the country properly understood what unemployment meant for its victims. To focus attention on the human problems of unemployment they organized a series of *hunger marches*. Groups of the unemployed undertook a march on foot from their home area to London. Their passing through towns and villages on their march and their orderly demonstrations in London at the end of the march did much to demonstrate the sadness of their plight. The most famous of these marches was the *Jarrow Crusade* of 1936, marching from the north-eastern town of Jarrow, where the all-important ship-building industry no longer provided jobs.

Government policies towards the unemployed were harsh. But other policies, designed to improve the country's economy, eventually helped to create more jobs. Fundamental to these policies was a firm government commitment to economic protection, which was now fully implemented by Neville Chamberlain, Chancellor of the Exchequer between 1931 and 1937. The earlier controversy over the relative value of free trade and economic protection now faded, as most of the country became convinced of the need to protect British industry from foreign competition. This policy would improve employment prospects, though the import taxes would inevitably lead to higher prices of imported goods. In February 1932 the Import Duties Act placed a general import duty of ten per cent on all goods entering the country and ensured that the percentage of this duty should be under constant review and adjusted appropriately when the interests of British industry seemed to require it. A special exception was made for goods entering Britain from Commonwealth countries. Later in 1932, at the Canadian capital of Ottawa, a conference of Commonwealth countries was held and favourable terms were agreed for trade within the Commonwealth.

Hunger marches by men from the depressed areas were an effective demonstration of the plight of the unemployed in the 1930s. This photograph shows the men from the north-eastern ship-building town of Jarrow on their way to London.

Economic planning was also partly adopted by the government. In this respect, government policy was much influenced by the ideas of the leading economist of these years, J. M. Keynes, who had earlier criticized the reparations system imposed by the Versailles treaty. Keynes urged that the government should take on a much more powerful role in the direction of the country's economy; in doing this, he urged nationalization and a more equal distribution of incomes. The National government, with its strong Conservative majority, was unlikely to implement these policies completely, but it was nevertheless influenced by Keynes' idea of overall economic planning by the government. In 1933 London Transport was created as a public body taking control of the different private companies which had previously provided the capital's transport services. In 1939 another public body came into existence, the British Overseas Airways Corporation. Commercial airflights were beginning to be developed in the 1930s and from the start this form of transport came under government control. In coal-mining, some progress was made towards reorganizing the industry by the amalgamation of a number of mines. In agriculture, different marketing boards were established to oversee the production and distribution of different agricultural products.

Another basic economic idea of J. M. Keynes was that money paid in interest on a loan should be as low as possible. In this way, businesses would be encouraged to borrow the money in order to expand their work, thus contributing to the economic prosperity of the country and creating more jobs. Throughout the 1930s the National government adopted this policy of low interest rates, producing, as a result, an expansion of private industry. The building industry benefited most from this policy. Throughout the 1930s home construction was undertaken on a vastly increased scale, though much of the development was unplanned and much of it was criticized for being monotonous in design. But quite apart from providing employment, these developments also provided many people with far better living

This suburban road shows the general style of housing that was constructed during the 1930s. The boom in private house-building at that time was a sign that Britain was emerging from its economic difficulties.

accommodation than they had previously enjoyed. The suburban areas of many British towns still provide direct evidence of the house-building boom of the 1930s. The building industry was not alone in experiencing success: the increasing popularity of consumer goods such as cars, telephones, radios and electrical goods led to a sharp expansion of these comparatively new industries.

Economic protection, economic planning and low interest rates all contributed to gradual improvement in the country's economy and the unemployment problem. But unemployment nevertheless remained. The new industries tended to avoid the old industrial areas and could not therefore absorb the unemployed where they were most numerous. Some government policies were specifically designed to assist the unemployed. In 1934 the areas where unemployment was still a serious problem were designated as *special areas* and were given grants to assist their recovery though it is doubtful whether this government action made much difference.

Political developments in the 1930s

Ramsay MacDonald continued as Prime Minister until his retirement in June 1935. Throughout the 1930s most members of the

Labour party continued to feel bitter towards him on account of his role in the events of 1931 and his leadership of a predominantly Conservative government. Baldwin succeeded him as Prime Minister and felt the time appropriate to hold a general election. This election confirmed the Conservative-dominated National government in power, though the Labour party, now led by Clement Attlee, increased its representation significantly on its 1931 performance.

1935 General Election	
Conservatives	432
Labour	154
Liberals	20

In the event, due to the Second World War, the 1935 election was the last for ten years. Baldwin retired in May 1937 and Neville Chamberlain became Prime Minister. Though he continued to show concern for domestic matters, the serious problem created by Nazi Germany now demanded most of the government's attention. The part played by the British government in the events leading to the outbreak of war in September 1939 is considered in the following chapter.

A new political movement developed in the 1930s, the British Union of Fascists. Its founder was Sir Oswald Mosley, who had been a junior minister in the second Labour government, from which he had resigned after his plans for reducing unemployment were rejected by the government. Italian Fascism rather than German Nazism was used by Mosley as the model upon which British Fascism was to be based, and in his book *The Greater Britain* Mosley put forward such typical Fascist ideas as the need for discipline and nationalism. Uniformed, black-shirted Fascists paraded at meetings and marches, attracting much interest and much opposition from the left-wing. In the late 1930s anti-semitism was openly adopted by British Fascism and Fascist demonstrations in east London often developed into scenes of violence between the Fascists and their opponents. By the late 1930s British Fascism was already in decline. The gradual return to prosperity had caused it to lose the support of the discontented, and in 1936 the Public Order Act, by forbidding the wearing of political uniforms, deprived the movement of one of its more theatrical attractions. At the outbreak of war in 1939 leading Fascists were considered a security risk and were imprisoned for the length of the war.

The British monarchy was a cause of much controversy during the mid-1930s. King George V's reign of more than a quarter-century ended in January 1936, when he was succeeded by his bachelor son Edward VIII. The new King built upon his earlier popularity by adopting a less traditional approach and by showing concern for the plight of the unemployed. Government ministers were worried by what they considered to be his irresponsibility and were particularly concerned at his close friendship with an American woman, Mrs Wallis Simpson. In the autumn of 1936 Mrs Simpson was divorced for a second time and it became apparent in government circles, though not to the public at large, that the King intended to marry her. The proposed marriage was strongly opposed by the Prime Minister, Stanley Baldwin, and by the Archbishop of Canterbury, Cosmo Lang. When the matter became public knowledge in early December 1936, it was thought that majority opinion within the country and within the Commonwealth was opposed to this marriage. The opposition was mainly based on Mrs Simpson's divorced status and partly based on her American nationality. Baldwin insisted that the King must either abandon the idea of this marriage or abandon the throne. The King's devotion to Mrs Simpson was so strong that he took the latter course, abdicating in favour of his brother, the Duke of York. The crisis surrounding the abdication had put the monarchy to a severe test but the new King, as George VI, though he did not have his brother's popular appeal, proved conscientious and devoted and did much to revive people's confidence in the monarchy.

Many of the issues of these years were concerned with Britain's external relations, with the problems of India and Ireland and, increasingly, with the problem of Germany. The government's policy of *appeasement* is considered in its wider setting in the following chapter. The government's pursuit of appeasement is partly explained by the strength of the pacifist movement under the leadership of men such as George Lansbury of the Labour party and Canon Dick Sheppard of the Church of England. The extent of support for pacifism was shown in the summer of 1935 when a nationwide peace ballot was held revealing widespread support for the reduction of armaments and, among a fifth of those questioned, support for the idea that even in the event of armed aggression, Britain should make no retaliation whatsoever. Pacifism confronted governments of the late 1930s with a serious problem. As the German situation became increasingly threatening, it seemed essential to protect Britain's interests by a policy of rearmament. But such a policy was clearly not favoured by a majority in the country. Nevertheless the government began rearmament under Baldwin's lead in March 1936. Even though rearmament was pursued even more vigorously after the Munich conference of September 1938, the country was still not properly prepared for war when it came a year later.

Questions

28. Study the poster on page 98 and then answer questions (a) to (e) which follow.
    (a) (i) Name the Prime Minister who gave this message, and the political party which he led.
        (ii) Give the month and year in which this poster appeared.
            (2)
    (b) (i) What is meant by the assertion made in heavy print on lines 3 and 4 of this poster?
        (ii) Name the industry whose problems led to the events referred to in this message.
        (iii) Trace the development of the problems of this industry during the five years before the publication of this poster.
            (2+1+4)
    (c) Describe the measures taken by the government and its supporters to defend itself against the attack the Prime Minister is referring to in lines 3 and 4 of this poster.
            (3)
    (d) Show how the events referred to in this message were brought to an end.
            (3)
    (e) Describe the effects of this outcome on
        (i) the trades union movement, and
        (ii) the workers in the industry named in (b) (ii).
            (5)
29. Describe and explain the increasing political importance of the Labour party during the 1920s. What did it achieve during the ministries of 1924 and 1929–31?
30. Why was unemployment such a serious problem in Britain during the early 1930s? Show how, and with what results, the National government attempted to assist the unemployed and reduce their number.

11
The causes of the Second World War

German rearmament

The government of the Weimar republic never adhered strictly to the disarmament clauses of the Versailles treaty. German rearmament had therefore already begun when Hitler became Chancellor in January 1933. It was now felt in Europe that Germany had been unfairly discriminated against by the Allies over the matter of armaments after the First World War. Hitler felt that he could use this change of opinion to Germany's advantage. He put forward at the Disarmament Conference of the League of Nations that Germany would only consider disarmament within the context of a general European disarmament. When it was apparent that the League would not accept this view, Hitler withdrew Germany from League membership in October 1933. Thereafter German rearmament was pursued more openly and more vigorously, because this policy appeared to the German people to be a means both of absorbing unemployment and of defying the hated Versailles treaty. In March 1935 German rearmament was taken further by Hitler's denunciation of the Versailles clauses restricting the size of the German army and by his introduction of conscription. This caused acute concern among the Versailles signatories and in April 1935 at Stresa, the prime ministers of Britain, France and Italy formed the Stresa Front to oppose revived German militarism; it was the last occasion on which these major First World War allies, combined together against their former enemy. Shortly afterwards pacts between Russia and France and between Russia and Czechoslovakia were made, prompted by fears arising from German rearmament. These were the countries which had most to fear from a German military revival. It seemed possible that Europe was at last waking up to the threat of this revival.

But in June 1935 this resistance to German rearmament was broken with the signature of the Anglo-German naval agreement by which Britain agreed that the size of the German submarine force could equal that of Britain and the size of the rest of the German fleet could equal 35 per cent that of Britain. Though this agreement had the appearance of a friendly understanding in fact it was an acknowledgement by Britain that Germany had the right to rearm. In this matter Britain had acted alone and so the Stresa Front collapsed. By accepting Germany's right to rearm, Britain showed that the Allies were no longer united in their approach to Germany.

In January 1935 the people of the Saar were allowed their right, promised at Versailles, to vote by referendum on their future status. By a large majority they voted for union with Germany, thus showing their willingness to support the country which the majority felt they belonged to and which appeared at last to be under strong leadership. Though the acquisition of the Saar was neither planned nor carried out by Hitler, as it occurred at the same time as he was successfully rearming the country, it enhanced his standing among the German people.

Agreements with Italy and Japan

Hitler was impressed by Mussolini's conquest of Abyssinia between October 1935 and May 1936, already considered in chapter 5, and he stood aside from the general condemnation of Mussolini's actions in Abyssinia. The example of the comparatively slight resistance of the major world powers to this aggression was not lost on Hitler. In March 1936 he ordered German troops to enter the Rhineland and thus end its demilitarized status. His action was another breach of the Versailles treaty, a direct challenge to France and, to a lesser extent, to Britain. Yet neither country did anything positive to prevent the entry of the German troops. Within Germany, Hitler's bold and successful actions against one of the most hated terms of the Versailles treaty brought him renewed prestige.

Though in the early years of Hitler's chancellorship, relations between Germany and Italy had been uneasy, as had been shown by differences over Austria in 1934 and by the Stresa Front in 1935, both systems of government shared many similar characteristics. Their mutually-favourable response to each other's actions in Abyssinia and in the Rhineland led them to see the value of reaching a friendly understanding in a world that seemed hostile to them and yet unwilling to stand up to them. They were further encouraged in this way by the involvement of both of them on the Nationalists' side in the Spanish Civil War. In October 1936 Italy's new Foreign Minister, Count Ciano, was the man chiefly responsible for reaching an understanding between Italy and Germany, known as the Rome-Berlin Axis. There were no precise terms to the agreement, but it signalled the beginning of cooperation. In May 1939 the terms of the so-called Pact of Steel made the cooperation closer and committed Italy to the dangerous agreement of giving military support to Germany whenever Germany should declare war.

In November 1936, only a month after the conclusion of the Axis agreement, Germany reached an understanding with Japan's military régime by signing with them the Anti-Comintern pact. Its name shows that it was specifically intended to oppose the Comintern, the international organization whose purpose was to spread Communism throughout the world. A year later, in November 1937, Italy also joined this pact. The three powers were thus associated together and the bonds between them were made firmer by another agreement in September 1940 known as the Rome-Berlin-Tokyo Axis pact, considered in more detail at the beginning of chapter 13. These understandings with Italy and Japan strengthened Hitler's position as he embarked on further policies of aggression in the late 1930s. At the same time he was increasingly aware that the response of the Western powers was likely to be weak.

Appeasement

The foreign policies of both the British government and the French government in the late 1930s were dominated by the attitude known as *appeasement*. At its best, appeasement involved rectifying the grievances resulting from Germany's treatment after the First World War. In practice, appeasement made the foreign policies of the Western powers appear weak, and encouraged Hitler to imagine that in spite of whatever aggression he undertook, the Western powers would not resist him.

The policy of appeasement is linked especially with the name of Neville Chamberlain, Britain's Prime Minister between 1937 and 1940. Chamberlain came from a wealthy Birmingham family which had already made a name for itself in British political life. As a former Minister of Health and a Chancellor of the Exchequer, Chamberlain had made valuable contributions. After succeeding Baldwin as Prime Minister, it was he who dominated Britain's foreign policy rather than the Foreign Secretary, Lord Halifax. The French government also practised appeasement during these years under the leadership of their Prime Minister, Edouard Daladier, and their Foreign Secretary, Paul Bonnet. The French and the British governments now had an identical approach to Nazi Germany and, though its policy was still definitely isolationist, the United States also tended to encourage appeasement.

Public opinion in Britain and France supported appeasement. In the late 1930s there was a widespread feeling that the Versailles treaty had treated Germany unjustly; appeasement was seeking to correct this unjust treatment and it seemed therefore the right policy to pursue. In the late 1930s there was also a widespread fear of the devastating effects that a war might bring, especially from aerial bombardment such as had taken place at Guernica during the Spanish Civil War; if appeasement could prevent this sort of thing happening on a large scale, then it was a policy well worth pursuing. Apart from any other consideration, the virtual failure of the League of Nations led many to feel that there was no way of preserving peace other than by supporting the policy of appeasement in the late 1930s.

Early instances of the practice of appeasement are to be found in the mid-1930s in the Anglo-German naval treaty, in the Hoare-Laval plan for Abyssinia, and the easy acceptance of the remilitarization of the Rhineland. Later, in 1938, the policy of appeasement was more fully developed as the response of the Western powers to the German policies towards Austria and Czechoslovakia.

The Anschluss with Austria

Though Germany and Austria had close ties in language and culture, *anschluss* (union) between them was prohibited by the terms of the Versailles treaty. In spite of this prohibition, two attempts were made in the early

Germany and her neighbours before the Second World War

107

1930s to bring the two countries together. An attempt in 1931 to create a customs union between them was opposed by the League of Nations and by the Versailles signatories: the attempt came to nothing. After Hitler became Chancellor, he made the creation of *anschluss* an immediate objective, as in his view the racial identity of the Austrians made it right that they should be fully unified with Germany. He gave support to the Austrian Nazi party in their bid to overthrow the Austrian Chancellor, Dollfuss, who vigorously opposed *anschluss*. An attempted coup by the Austrian Nazis in July 1934 was a bloody affair, in the course of which Dollfuss was captured and killed by the Austrian Nazis. But the coup failed to lead to *anschluss*: support in the country withered and in neighbouring Italy Mussolini showed his strong opposition to *anschluss*. At this stage Mussolini still saw Germany as Italy's enemy and was alarmed at the prospect of increased German power on the borders of his country. As a gesture of protest and opposition, he moved troops to the Brenner, the mountain pass connecting Italy with Austria.

By the time Hitler made his next attempt at *anschluss*, in the spring of 1938, Austria had become isolated. As shown earlier, Italy had signed the Axis agreement with Germany, so Austria could not now expect Italian support. Little support would be given by other neighbouring countries. Czechoslovakia, Romania and Yugoslavia, the three members of the *Little Entente*, united by mutual hostility to Hungary, were no longer closely linked with Austria. Nor was there support for Austria from France, now fully pursuing the policy of appeasement. In February 1938 discussions took place between Hitler and the Austrian Chancellor, Schuschnigg, in which Hitler demanded that the Austrian government should treat the Austrian Nazis more favourably and that their leader, Seyss-Inquart, should become Minister of the Interior. Schuschnigg left the discussions with the feeling that Hitler was intent on securing *anschluss* by bullying techniques. After his return to Austria, Schuschnigg announced that he would hold a referendum to show whether the Austrian people did or did not want *anschluss* with Germany. He expected that a majority would vote against *anschluss*. This would be a source of strength in future negotiations with Hitler. The idea of the referendum worried Hitler: he now threatened a German invasion into Austria if the referendum was not cancelled. Schuschnigg was concerned at this threat and cancelled the referendum; but Hitler then raised his terms by demanding that Seyss-Inquart should replace Schuschnigg as Chancellor. On the refusal of the Austrian President to agree, the order was given for the German army to invade on 12 March 1938.

Very little bloodshed occurred during the invasion and many newsreel films of the event show the German army receiving a rapturous welcome from the Austrian people. Undoubtedly many Austrians did welcome the *anschluss*, though Schuschnigg was probably correct in his view that a majority would still have preferred independence, had they been allowed to express their opinion on the matter. On this occasion, Mussolini made no opposition to Hitler's action. As for Britain and France, the *anschluss* well illustrates the practice of appeasement: they made formal protests, but did nothing more. The country most affected by the events of March 1938 was Czechoslovakia, as its entire western frontiers were now surrounded by Nazi territory.

The problem of Czechoslovakia

The racial and linguistic differences existing in Czechoslovakia at the time of its creation after the First World War have been considered earlier in chapter 2. By the late 1930s through the dedicated leadership of Thomas Masaryk, its President until 1935, and his successor Edward Benes, the new republic had progressed well. But the minorities problem had continued to disturb the republic. The German success in Austria encouraged the demands for self-government made by the Germans in the Sudetenland area of Czechoslovakia, under their leader Konrad Henlein. Throughout the summer of 1938 Hitler gave his open support to these demands and Henlein received financial aid from Nazi Germany. The distinct possibility of direct military help by Nazi Germany for the Sudetenlanders was a source of concern to France, which had earlier agreed to assist Czechoslovakia in the event of attack. It also worried Britain, whose status as a great power would make it difficult for her to stand aside if a further act of Nazi aggression took place, even though Britain had no similar agreement with Czechoslovakia.

In the summer of 1938 Britain made an attempt to solve the problem by sending a special mission under the leadership of Lord Runciman to try to produce a settlement between Henlein and the Czech government and thus forestall a possible Nazi take-over. But the Runciman mission failed completely. Chamberlain then himself took on the direct responsibility of seeking an international settlement that would prevent the outbreak of war which, it seemed, would inevitably follow if German troops entered Czechoslovakia. On three occasions in September 1938 Chamberlain met Hitler: at Berchtesgaden and at Godesberg, Hitler and Chamberlain met alone, and at the summit conference at Munich the two met together with the leaders of Italy and France.

At the first of these meetings, at Hitler's mountain retreat of Berchtesgaden, Chamberlain received an ultimatum from Hitler to the effect that war would follow if the Sudetenlanders were not allowed self-government, it being understood that the granting of self-government would lead inevitably to the take-over of the Sudetenland by Germany. Chamberlain then discussed the issue with Daladier, the French prime minister, and between them a solution was reached, and was accepted also by the Czech government, whereby those areas of the Sudetenland in which the population was 50 per cent or more German should be incorporated in Germany. Chamberlain returned to Hitler for a second meeting at Godesberg, in the Rhineland: here he informed Hitler of the suggested solution. But Hitler now raised his demands by insisting that the whole of the Sudetenland should be incorporated

into Germany. He was particularly angered when the news was brought to him, actually during the course of his meeting with Chamberlain at Godesberg, that the Czech army had mobilized, though such action by Czechoslovakia was, under the circumstances, only a sensible precaution. Meantime, to make matters worse, Hitler was encouraging Hungary and Poland to make demands on behalf of their own minorities within Czechoslovakia and he was encouraging the Slovaks to press for their own independence from the Czech government. After Godesberg the situation was particular tense and the prospect of war loomed dangerously.

The Munich conference

Mussolini's suggestion of a four-power summit meeting at Munich removed the immediate threat of war. Czechoslovakia, with whose future they were directly concerned, had no representation at the conference at all. Nor was there a Soviet representative, in spite of the Soviet Union's concern at Hitler's aggression. There was little purposeful discussion at the conference anyway, and the agreement which was signed in the early hours of 30 September 1938 gave way to Germany on almost every point. It provided for a German take-over of the Sudetenland between 1 and 10 October. This take-over was to be supervised by an international commission, which was also responsible for the holding of a referendum in some areas and for the drawing of the final boundaries; in practice, the international commission undertook its tasks at Germany's dictation. It was also agreed that the Polish and Hungarian claims against Czechoslovakia were to be satisfied.

For Czechoslovakia, the effects of Munich were devastating. By it, Czechoslovakia lost valuable defensive frontiers and major industrial regions, whilst the communications system in the country was seriously disrupted. Germany's success duly led to the satisfying of the Polish and Hungarian claims: within a few weeks Teschen was occupied by Poland and the southern part of Czechoslovakia was occupied by Hungary, which also, with no difficulty, seized the territory of Ruthenia in the east of Czechoslovakia in March 1939. The Slovak bid for independence was much strengthened by the clear helplessness that overhung the Czechoslovak government.

Before returning to England, Chamberlain obtained Hitler's signature to a declaration asserting the fundamentally peaceful nature of Anglo-German relations. It was a curious postscript to so one-sided a conference. Chamberlain made much of this declaration when he returned to Britain, anxious to show that he was taking all the steps he possibly could to ensure peace. In the light of later events, the declaration reads pathetically:

We the German Führer and Chancellor and the British Prime Minister have had a further

meeting today and are agreed in recognizing that the question of Anglo-German relations is of the first importance for the two countries and for Europe.

We regard the agreement signed last night and the Anglo-German naval agreement as symbolic of the desire of our two peoples never to go to war with one another again.

We are resolved that the method of consultation shall be the method adopted to deal with any other questions that may concern our two countries, and we are determined to continue our efforts to remove possible sources of difference and thus to contribute to assure the peace of Europe.

The Munich settlement was greeted with widespread relief by the people of Britain and France and also by the people of

German troops enter the Sudetenland in October 1938, after Hitler's triumph at the Munich conference. Though these events were welcomed by some in the Sudetenland, those in this photograph give their new rulers an unfriendly reception.

Germany and Italy; for all of them, war had seemingly been prevented. At the time of Munich, very few people were critical of the agreements reached. In Britain, two government ministers resigned and Winston Churchill, then a back-bench MP and generally considered a warmonger, denounced Munich as 'a total and unmitigated defeat' and warned Britain: 'do not suppose that this is the end; it is only the beginning.'

Munich had by no means banished the threat of war. Britain and France intensified their efforts at rearmament, which had begun in the mid-1930s. Later, when war did eventually break out, many argued that the Munich agreement had given Britain extra time in which to rearm; but it must be remembered that the extra time was also available for use by Germany and Italy. The real importance of Munich is its vivid demonstration of the British and French commitment to appeasement. The events of the autumn of 1938 suggested to Hitler that further German expansion could be pursued without any real opposition from the great powers of Western Europe.

Prime Minister Chamberlain, on arrival in England from Munich, reads the Anglo-German declaration reproduced on page 110. Chamberlain was anxious to show that he had taken all possible steps to secure European peace.

The abandonment of appeasement

The Munich settlement did not last long. Six months later Hitler seized the opportunity of an internal Czech crisis to complete the country's dismemberment. In March 1939 German troops entered the western provinces of Bohemia and Moravia. Hitler's threat to mount an aerial bombardment of Prague was sufficient to ensure that the invasion was not resisted. The protectorate of Bohemia-Moravia was created as a Nazi puppet-state; Slovakia was allowed the independence for which it had long agitated, though the exchange of German domination for Czech domination may not have been entirely welcome. No suggestion could be made, as it was with some justice in the earlier cases of Nazi expansion, that these areas consisted of Germans who wished to be united with Germany. In the same month, the small territory of Memel was taken by Germany from Lithuania and linked to East Prussia.

It was this dismemberment of Czechoslovakia in March 1939 that made the British government realize that its policy of appeasement of Nazi Germany was not working. Chamberlain and his government resolved that the policy must be abandoned, that positive promises of British aid to newly-threatened countries must be made, and that Britain must declare war against Germany if Nazi aggression continued. France also abandoned appeasement at the same time. In March 1939 Britain and France gave guarantees of support to Poland, as a possible future victim of Nazi aggression. In April, further guarantees were given by both countries to Greece and Romania, both of which were disturbed by the Italian seizure of Albania, which had taken place in that month and which showed that the other Axis partner was following Germany's example of aggression. In May 1939 the Pact of Steel linked Germany and Italy even more firmly.

Poland, the Nazi-Soviet pact and the outbreak of war

Poland had, throughout the interwar years, a strong and dictatorial government, which shared some characteristics with the Nazi government in Germany with which, since a German-Polish non-aggression pact of January 1934, it had maintained reasonable relations. It also had reason to be grateful for Germany's role in the Munich settlement, as the valuable area of Teschen had been acquired by Poland as a result. But inevitably, once Nazi ambitions against Czechoslovakia had been fulfilled, Poland would be the next victim, as it possessed substantial German minorities.

Hitler had two main demands against Poland. He wanted the restoration to Germany of the international city Danzig, predominantly German in population. He also wanted German control of all road and rail communications across the Polish Corridor. By the spring of 1939 he had already decided to attack Poland on 1 September of that year if these demands had not been met by then. He was angered by knowledge of the Franco-British guarantees to Poland, but in the light of the French and British practice of appeasement, he was not particularly worried by them. He would simply risk the possibility of their declaring war in Poland's support: the problem would be met if and when it arose. Meantime, as the summer months passed, negotiations between the German and Polish governments on these issues made no progress.

In August 1939 one of the most surprising agreements of the twentieth century was concluded between Nazi Germany and the Soviet Union: the two countries whose governments represented opposite political extremes came together in a pact designed to further the ambitions of each. Ever since the formation of a National Socialist government in Germany, the Soviet Union had been worried at the possibility of a German invasion. The Nazi successes of 1938 and early 1939 made the situation appear more threatening. The fundamental political differences between the practice of democracy by the Western powers and the practice of Communism by the Soviet Union made it difficult for an effective alliance to be made between them, even though such an alliance would have been a most serious threat to Nazi Germany. The Soviet Union's suspicion of the Western powers had been confirmed by the West's exclusion of the Soviet Union from the Munich conference. Further, the Western policy of appeasement encouraged the Soviet view that even if there were a Soviet-Western alliance, the Western powers would possibly leave the Soviet Union to bear the weight of a war with Germany. Poland was a country in which both the Soviet Union and Germany had claims of territory and it was this common interest in Poland that brought them together. The replacement of the pro-Western Litvinov by the more forthright and more ruthless Molotov, as Commissar for Foreign Affairs, in May 1939 signalled a change in Soviet policy. Highly secret negotiations took place between Molotov and Ribbentrop, the German Foreign Secretary, throughout the summer months. Germany entered readily into these negotiations, since an alliance with the Soviet Union would remove the threat of war both to the east and to the west of Germany, a problem which had occurred during the First World War.

At the end of August a Nazi-Soviet non-aggression pact was signed between the two countries, and in a secret additional pact, agreement was reached on the division of Poland between them, and on the re-establishment of Russian influence in the Baltic states, Finland and Bessarabia. Hitler was now completely confident to go ahead with his invasion of Poland on 1 September 1939, as planned, before the autumn rain could hinder the progress of his army. The fact that Mussolini judged Italy to be militarily unready to join Germany in the invasion did not deflect Hitler from war. When Britain and France both declared war on 3 September 1939 he simply accepted the inevitable, whilst professing he had no particular quarrel with either of them. Popular opinion in the countries now at war, in Germany as well as in Britain and France, showed no enthusiasm for the coming struggle.

Chamberlain, speaking at a special session of the House of Commons on that fateful Sunday morning, 3 September 1939, summarized the feelings of all Europe.

> This is a sad day for all of us, and to none is it sadder than to me. Everything that I have worked for, everything that I have hoped for, everything that I have believed in during my public life has crashed into ruins. There is only one thing left for me to do: that is to devote what strength and powers I have to forwarding the victory of the cause for which we have to sacrifice so much. I trust I may live to see the day when Hitlerism has been destroyed and a liberated Europe has been re-established.

On that day only three countries, apart from Poland, were at war, but behind each of them stood colonial empires, or allies, or both. Quite soon, more countries became involved in the conflict so that by December 1941 almost the whole world was at war.

Questions

31. Study the document on page 110 and then answer questions (a) to (d) which follow.
    (a) (i) Name the *German Chancellor and Führer*, and
        (ii) show in what ways he pursued what might be described as an aggressive foreign policy, up to the spring of the year in which this document was signed.
        (1 + 3)

(b) (i) Name the *British Prime Minister*,
    (ii) give the name usually applied to the policy adopted by this Prime Minister towards *Anglo-German relations* at this time, and
    (iii) explain the reasons which he felt justified this policy.
    (1 + 1 + 3)
(c) (i) With which country was *the agreement signed last night* principally concerned?
    (ii) Name the two other statesmen who took part in this agreement.
    (iii) Describe the events which led to the signing of the agreement and the principal provisions made by the agreement.
    (1 + 2 + 4)
(d) Describe the later developments which caused the British Prime Minister who signed this document to abandon the policy named in (b) (ii).
    (4)

32. Describe each of the following and show its importance in contributing to international tension during the 1930s: (a) the attack by Japan on China, (b) the attack by Italy on Abyssinia and (c) the developing relations between Germany, Italy and Japan.

33. Show how events in Europe during the previous eighteen months led to the outbreak of war in September 1939. How would you apportion responsibility for this outbreak?

12
The course of the
Second World War (1)

The period of the Phoney War

Germany invaded western Poland on 1
September 1939. So swiftly successful was
this invasion that on 17 September the Soviet
Union invaded eastern Poland, fearing that
the relentless German advance might sweep
on into the eastern areas which the Nazi-
Soviet pact had allocated to the Soviet Union.
The German success was due partly to the
favourable geography and the favourable climate of the area, as well as to German military superiority. The border between Poland
and Germany was lengthy, thus allowing the
German forces to invade simultaneously in
many different parts of the frontier. The September weather was dry, thus making it possible for the German tanks and armoured
vehicles to advance across open fields, without being impeded by road blocks and
defences. The Germans used infinitely superior equipment; the Poles, though they themselves considered their country to be a great
power, and though they displayed determined resistance, were ill-equipped, the
Polish army still relying largely on horse-
drawn equipment. Poland's final surrender
came on 27 September 1939, when the
country was divided between Germany and
the Soviet Union. Thus the Second World
War began with a spectacular military success for Germany, against which Britain and
France, in spite of their declaration of war,
were unable to provide any resistance.

The Soviet Union wanted to establish an
effective barrier between itself and Germany.
The favourable outcome of the Polish campaign was therefore used for further Soviet
advance. The three Baltic states of Estonia,
Latvia and Lithuania, which had maintained

*German and Soviet gains in the early months of the
Second World War*

a precarious independence during the interwar years, now found themselves under Soviet control. All three accepted so-called mutual assistance pacts, which they were powerless to resist.

Like the Baltic states, Finland had earlier been under the control of tsarist Russia, but Soviet pressure for the imposition of a mutual assistance pact on Finland was resisted. When the Russo-Finnish negotiations on this issue broke down at the end of November, the Soviet Union invaded Finland. The Finns fought with dogged determination against their invaders, but were unable to match the Russian superiority in numbers and equipment. The *Winter War* between Finland and the Soviet Union lasted for some three months, ending in a Finnish defeat in March 1940. In the subsequent treaty, border territories were transferred to Soviet control and the port of Hankö was leased to the Soviet Union, thus providing Soviet access to the Baltic via the Gulf of Finland.

While these Nazi and Soviet conquests were taking place in the east, a curious situation of inaction developed in the west, which western journalists described as the 'Phoney War'. French military strategy had been dominated during the interwar years by the requirements of defence against enemy attack rather than those of French attack against enemy defences. The French Maginot Line, constructed in the early 1930s along the Franco-German frontier, was an example of a solid defence system, but it was unsuitable as a base for attack. At the beginning of the war, the French therefore made only very minor advances into German territory and the British, who had sent an expeditionary force to France on the outbreak of war, followed the same policy. Inaction by the west in the autumn of 1939 was to Germany's advantage. Hitler was employing his best troops in the attack against Poland and had left the western areas of Germany with comparatively poor defence; had France and Britain made a concerted attack at that time, they may well have had more success than the leaders of either country felt was possible. At the beginning of October 1939, encouraged by the success of his Polish campaign,

Hitler offered peace to the West, stressing that, as distinct from eastern Europe, he had no territorial ambitions in western Europe. Though popular opinion in both France and Britain found Hitler's offer of peace attractive, it was firmly rejected by both Western governments which were determined to defeat Hitler. Nevertheless, little action followed. German troops in their Siegfried Line faced the French troops in the Maginot Line in nervous stalemate, with neither side bold enough to take the first positively aggressive steps. But with the rejection of his peace offer in October, it was only the poor winter weather that prevented the launching of the full-scale attack which Hitler then planned. Meantime, German defences in the west of the country were vastly increased and improved.

The German attacks in the west

The neutrality adopted by Scandinavia and the Low Countries did not shield them from Nazi attack when, largely for strategic reasons, this was felt necessary by Hitler. With the arrival of better weather in early April 1940, an attack was launched against Denmark and Norway. Denmark collapsed in a matter of days with minimal casualties; Norway put up a stronger resistance and, aided by the country's mountainous terrain and some Franco-British support, the Norwegians battled for over two months against the invasion. Hitler was anxious to secure control in this area before he launched his main attack on the west, as he and his advisers were aware that Germany would be dangerously exposed to attack if the British were to occupy Norway, an event which seemed highly probable early in 1940.

In early May 1940, a month after the commencement of the attack on Scandinavia, Hitler launched his attack on the Low Countries of Belgium and Holland, as a preliminary to the attack on France and then on England. The attack was launched at a time of poor morale in France and Britain. New prime ministers had been appointed in the spring of 1940: in March Paul Reynaud succeeded Daladier as Prime Minister of France and in May Winston Churchill succeeded Chamberlain as Prime Minister of Britain. Both men were, in their different ways, better suited to war leadership than their predecessors, but at this stage were unable to raise the morale of their fellow-countrymen. The people of France, already disillusioned with the Third Republic and now facing the immediate prospect of invasion by land, were gripped by a sense of defeatism. Nor were military relations between the two countries as harmonious as the grim circumstances required.

The Nazi attack on the Low Countries in May was swift and ruthless. Casualties were especially heavy in Holland, where the city of Rotterdam was subjected to relentless aerial bombardment which recalled the bombardment of Guernica, and was a foretaste of the destruction of other European cities during the following five years. The main German thrust was across southern Belgium and towards the French town of Sedan, thus avoiding the Maginot Line, which did not run along the Franco-Belgian frontier. This military move was an impressive German success and was continued by a further thrust towards the northern coast of France, which was reached by German forces before the end of May.

These German successes had a devastating effect on the British and French troops and on the demoralized people of France. The German advance in northern France caused the British government to withdraw its troops from France. During little more than a week, in late May and early June, 200,000 British and 130,000 French troops were evacuated from the beaches of the French resort of Dunkirk. Many different types of sea craft collected refugees and brought them across the Channel to Britain, while German forces continued to attack the retreating troops by air. As the Germans did not wish to risk their tanks in the difficult countryside around Dunkirk, there was a comparative absence of land attacks around Dunkirk and the evacuation of the troops was thus made a little easier.

Chaos increased throughout France as the German forces now made their way westward. Meantime Mussolini, judging that the time had come for Italy to join the war on what appeared to be the winning side, declared war against France in early June. In the next few weeks, Italian forces advanced only a few miles inside southern France; along some parts of the Franco-Italian frontier, French forces made successful advances into Italian territory. The Italian invasion was therefore a comparatively minor

Western Europe in 1940

problem for the French, but the German invasion was proving a totally different matter.

The French government abandoned Paris and allowed the Germans to enter, thus sparing Paris the fate which only a month previously had overtaken Rotterdam. The French government moved temporarily to Tours in the Loire valley and then to Bordeaux on the Atlantic coast. The roads of France were crammed with refugees, also moving westward. The evidence of defeat within France was total. Reynaud's government realized that there was little they could do but sign an armistice with the invading forces. The only possible alternative that existed was the continuation of the struggle from the French north African possessions of Tunisia, Algeria and Morocco, though few gave support to this idea. Churchill, anxious for Britain's sake that France should continue the struggle, offered joint-citizenship to the French people, but this offer had little practical value under the circumstances. The French government signed an armistice with Germany on 22 June 1940.

The Vichy régime

The armistice imposed on defeated France in 1940 was not so severe as that imposed by Nazi Germany on defeated countries elsewhere. The comparative leniency was partly due to the large size of France, which would make total subjection of the country difficult even for Nazi administration. It was also partly due to the extent of the French colonial possessions in both Africa and Asia, which could be kept at least from outright hostility to the Germans if the treatment of defeated France was reasonable. By the terms agreed on 22 June 1940, Germany was to occupy and control the northern and western parts of France, while a French government allied with Germany was to have control of the southern parts. To ensure the cooperation of the French government, those French who had been captured during the fighting and were now prisoners of war, were to remain in German hands.

Reynaud had fallen from power a few days before the armistice was signed. Marshal Philippe Pétain was the new premier. Eighty-four years old in 1940, Pétain symbolized many qualities which the French sought in their hour of defeat. He was a hero of the First World War, famed for his determined defence of the fortress of Verdun. He was a symbol of the traditional values of French society, loyal to the Church and a supporter of order. Further, his advanced age (as a boy he had learnt his church catechism from a priest who had served as a chaplain in the Napoleonic Grand Army, which had invaded Russia in 1812) enhanced the aura of respect that surrounded him. Pétain and

A Russian cartoonist's view of wartime France (from left to right the puppets are Pétain, Darlan and Laval). Hitler controlled similarly the strings of a number of collaborationist régimes during the Second World War.

ministers such as Laval and Darlan, who served with him and supported him, were anxious not only for a favourable armistice but also for a restructuring of the French state. They sought the abolition of the despised Third Republic, whose incompetence had been especially emphasized by the swift collapse of France during the previous few weeks.

The fashionable watering spa of Vichy was chosen as the headquarters of the new French government. Here in early July 1940 the two chambers of the Third Republic, by a very large majority, passed a law which abolished the Third Republic and created what was technically known as *L'État Français* (The French State) and more usually known as the *Vichy régime*. From the circumstances

Winston Churchill visits the bombed cathedral at Coventry towards the end of 1940, accompanied by the Provost (in gaiters) and Mayor (in his chain of office). Visits by the Prime Minister to bombed areas such as this helped strengthen the support which he received from the British people for the war effort against Germany.

of its origin and from the nature of its constitution, Vichy was a right-wing totalitarian régime of a pattern increasingly seen in Europe during the interwar years and, until the events of late 1942, it had close and friendly contacts with Nazi Germany.

The battle for Britain

Hitler anticipated a political crisis in Britain after France had fallen: he believed that Churchill would be replaced and the way made easy for the establishment of German control. In his estimation of the situation, Hitler badly misinterpreted the mood of Britain in the summer of 1940. Increasingly, Britain was rallying to the inspiring leadership of its new Prime Minister, and possessed in any case the natural advantage of the English Channel. Before any landing could be made in Britain, it was essential that Germany should have control of the air, to prevent their invasion force from being bombed.

Goering's air force started in the first instance to make attacks on British air bases but failed to sustain the attacks for long enough to make them effective. Then the German air force unwisely changed to attacking factories and cities, a change of tactic which did not in any way advance their immediate objective of securing control of the air. The Royal Air Force (RAF), under the direction of Hugh Dowding, successfully repelled many of the German air attacks. In achieving this success, the RAF had the advantage of the recent British discovery and application of radar, which gave early warning of attacks and made possible a more efficient use of the RAF's resources. Although not so extensive as those of the German air force, the RAF's resources were not so small as was popularly thought. British fighter aircraft, the spitfires and the hurricanes, were swifter and more effectively armed than were most of the German planes. By mid-September 1940 Hitler postponed plans for the invasion of Britain, though aerial attacks against British cities continued throughout the winter of 1940–41.

North Africa and the Balkans

In contrast with the impressive advances of the spring and summer of 1940, leading to the fall of five west European countries in rapid succession, there followed a ten-month period lasting until April 1941, during which time little progress was made by German forces. By the summer of 1940 Hitler was clear in his mind that the next major German invasion must be directed at the Soviet Union. This objective was postponed until June 1941, however, largely as a result of the diversion of German military resources to north Africa and the Balkans, where it was necessary for the Germans to give aid to their Axis partner, Italy.

Mussolini defined Italy's war after 1940 as a *parallel war* with that waged by Germany. He wanted to see Italy make a contribution similar to that made by Germany and had no wish to see Italy as a junior partner in the Axis alliance. But events placed his country in this subordinate position. Undismayed by his near total failure in France,

The Axis Powers in North Africa and the Balkans, 1940–41

Mussolini gave orders in September 1940 for the invasion of British-held Egypt from neighbouring Italian-held Libya. Encouraged by the initial success of his forces in this invasion, he ordered the invasion of Greece from Italian-held Albania. His forces here were at once turned back by the Greeks, with the British aid originally promised to Greece in the months just before the outbreak of war. This defeat in Greece was then followed by defeat in Egypt during the winter of 1940–41, when British troops stationed in Egypt defeated the Italians, and launched a counter-offensive into Libya, conquering half of the country by February 1941.

Thus two ambitious Italian assaults had led to total defeat. Consequently, Germany had to come to the aid of her ally in both areas. In February 1941 Hitler sent Field-Marshal Rommel and the Afrika Corps to Libya to direct a new offensive against the British in Libya and in Egypt. Rommel, though later in the war persuaded to take part in a plot against Hitler, was at this time loyal to the Führer. He was a soldier of exceptional ability, concerned (as were many military leaders on both sides, who as young officers had gone through the pointless slaughter of the First World War) with preserving lives whenever it was possible to do so. Under Rommel's direction, by April 1941 the British were expelled from Libya.

German aid to retrieve Italian failure in the Balkans was similarly successful. Pressure was put on Bulgaria and Yugoslavia to permit the passage of German troops going to the aid of the Italians in Greece. The Bulgarian government, sympathetic towards the Nazi government, agreed readily. The Yugoslavian royalist government was unseated by a military coup after it had given its agreement in March 1941; the new government immediately repudiated its predecessor's agreement, thus presenting a brave challenge to Germany. Hitler retaliated by ordering the invasion of Yugoslavia. This provided the most spectacular example of Nazi *blitzkrieg* attack, as the country was conquered in the space of eleven days. Yugoslavia was surrounded by countries allied to Germany or occupied by Germany, thus making possible simultaneous attack along the entire inland frontier, while Italy launched attacks from the coastal Italian towns of Fiume and Zara. Germany followed the success in Yugoslavia by a swift invasion of Greece, which fell completely to Germany before the end of April.

The invasion of the Soviet Union

Germany eventually paid a heavy price for its spectacular successes in the Balkans and north Africa during the early months of 1941. The extensive deployment of the troops and equipment and the need to overhaul the equipment after use during these campaigns made for a fatal delay in the already-planned attack on the Soviet Union.

Hitler's unprovoked attack of the Soviet Union in June 1941 was caused partly by his belief that defeat of the Soviet Union would remove all hope of assistance to Britain and partly by his hatred of Communism and of Russia itself. But the *blitzkrieg* attacks he had earlier launched so successfully in quite large countries, such as France and Yugoslavia, foundered in the vast stretches of the Soviet Union. The German invasion force of 22 June 1941 was the largest ever deployed in the history of Europe: four million men, over three thousand tanks and five thousand aircraft. During the first four months substantial advances were made; important cities such as Kiev fell to the Germans and much of Russian agriculture and industry came under their control. But by December 1941 the German advance was halted. By this time the bitterness of the Russian winter was taking its toll among the exhausted German troops: had there been an earlier start on this long campaign, the troops might have made further advance before winter fell. The opposing Soviet troops were now strengthened by the transfer to Russia's west of troops stationed earlier in the east as a precaution against possible Japanese invasion. Stalin's efficient espionage system correctly assured him that the Japanese, in spite of

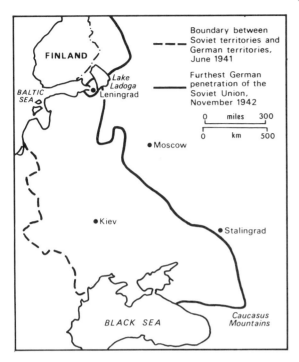

The German Invasion of Russia, 1941–42

some troops from the south of Russia and transferred them to the attacks on Leningrad and elsewhere. This transfer was unwise. In the autumn of 1942 the Germans began the assault on the southern city of Stalingrad, where eventual defeat of the German forces led to the collapse, not only of Hitler's ambitions in the Soviet Union, but also of the precarious empire which, by shifty diplomacy and brute force, he had created throughout Europe.

The Third Reich at its fullest extent

Seven European states were able to preserve their neutrality throughout the Second World War: Spain, Portugal, Eire, Switzerland, Sweden, Turkey and the Vatican. All other European states, with the exception of Britain, came to a greater or lesser degree under the control of Germany at one time or another during the war. The high point of German control was in the autumn of 1942, just prior to the reversals that followed later that year in the Soviet Union and in north Africa.

Of the remaining countries, five were allies of Nazi Germany. Italy was the closest ally though, as has been seen in the Balkans and north Africa, by no means militarily reliable. Hungary and the Balkan states of Bulgaria and Romania also felt their best interests were served by a German alliance, foundations for which had been laid by economic links with Germany before the war. After the German invasion of the Soviet Union, Finland became a minor ally of Germany, because she wanted to regain the territories conquered by the Soviet Union during the Winter War of 1939–40.

In other countries, Nazi control was exercised through a government composed of the country's own nationals prepared to collaborate with the German authorities. Such a system had advantages for the country in that, within limits, it was permitted a degree of independence. The most important example of a collaborationist régime of this type is the Vichy régime in France, though its control was limited to the southern part of the

expansionist ambitions in many directions, did not intend to invade the Soviet Union and no purpose was to be served by keeping large numbers of troops guarding the east.

During the next year, 1942, Hitler felt confident that he would achieve success in the Soviet Union. In spite of the poor condition of his troops, he firmly refused any permission for retreat. By the spring of 1942 the German forces had been considerably reinforced. Hitler made no direct assault on Moscow, but directed attacks in the north against the besieged city of Leningrad, where more than half a million inhabitants had died during the winter of 1941–42, and in the direction of the Caucasus in the south with the aim of seizing the extensive Soviet oil wells in that area. In the summer months of 1942 the German military successes of the previous summer were repeated and it seemed possible that the Soviet Union would fall to the Germans.

So confident was Hitler that he withdrew

country. All Greece came under the control of a collaborationist government and Norway was under the control of a government of Norwegian Nazis headed by Quisling; both these governments were strongly linked with Nazi Germany. Different parts of Yugoslavia and Czechoslovakia were governed by collaborationists; in the case of Czechoslovakia this situation had been established in 1938–39, before the outbreak of war.

Territories which were neither allied to Nazi Germany nor under governments compliant to Nazi Germany, suffered direct occupation and Nazi administration. Denmark, Holland, Belgium, northern and western France, the large central areas of Poland and the conquered territories of the Soviet Union all came within this category. Territories where there was a significant German element within the population were fully incorporated into Germany: large areas of western Poland, the controversial area of Alsace-Lorraine, smaller areas on the Belgian border and the area of Slovenia in northern Yugoslavia were all fully incorporated as a part of Germany in this way.

The New Order: race

The phrase *The New Order* was first used by the Nazis during the conquests of 1940. Essentially, the phrase referred to the postwar organization and economic integration of what was expected to be German-dominated Europe. As Germany lost the war, it is not possible to see what the New Order would have been like in times of peace. What was seen of the wartime New Order was so cruel that it cannot be considered a basis for any reasonable or humane postwar development.

Nazi attitudes towards race had been applied in Germany before the outbreak of war, as has been shown in chapter 6. As so much of Europe had come under Nazi control by the end of 1942, Hitler's government was able to impose its racial policies more widely. It was a matter of concern to the Nazi government that a number of people of pure 'Aryan' descent were to be found living outside the boundaries of Germany. The migration of their ancestors to other areas had taken place for differing reasons centuries previously, but they had nevertheless maintained a German identity. As Germany secured control over areas of earlier German settlement, such as the central areas of Poland, Bessarabia and the Russian Don valley, the government encouraged the transfer of these Germans back to Germany itself. Certain other European races, such as the Scandinavians, Swiss and Dutch were favourably regarded by the Nazi government as being racially similar to the Germans and therefore also within their definition of 'Aryan'. Races in countries allied with Germany were accorded a favourable position in the Nazi racial system, even though in the case of the Italians and the Japanese they were racially dissimilar to the Germans. The entire Nazi structure of racial acceptability was total nonsense, unworthy of serious consideration were it not for the deadly effects that it had on those who were held to be outside it.

Among those whom the Nazis rejected on racial grounds, two drew out their particular hatred: the Slavonic people found in eastern Europe and the Jewish people scattered throughout the whole of Europe. From the time of the conquest of Poland and parts of the Soviet Union the treatment of the Slavonic people was in the hands of the SS. Some of the worst Nazi excesses took place against Slavonic people in the Soviet Union, where SS Action Teams killed tens of thousands of Russians within the newly-conquered territories. Conditions in German prisoner-of-war camps in the Soviet Union were atrocious, the prisoners being herded into exposed barbed wire encampments and left there to suffer the bitter weather; it has been estimated that almost two million Russian prisoners-of-war died while in captivity.

In the early stages of the war, Jewish people in conquered territories were taken to Poland and herded into ghettoes. After the German invasion of the Soviet Union, more and more Jews came under Nazi control and in order to solve this 'Jewish problem', as it was termed by the Nazis, the *Final*

Solution was approved by the Nazi government in January 1942, requiring the extermination of all Jews in Europe. For the following three years, until shortly before the end of the war, squalidly-packed cattle-trucks brought Jews by rail from all over Nazi-held Europe for extermination in the camps established for this purpose, most of which were in Nazi-held Poland. Estimates of the number of Jews slaughtered in this way during the Second World War vary, but the figure of six million is not an exaggeration.

The ruthless and thorough application of Nazi racial theories during these years is probably the most horrific aspect of the history of the world in the twentieth century. Subsequent generations have asked why it was allowed to happen. Although those who lived near the camps must have had some knowledge of the atrocities, there was little they could do in the way of taking on the formidable Nazi administration. There was generally very little knowledge of what was happening and nothing positive that could be done about it even if there had been. The suggestion has been made that outside leaders should have spoken more vigorously against German action, but outside the Nazi-held areas there was little positive evidence available of these atrocities and in any case the Nazi government would have paid no attention to them. Nothing could be done until the war ended. The 'silence' of Pope Pius XII on this matter has become a matter of controversy, considered more fully in chapter 17.

The New Order: the economy

The circumstances of war favoured the German acquisition of goods. In Poland and the Soviet Union, outright seizure of property took place. In France and other western countries there was similar economic exploitation, though it was less forthrightly applied: the occupied country had to pay for the army of occupation and the exchange rate was fixed at a level that greatly favoured Germany, which in any case bought material on credit and in the event was never called

'We are leaving to work in Germany.' A Nazi wartime poster in occupied Belgium paints an attractive picture of employment prospects in Germany.

upon to make repayment.

Manpower throughout the German Reich was also exploited. The inhabitants of the conquered eastern lands were treated with less consideration than those from the west. By 1940 foreign workers from Poland were forcibly recruited. In western countries such as France and Belgium, recruitment was voluntary and encouraged by Nazi advertisements that painted an attractive picture of employment prospects in Germany; poor employment prospects at home were a further inducement. By the end of 1942 the need for foreign labour became more acute as it became apparent that the war was not coming to an end in the foreseeable future. An intensified campaign of recruitment was organized from May 1942 in which the weight of the campaign rested once more on the inhabitants of the conquered eastern territories; Slavs were increasingly compelled to work in the Third Reich. By the middle of 1944 there were as many as seven million foreign workers employed in Germany and another seven million were working on the German war effort in other countries.

The effects of German economic policies during the war were almost wholly disastrous. The traditional ills of a weak economy were all in evidence: inflation rocketed throughout the occupied territories, raw materials were in short supply, black market

123

dealings flourished while orderly, accepted forms of exchange declined. Hatred grew between those who collaborated readily with the German authorities and those who resisted.

The Nazi lead in economic matters was not undivided. As in the period before the war, Hitler preferred there to be overlap between the responsibilities of his ministers, as he found this a useful means of maintaining his own leadership. It is doubtful if this divided responsibility worked well in practice during the war. Albert Speer, who was placed in charge of armaments manufacture in 1942, found the overlap of responsibility between ministers, especially between himself and Goering, particularly awkward for orderly economic development.

Questions

34. Study the cartoon on page 117 and then answer questions (a) to (d) which follow.
   - (a) (i) Name the ruler shown pulling the strings of the puppets and name the country represented by the puppets.
       - (ii) Name the town on which this puppet government was based.
       - (iii) Give the year in which this puppet government came into being.
       - (iv) Describe the circumstances leading to the formation of this puppet government.

          $(1+1+1+3)$
   - (b) (i) Name *two* other countries in Europe which had similar puppet governments, and
       - (ii) describe the circumstances leading to the formation of *one* of these puppet governments.

          $(2+2)$
   - (c) Show the importance of the careers before the Second World War of *two* of the puppets in the cartoon.

          (4)
   - (d) In what ways and with what eventual results was this puppet government opposed by
       - (i) forces within the country, and
       - (ii) forces coming from outside the country?

          (6)

35. Describe and explain how Germany (a) achieved military success in Europe during the first two years of the Second World War and (b) governed occupied Europe during the war.

36. Show the importance of *four* of the following in the history of the Second World War: the defeat of Poland; the fall of France; the battle of Britain; the invasion of Russia; the Nazi New Order.

13

The course of the Second World War (2)

The war in the Pacific and the entry of the United States

The military government of Japan took advantage of the war in Europe to extend its Co-prosperity Sphere. The collapse of France in 1940 inevitably led to confusion in the French colony of Indochina. Japanese forces took over most of the country in the summer of 1940, completing the conquest, in alliance with Siam, during 1941. So many problems faced France and other Allied powers elsewhere, that resistance to the Japanese seizure of Indochina was minimal.

At this early stage of the war Japan's confidence in an inevitable German victory led her to seek closer association with Germany. The Rome-Berlin-Tokyo Axis pact signed by Italy, Germany and Japan in September 1940, united the three countries more firmly in their aggressive designs in Europe and in Asia.

Article 1. Japan recognizes and respects the leadership of Germany and Italy in the establishment of a New Order in Europe.
Article 2. Germany and Italy recognize and respect the leadership of Japan in the establishment of a New Order in greater East Asia.
Article 3. Germany, Italy and Japan agree to cooperate in their efforts on the aforesaid lines. They further undertake to assist one another with all political, economic and military means if one of the three contracting powers is attacked by a power at present not involved in the European War or in the Chinese-Japanese conflict.

This was a highly threatening pact, as the achievement of Article 2 would bring an end to the imperial hold in Asia of Western powers such as Britain, France, Holland and the United States. The most threatened among these powers was the United States, whose commercial interests in the Pacific area were being attacked by Japan's increasingly aggressive actions. Relations between the two countries, never very good between the wars, declined further: in the final months of 1940 the United States placed a series of embargoes on the export to Japan of essential goods, such as aviation fuel, iron and steel, and in 1941 froze Japan's investments in America, thus depriving the Japanese war economy of an essential source of income. In this way, the United States attempted to dissuade Japan from her course of aggression. But the attempt failed. Half-hearted negotiations took place and brought little improvement. In October 1941 General Tojo, the former Minister of War, became Prime Minister and it now seemed that under him, Japanese military aggression would be even more fully pursued.

Early on the morning of Sunday 7 December 1941 the Japanese armed forces struck directly against the United States. Within a few hours Japanese forces put out of action the American Pacific fleet, stationed at Pearl Harbor, Hawaii. The way was thus opened for a rapid advance of Japanese power in the Pacific in the early months of the following year, so that by May 1942 the American-held Philippine islands, the British colonies of Burma and Malaya, the Dutch East Indies and a large number of minor Pacific islands were in Japanese possession. Some bombings of northern Australia took place and there was fear (in the event, unwarranted) that Australia and New Zealand might fall before what appeared to be the relentless expansion of the Japanese Co-prosperity Sphere in the months after Pearl Harbor.

Pearl Harbor finally shocked the American people out of their interwar isolationist attitudes. Until March 1941 American policy towards the war had been within the limits of a policy known as *cash and carry*: American military supplies were available to Britain and France only if paid for and carried away by the country acquiring them. After March 1941 this policy was replaced by the more generous policy of *lend-lease*: supplies were now made available throughout the war, with no need for immediate cash settlement. In August 1941 Roosevelt joined with Churchill in issuing the *Atlantic Charter*, the result of a summit meeting between the two leaders, on board ship, off the Newfoundland coast. In this document, both countries supposed an eventual Allied victory would take place, and sketched out their plans for a postwar settlement which would give emphasis to the creation of fully democratic government and of an efficient system of international security. Thus, by the time of Pearl Harbor, there already existed substantial American aid for the Allied cause and an identity of outlook on war aims. Such was the shock that Congress voted overwhelmingly for entry into the war. The extensive contribution by a new, fresh and strong country to the Allied side became a decisive factor in the eventual Allied victory.

Allied success in north Africa and Italy

In Libya, during the early months of 1942, German forces under Rommel's lead had

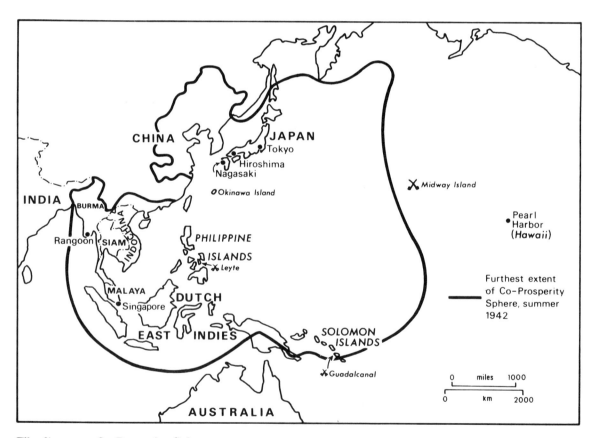

The Japanese Co-Prosperity Sphere

given decisive help to the Italian forces in driving the invading British and Commonwealth forces back into Egypt. In June 1942 the German advances into Egypt were at last halted. German forces were now within seventy miles of Alexandria. Though they had been successful, their strategic position was unfavourable: in the remote deserts of Egypt they were a long way from their sources of supply, while the opposing British forces had easy access via the Red Sea and were increasing in size and strength. In October 1942 the British Eighth army, under their new Commander, Field Marshal Montgomery, defeated the Germans in the battle of El Alamein. Starting with an intensive artillery barrage, the British forces had broken through the Axis lines within a week and had begun to pursue them westwards, out of Egypt and across Libya.

In November 1942, just a week after this Allied victory, Anglo-American forces made successful landings on the shores of the Vichy-held territories of Algeria and Morocco. The swiftness of the Vichy capitulation led the Nazi government to doubt the fundamental loyalty of the Vichy régime to the German cause: consequently the régime's limited independence was abolished. In north Africa, the Anglo-American forces from the west, and the British Eighth army from the east, were converging on Tunisia. Here, the German army intended to make a stand. But at the battle of the Mareth Line in March 1943 the Eighth army broke Axis resistance and then combined their forces with those from the west in a final struggle against the Germans, who lost their hold on north Africa in May 1943. The Allied leaders had agreed in the previous year that their north African campaigns had the purpose of preparing suitable ground for an assault on Italy, 'the soft underbelly of the Axis' as it was called by Churchill. In July 1943 landings were made in Sicily, which fell to the Allies with little opposition. But the subsequent campaign on the Italian mainland was hard and lengthy: it was to take almost two years before the Allies reached the north of Italy.

The immediate result of the collapse of Sicily in July 1943 was the fall of Mussolini. The Fascist Grand Council agreed that he should be deposed and imprisoned and that Marshal Badoglio, the hero of the Abyssinian campaign, should take his place as Prime Minister. During the war the military failures and the increased ruthlessness of Fascist government had deepened the unpopularity in which Mussolini had been held by most Italians since his declaration of war in June 1940. The corruption of the Fascist system had been starkly revealed during these years. There was a hatred of the unconcealed contempt in which the Germans held the Italians. The hope that the war would increase the Italian hold on the Mediterranean area had come to nothing, as by July 1943 the Mediterranean sea was almost controlled by British and American forces. Hitler showed a rare sense of loyalty to Mussolini. In September 1943 German parachutists rescued the former Duce from his imprisonment. Subsequently, again with strong German support, Mussolini was able to re-establish a Fascist government, this time in a republican form, based on the town of Salò in northern Italy.

The continued demand by the Allies for 'unconditional surrender' suggested to Badoglio that Italy's best interests were served by remaining loyal to the Axis. But in the weeks after Mussolini's fall, as the Allies advanced from Sicily to southern Italy, it became clearer to the Italians that they were on the losing side. In the meantime the German government had little faith that the Badoglio government would continue its loyalty to the Axis for very long. Consequently in these weeks the Italian peninsula was flooded with German soldiers, so that it became almost under German occupation. The uncertainty was shortly resolved by the Badoglio government: an armistice with the Allies was agreed in September and Italy entered the war on the Allied side in October. This helpful change of side caused the Allies to treat Italy more favourably, in spite of their earlier declaration of 'unconditional surrender'. The military situation was confusing: the Allied forces in Italy were now assisted by the official Italian forces, whose

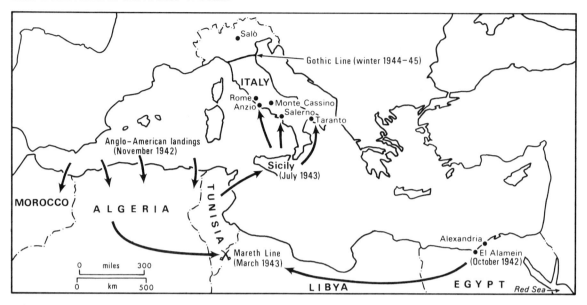

Allied advances in North Africa and Italy, 1942–45

government was based on the southern town of Brindisi, now held by the Allies. The German forces in Italy had been substantially increased and were assisted by Mussolini's less numerous supporters, based on Salò in the north.

The slow progress of the Allied forces northward through the Italian peninsula was marked by some major engagements. In September 1943 sea-borne landings were made on the beaches at Salerno and at Taranto: in spite of heavy loss of life and bitter fighting, the Allied forces were able to establish firm hold in these areas. A similar sea-borne assault on Anzio, seen as essential for advance on Rome, led to more protracted fighting in the early months of 1944. Also in the spring of 1944 a controversial Allied attack took place on the ancient hill-top monastery of Monte Cassino: repeated Allied assaults almost razed the monastery to the ground. The Allies believed that the Germans were using the monastery and that its destruction was essential, but later evidence suggests that the destruction served very little purpose in the overall Allied strategy in Italy. The Allied entry into Rome in June 1944 was not the end of the fighting: some compara-

tively swift northward progress was made in the summer of 1944, but the Allied forces were stopped during the winter of 1944 to 1945 at the Gothic Line, just north of Florence. Only with the retreat of the remaining German forces in April 1945 was there a successful breakthrough into northern Italy: Mussolini's Fascist republic of Salò, by then nothing more than a shoddy façade for German rule, was brought down and the former dictator was shot by Italian partisans at the end of April 1945.

By the time the Allies had been successful in northern Italy, more significant advances had been made against Germany, one from the direction of the Soviet Union and another from the direction of France. The Allied campaign in Italy had taken so long that it could not become the spring-board for an effective final thrust against Germany, as envisaged earlier by Churchill. The Italian campaign nevertheless had much value. To combat the Allied advances, the German government had had no alternative but to station many troops in Italy, even though they were desperately needed elsewhere. The German government also felt it was essential to keep troops in the Balkans, as an invasion there was expected to follow from an Allied success in Italy.

Soviet success on the Eastern Front: Stalingrad

The German forces, held down in Italy and the Balkans by the Allied campaigns in Italy, were desperately needed for fighting on the Eastern Front. In the autumn of 1942, at about the same time as the battle of El Alamein, the German forces besieging Stalingrad were aware of a stiffening of Soviet resistance. The Soviet forces were now beginning to show the value of the increased military production that had been taking place in the unconquered eastern areas of the Soviet Union earlier in the war. Substantial Soviet reinforcements were sent to the Stalingrad area. Unable to enter the city, they nevertheless encircled the besieging German Sixth army. Within the city, the inhabitants were prepared to last out the siege as long as need be and they fought desperately, aided by their city's natural advantage of the vast width of the Volga river, almost a mile wide in parts, which separated them from the besieging forces. Intense fighting took place around Stalingrad in the bitter winter of 1942–43. The German forces themselves suffered attack by the encircling Soviet forces and were desperately short of supplies. A strategic retreat by the Germans would have eased the situation for them, but in spite of the rising number of German deaths from injuries and from cold, permission to retreat was firmly refused. For the world at large, Stalingrad became a symbol of determined resistance to German aggression and a focus of hope that the tide of German success might at last be turning.

In January 1943 the German Commander at Stalingrad, von Paulus, realized that the situation was hopeless and gave orders to retreat. The Soviet forces began to pursue the German army towards the Black Sea and the west. Amidst much emotion, towns that had been earlier conquered by the Germans were now recaptured by the Russians. Although the German forces were able to make some effective counter-attacks, by the end of 1943 Soviet forces had reconquered two-thirds of the land occupied by the Germans, and by the spring of 1944 they had reached the borders of the east European and Balkan countries.

Romania and Bulgaria fell rapidly in September 1944. In Yugoslavia, the work of expelling the Germans had been almost completed by Tito's partisans before the Soviet forces arrived. The Balkans thus secured, an advance was made up the Danube valley towards Hungary. The advance was stopped here throughout the winter of 1944–45, as a last ditch stand was made by the German troops who had fully occupied Hungary and who had put up stern resistance, especially at Budapest. Poland was entered in August 1944. But no Soviet assistance was given to the rising of the Polish Home army which the Germans suppressed. The Soviet forces advanced later and entered the capital, Warsaw, in November 1944. At the start of 1945, the Soviet Union was poised for entry into the eastern parts of Germany.

The Second Front

The idea of opening a Second Front in France had been under discussion since 1942, and was eagerly sought by the Soviet Union, as it would afford relief to their own fighting. The Second Front had to wait until the Allies had complete control of the sea. Only by the summer of 1943 did the Allied forces have this complete control, having by then won the extended Battle of the Atlantic, which had continued throughout the early years of the war. With no more threat of German submarine attacks, the massive invasion force could be successfully launched from the southern shores of England to the northern shores of France. Apart from the time needed to complete the Battle of the Atlantic, much preparatory work was needed on the organization of the vast invading force of the American, British and Commonwealth soldiers. Prefabricated 'Mulberry' harbours for the landing of troops, and an oil-supply system by means of 'Pipe Lines under the

Allied advances, 1944–45

Ocean' (PLUTO) were among the more important devices which the Allies prepared. The Germans meantime had strengthened their defensive Atlantic Wall in northern France and were attempting to guess where the expected landings would take place: most of the German leaders anticipated that the shorter crossing in the Calais region was the most likely. But the final Allied decision was to take a longer crossing and land further west in the Normandy region.

The date for these 'D Day' landings was 6 June 1944. The fact that the weather was appalling and the sea exceptionally rough did not allow it to be postponed: the defenders of the Atlantic Wall were taken by surprise, not only by the place of the landing but also by its timing. Within a couple of days 200,000 Allied troops had landed and had firmly established their hold in the coastal areas of Normandy: they were followed by more within the next fortnight so that the total number of troops landed was approximately 650,000. Hitler's plan was to allow the landings to take place and to fight against the invaders later, in the interior. But by the time the Germans had

launched a strong attack, the invaders had established such a strong hold that the German forces were unable to stop their further advance. French resistance forces gave active help to the Allied forces in their continued advance. In August 1944 Paris fell and General de Gaulle, the leader of the Free French, formed a provisional government.

The successful advances of the Second Front from the west, and of the Soviet forces from the east, made it seem possible that Germany would be defeated before the end of 1944. But the stubborn German resistance slowed down progress towards the end of the year and the campaign became more protracted. Inter-Allied differences on strategy sapped their military unity: the British command, under Montgomery, wanted a direct thrust through the German industrial areas to Berlin, but the American command, under Eisenhower, wanted an equal advance on a broad front. As Eisenhower also had overall command of the entire Allied strategy, it was his views which prevailed. Nevertheless, he authorized Montgomery to attempt part of his plan by seizing bridges across the river Rhine in Holland. This led, in September 1944, to the ill-fated Arnhem expedition, in which British paratroopers were unlucky enough to land in an area strongly controlled by German troops. The failure of this campaign and the difficulties now experienced in furnishing the enormous Allied army with supplies, resulted in comparatively little advance in the closing months of 1944.

Whilst the Allied forces were thus on the defensive, a spirited attempt was made by some young German officers in the Ardennes mountains of southern Belgium to reverse the Allied advance. Their immediate aim, in what is sometimes called 'the Battle of the Bulge', was to reach the Allied supply port of Antwerp, but within ten days of launching their assault, in December 1944, they had been decisively defeated: the cost in men and supplies for an army that was clearly in the last stages of defeat was very serious. By the spring of 1945, with better weather and fuller supplies, the Allied forces were ready for the final thrust against a disintegrating Germany.

After four years as a Nazi-controlled city, Paris was liberated by the armies of the Second Front in August 1944. This photograph shows the triumph of that occasion, as American troops march confidently along the Champs-Élysées.

Allied aerial bombardment

The final western advances in the spring of 1945 were accompanied by a devastating aerial bombardment of Germany, the climax of Allied policies begun earlier in the war. Two methods were used by the Allies in their bombing of Germany. In the early stages, *precision bombing* was employed: targets of economic, military or strategic importance were selected and they alone were to be bombed. By 1941 the British government realized that precision bombing was not working, as the aircraft crews, who for purposes of cover worked only at night, were unable to locate their targets precisely. After the American entry, their crews employed daytime precision bombing, often securing successful results but risking the obvious chance of detection. In 1941 the British government shifted to *area bombing*: well-populated towns were now to be bombed indiscriminately in an attempt to lower the morale of the German people. This was a ruthless policy which had been earlier employed by the Germans in their attacks on Poland in September 1939 and on Britain in the winter of 1940–41. But this shift of policy by Churchill's government was never made clear to the British people, who were told that the bombers were aiming at strategic targets and that civilian casualties were merely accidental.

The head of Bomber Command, Sir Arthur Harris, put the new policy into practice with devastating loss of civilian life in Germany. The bulky shape and swift movement of the new Lancaster planes made them particularly suitable for this new method of area bombing. Many German cities suffered: the worst casualties, in each case numbering substantially more than a hundred thousand deaths, occurred in July and August 1943 at Hamburg, and in February 1945 at Dresden.

The military value of these raids was mixed. The destruction of some targets, such as the Schweinfurt ball-bearing plants and the launching pads for the V2 rockets, had undoubted value, but German production was only marginally reduced by the campaigns overall. The worst human casualties were brought about by area bombing, which

The loading of a Lancaster plane with bombs destined for Germany in the closing stages of the Second World War. The usefulness of much of the aerial bombardment of Germany has subsequently been questioned.

did very little to achieve its aim of reducing German morale. The German civil defence system, though seriously strained towards the end of the war, worked efficiently to relieve the suffering of German civilians. Hitler himself, who in prewar days enjoyed successful public appearances, never visited the bombed areas where the people for whom he was responsible were suffering cruelly.

The final German collapse

With the continued advance of well-supplied forces of the Soviet Union from the east, and of British and American forces from the west, all hope of German victory was lost. Even under these hopeless circumstances, Hitler insisted that Germany should fight to the last and should never follow the example of the First World War generals by giving in to the enemy. In defeat, Hitler became quite irrational, placing unfounded hope on the invention of new weapons to destroy the encircling enemy forces. He was encouraged in the summer of 1944 by the German use against Britain of the V1 flying bombs and the V2 rockets. Though these inflicted serious casualties in the London region, it would have been a more purposeful strategy to employ them against the advancing armies. The Allies took countermeasures against these attacks and later in 1944 destroyed the launching bases of the V1s and V2s.

As defeats surrounded them and as Hitler's government acted so irresponsibly and so irrationally, internal German opposition developed. In July 1944 some members of the army took the lead in an attempt to assassinate Hitler. The plan was to plant a time bomb during one of Hitler's meetings at his military headquarters in East Prussia: after Hitler had been killed in this way, a military government would be set up and would at once seek an armistice. The bomb was placed in the headquarters by a military aristocrat, Colonel Count von Stauffenberg, who heard it explode as he was leaving the headquarters site. The blast was so strong that he naturally assumed Hitler to have been killed by it: consequently the new opposition government was proclaimed. But Hitler was not killed in the blast. Fortunately for him, the meeting was held in a room above ground and not underground in the bunker, where meetings were normally held and where the force of the blast would have been more considerable. Also, after Stauffenberg's departure, the briefcase containing the

In this last photograph taken of him, Hitler greets the boys who were recruited for the hopeless task of defending Berlin early in 1945. Contrast Hitler's broken style with that of the confident prewar years, as shown in the photograph on page 60.

bomb had been moved to a different place in the room, so that Hitler was not so close to the blast. Stauffenberg and other conspirators were shot later in the day: others were discovered later and suffered brutal execution. Hitler's escape from death was amazing, but the shock of the July plot affected him badly and he became increasingly withdrawn, neurotic and suspicious.

In the early months of 1945 Hitler's government was unable to give any active direction to the hopeless task of defending Germany against attacks. In the early weeks of the year Soviet forces entered eastern Germany and in February Budapest fell to the Soviet forces in Hungary. In March the west-

ern Allies crossed the Rhine and cut off the industrial Ruhr area from the rest of Germany. To carry out Hitler's policy of defence to the very last, old men and sixteen-year-old boys were recruited into the German army. In mid-April, Soviet forces entered Berlin. At the end of April Hitler, realizing that Germany was now defeated, committed suicide, designating Admiral Doenitz as his successor. Doenitz' obvious task was to end the war and, after unsuccessful attempts to seek a separate understanding with the Western powers, in the hope that they would treat Germany more leniently than would the Soviet Union, he surrendered unconditionally on 8 May 1945.

Churchill, Roosevelt and Stalin, with their aides grouped behind them, at the Yalta meeting in February 1945. As the war drew to an end, differences between the wartime Allies were already beginning to emerge.

The conferences at Yalta and Potsdam

A series of high-level conferences were held between the Allied countries during the Second World War. Most of them were concerned with the coordination of military strategy and the most important were at Casablanca in January 1943, when the invasion of Italy was agreed, and at Teheran in November 1943, when the opening of the Second Front was agreed. Towards the end of the war, further conferences were concerned less with the military strategy and more with the future peace. The conference at Yalta, a resort in the Crimea, was attended in February 1945 by Roosevelt, Churchill and Stalin. The conference at Potsdam, a suburb of Berlin, was attended in July 1945 by Truman, Attlee and Stalin.

At Yalta, the Allied leaders were aware that their wartime alliance had led to the victory over Nazi Germany, which by then they had almost achieved. Already, however, there were signs that the alliance would not long survive the end of the war. The Western

leaders were disturbed at the strong influence of the Red Army in many of the parts of eastern Europe which it had freed from Nazi control; they were particularly concerned at the situation in Poland, where the Soviet Union was already establishing a Communist-dominated government, in total disregard of the non-Communist Polish government-in-exile. They attempted at Yalta to resolve their differences on these issues, but in its negotiations the Soviet Union was in a strong position, as its army occupied most of the territories under discussion.

Agreement was reached on the future of Poland, by which the country was effectively moved westwards: Poland was to secure land from Germany as far as the Oder and Neisse rivers, while the Soviet Union was to secure land from Poland almost as far as the old Curzon Line. Though the Soviet Union promised to allow free elections within Poland and to allow members of the Polish government-in-exile to join the new government in Poland, in practice, little progress was made in putting these provisions into effect over the following few months. Mindful of the German invasion of their country through Poland in 1941, the Soviet Union sought to create, both by the drawing of Poland's frontiers and by the composition of Poland's government, a land which would be securely under Soviet influence. This Soviet concern for security was the main reason that underlay their further insistance that Germany should be partitioned and that the Soviet Union should secure reparations from their part of Germany. Though the United States and Britain were also generally unsympathetic towards Germany, they were beginning to doubt whether a severe policy against Germany was the best way in which to secure the future peace of Europe. Nevertheless, agreement was reached in principle on the division of Germany into zones, to be administered by the occupying powers until such time as a peace treaty was signed with Germany by all the victorious powers. By its *Declaration on Liberated Europe*, the conference agreed that democratic elections should take place in the countries liberated from Nazi control. The progress of the war in

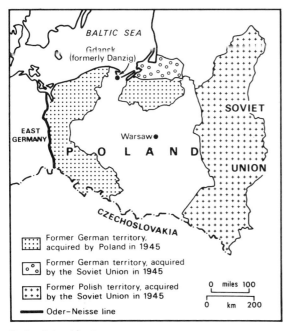

BALTIC SEA

Gdansk
(formerly Danzig)

EAST
GERMANY

Warsaw

P O L A N D

SOVIET

UNION

CZECHOSLOVAKIA

Former German territory, acquired by Poland in 1945

Former German territory, acquired by the Soviet Union in 1945

Former Polish territory, acquired by the Soviet Union in 1945

Oder–Neisse line

0   miles 100

0   km   200

Poland in 1945

the Pacific was also discussed. The Soviet Union had not involved itself so far in fighting against Japan, but at Yalta Stalin promised to join the war in the Pacific within three months of the ending of the war in Europe.

By the time of the Potsdam meeting in July, though the struggle against Japan continued, the war in Europe was over. The treatment of Germany was the main issue, and agreement was finalized on the division of the country into four zones, Soviet, British, American and French, and on the similar division of the city of Berlin, itself within the Soviet, eastern sector. Little progress was made on Poland, which was by then firmly under Soviet control. Truman was a more forceful opponent of Stalin than Roosevelt had been and he was openly critical of the continuing Soviet influence in eastern Europe and the apparent disregard by Stalin of the Yalta *Declaration on Liberated Europe*. It was now clear that there was no chance of continuing the wartime alliance and that a state of Cold War between the Soviet Union and the United States was fast developing.

The use of the atomic bomb

The Japanese had expanded swiftly over such a large area in the months after Pearl Harbor that the task of defeating their Co-prosperity Sphere was likely to be slow and

American troops in the Philippines towards the end of the Second World War proudly display a flag captured from the enemy.

costly. The first major victory against them had come in June 1942 with the American naval victory off Midway island, when substantial damage was done to the Japanese fleet. The myth of Japanese invincibility was broken at Midway. Much of the subsequent American fighting was at sea. While Guadalcanal in the Solomon islands later in 1942, and Leyte in the Philippine islands in the autumn of 1944, were important American victories, most of the fighting against Japan consisted of a slow reduction of the area of the Pacific under Japanese control. Between 1944 and 1945, the British conducted an extensive land campaign against the Japanese in Burma. They entered this enemy territory from neighbouring India in the spring of 1944 and, after the successful battles of Kohima and the Imphal Plain, they secured their position in the north and advanced steadily southwards, reaching Rangoon in May 1945.

But the Japanese were resilient fighters and defended their earlier conquests with a fixed determination, unmatched elsewhere in the Second World War. Many Japanese soldiers preferred suicide to surrender. As the Allies gradually closed in, Japan's resources became hopelessly inadequate to provide for her population. In the spring of 1945 the island of Okinawa fell to the American forces, who were then well placed for launching an invasion of Japan itself. But Okinawa had been a hard-won victory for the Americans and it was generally considered by their military leaders that any landings in Japan would most probably encounter even greater resistance. In the meantime, extensive bombing raids on Tokyo appeared to have little effect on the Japanese determination to continue the struggle.

There was therefore widespread fear that the war against Japan would drag on for a long time. This was the main reason for the American decision to use the atomic bomb against Japan. Research into the making of an atomic bomb had been taking place secretly in the United States throughout the war. In the summer of 1945 this research was brought to a successful conclusion with the testing of an atomic bomb in the desert

regions of the United States. The application of atomic energy for destructive purposes was a revolutionary development in methods of warfare, as the release of atomic energy in this manner created an explosion infinitely more devastating than anything achieved by conventional bombs. Destruction would be on a massive scale. A further effect of an atomic explosion, though this was not well understood during the experimental stages, was the emission of radioactive fallout, which would produce a suffering and lingering death for those who happened to be in the wide area contaminated by it. In some circumstances, the effects would reach even the following generation.

When President Truman attended the Potsdam conference in July 1945 he was aware that his country could use an atomic bomb successfully against Japan. After consultation with the leaders of Britain and China, the other major powers fighting against Japan, a joint ultimatum was delivered to the Japanese government.

> Japanese sovereignty shall be limited to their islands. The Japanese military forces, after being completely disarmed, shall be permitted to return to their homes. . . We do not intend that the Japanese shall be enslaved as a race nor destroyed as a nation. . . The occupying forces of the Allies shall be withdrawn as soon as there has been established, in accordance with the freely expressed will of the Japanese people, a peacefully inclined and responsible government. We call upon the government of Japan to proclaim now the unconditional surrender of all the Japanese armed forces. . . The alternative for Japan is complete and utter destruction.

The last sentence of this ultimatum seems less clear about what it meant by 'complete and utter destruction' than it might have been. The Japanese government rejected the ultimatum and total disaster followed swiftly for their country. On 6 August 1945 an American plane dropped an atomic bomb on the Japanese town of Hiroshima, completely destroying the city and killing tens of thousands of people. On 7 August the Soviet Union declared war on Japan, thus fulfilling the promise Stalin had given at Yalta. On 9 August a second atomic bomb was dropped on the Japanese city of Nagasaki, with effects equally as devastating as those created three days earlier at Hiroshima. The resistance of the Japanese government was now totally broken and a few days later the government announced its surrender.

Since the dreadful events at Hiroshima and Nagasaki, debate has continued on the extent to which the government of the United States was justified in this use of atomic weapons. Popular opinion in the United States and Britain at that time responded with satisfaction that at least the atomic bombs had ended the war in Japan, though with this satisfaction was mixed a sense of horror as the full effects of the bombs became better known. It can be suggested that the American action saved the lives of many Allied soldiers who would have been killed in the continuing war against Japan. It is also certain that the American government did not fully understand the importance of radio-

active fallout. But it is doubtful whether it was necessary to be quite so purposefully destructive. The promised Soviet intervention would improve the chances of a swifter end to the war in the Pacific. Further, there was no real need to destroy two highly-populated cities, as an explosion in open countryside would have been sufficient demonstration to the Japanese government of the sort of weapon the Americans now had. The most compelling reason against the use of the atomic bomb is the example it set of human destruction and human suffering on a massive scale, sad features of the twentieth century which were more fully in evidence throughout the globe in 1945 than in any other year in the history of the world.

Questions

37. Study the photograph on page 136 and the photograph on this page and then answer questions (a) to (d) which follow.
    (a) (i) Name the country whose flag is shown in the photograph on page 136.
        (ii) Give an account of this country's aggression during the four years before the event shown in the photograph on this page.

        (1+5)
    (b) With reference to the photograph on page 136,
        (i) what evidence in the photograph suggests the place where the photograph was taken?
        (ii) what is the nationality of the soldiers shown in the photograph?
        (iii) Describe the main military tactics these soldiers would most probably have used in order to reach this place.

        (2+1+2)
    (c) With reference to the photograph on this page,
        (i) name the weapon that is being used,
        (ii) name the two cities which were destroyed by the use of this weapon,

The atomic cloud that brought the Second World War finally to an end. Later development of nuclear weapons has meant that in any future world war, destruction could be both widespread and swift.

(iii) give the month and year in which these two cities were destroyed, and

(iv) explain the ways in which this photograph suggests that this weapon is different from conventional weapons of war.

$$(1+1+1+2)$$

(d) Describe the attempts that have been made since the time of the event shown in the photograph on page 138 to reduce the possibility of the further use of this weapon of war.

(4)

38. Show the importance of *three* of the following in leading to the defeat of the Axis powers in the Second World War: the fighting in north Africa and Italy; the progress of the Second Front; the campaigns of the Soviet Union; the Allied aerial bombardment.

39. 'From Allied harmony to Cold War.' With reference to the years between 1944 and 1949, trace the changing relationships among the Allied powers in the light of this statement.

14
The Soviet Union since 1945

The Soviet Union emerged from the Second World War an enlarged country, prepared to involve itself far more actively in world affairs. As has been shown in the previous chapter, the country's European boundaries had been extended westwards and the continuing presence of the Red Army in central and eastern Europe became a significant factor in the development of Communist-dominated governments in these areas, a matter considered in the following chapter. Whilst a number of European governments which had risen and flourished during the interwar years had now collapsed, the Communist government in Russia was in a position of great strength. But during the Great Patriotic War the Soviet people had suffered bitterly and the country itself had been extensively devastated. The immediate task was reconstruction.

Stalin's last years

Under the fourth five year plan (1946–50) and the fifth five year plan (1951–55) the Soviet Union made good what their economy had lost during the war. Emphasis was given to the reconstruction of the damaged cities, to the development of heavy industry and to the formation of even larger collective farms. The reparations demanded from defeated Germany and the hard work of the victorious Russians made for the considerable success of these plans. But for most Soviet citizens postwar life was hard: overcrowded living conditions, long hours of work and queues for basic foodstuffs were widespread. Whilst the plans were sensibly directed to-

wards reconstruction, the schemes which took most money and labour, such as the Volga-Don canal, were not well thought-out, even with a view to the country's long-term needs.

These years saw the continuation of the dictatorship which Stalin had created for himself in the 1930s. Stalin's war leadership had led to a marked increase in his popularity. It was therefore thought that after the war he would have less recourse to purges than he had earlier. But his old ways soon reappeared. Censorship and repression were directed mainly by his loyal assistant Zhdanov, who was also largely responsible for the development of a lavish personality cult of Stalin, building on the Soviet leader's increased popularity during the war. Zhdanov was foremost among those who encouraged the people of the Soviet Union to give undivided loyalty to Stalin as a leader who could do no wrong. Meantime, any who were suspected of thinking otherwise were purged. During the few months before his death in March 1953, Stalin was planning an extensive purge that would probably have rivalled those in the 1930s in the number of its victims.

During Stalin's last years the divisions of the Cold War developed and deepened. The Soviet refusal to allow the economic benefits of Marshall Aid to be accepted by the satellite states in 1947 marked a further break between the Soviet Union and the United States. In the same year the *Cominform* (Communist Information Bureau) was created as a body designed to further Communist interests in non-Communist countries and to link the satellites of eastern Europe more firmly to the Soviet Union. Such incidents as the Communist coup in Czechoslovakia in February 1948 (see page 153) and the blockade of Berlin of 1948–49 (see page 159), both of which were direct results of Soviet policy, led to the creation of NATO and an increase in the tensions of the Cold War. In Korea in the early 1950s, tensions broke into open warfare, with strong Russian encouragement and support of the North Koreans in their campaign against the South and its American and United Nations assistance, as shown in chapter 26.

Thus at the time of Stalin's death in March 1953, the government of the Soviet Union was suspicious both of those outside the Soviet Union and of many within. For more than a quarter of a century Stalin had been a dominating and frightening figure, not just within his country, but throughout the world. His death marked the end of an era. It was unlikely that his successors would wish to or would be able to follow a similar course.

The thaw

It was not until five years later, early in 1958, that the Soviet Union again had one leader: Nikita Khrushchev. It was clear from 1953 that the new Soviet leaders intended to get rid of the worst features of Stalinism. A collective leadership, in which Malenkov as Prime Minister and Khrushchev as Party Secretary were the dominant figures, showed a desire to soften the rigidity of recent years. The most noticeable early sign of this more relaxed approach, sometimes known as *the thaw*, was the removal and execution of the former police chief, Beria, a devoted Stalinist who had hoped to succeed his master as sole ruler of the Soviet Union. As Party Secretary, Khrushchev was able to build up a following of his own in the mid-1950s, just as Stalin had in the same office in the mid-1920s. In February 1955 Malenkov was replaced as Prime Minister by Bulganin, with whom Khrushchev worked in harmonious partnership. The softening of Soviet attitudes was vividly demonstrated by visits of Bulganin and Khrushchev to a number of non-Communist countries, including a visit to Britain in the summer of 1956. Khrushchev became increasingly the dominant partner,

and in March 1958 was able to combine his post of Party Secretary with that of Prime Minister.

Khrushchev was closely associated with the thaw throughout the mid-1950s. His most dramatic contribution to the changed approach in the Soviet Union came with his speech to party officials at the twentieth party congress in 1956. In this speech he made a complete condemnation of Stalin's policies. He started by referring to the suspicions held by Lenin about Stalin's suitability for high office, but the bulk of his speech was concerned with condemning the tyranny which Stalin had created.

> Stalin used extreme methods and mass repression at a time when the Revolution was already victorious, when the Soviet state was strengthened, when the exploiting classes were already liquidated and socialist relations were rooted solidly in all phases of national economy, when our party was politically consolidated and had strengthened itself both numerically and ideologically. Considering the question of the cult of the individual, we must first of all show everyone what harm this caused to the interests of our party.

Details were given of the purges, the police activity, the staged trials and the vast number of executions that had been common under Stalin. Even his leadership during the Second World War was criticized: the early defeats were attributed to his purge of army leaders and a number of later campaigns were described as an unnecessary waste of human lives. The breakdown of Soviet relations with Yugoslavia was said to have been caused by Stalin's high-handed attitude towards Tito.

The speech covered dangerous ground for the Soviet leaders, as many of them had been associated with Stalin and his policies at an earlier stage; Khrushchev himself was among them. Conveniently, Khrushchev did not refer to this matter in his speech, though he did hint at the guilt of others. The real impact of the speech was among the vast population of the Soviet Union, all of whom had been trained for decades to regard Stalin as a leader who was almost incapable of error. This changed view had an unsettling effect on many who had previously been under Stalin's authority, though the effect of this was more noticeable outside the Soviet Union, among the satellite countries. Already the Soviet thaw had sparked off risings in East Germany in 1953. Shortly after Khrushchev's speech in 1956 more serious risings occurred in Poland and in Hungary, as shown in the following chapter. The vigorous Soviet response to the Hungarian uprising was clear evidence that there were limits to the Soviet thaw: Stalin had been removed from his pedestal, but the Soviet system was to continue.

Social and economic life under Khrushchev

One fundamental feature of Soviet life which continued under Khrushchev was the planned economy. The government put forward five-year and seven-year plans, sometimes overlapping in their time spans; the sequence of the plans was less clearly defined than in Stalin's time. The objectives of the plans were also somewhat different. More attention was now given to the development of previously neglected industries. No longer was there such solid concentration on the heavy industries of iron, steel and coal. Instead, the developing chemical industry, and consumer production, were given most attention. There was also a change in the organization of the economy. Whereas previously this had been highly centralized from Moscow, fuller initiative was now allowed to local managers under the general supervision of regional councils for industrial production. More attention was given to improving the living and working conditions of the industrial workers. No longer was there the stern concentration on output, regardless of the human toll that it might take. Under Khrushchev, working hours were reduced, wages for many workers were increased and fuller attention was paid to the views of Soviet trade unions on working conditions. A concerted drive was made to improve the deplorably overcrowded housing conditions that still existed in the Soviet Union. In

During a visit to the United States in 1959, Nikita Khrushchev displays a characteristic interest in agriculture.

all of these different ways, the people of the Soviet Union were able to benefit more fully from the government's economic policies.

Much attention was given by Khrushchev to agriculture, an area of the economy which had been beset with difficulties in both tsarist and Communist times. Khrushchev's policies for agriculture were essentially similar to his policies for industry. There was no change from the system of collective farming. But to improve their efficiency, a number of the farms were amalgamated into larger units and they were freed from rigid Moscow-centred direction. Khrushchev's greatest innovation in agriculture was the development of the virgin lands, those areas of the Soviet Union which had not previously been under cultivation. This was essentially a sound policy, but it was undertaken too rapidly and without sufficiently careful use of the new soil. Often it appeared that Khrushchev's enthusiasm for certain agricultural developments, for example, his encouragement of maize cultivation, outran their practical usefulness.

The comparatively liberal nature of Khrushchev's policies towards industry and agriculture were matched in other areas of Soviet life. To assure the people of the Soviet Union that there would be no return to Stalinist methods, the power of the police was restricted and the holding of secret trials was abolished. Encouragement was given to maintaining the regional differences that existed within the Soviet Union. There was a general relaxation of censorship. Books appeared which would certainly have been banned in earlier years: Solzhenitsyn's *One Day in the Life of Ivan Denisovich* revealed the grim horrors of life in a labour camp during the Stalin years, and Pasternak's *Doctor Zhivago* had vivid descriptions of the difficulties of the civil war period. But censorship was still applied. A number of books were banned and Khrushchev himself was particularly critical of modern art, which he judged to be essentially anti-Communist.

These years were marked by some spectacular Soviet exploits in outer space. It was the Soviet Union which launched the first space satellite in 1957 and the first man in space in 1961. Though it was the United States which landed the first man on the moon in 1969, Soviet space technology was nevertheless impressive. Many of these advances were attributable to the thorough attention given to education both under Khrushchev's leadership, and before. As a boy in tsarist Russia Khrushchev had received no formal education, and he had a close concern that well-educated citizens should not become a class apart from others. He began a scheme by which students in higher education were compelled to take part in industrial or agricultural work during the course of their studies.

Khrushchev's foreign policy

Probably no other Soviet leader played so important a part in foreign affairs as Khrushchev did. The term generally applied to his policy was *coexistence*, implying a desire to live harmoniously with other countries in spite of the different political systems that each pursued. Chinese Communists applied the term *revisionism* to this approach, which

they saw as a watering down of the Marxist-Leninist drive for the spread of Communism throughout the globe. This conflict over foreign affairs became an early point of difference between the Soviet Union and Communist China.

In practice, Khrushchev was inconsistent in his pursuit of coexistence. Two of the most serious crises of the Cold War took place while he controlled the Soviet Union: the protracted crisis over Berlin, considered in chapter 16, and the serious crisis over Cuba, considered in chapter 24. Though in both these Khrushchev eventually revealed his desire for coexistence with his enemies, many of his attitudes during the crises were distinctly provocative. At the Paris summit conference of 1960 (page 162) and also at a meeting in Vienna with Kennedy in 1961, Khrushchev further revealed provocative and intolerant attitudes, though the faults were not entirely on his side.

There were nevertheless significant contributions by Khrushchev towards coexistence. His attitude towards Yugoslavia was far less rigid than that of Stalin. The abolition of the Cominform in 1957 was welcomed by the Tito government, whose relations with the Soviet Union improved. Visits abroad by Khrushchev often led to a more relaxed and friendly atmosphere: his visits to Britain in 1956 and to the United States in 1959 were particularly important in this respect. In 1963 the Soviet Union signed the Test Ban treaty with the United States and Britain, thus ending the dangerous testing of nuclear weapons in the atmosphere.

It was essentially his foreign policy which led to his fall from power in 1964. Whilst Khrushchev was on holiday in October 1964, other leading members of the Communist party met in Moscow and agreed that he should be removed from power. His development of a personality cult and the failure of his virgin lands scheme were both held against him. But it was his foreign policy that was most condemned: the ill-judged handling of the Cuban crisis, the deteriorating relations with China and Khrushchev's flamboyant behaviour abroad were all held to have been against the interests of the

Soviet Union. There was little that Khrushchev could do to rally support. His enemies moved swiftly and he had no alternative but to resign, allegedly on grounds of ill-health, and to enter quietly and modestly into retirement on a state pension.

Brezhnev and Kosygin

The new Party Secretary was Leonid Brezhnev and the new Prime Minister was Alexei Kosygin. Neither became totally dominant over the other during the rest of the 1960s and throughout the 1970s while they continued to hold power. But it seemed that Brezhnev, as Party Secretary, possessed slightly more authority than Kosygin. The changed leadership brought no major changes in policy. Generally, in both domes-

tic and foreign affairs, the policies followed by Khrushchev were also followed by his successors. Though there was no return to Stalinist methods, the Soviet system developed along more rigid lines in these years. Stalin was no longer presented as the complete tyrant portrayed by Khrushchev and some of his undoubtedly valuable work for his country was given its due importance.

More significant was the persecution of those who were termed *dissidents*, writers and thinkers who were critical of the totalitarian nature of the Soviet system. In 1966 Sinyavsky and Daniel were tried on charges of anti-Soviet activity, the most important aspect of which had been the publication abroad of articles critical of the Soviet government. After a government trial the two accused were sent to work in labour camps. Other trials followed a similar pattern in the 1970s. Some dissidents, not even

This photograph, taken secretly in a Soviet court room, shows Sinyavsky and Daniel on trial for anti-Soviet activities. Such trials showed that in the 1960s and 1970s the Soviet Union was still unprepared to allow full human rights.

allowed a trial, were held against their will in psychiatric hospitals. In the 1970s the writer Solzhenitsyn and the scientist Sakharov became important dissident leaders. Solzhenitsyn's *Gulag Archipelago*, with its sharply-observed descriptions of life in Soviet prison camps, was widely acclaimed in the West, but was condemned by the Soviet authorities as 'unfounded slander'. Subsequently Solzhenitsyn fled to the West. Throughout the 1970s there was continuing evidence of Soviet anti-semitism and many Jews were prevented from leaving the Soviet Union and settling in Israel.

At Helsinki in 1975 the government of the Soviet Union signed a collective agreement on the future security and peace of Europe. A part of this agreement concerned the issue of human rights:

> The participating states will respect the equal rights of peoples and their right to self-determination, acting at all times in conformity with the purposes and principles of the Charter of the United Nations and with the relevant norms of international law, including those relating to territorial integrity of states.

In the late 1970s the Soviet Union's continued disregard for human rights became an issue which concerned many Western governments more acutely than before. As examples of the denial of human rights continued, these Western governments became more forceful in their criticisms, though their views had little practical effect on Soviet policy and were of little practical help to the persecuted dissidents.

In relations with the West, détente became the goal of the Soviet Union. Visits were paid by Soviet leaders to Western countries. The agreements of the early 1970s between East and West Germany were encouraged. Though the Soviet Union proved a tough negotiator, as shown in the final chapter, progress was made at the Strategic Arms Limitation Talks in the late 1970s. A more serious aspect of foreign affairs from the Soviet Union's point of view was the continuing decline of relations with Communist China, a decline which became even more serious as Communist China sought an even closer understanding with the West.

Questions

40. Study the extract on page 141 from a speech by a Soviet leader and then answer questions (a) to (d) which follow.
    (a) (i) Give the year in which this speech was delivered,
        (ii) name the Soviet leader who delivered it, and
        (iii) outline the rise to power of the Soviet leader named in (a) (ii).
        (1+1+3)
    (b) Explain the circumstances to which the speaker is referring in his first sentence in this extract.
        (5)
    (c) (i) What do you understand by the *cult of the individual*?
        (ii) Name *one* other Communist leader, *outside* the Soviet Union, who may be said to have developed such a cult.
        (iii) Show to what extent the speaker named in (a) (ii) developed such a cult during the years after this speech.
        (1+1+4)
    (d) Show the importance of the work of this speaker in the development of the economy of the Soviet Union during the years after this speech.
        (4)

41. Show how Stalin continued to rule the Soviet Union as a dictatorship during the years after the Second World War. To what extent was there a relaxation of this dictatorship under Khrushchev?

42. Examine the significance within the Soviet Union during the years since 1945 of (a) the development of the agricultural and industrial economy of the country and (b) the suppression of the political and civil liberties of its citizens.

15
Communism in eastern Europe

Of all the countries involved in the Second World War, the Soviet Union suffered the greatest loss of life and after the war made the greatest gains in both influence and territory. In 1945 Communist governments came into being in what were often termed the Soviet *satellites* of Poland, East Germany, Hungary, Romania, Bulgaria, Yugoslavia and Albania. In 1948 Czechoslovakia also became Communist. Soviet influence was asserted in the areas of the Middle East and of the Far East which bordered on the vast Soviet land mass. The immense efforts of the Great Patriotic War had not been without their reward.

Attempts at union among the Communist states

As the Soviet Union's alliance with the Western powers collapsed towards the end of the Second World War, the old interwar hostility between the Western powers and the Soviet Union developed into a situation of Cold War. It became essential for the Soviet Union to be certain of its control of the countries of eastern and central Europe. In spite of the existence of many economic and cultural differences between these countries, the Soviet Union sought to create a closer union among them and a closer dependence by them on the Soviet Union. In 1947 the *Cominform* (Communist Information Bureau) was created. It was in some respects a successor to the earlier *Comintern*, which had aimed to spread Communism, and which had been abolished in 1943 as a gesture of friendship to the West, prompted by the common wartime struggle. In Stalin's time the Cominform developed as an effec-

tive instrument for maintaining control of the satellites, though its importance declined after his death, and the Cominform was abolished in 1956.

Comecon (Council for Mutual Economic Aid) was established in 1949 but, in contrast to the Cominform, it was relatively insignificant in Stalin's time and its importance increased only after his death. Yugoslavia was an associate member, but the other satellites were full members of Comecon, whose purpose was to foster economic cooperation among members. Under Stalin, Comecon asserted a highly dictatorial policy throughout the satellites, insisting on rapid industrialization and collectivization and forcibly transferring goods to the Soviet Union on terms which were unfavourable to the satellites. Part of the 1956 de-Stalinization programme admitted that Comecon had earlier been employed dictatorially against the satellites. Thereafter it developed a new role and worked more wholeheartedly for the interests of all its members. Loans were made to members by the Soviet Union, technical information was freely exchanged between members and flexibly-applied planning made it possible for some countries to specialize in certain products. As a result of these more helpful policies, Comecon was able to give valuable assistance in the development of trade within eastern and central Europe. Though there were marked differences between the Communist-based Comecon and the capitalist-based EEC, they both developed at the same time and Comecon may be regarded, with some reservations, as the Communist response to the developing EEC.

Similarly, the Warsaw Pact may be regarded as the Communist military response to the development of the North Atlantic

Treaty Organization (NATO), considered in chapter 20. The immediate reason for the Warsaw Pact was the entry of West Germany into NATO, a move which the Soviet Union had consistently opposed. Two months after West Germany's entry into NATO, in May 1955, the satellite states, again with the exception of the rebellious Yugoslavia, signed a treaty of Friendship, Cooperation and Mutual Aid. The Warsaw Pact gave formal recognition to the presence of Soviet troops in satellite countries and it allowed for a strengthening of the defences of the satellite states. Like NATO, its form of agreement was acceptable to the United Nations. But the Warsaw Pact had a particular value to the Soviet Union at times when satellite states were in rebellion, as any participation in suppressing rebellion by the Warsaw Pact members could be seen as common action by the forces of all the member countries.

Poland

Reasons of strategy, considered towards the end of chapter 13, made the Soviet Union determined to establish and maintain firm control of Poland. In 1945 the frontier changes of Poland and the Communist government therein were both imposed at virtual Soviet dictation which the Western powers had done little to resist. This seemingly dictatorial behaviour deepened the traditional hostility between the government of the Soviet Union and the people of Poland. To keep its control of the country, the Soviet Union practised policies of repression of the Polish people.

More than in any other east European country, the Roman Catholic church became a strong opponent of the Communist government, its leader, Cardinal Wyszynski, being particularly outspoken in his condemnations of the state. The underlying opposition of the Polish people towards Soviet control waited only for the opportunity which came when the de-Stalinization policies of 1956 suggested a slackening of the Soviet hold. Rioting in the town of Poznan in June 1956 was the first open demonstration of the wish

of the Polish people for fuller control of their own country. Though the riots were suppressed by the Polish government itself, the new Polish Communist leader, Gomulka, showed a spirited, if limited, independence of Moscow by refusing to reinstate some of the more repressive ministers after the rioting had been ended.

Gomulka continued in power for the next fourteen years. Many who had supported him in 1956 became disappointed by the heavy-handed direction which his rule increasingly employed. In foreign relations, Gomulka took important steps towards a better understanding between Poland and West Germany, considered in more detail in the following chapter. But the internal Polish situation worsened in the late 1960s, many Poles becoming discontented with the declining economy and the increasing political repression practised by the government. Young people in particular were critical of the Polish civil service; writers were becoming more outspoken in their criticisms. Price rises led to food riots and strikes, especially in the north of the country, in December 1970. Though strong tactics were used to suppress disorders, Gomulka was compelled to resign.

The new Party Secretary, Edward Gierek, made a successful appeal to the Poles for support for Communism and their country's links with the Soviet Union. He promised to involve the Poles more purposefully in the country's economic and political development and took steps to fulfil this promise in subsequent years. The 1970s, though not free of some strikes and disorders, were less troubled than the 1960s. But the election of the Polish Cardinal Wojtyla as Pope John-Paul II, in October 1978, received a widespread and enthusiastic response from many Polish people, vividly demonstrating the continued Catholic nationalist feelings.

Hungary

Hungary was the only satellite to have had an earlier experience of Communist rule at the time of Bela Kun's short-lived government in 1919. As has been shown earlier, Hungary was an ally of Germany before and during the Second World War and it was the scene of some bitter, last-ditch fighting by the Germans in the spring of 1945. As Hungary had been an ally of Germany, it is not surprising that it failed to submit readily to Communism. However, an important factor leading to the Hungarian acceptance of Communism was the continued presence of the Red Army in the country during the postwar years. Elections later in 1945 returned a coalition government in which the Communists were represented. In the 1947 election the Communists increased their vote, and in the following two years opposition political parties were forcibly dissolved. At the time of the election of May 1949 the electorate was presented only with a single list of candidates of the People's Front, which consisted of the Communists and their political allies.

The road to full control in Hungary had therefore been a more difficult one for the Communists in Hungary than it had been for Communists in other east European countries. The Red Army and secret police silenced opposition, but did not destroy it. Declining living standards, the result of imposed, Soviet-orientated economic policies, kept opposition alive. As in Poland, a focus of opposition existed in the Roman Catholic church, then under the leadership of Cardinal Mindszenty, whose outspoken condemnation of the Communist régime led to his public trial and imprisonment in 1949.

The de-Stalinization programme of 1956 afforded the opportunity for rebellion. Popular opposition led to the resignation in July 1956 of Rakosi, a Stalinist and one of the most hated of the government ministers. Further modest concessions did nothing to quell the mounting opposition and increasing demands for a more democratic system within Hungary. In late October, as a result of the government forces opening fire on demonstrators, opposition became more widespread and the government resigned. Imre Nagy, a supporter of a more liberal and independent form of Communism for Hungary, was appointed Prime Minister. He used the opportunity of his popular, revolutionary support to declare political freedom in Hungary and to demand from the Soviet Union the withdrawal of Hungary from the Warsaw Pact and the establishment of Hungary as a neutral state. If the Soviet Union submitted to these demands, then Hungary would be lost as a satellite. On 4 November 1956, on the excuse that their action was to suppress right-wing Fascist elements, Soviet tanks were sent to suppress the Hungarian rising. Bitter fighting and much loss of life took place in the streets of Budapest until, a week later, the situation was firmly under Soviet military control. Janos Kadar, an earlier Nagy supporter who had turned against him during the revolution, was created Prime Minister and, with the support of the Soviet forces, began persecution of those who had been prominent in the revolution. Many people were arrested and many were executed, including Imre Nagy.

No positive response was made by the Western world to the events in Hungary in November 1956. The leading powers of the West were occupied with the Anglo-French invasion of Suez, which occurred on the very same days as the Soviet invasion of Hungary. Nagy's appeal to the United Nations went virtually unheeded. Many non-aligned countries, conscious of the value of Soviet economic aid, refused to vote for the withdrawal of Soviet troops from Hungary when the motion was put in the United Nations. Had the West not been so preoccupied by Suez, it is possible that stronger protests may have been made at the Soviet action, but it is unlikely that any intervention would have been made to forestall it, as such action could have risked world war. The most that Western countries did was to try to accommodate the large numbers of refugees who fled from Hungary as the Soviet invasion took place.

Kadar's government began in sad circumstances. In practice his work as Prime Minister between 1956–58 and between 1961–65 was of much practical value to Hungary. He gave much concentration to the development of the Hungarian economy and to the improvement of living standards, thereby

The head of a statue of the former Russian dictator lies smashed in a Budapest street during the Hungarian rising of 1956. But the new rulers of the Soviet Union had no intention of allowing Hungary's bid for independence to succeed.

removing one of the main sources of the 1956 discontent. While remaining totally loyal to Moscow, he gave no encouragement to Stalinist-type politicians and carefully relaxed some of the rigid suppression reimposed just after the revolution.

Yugoslavia: the creation of a unique Communist state

Yugoslavia, 'the land of the southern Slavs', was created at the end of the First World War, as has been shown in chapter 2. When the Germans invaded in April 1941 the country was therefore still comparatively young and it still showed signs of tension between different Slav groupings, especially between the Serbs of the south and central areas, and the Croats of the northern areas. But the German invasion brought the different groups together in a spirit of resistance that was virtually unequalled in any other part of Nazi-dominated Europe. The mountainous terrain of much of the interior of the country made wide-spread guerrilla warfare highly effective.

There were two resistance movements. In the earlier stages of the war the more important were the *Chetniks*, led by Mihailovic.

This group showed a strong sense of traditional nationalism, had links with the exiled royal family, and tended to represent rather narrowly the interests of the Serbs: not all of its members proved fully reliable, as some Chetniks collaborated with the invaders. Members of the other group were known as the *Partisans* and were led by the Secretary of the Yugoslav Communist party, Josip Broz, who acquired the nickname of Tito. The Partisans aimed not only to drive the invaders from Yugoslavia but also to create a Communist government, an objective which they had planned before the war had started. Though much of their internal support came from the Croats, they did not seek to represent only Croat interests. The importance of Tito's fight against the Nazis was recognized by Western leaders and by Soviet leaders between 1944 and 1945, and Tito was in constant touch with both sides. By the time the Red Army entered Yugoslavia in October 1944, the Partisans had effectively rid their country of the Nazis.

At the end of the war there was no real prospect of the monarchy returning. Tito's Partisans received immense popular support in elections held towards the end of 1945. Yugoslavia was created a republic and Tito then sought to bring about the changes in the Yugoslavian economy and society to which the Partisans had pledged themselves during the war. Meantime his popular support throughout the country was increased by the Yugoslavian acquisition of the Istrian Peninsula from defeated Italy.

In establishing and developing his Communist government, Tito took steps to maintain the independence of his country from Russian domination. The geographical situation of Yugoslavia made achievement of an independent policy easier for Tito than it was for other east European leaders, but it was nevertheless a brave course for an infant Communist state to follow. Tito planned that the economy of Yugoslavia should be developed for the benefit of Yugoslavia itself and should not necessarily be linked to Soviet economic objectives. He was prepared to accept United Nations aid in order to achieve the much needed improvement in the Yugo-slavian standard of living. He refused to permit the presence of Russian police inside Yugoslavia. He also embarked on an independent foreign policy towards the neighbouring Communist states of Albania and Bulgaria.

For the first time, the Soviet Union was confronted by a minor Communist state refusing to accept dictation from Moscow. The extension of Communism into so many neighbouring countries in the postwar years made it essential for the Soviet Union to correct this example of insubordination. An exchange of letters between Moscow and the Yugoslavian Communist leadership took place, but the Soviet Union was unable to bring about any change in the Yugoslavian attitude. Nor was the Soviet Union able to develop any internal Communist opposition to Tito, despite considerable efforts at both objectives. In June 1948 the Soviet Union arranged for the expulsion of Yugoslavia from membership of the Cominform.

The Cominform condemns these anti-Soviet conceptions of leading members of the Yugoslav Communist party as incompatible with Marxism-Leninism and as suitable for Nationalists. The leading members of the Yugoslav Communist party are slipping off the Marxist-Leninist path to the Nationalist, Kulak road.

Tito's Yugoslavia

Despite this doctrinal emphasis, the real cause of the expulsion was Russian anger at Yugoslavian defiance. The expulsion was followed by the placing of a Soviet economic and military blockade on Yugoslavia, but this had little practical effect. For the remainder of the Stalin years, Yugoslavia was regarded as an outcast from the Communist bloc.

Development under Tito

In practice, being an outcast did no great harm to the Yugoslavian people. The economy was already organized to serve Yugoslavian interests and Yugoslavia continued to receive United Nations and Western assistance. Political life, though never deviating from Communism, was able to develop along lines that were far more liberal than those found in the Soviet Union or in the other satellite states. Greater freedom of discussion was allowed and there was more genuine worker participation in industrial and agricultural development. Repression, though less heavy than in other Communist states, was not entirely absent: much international tension was focused in the early 1950s on the case of a friend of Tito and a leading member of his government, Milovan Djilas, whose outspoken criticisms of Yugoslavia's ruling hierarchy led to his imprisonment. His most important publication, *The New Class*, was a highly-perceptive study of the Communist administration of the satellite countries during the postwar years.

The thaw which occurred after the death of Stalin gave the Soviet government an opportunity to seek a renewed understanding with Yugoslavia. In May 1955 the Soviet leaders Khrushchev and Bulganin paid a visit to Yugoslavia in the course of which they acknowledged Soviet responsibility for the quarrels of the late 1940s. In April 1956 a further gesture of reconciliation was made with the abolition of the Cominform. The reconciliation, however, was neither fundamental nor long-lasting. In the late 1950s Soviet-Yugoslavian friction again arose, begun this time by Soviet condemnation of

what the Soviet Union termed Yugoslavia's *revisionism*, its attempts to adjust the practice of Communism to Yugoslavia's requirements. Since then the relationship between the two countries has remained unsteady. The Soviet Union's ready military response to opposition in the satellite countries, shown most notably in Hungary in 1956 and in Czechoslovakia in 1968, suggests that it has been only the physical difficulty of launching an invasion of Yugoslavia that has prevented the Soviet Union from doing so. Such an attitude cannot be the basis of a satisfactory international relationship.

In the years since 1945 Yugoslavia has many other achievements to its credit, some of which are a result, in one way or another, of the independent, liberal type of Communism which Tito has developed. The standard of living of many Yugoslavians was improved by Tito's flexible application of Communist economic theory to his country's needs. Agricultural cooperatives have existed in Yugoslavia, but membership of them has not been compulsory. Cooperatives for the loan of agricultural machinery have been widely used, but the usual pattern of development has remained individual holdings and a market economy. As may be expected in a comparatively new area of the economy, industry has developed within a stricter Communist framework, with all major industry nationalized and with worker participation in its direction. Foreign tourists found their comparative freedom of movement an added attraction to visiting the country, and the Yugoslavian economy has benefited considerably from tourism.

In a country of mixed Slav races such as Yugoslavia, it would be impossible to eliminate all friction between the different regions. Economic differences have contributed to these frictions. The northern industrial areas of Croatia and Slovenia have felt that their more advanced economy has been used to subsidize the more backward economy of the central and southern agricultural areas of Serbia and Macedonia. Parts of the country have also felt that as the Yugoslavian capital of Belgrade is also the Serbian capital, the influence of Serbia has

The Communist leader Tito speaks at a political rally in Yugoslavia. In spite of Soviet pressure, he continued to develop his country as a leading non-aligned state in world affairs.

come to dominate the country. The creation of six regional parliaments has shown Tito's wish to diminish these differences and strengthen Yugoslavian unity.

Tito's foreign policy has fluctuated. Though at times expressing support for the Soviet Union, the policy that he has followed most strongly is that of *non-alignment*. Yugoslavia has not joined either the Warsaw Pact or NATO. In the 1960s and 1970s links were forged with the non-aligned countries of the third world. Many international conferences that have been concerned with the interests of the non-aligned countries have taken place in Belgrade, such as those in the autumn of 1961 and in the autumn of 1976, when the Helsinki agreements of the previous year were renewed.

Yugoslavia owes more to the dedication and fearlessness of its leader than does any

other Communist country in Europe. For a European country, it has developed in a unique way. The question that inevitably overhangs the future of Yugoslavia is whether this unique experiment will survive the death of the man to whom it owes so much.

Czechoslovakia: the 1948 coup

The country of Czechoslovakia had little cause to feel gratitude towards the Western powers after the Second World War. The abandonment of this small, central-European country by the West at the time of the Munich crisis in the autumn of 1938 had done nothing to prevent the eventual outbreak of war in Europe, and had resulted in a Nazi occupation of the whole of their country by the

spring of 1939. Resistance to the Nazi-occu-
pation had started even before the outbreak
of the Second World War and both Communist and non-Communist elements
became increasingly active. The Communists
joined forces with the Soviet armies as they
entered the country in the war's closing
months. After the war, the Soviet Union
accepted the return of the exiled Benes as
the Czechoslovak President, provided he
included Communists in his government.
Supported by the presence of the Red Army,
these Communist members, though few in
number, were able to assert much influence:
the postwar social and economic reforms,
the banning of the prewar right-wing parties
and the increased powers of the local Communist-based *national committees* were all the
result of their work. Further, Benes had no
alternative but to accept the loss to the Soviet
Union of the eastern province of Ruthenia,
on the grounds that the national committees
in that province had voted to be united with
the Soviet Union. In these circumstances,
the chances of Czechoslovakia achieving
genuine independence were slim.

The Soviet Union prevented Czechoslovakia from accepting the American offer of
Marshall Aid in 1947. This Soviet dictation,
based solely on the will to maintain Soviet
influence in Czechoslovakia, regardless of the
economic advantages that Marshall Aid
offered to a war-stricken country, reduced
the support of the Communist party within
the country. It seemed likely that in the
elections due to be held in the spring of
1948, the Communist party would do badly.
In February 1948, in order to prevent its
possible electoral defeat, the Communist
party staged a coup, which resulted in the
establishment of a Communist government.
It may be that the coup owed something
to Soviet encouragement, though its role in
the events of February 1948 is not absolutely
clear.

Probably no other move in the Soviet satellite states was of such importance to the
West as this coup in February 1948: its impact
on the military thinking of western Europe
is considered in chapter 20. For Czechoslovakia, shortly after the coup, a new Com-

munist constitution was issued. Benes, whose
popularity was so great that he was allowed
to continue as President, refused to accept
the new constitution, resigned in June 1948
and died shortly after. The body of the other
leading non-Communist politician, the Foreign Secretary, Jan Masaryk (son of the
founding father of Czechoslovakia, Thomas
Masaryk), was found a few days after the
coup on the pavement below an open win-
dow. It has never been established whether
depression at the events of the coup had
led to his suicide or whether he had been
killed by those working for the coup. The
elimination of Benes and Masaryk removed
the two leaders around whom there could
have developed an opposition to the Communist government. There was little possibility in 1948, the year of the Soviet condemnation of Tito, of any deviation from strict
Moscow allegiance. Not until 1968, twenty
years later, was this situation to show any
significant change.

Czechoslovakia: the Prague Spring and its aftermath

Under the rule of Novotny, who combined
the role of President of Czechoslovakia with
that of First Secretary of the Czechoslovak
Communist party, the country's political and
economic life remained firmly linked to and
dominated by the Soviet Union. The first
stirrings of dissatisfaction with these close
Soviet connections were heard when the
Czechoslovak economy virtually collapsed in
the mid-1960s. Dissatisfaction was expressed
by the central committee of the Czechoslovak
Communist party in the autumn of 1967,
and the demand was swiftly made for the
separation of the posts of President and First
Secretary. In early 1968 Novotny retired
from politics. General Svoboda, a respected
military hero, became President, and Alexander Dubcek, who had a strong, popular
following in Czechoslovakia, became First
Secretary. The new administration embarked
on a thorough reformulation of the country's
policies. Dubcek's policies were concerned
initially with the economy, which he decen-

tralized and freed from the rigid organization that for some years had stifled its development. Other changes followed. The press was no longer censored; at Communist party and trade union meetings full participation by members was encouraged; the activities of the secret police were curbed and political prisoners were released. There were limits to the new policies: Dubcek was a committed Communist and it was no part of his policy to go so far as to allow opposition political parties or sever completely Czechoslovakia's connections with the Soviet Union. The Dubcek administration aimed to create 'Socialism with a human face', and the Czechoslovak people in the spring of 1968 gave this new type of Socialism a spontaneously warm welcome.

But the government of the Soviet Union was much concerned by these events in Czechoslovakia, which it judged to be getting beyond the control of the Dubcek administration. In spite of Dubcek's prohibition of opposition parties, some Czechoslovak political groups were nevertheless emerging, and only a short step would be needed to transform these political groups into opposition parties. If this process were then copied by other east European satellites, Soviet control could be seriously undermined. Czechoslovakia's new attitudes were most likely to lead to an easing of her relations with western Europe, which might endanger the defences of the Warsaw Pact, and the trading arrangements of Comecon. Soviet dissatisfaction was shown by extensive manoeuvres by the armies of the Warsaw Pact countries on Czechoslovak soil throughout the summer of 1968. Meantime in a series of meetings with the Soviet leaders, Dubcek attempted to assure them that they had no cause to view the events in his country with any anxiety. His efforts appeared to have succeeded when in early August 1968 a meeting of the Warsaw Pact powers was held in relaxed circumstances at Bratislava, in Czechoslovakia. Here it was agreed, among other matters, that the military manoeuvres in Czechoslovakia should end.

But the Bratislava meeting was merely a feint. Quite unexpectedly, during the night of 20–21 August 1968, Soviet tanks and troops, assisted by those of some other Warsaw Pact countries, invaded Czechoslovakia, on the excuse that they had been called in to suppress counter-revolution. The troops took over the administration of the country and arrested Dubcek and most of the other leaders. The Czechoslovak people were outraged. They attempted to persuade the invading troops that the invasion was uncalled for and they adopted attitudes of passive resistance; some thousands fled from the country as refugees. Dubcek and the other leaders had meanwhile been taken to Moscow where they were compelled to sign an agreement to abandon many of the features of their new programme. They had little choice but to comply. Later in the year a further agreement was imposed, allowing for the permanent stationing of Soviet troops within Czechoslovakia.

The Czechoslovak people continued to show their opposition to the invasion and to the Soviet dictation of their country's policies. In January 1969, Jan Pallach, a young Czechoslovak student, committed suicide by burning himself alive in the central square of the city of Prague, as a gesture of protest against Soviet policies in his country. Jan Pallach's funeral became an occasion of a widespread and moving protest against the Soviet Union. In March 1969 anti-Soviet rioting broke out in Prague, sparked off by a Czechoslovak victory against the Soviet Union in an ice-hockey match played in Stockholm. The Soviet Union interpreted this as a sign that Dubcek could still not control the country adequately and they deposed him from his post as First Secretary, putting in his place Gustav Husak, a Communist leader of the earlier Novotny type. Dubcek was shortly afterwards expelled from the Communist party.

The Prague spring was an occasion, initially, of great hope and, ultimately, of bitter disappointment. Little of the work of the Dubcek administration survived: many of the old problems reappeared. Husak proved a loyal servant of Moscow: by means of political repression, he took all possible steps to ensure that the country did not again

A Prague citizen attempts to reason with one of the Russian soldiers sent to resecure Soviet control of Czechoslovakia after the upheavals of August 1968.

deviate in the way it did between 1968–69. Opposition to the Husak régime was for some years almost non-existent, but at the beginning of 1977 a group of Czechoslovak dissidents formed an organization called *Charter 77* which pledged itself to work for the restoration of human rights in Czechoslovakia. The particular method they adopted was to publicize details of fellow-countrymen who were imprisoned by the authorities or subject to disabilities in their education or work. Thus the issue of human rights in Czechoslovakia was effectively revived.

The emergence of Charter 77 had been preceded by the Helsinki agreement of 1975 and the review of the agreement at Belgrade in 1976: it was therefore part of a wide assault on Soviet inflexibility towards the human rights issue. Nevertheless, the thousand or so Czechoslovaks who, by the end of 1978, had given active support to Charter 77, were subject to police harassment and other disabilities.

Questions

43. Study the photograph on page 149 and the photograph on page 155 and then answer questions (a) to (d) which follow.
    (a) Name the country against whose influence the people in both these photographs were protesting.

    (1)
    (b) With reference to the photograph on page 149:
        (i) name the former ruler of the country referred to in (a), the head of whose broken statue is shown here.

        (ii) account for the hostility shown by the people of this city towards this former ruler.
        (iii) how do you account for the action of these people in this year?
        (iv) show how the actions of these people were eventually suppressed.

        (1+2+2+3)
    (c) With reference to the photograph on page 155:
        (i) trace the events during this year which led to the situation shown in the photograph.
        (ii) suggest what might be the main points being made by the protester in the foreground.
        (iii) show how the country represented by the man on the right was able to reassert its control.

        (3+2+2)
    (d) Outline the history of *one* of these two protesting countries from the time of the photograph to the present day.

    (4)

44. Trace the rise to power of Tito. Show how far he succeeded as President of Yugoslavia in his work of (a) improving his country's economy, (b) resisting pressure from the Soviet Union and (c) developing a non-aligned foreign policy.

45. How do you account for the establishment of Soviet influence in eastern Europe during the years between 1944 and 1949? Show how and with what results, *one* of the east European countries has attempted to throw off Soviet control.

16

Germany and France since 1945

Postwar Germany

Quite apart from the psychological impact of military defeat and knowledge of their government's horrific racial extermination programme, the German people faced severe practical problems in the immediate postwar years. Foremost was finding basic means of subsistence and survival. The land advances and the aerial attacks of their enemies had seriously dislocated the German economy. The forced transfer of German minorities to Germany from neighbouring countries, especially Poland and Czechoslovakia, added to these problems. Life in these desperate circumstances was a struggle for survival.

Defeated, humiliated and impoverished, the German people were also divided into the four zones agreed by the Allies at Yalta and Potsdam, as shown at the end of chapter 13. Though sharp differences were later to emerge between the Allied occupants of the zones, immediately after the war their collective attitude towards Germany was unsympathetic. This was shown especially in the seizure of German goods as reparations. Leading members of the Nazi party were tried by the Allies at Nuremberg, and a strict pursuit of a policy of de-Nazification imposed restrictions on any who had been members of the Nazi party.

Gradually Germany's economic plight improved. As it did so, differences between the Allies began to develop. In the autumn of 1946, the United States began to help in the reconstruction of Germany, and in the spring of 1947, the economies of the American and British zones were combined, the French zone joining them later in the year. Thus West Germany began to take shape, and from 1947 differences between this part of Germany and the Soviet zone of East Germany developed. In the same year, the granting of Marshall Aid further aligned the western zones of Germany with the Western powers.

As the division of Germany became more definite, the prospect of re-uniting the country became increasingly unlikely. Without a united Germany there could be no German peace treaty.

The Berlin Airlift

By 1947 Germany was a crucial area of Cold War conflict. In East Germany, the Soviet Union sought to create a Communist system, under the rule of Walter Ulbricht.

German divisions after 1945

This insipid German Communist, who had been exiled in the Soviet Union during Hitler's rule, was returned to Germany in 1945 by the Soviet authorities. The support of the Red army enabled the Communist party to dominate the politics of East Germany.

In the West, the occupying powers helped towards the gradual re-emergence of German political life and of the two parties which were to play an important role in the West German revival: the Christian Democrats and the Social Democrats. The Christian Democrats were the successors of the Centre party that had flourished on German Roman Catholic support before Hitler's time. Its appeal now was wider: it represented moderate Conservative opinion and it aimed at a political and economic revival of Germany. The Social Democrats were the party of the left, successors of the prewar Socialist party; they aimed to realize Socialist goals but they were firmly opposed to Communism. The Free Democrats were a small, moderate third party. Politically, therefore, the two parts of Germany were developing in very different directions.

Economic issues sharpened these differences. In February 1948 the occupying powers in the western zones set up an economic advisory council to oversee the economic development of their zones. This appeared

An aeroplane arriving in West Berlin to help sustain the city during the Soviet siege between 1948 and 1949. Notice the evidence of bomb damage, caused a few years earlier partly by those powers which now gave invaluable aid and support.

to be the beginnings of a German government for the western zones. In June, in order to encourage the development of the West German economy, the currency in the western zones were reorganized. This policy eventually helped to produce the desired results for the economy in the West, but it was viewed unfavourably at the time by the Soviet Union as another hostile move.

The developing conflict became focused on the divided city of Berlin. Earlier in 1948 the Allied Control Commission, which administered the city, and on which all the occupying powers were represented, had broken up in disagreement over their conflicting policies. Now the currency reorganization led to a complete breakdown in relations. As Berlin lay within the Soviet zone of Germany, the Soviet authorities were able to take action there. In late June 1948 they placed a. blockade on all traffic by road, rail and canal from West Germany to West Berlin, thereby placing the people of West Berlin in a state of siege, as the West Berliners normally relied heavily on West German supplies. The Western powers interpreted these Soviet moves as threatening a Soviet takeover of West Berlin, and as another move in the advance of Soviet power in Europe.

The United States and other leading Western powers felt that they must take steps to preserve their presence in West Berlin. The situation was so dangerous that if the Western powers had taken military action to end the blockade, the conflict might have grown into a major war. They therefore decided on the more moderate policy of the Berlin airlift, supplying West Berlin by air. The people of West Berlin, who showed every wish to remain under the protection of the Western powers, cooperated fully with this airlift, extending the two airports of West Berlin and constructing a third to accommodate the vastly increased air traffic. The airlift was a costly venture, borne mainly by the United States, but the advantages to the Western powers were twofold. It avoided a major great-power confrontation, and demonstrated the determination of the West to preserve its position in West Berlin. In May 1949, after the airlift had been operat-

ing for eleven months, the Soviet Union gave way and lifted their blockade of the city.

The Berlin blockade of 1948–49 was a major incident in the Cold War. It had significant consequences for both great-power relations and internal German development. It had demonstrated the need for the Western powers to combine forces to prevent Communist aggression such as that threatened at Berlin, and it was therefore one of the strongest factors encouraging the formation in 1949 of the North Atlantic Treaty Organization (NATO), as shown in chapter 20. It had also deepened the divisions of Germany to such an extent that there was now no prospect of the country being reunited in the foreseeable future. Both East Germany and West Germany took steps to strengthen their positions.

West and East Germany

Building upon the developing life in West Germany and upon the encouragement of the Western powers, shown especially in the currency reorganization of June 1948 and the support during the Berlin blockade, steps were taken to establish the *Federal Republic of Germany*. During 1949 under close Western supervision, the Germans framed a constitution, taking care to avoid the difficulties into which the Weimar Republic had fallen. The basis of the new constitution was the federation of the eleven *länder* (provinces) into which the western zones were divided. All local affairs were to be conducted by the *landtag*, the local parliament that each province possessed. The federal parliament, at Bonn, was to consist of two houses: the *Bundestag*, elected by universal suffrage to represent the people of West Germany, and the *Bundesrat*, composed of at least three members of each province, representing the opinions of the various *landtag*. The President was to be elected by both houses for a period of five years, but his powers were less important than those of the Federal Chancellor, who was elected by the Bundestag. Parties securing less than five percent of the votes cast in an election were to be excluded from parliament, and in this way it was hoped that the Federal Republic would avoid the confusions typical both of the Weimar Republic and the French Fourth Republic.

At the same time the régime in East Germany also became more firmly established. The East's response to the creation of the Federal Republic in West Germany was to bring into being their own *German Democratic Republic* in October 1949. When elections were held later in the year, Ulbricht's Socialist Unity party was the only party allowed to put up candidates. Life in the German Democratic Republic showed few of the economic benefits found in the Federal Republic. The economic plight of East Germany worsened still further as the Soviet Union continued to demand reparations.

Discontent with this situation in East Germany showed itself in a number of ways. In June 1953 strikes in East Berlin developed into riots similar to those which took place in neighbouring Poland at the same time. Only the intervention of Soviet troops brought about the suppression of these riots. The steady flow of refugees from East to West Germany and from East to West Berlin throughout these years provided continuing evidence of the unacceptability of life in the German Democratic Republic.

Christian Democrat government in the Federal Republic

The first general election for the government of the new Federal Republic was held in August 1949. The Christian Democrats won by a narrow majority and their leader, Konrad Adenauer, became Chancellor. Already 73 years old, he was destined to remain Chancellor for the next fourteen years. He had been active in local government during the Kaiser's rule in Germany, and in 1917 had become Mayor of Cologne. His opposition to National Socialism had been vigorous and he had twice been imprisoned for short periods by the Nazis. In 1945 he was re-appointed Mayor of Cologne by the Americans and subsequently gave active

support to the newly-formed Christian Democrat party. Under Adenauer, and under his two Christian Democrat successors, Ludwig Erhard (1963–66) and Kurt Kiesinger (1966–69), the Federal Republic made outstanding advances in economic development and successfully played a part in European and world affairs.

Throughout the 1950s industrial production within the Federal Republic expanded to an extent unparalleled elsewhere in Europe. Unemployment figures dropped to a virtually non-existent level and agricultural output far exceeded the prewar achievement. How did this remarkable economic 'miracle', as it was called, come about? Raw materials and labour were in good supply in West Germany: new economic developments therefore had plentiful resources on which to build. Many foreign workers from poorer European countries were attracted by employment prospects in Germany. West Germany inherited a long-established tradition of German industrialization which the war had seriously interrupted but not totally broken. In some respects there were advantages to be gained from starting with new factories and new equipment, which wartime devastation had made necessary. The policy pursued by Ludwig Erhard, Adenauer's Minister for Economic Affairs, was to encourage the economic development and to impose only slight government direction and intervention. The revived trade unions pursued moderate policies, discouraging strikes and industrial unrest, thus contributing further to the stable and purposeful atmosphere in which the economy was able to flourish. Though in the mid-1960s an economic decline set in, leading to an increase in unemployment and a decrease in industrial output, the advances of the previous decade had created a position of economic strength which enabled the Federal Republic to weather these temporary difficulties.

The stable, successful development of West Germany in these ways made it easier for the Federal Republic to become involved in European affairs in the 1950s. It was one of the leading members of the European Coal and Steel Community from 1952, and of

President de Gaulle and Chancellor Adenauer, with interpreter in the middle, negotiate details of the 1963 treaty of friendship. The policy of both men in seeking amicable relations between their countries was a bold attempt to end deeply felt suspicions.

the European Economic Community from 1957, its own economic progress being assisted by the slackening of trade restrictions which these organizations encouraged. Closer relations were established with France. De Gaulle's strong support for the position of the Federal Republic in relation to the Democratic Republic was the basis of sound Franco-German relations during these years, helped further by the personal understanding that de Gaulle and Adenauer had for each other. In 1963 a treaty of friendship was signed between the two countries. No longer were Franco-German relations as troubled and as dangerous as they had been on many earlier occasions: one instance of this was the lack of controversy surrounding the transfer to the Federal Republic in January 1957 of the Saarland, earlier linked economically to France.

The rearmament of Germany became a highly controversial issue in the 1950s. Many Germans associated re-armament with the aggression of National Socialism and preferred the Federal Republic to remain unarmed; others took the view that only by achieving equality with other nations regarding armaments could the Federal Republic attain real equality of status. The United States government considered that the Federal Republic ought to be re-armed and thus made ready for possible conflict: West Germany was located dangerously near to the Soviet bloc and had already been an area of serious Cold War conflict, at Berlin between 1948–49. In the early 1950s the creation of the European Defence Community was an attempt to make German re-armament appear acceptable to international opinion, by ensuring that Germany would work jointly with others under the control of an international body. As is shown in chapter 20, this attempt failed, but Germany was subsequently admitted to the West European Union and to NATO, where her forces acted jointly with those of other countries.

The Berlin wall

In the 1950s political, economic and military developments aligned the Federal Republic even more firmly with the Western powers. Meantime the continued strengthening of NATO and the Warsaw Pact showed that the tensions of the Cold War had not relaxed. The Federal Republic's *Hallstein doctrine* (named after a senior official at the German Foreign Office) suggested a hardening attitude towards the Democratic Republic: by this doctrine the Federal Republic refused to give its recognition to any country which recognized the German Democratic Republic.

In the late 1950s, as in the late 1940s, tension again focused on Berlin. In November 1958 the Soviet leader, Khrushchev, demanded that the future status of Germany and of Berlin should be the subject of direct discussion between the Federal Republic and the Democratic Republic, an impossible demand in view of the Federal Republic's known, firm refusal to recognize the Democratic Republic. He warned that if after six months the situation remained unresolved, the Soviet Union would itself sign a peace treaty with the German Democratic Republic, an event which could possibly lead to a demand by the Soviet Union for control of West Berlin. In the event, Khrushchev quietly forgot about his six months deadline. Though the atmosphere remained tense, it was eased by a comparatively successful visit that Khrushchev paid to the United States in the summer of 1959. But the government of the Federal Republic became concerned that the comparative harmony between the Soviet Union and the United States might lead to a slackening of the American resolve to defend West Berlin.

A four-power summit conference, attended by Khrushchev and Eisenhower together with President de Gaulle of France and Prime Minister Macmillan of Britain, took place in Paris in May 1960. Its main purpose was to resolve the German problem and prepare the way for a joint peace treaty. Another major issue for discussion was disarmament. Though much hope was placed in the outcome of this conference, in the event it dispersed in confusion and ill-will. The United States had recently put into use over Soviet territory the U2 spy plane, capable of flying with its sophisticated equipment at heights of as much as six kilometres in order to avoid detection. At the start of the conference Khrushchev announced that a U2 plane and its American pilot had been brought down over Soviet territory and he demanded an apology from Eisenhower before he would continue with the conference's main business. On Eisenhower's refusal to give this apology, the conference came to an abrupt end.

The tension over Berlin continued in the succeeding months, while an increased number of atomic tests were held by both the Soviet Union and the United States. In June 1961 an unsuccessful meeting at Vienna between Khrushchev and the new American President, John Kennedy, merely added to the tension. Meanwhile in Berlin itself, the refugee problem was reaching crisis proportions as more and more East Germans fled to the West. Though dangerous and punishable by the authorities of the German Democratic Republic, it was still comparatively easy for East Berliners to cross to the other side. In August 1961, under Soviet direction, the East German authorities began to erect a wall along the forty-kilometre frontier between the two parts of the city. This effectively stopped the flow of refugees, but it did nothing to reduce the tension which continued to overshadow the city for more than another year. Only with the diplomatic conflict over the missiles on Cuba in October 1962, considered in chapter 24, did the threat of war over Berlin slacken.

The wall has remained one of the most dramatic symbols both of a divided Germany and of a divided world. Many East Germans

Checkpoint Charlie, the major crossing point in the divided city of Berlin. Notice the military-style defence on either side, suggesting close scrutiny of people wishing to cross the border.

have been shot in attempting to flee across it to the West. It has been a vivid reminder that the division of Germany is now almost permanent and that the wartime Allies have still been unable to agree a satisfactory peace settlement with Germany. But the Allied powers and the Berliners have both learnt to live with the wall and to accept the absence of a peace settlement. Since the early 1960s the dangers inherent in the division of Germany and of Berlin have lessened. This has followed partly from the acceptance by both sides that little can be done to heal the division and partly from the pursuance of the more conciliatory policies of West Germany's *Ostpolitik* in the late 1960s.

Willy Brandt: the Ostpolitik

In October 1969, for the first time in the history of the Federal Republic, the Social Democrats formed a government and their leader, Willy Brandt, became Chancellor. He only succeeded, however, due to the additional support of the Free Democrats, whose leader, Scheel, became Foreign Minister and Vice Chancellor. The new Chancellor had been well known in Germany as a popular and effective Mayor of West Berlin in the late 1950s and the 1960s. From an early age he had been a committed Socialist and had spent the Hitler years in self-imposed exile in Scandinavia. On appointment as Chancellor in 1969 he announced his programme of moderate reform within Germany and of seeking a better relationship with East European countries and with the German Democratic Republic. It was this latter policy, known as the *Ostpolitik* (the East Policy), that became the distinguishing feature of Brandt's chancellorship in the years between 1969 and 1974.

Positive results of the Ostpolitik came in 1970, with the signing of a treaty with the Soviet Union in August, and with Poland in December. By these treaties, the Federal Republic made clear its acceptance of the frontiers of Europe as they then existed and, in particular, the boundary between the two parts of Germany and the boundary of the Oder-Neisse line between East Germany and Poland. Negotiations were more difficult with East Germany. In March 1970 Brandt became the first Chancellor to visit East Germany when he travelled to Erfurt, where he met Prime Minister Stoph, who in May 1970 paid a return visit to the West German town of Kassel. Both leaders showed their desire for a settlement, and in December 1972 a basic treaty was signed by which they agreed to recognize the permanence of the division of Germany for the time being and to adopt what the treaty called, 'good neighbourly relations'. Not all West Germans approved of this treaty; many were concerned at the apparent abandonment of the Germans in the East. The policy continued in December 1973 with a treaty with Czechoslovakia which brought closer relations and greater harmony in a traditional area of friction. By other less important agreements, the Federal Republic established diplomatic relations with almost all the other east European countries. The Ostpolitik had certainly produced a more peaceful relationship than had existed a decade previously.

Brandt resigned in May 1974, after he had accepted responsibility for allowing a suspected East German spy to continue to work in government offices. The Ostpolitik had been his greatest contribution as Chancellor; his work in domestic affairs had become less effective than was at first hoped. His successor, Helmut Schmidt, also a Social Democrat, gave his main attention to domestic issues during his years as Chancellor.

The Federal Republic in the 1970s

West Germany had her share of the economic problems that troubled most Western nations in the 1970s. In the mid-1970s unemployment rose as high as a million, consumer demand decreased, strikes became more common, and inflation rose. Soon after his appointment, Schmidt cut government expenditure and raised taxation, in an endeavour to restimulate the economy. These, and later measures, helped the economy to improve in some directions. Unemployment remained at about the level of one million but West Germany continued to be one of the leading members of the EEC, and her economy weathered the economic problems of the 1970s more successfully than any other European country. Germany's currency, the Deutschmark, was the leading European currency by the end of the decade.

For the first time since the war the problem of political extremism of the right and of the left became acute. On the right, in the late 1960s, the National Democratic party developed under the leadership of Adolf von Thadden. Though some of its members were former National Socialists and though it wished to place a stronger emphasis on German nationalism, it was not as formidable, at least in its outwardly expressed policies, as prewar National Socialism. Though it had some success in local elections, it never succeeded in achieving the five percent needed in general elections for membership of the Bundestag.

On the left, a terrorist group known as the Baader-Meinhof gang developed, and in the 1970s committed a number of violent outrages, such as the bombing of administrative centres and the kidnapping and murdering of prominent Germans. The objectives which underlay their outrages were muddled. Many observers interpreted the gang's activities in social terms, as a revolt of young, middle-class West Germans against the materialism of life in the Federal Republic. It could also be seen as a revolt against the dominance of the Christian Democrats in the *länder*. For this reason the movement received some limited support in student circles. Though in 1972 the ringleaders were imprisoned, nonetheless the gang's activities continued and in a more ruthless manner. In 1977 Hanns-Martin Schleyer, President of the Employers' Federation, was kidnapped by terrorists, who demanded the release of imprisoned members of their gang in return for his life. The international nature of terrorism in the 1970s was vividly illustrated when a German airliner was hijacked by Arab terrorists, acting in support of the Baader-Meinhof gang. The airliner was eventually landed at Mogadishu in Somalia where, with the agreement of the Somali government, it was successfully stormed by an anti-terrorist unit of the German army in what was the first military action outside Germany by German troops since the end of the Second World War, 32 years earlier. After the news of the success at Mogadishu, Schleyer was murdered by his captors and many of the imprisoned Baader-Meinhof gang committed suicide. Chancellor Schmidt acted throughout with the full agreement of the other political parties and his handling of the situation won him widespread respect.

By the late 1970s, the problems that had concerned the Germans immediately after their wartime defeat, no longer appeared so significant. The problems of the economy and of terrorism were more immediate. But though the Federal Republic has managed to accommodate itself to the divisions of Germany and the lack of a peace settlement, these unresolved issues remain the foremost problems of the West German government.

Postwar France

As the Western Allies advanced across France in the summer of 1944, what remained of the Vichy régime collapsed. Those who during the German occupation had cooperated closely with the enemy were denounced and humiliated. Laval and some 700 other Vichy politicians were executed, Pétain being spared the same fate only on account of his extreme age. After the bitter wartime experience, French political life was inevitably much changed. In the closing stages of the war, Charles de Gaulle, the leader of the Free French, formed a provisional government. But it was the political forces of the left that were strongest, largely because of their leading role in the struggle against Vichy. Meantime the right, which had generally supported Vichy, was discredited: long-established right-wing parties were now in serious decline. But though the left was politically dominant, de Gaulle himself, who continued as President, was distinctly a man of the right.

The history of France during the previous 25 years had shown the inadequacy of the constitution of the Third Republic. As the constitution of the Fourth Republic, adopted after a referendum in October 1946, differed only slightly from the earlier constitution, many of the reasons for instability under the Third Republic were continued under the Fourth. The President was still to be a mere figurehead. Real power continued to be held by the two-chamber assembly, and especially by the lower house. The left naturally welcomed this power balance, as in it, the government would be more directly responsible to the electorate.

In January 1946, while the constitution was being prepared, but before it had been formally accepted, de Gaulle resigned from the presidency. Relations between himself and the assembly on a number of issues, especially the President's concern for a strong French army, were strained. It was already clear that the new constitution would rob the presidency of the powers which de Gaulle felt essential for the maintenance of stability in France. For more than a year, he had little to do with French politics. Then in April 1947 he launched the *Rassemblement du Peuple Français* (RPF, the rally of the French people) as a national movement under his leadership. In local and in general elections the success secured by the RPF demonstrated the continuing support for the policies de Gaulle advocated and for the leadership which, for many of the French, de Gaulle alone could satisfactorily give. Support for the movement declined in the early 1950s, but revived later as the prospect strengthened of de Gaulle becoming President once more.

Political and economic life under the Fourth Republic

The entire history of the Fourth Republic is characterized by political uncertainties unparalleled in any of the major European countries during the postwar years. General elections were held in 1947, 1951 and 1956 and all of them produced assemblies which were divided on most political issues. To the prewar French parties such as the left-wing parties of the Socialists and Communists, the traditional centre party of the Radicals, and the right-wing Republican party, were added the new postwar French parties such as the *Mouvement Republicain Populaire* (MRP, the Republican popular movement) and the Gaullist RPF. In the 1956 election another new party gathered support: the Poujadist party, led by Pierre Poujade. It was based on the support of shopkeepers and people of moderate incomes. As the representation of these different parties in the assembly was approximately equal, governments were able to maintain themselves in power only so long as their policies were acceptable to a majority of the deputies representing the different parties in the assembly. The problems confronting France in these years were so varied that it is not surprising that government changes were frequent, and prime ministers lasted sometimes for only a few weeks. Further, the fact that the governments were so short-lived resulted, in many instances, in these problems remaining unresolved.

In spite of this political uncertainty, some governments of the Fourth Republic did take important policy decisions. It was the French Foreign Minister, Robert Schuman, who proposed the formation of the European Coal and Steel Community, details of which had been worked out by Jean Monnet. From this stemmed the European Economic Community. It was one of the greatest of the Fourth Republic's prime ministers, Pierre Mendes-France, who led his government in 1954 to a retreat from the intolerable position which the French faced in Indochina, considered in chapter 26. In economic matters, in spite of the political divisions between the values of private enterprise and nationalization, substantial economic progress was made. This was very largely attributable to the emphasis given to the planning of the French economy, a matter to which the French gave their attention much earlier than most other West European countries, and which was taken later as a model copied elsewhere. Jean Monnet was an early director of this planning, which besides providing a framework for the much-needed modernization of French industry, also rid France of the economic injustices associated especially with the influence of the 'two hundred families' in the governments of the Third Republic. As a consequence of the importance given to planning, the French industrial production by the mid-1950s had increased on prewar production by approximately 50 percent.

Nevertheless, quite apart from the political chaos, France did face disturbing problems. Agriculture lagged seriously behind the development of industry. Postwar re-housing was not given adequate attention; urban development was neglected. The role of the French government in the Suez crisis of 1956, considered in chapter 22, brought discredit upon the republic. But it was the problem of Algeria which brought the insecure Fourth Republic to its final collapse.

Algeria and the fall of the Fourth Republic

The extensive French Empire at the end of the Second World War was in widespread revolt. In the immediate postwar years, the French fought against the movements for independence in Indochina, and the manner in which Indochina was eventually lost at Dien Bien Phu in 1954 is shown in chapter 26. Other overseas areas were also abandoned in these years: the French mandates of Syria and Lebanon in 1946 and the French colonies of Tunisia and Morocco in 1956. The French still held control of most of their colonies in West Africa, where agitation for independence was comparatively slight. Also, they still held control of Algeria, where immense problems challenged the

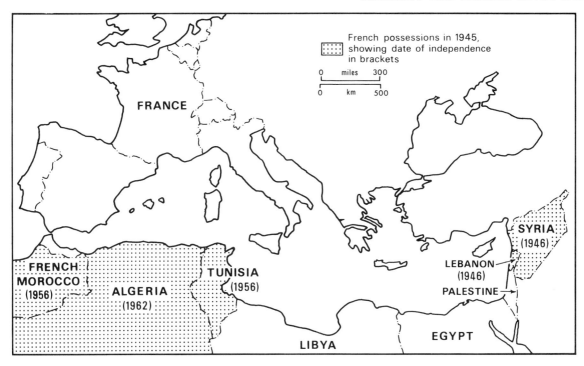

French possessions in North Africa and the Middle East

governments of the Fourth Republic in the late 1950s.

Algeria had been held by the French since the early nineteenth century, longer than any other French overseas possession. Geographically it was closer to France than any other colony. Generations of French people, known as the *colons* and numbering about a million in the mid-twentieth century, had settled in Algeria and regarded Algeria as their home. Algeria's constitutional links with France were unique among the French overseas possessions, as representatives elected by the colons were returned direct to the French assembly in Paris. For all practical purposes, Algeria was regarded as a part of France.

Opposition to the French in Algeria began seriously in 1954. It was led by the National Liberation Front directed by Ben Bella and assisted by Egyptian aid. It held much sympathy in other parts of the world. Inevitably, independence was most vigorously resisted by the colons, who feared that after independence they would lose their privileged status

in Algeria. French troops, released in 1954 from the campaign in Indochina, were sent to quell a highly-effective terrorist campaign in Algeria and to suppress instances of terrorism which occurred within France itself. The colons fought alongside the army against the terrorists but the lengthy campaign, marked by appalling violence and extreme cruelty on both sides, further weakened the Fourth Republic. As government succeeded government in the mid-1950s, none was able to deal adequately with Algeria. It was clear that the French were not winning, but it was equally clear that because of the number and position of the colons, it would be difficult to abandon this overseas possession, even though world opinion, expressed in a United Nations vote in 1955, appeared to favour such a course. An added difficulty was the determination of the French army, particularly the crack paratroop regiment, to maintain control of Algeria, even if the French government were to abandon it. Any French government that made concessions to the Algerians was therefore likely to encounter a revolt by the army.

In the spring of 1958, after a period of much political instability, another new government in France appeared to be on the point of abandoning Algeria. This government encountered in Algeria violent demonstrations by both the colons and the army. Throughout their demonstrations they constantly shouted their slogan and objective: *Algérie Française* (French Algeria). A revolutionary committee representing their cause, known as the *Committee of Public Safety*, seized control in Algeria and thus threatened the credibility of the French government. In this time of crisis, de Gaulle held himself in quiet readiness at his country retreat of Colombey-les-deux-Églises, to assume power once more. Disillusion with the political weakness of the Fourth Republic caused many to feel that de Gaulle's solution of a strong presidency would save France from chaos and would somehow resolve the problem of Algeria. Many in the army were conscious of de Gaulle's own connections with the army and were confident that he would save Algeria for France. The left were not so ready to welcome him, but were over-ruled in the assembly, which voted to ask de Gaulle to become Prime Minister. He accepted at once, insisting that he should be given full powers of government, but taking care to make no specific promises about Algeria.

The Fifth Republic and de Gaulle's solution for Algeria

Four months after his appointment, de Gaulle presented to the French people in September 1958 the new constitution for what was now called the Fifth Republic. Its most important feature was that it increased the power of the French President and reduced the power of the French assembly. The President was to be elected by universal suffrage for a period of seven years and was to make his own free choice of Prime Minister. Key policy decisions would in future be made by the President. At the

De Gaulle speaking in Algeria shortly after his appointment as Prime Minister in 1958. Notice that the Algerian French continued to use the revolutionary banner 'Committee of Public Safety', but also decorated their building with the Lorraine cross, the symbol associated with de Gaulle's Free French movement during the Second World War.

time the constitution was accepted, de Gaulle ceased to be Prime Minister and became President, successfully appealing to the French people in a referendum, for acceptance of the constitutional changes he had made. De Gaulle's personal following in the early years of the Fifth Republic was strong, assisted by a new party, officially called the

Union for the New Republic but more usually referred to as the *Gaullist party*. The Conservative element in France, previously dispersed in a number of parties, was now effectively united in the Gaullist party.

In Algeria, de Gaulle's main concern initially was to reduce the atmosphere of tension among the colons and within the army, all of whom were confident that this new military leader of France would ensure the survival of *Algérie Française*. De Gaulle withdrew some troops from Algeria and took steps to improve the Algerian economy. But in September 1959, de Gaulle announced that the people of Algeria would be given the opportunity to vote on the future of their country. The vote was to be delayed for four years, as in the meantime de Gaulle wished to reduce further the atmosphere of tension.

As the majority of Algerians outnumbered the colons, and as they would undoubtedly vote in favour of self-government, the declaration of September 1959 was in effect an abandonment of Algeria by France, and it aroused much opposition from the colons and from the army. The strongest opposition came from *L'Organisation de l'Armée Secrète*, (OAS, the Secret Army Organization), a right-wing military organization, in which a former French Commander-in-Chief in Algeria, General Salan, had much influence. Its methods both in Algeria and in France were too violent for it to win public support. The French army, whose loyalty on the Algerian issue had previously been doubtful, now gave full loyalty to de Gaulle. Terrorist tactics that had been used by the French army in Indochina and in Algeria were now employed by the OAS in both France and Algeria in an attempt to bring down the Fifth Republic. The main effect of the OAS terrorist campaign on de Gaulle was to make him speed up granting independence to Algeria as a means of bringing the violence to an end. It certainly did not achieve the terrorists' aim of maintaining French control of Algeria.

There had already existed since the later 1950s a provisional government for Algeria, consisting of the main Algerian rebel leaders and based temporarily in Cairo. They naturally welcomed de Gaulle's declaration of September 1959 and sought negotiations with the French government. These eventually took place between May 1961 and March 1962, when, at Evian in Switzerland, agreement was reached on a cease-fire between the Algerians and the French. Algeria was to become independent, though it was to cooperate with France over military affairs and over the exploitation of the Sahara's resources. The Evian agreement was accepted by a large majority of the Algerian people in a referendum in the summer of 1962. Most of the colons realized the impossibility of maintaining *Algérie Française* and preferred to return to France rather than live in the newly-independent country. OAS opposition continued for a while, but gradually came to an end in the mid-1960s.

The foreign and domestic policies of de Gaulle

In solving the problem of Algeria, de Gaulle had solved the most troublesome and the most dangerous problem facing France: it was his greatest achievement. It was matched by his realistic decision to withdraw France from the territories in West Africa, most of which had been held as French colonial territory since the late nineteenth century, or as mandates after the First World War. It seemed realistic to grant independence at this stage rather than await the inevitable development of opposition within the colonies. In the late 1950s and early 1960s many independent African republics came into being from the former French territories, the largest being the republics of Guinea, Cameroon, Niger, Upper Volta, Chad, Ivory Coast, the Central African Republic, Senegal, Mali and Mauritania. Some, but not all, of these republics continued to be members of the French Community and thus secured some continuing support in their early years of independence. Thereafter in the development of his foreign policy, de Gaulle had one clear objective: the restoration of French greatness in Europe and throughout the world. He sought to revive the great power status which France seemed to have lost under the Fourth Republic. So far as he was concerned, this meant breaking the strong French dependence on the United States and making France the leading political and economic power in Europe.

In January 1963 de Gaulle rejected Britain's application for membership of the EEC and at the same time accepted West Germany's proposals for a Franco-German treaty. His rejection of the British application is considered more fully in chapter 20: his fundamental reason was his fear that the leading position of France would be lessened if Britain, together with its 'special relationship' with the United States, were to enter. By his pursuit of the agreement with neighbouring West Germany he showed a similar concern for the position of France in Europe. By allying with the other major power in continental Europe he was creating a European power bloc which would be in a position to resist American pressure. The basis of the treaty of friendship with West Germany was the close personal understanding between de Gaulle and Adenauer, but it remained firm throughout the 1960s, after Adenauer had ceased to be the West German Chancellor. De Gaulle withdrew French troops from NATO in 1966 and rejected Britain's second application for EEC membership in 1967: both events give further evidence of his desire to reject influence from outside continental Europe and to continue to assert the importance of France as a great power.

His view of Europe was a wide one. By the mid-1960s he spoke of a Europe that stretched as far as the Russian Ural mountains, and his search for an understanding with the Communist bloc caused some disquiet among his West German allies. In the summer of 1966, shortly after the withdrawal of French troops from NATO, de Gaulle was given a warm reception in Moscow, and he paid visits to east European countries. Though the visits led to some slackening of tension they failed to create any really significant change for continental Europe. Nor in the mid-1960s did his visits out-

side Europe achieve significant results, apart from alienating major powers. He condemned the role of the United States in Latin America during a visit there in 1964, and its role in Vietnam during his visit to neighbouring Cambodia in 1965; he gave outspoken support to the Quebec French-speaking separatists during a visit to Canada in 1967, thus further alienating Britain.

The strong government which de Gaulle established in 1958 restored stability to France. The economy also developed along more stable lines. Devaluation of the franc together with the creation of a new French franc, equal to one hundred of the old, had occurred just before the Fifth Republic was established: this helped to increase French exports in the early years of the Fifth Republic. Another legacy of the Fourth Republic that was successfully developed by de Gaulle was the system of economic planning worked out by Jean Monnet. But the Gaullist government was more successful in achieving the objectives of the planning than the weak governments of the Fourth Republic. Though there was a generally successful development of the French economy during these years, some of de Gaulle's economic policies were widely criticized. The expense of developing a nuclear deterrent, which the President considered essential if France was to secure great power status, was felt by many to be a considerable waste of France's economic resources. Others doubted the value of the President's policy of amassing gold and his wish to restore the gold standard.

The rioting of 1968 and de Gaulle's retirement

Thus in economic matters as in foreign policy, early success gave way to some disillusion among the French people in the mid-1960s. The style of de Gaulle's government seemed remote from most of the population of France. Its reliance on a small group of loyal Gaullists, foremost among whom were men such as Georges Pompidou and Couve de Murville, was felt to be too narrow a basis, while de Gaulle's grand, patrician manner was condemned by younger people as more appropriate to a bygone age of French greatness. Dissatisfaction was shown especially in 1965 when the left-wing candidate, François Mitterand, presented a real challenge to de Gaulle in the presidential election, and in 1967 when in a general election, the Gaullists only narrowly maintained their majority.

The early summer of 1968 was a period of acute crisis for de Gaulle's government. Student riots occurred in Paris, largely caused by well-justified complaints about their conditions of work and the refusal of the authorities to do anything realistic about them. Agitation then spread among workers and a series of strikes occurred throughout France on a scale not yet seen in the postwar years. Clashes of students and workers with

the riot police became more serious, and a revolutionary situation developed. De Gaulle's political answer to the disorders was to seek support from the mass of the French people in a general election held in June. The main issue in the election was the disorder in which France appeared to be plunged, and de Gaulle's assertion that only by supporting his party could the French be assured of a return to stability. The election campaign worked with considerable success for the Gaullists, who were returned with an overall majority. A new Prime Minister, Couve de Murville, was appointed, and concessions designed to satisfy students and workers were promised. Though these concessions did not go so far as many of the rebels had wished, in combination with the clear electoral success of the government, they did help to bring the disorders to an

An incident between students and riot police in a Paris boulevard during the summer of 1968. The disturbances of that year brought to the surface many tensions in French society and contributed to de Gaulle's fall from power in 1969.

end. Idealistic hopes by some students of their further and deeper involvement with the workers in a fully-revolutionary movement came to nothing.

The work of administrative reform of France continued as a priority of the Gaullist government. Early in 1969 de Gaulle issued a comprehensive plan of reform, designed to decentralize the government of France. He submitted these reforms to the French people in a referendum. In themselves the reforms were moderately progressive, but the referendum of April 1969 became really a vote of confidence in de Gaulle himself. By a narrow margin, the people of France voted against his proposals. De Gaulle at once resigned as President. He retired for the last time to his country retreat of Colombey-les-deux-Églises where he died in the following year, having taken no further part in French political life.

The Fifth Republic in the 1970s: Pompidou and Giscard d'Estaing

Though France had narrowly rejected de Gaulle in April 1969, Gaullism continued to be a powerful force in the country, and the presidents who followed, until 1974 Georges Pompidou, and thereafter Valéry Giscard d'Estaing, were both Gaullists. Pompidou, a man of academic background, had become associated with de Gaulle during the Second World War and had been his Prime Minister in the years between 1962 and 1968. In supporting him in the presidential election of June 1969, the French people showed a desire to maintain the stability that had developed earlier under the Fifth Republic. In his approach to politics, Pompidou was less rigid than de Gaulle and his five years as President showed that the Fifth Republic was capable of surviving its founder and adapting itself to changing circumstances at home and abroad. He abandoned some of the more controversial and less purposeful objectives of his predecessor's foreign policy, and he adopted an easier approach to Britain's third application for EEC membership, meeting at Paris on friendly terms with Prime Minister Heath in May 1971. Planning in

economic affairs continued and French exports were assisted by Pompidou's decision to further devalue the franc, a move which for reasons of prestige, de Gaulle had refused to make.

For the last year of his presidency, Pompidou was a sick man, and his government was less secure than earlier. After his death in office in April 1974, Giscard d'Estaing was elected to succeed him by an exceptionally narrow margin. Mitterand, the left-wing candidate, again proved a close challenger for the presidency. Pompidou had shown the durability of the Fifth Republic, and Giscard d'Estaing was concerned with the introduction of fuller reform in all aspects of French life, though his slender political support in the assembly was a continuing problem. In August 1976 political differences led to the dismissal of the Prime Minister, Chirac, and to the assumption of fuller presidential power by Giscard. In foreign affairs, Giscard had moved significantly from de Gaulle's position. Closer relations were established with the United States and with NATO, while the French control of an independent nuclear deterrent was diminished. Despite the economic problems that plagued Western Europe in the mid-1970s, under Giscard's presidency, the French government continued to address itself to reform and to a more realistic view of the French position in the world.

Questions

46. Study the photograph on page 163 and then answer questions (a) to (d) which follow.
    (a) Name
        (i) the capital city in which this photograph was taken,
        (ii) the sector of the city in which it was taken,
        (iii) the sector of the city beyond the large notice on the right, and
        (iv) the *two other* sectors that existed in this city just after the Second World War. (4)

(b) (i) What evidence does this picture contain to suggest that this sector boundary was closely controlled by both sides?

(ii) How do you account for this close control?

(5)

(c) Describe the events which led to international boundaries in this city being
    (i) established in 1945,
    (ii) challenged in 1948–49, and
    (iii) strengthened in 1961.

(6)

(d) Show to what extent in the years

since 1961 the relations within this divided country have improved.

(5)

47. Examine the circumstances which led to the creation in France of the Fifth Republic in 1958. To what extent did France benefit from the rule of de Gaulle thereafter?

48. Show the importance in the years since 1945 of *four* of the following: political instability in the Fourth Republic; *Algerie Française*; Brandt's *Ostpolitik*; the 1968 disturbances in Paris; President Pompidou; the Baader-Meinhof gang.

17
Mediterranean Europe since 1945

Postwar Italy

The gradual liberation of the southern and central parts of the Italian peninsula between 1943 and 1945 meant that political life had time to revive there before the Germans had been completely defeated in April 1945. A number of politicians opposed to Fascism revived the parties which had been persecuted during the Fascist era. Three parties became particularly important: the Socialists, the Communists and the Christian Democrats. The Socialists were initially dangerously divided. The Communists grew considerably in power during the postwar years. They had gained prestige by their active role in wartime resistance, and in Palmiro Togliatti they had an inspiring leader who lacked the rigidity of other Communist leaders in the postwar years and who was prepared to adapt Communism to the requirements of Italy. The Christian Democrats were the successors of the pre-Fascist Popular party. Their development had been much encouraged by the Roman Catholic church during the war years as a party capable of providing a stable, progressive and Christian government for the peninsula. Their leader, Alcide de Gasperi, had passed the war years as a refugee in the Vatican. His party and his personality were to dominate Italian politics in the postwar years. The Italian monarchy had been brought into discredit by King Victor Emanuel III's role in assisting the Fascist seizure and in maintaining their power: he abdicated in favour of his son, Umberto II. When a referendum was held in June 1946 on the future of the monarchy, the Italian people voted, by a narrow majority, in favour of a republic.

The Allied powers adopted a severe attitude towards Italy at the end of the Second World War, apparently giving the Italian government little benefit for its change to the Allied side in September 1943. Peace negotiations between the victorious powers were held at Paris during 1946 and led in February 1947 to a peace treaty which was imposed on Italy. By it, the Italian government was compelled to pay financial indemnity to the countries which it had attacked, and to accept the loss of all the overseas possessions acquired during and before the Fascist period. There were some minor boundary changes to France's advantage, and some major boundary changes to Yugoslavia's advantage. The Istrian peninsula together with the city of Fiume, were to be incorporated into Yugoslavia; the city of Trieste and the countryside around it, where the population was more mixed, were initially created a free territory under the control of the Allied powers.

At the same time as this treaty was imposed on Italy, the country began to receive useful financial and diplomatic aid from the United States. This was prompted by the increasing tension of the Cold War in 1947 and by concern that the developing strength of the Communist party in Italy might lead to Italy becoming another Communist country. Marshall Aid was generously given to de Gasperi's government and was invaluable in assisting the recovery of Italian industry, which continued to be organized on lines of private enterprise. In diplomacy also, the United States proved a valuable friend: it was their influence among the wartime Allies which was responsible for a solution of the problem of Trieste, finalized eventually in 1954, on terms which permitted Italy to retain the city but to lose the surrounding countryside. The Italians appeared to realize that some return was expected for this help: in 1949 Italy became a founding member of NATO and American forces were allowed bases in Italy. The United States also made it clear that the coming to power of a Socialist or Communist government in Italy would lead to an ending of American aid, a factor which further assisted the Christian Democrats in their continuing hold on power.

Christian Democrat rule did not only bring stability to Italian politics after the postwar chaos. It also laid the foundations of the Italian economic boom of the 1950s and early 1960s. Italy sought entry into the Coal and Steel Community in 1951 and saw economic advantage later in membership of the EEC. Productivity and exports were encouraged both by EEC policies and by government policies in these years. Similarly the poverty of the south was, to an extent, relieved by aid from the Italian government's *Fund for the South* and aid from the EEC's regional fund. Agriculture had lagged behind industry in the postwar economic revival and in the 1950s fuller attention was given to the reform of land-holding. Industry continued to expand at a generally faster rate than in most other European countries.

Italy in the 1960s and the 1970s

De Gasperi's successors, after his retirement in 1953, found it harder to maintain the dominance of the Christian Democrat party. In the early 1960s, under Aldo Moro, the party sought to ally itself with Nenni's Socialists, with whom it formed a series of coalition governments. The relaxation of the earlier Cold War tensions and the more liberal attitude of Pope John XXIII contributed further to the *opening to the left* as this new Christian Democrat policy was termed. Under the rule of these coalition governments in the 1960s, more progressive policies were pursued. Moves were made to nationalize essential industries such as electricity and parts of the steel industry. Reforms were undertaken in education, which still retained

out-of-date features from Fascist and pre-Fascist years. A start was made on the long-delayed plan for regional government, a matter of considerable importance in a country with a strong sense of regionalism. The economy continued to flourish throughout the 1960s, more emphasis being given to the planning of the economy than to allowing its free development.

By the end of the 1960s and the early 1970s the Christian Democrat–Socialist alliance became seriously strained, at times breaking up completely. Italy was plunged into economic and social difficulties as well as political difficulties. Uncertain economic progress led to some severe strikes, especially in the autumn of 1969. The rate of inflation increased alarmingly during the 1970s. Crime plagued many Italian cities, kidnapping of wealthy hostages being a profitable activity of a number of criminals, some of whom were very probably connected with the Mafia organization. The Red Brigades of the extreme left became notorious for their murdering or kidnapping of prominent Italian politicians and businessmen: in early 1978 former Prime Minister Moro was kidnapped by this organization and was murdered when the Italian government refused to accept the terrorist terms for his release. Many Italians showed more strongly than earlier their opposition to the links between church and state established by the 1929 concordat: in the 1970s laws legalizing divorce and abortion were eventually passed by the assembly only after stormy passage, in which the church condemned them as contrary to the spirit of the concordat.

Against this restless social and economic background, Italian political life developed chaotically. At times, the Italian government was held by a Christian Democrat–Socialist coalition; at other times it was controlled by the Christian Democrats alone. Extremist parties of the right and left flourished: the neo-Fascist Italian Social Movement gained support, though a more spectacular increase in strength was achieved by the Italian Communist party under the lead of Enrico Berlinguer. The Italian Communist party, with its willingness to apply its policies flexibly and seek understanding with other parties of the left, became the centre of *Euro-Communism*. It was widely forecast that the Communists would form a government after the general election of June 1976. Much anxiety was aroused at this prospect. In the event, the Christian Democrats won the election, but the Communist vote had increased substantially and their party was now the second largest party in the Italian assembly. A Christian Democrat, Giulio Andreotti, was appointed as Prime Minister of a government that inevitably relied on Communist support. Andreotti dismissed a number of formerly prominent Christian Democrat politicians. By working cautiously with Berlinguer, he established a stable government.

The postwar Papacy

Pope Pius XII (1939–58) was the last pope to reign in the fully-autocratic manner employed by so many of his predecessors over the centuries: his long pontificate of almost twenty years has subsequently become subject to much controversy. Born into the well-established Roman family of the Pacelli, he appeared destined from his youth for high office in the church. As a Cardinal, he had served as Papal Nuncio (Ambassador) to Weimar Germany, and in the 1930s he became Vatican Secretary of State. It was widely expected that he would be elected Pope during the conclave held after the death of Pius XI in 1939.

The early years of his pontificate were filled with the problems arising from the Second World War and the need for Vatican neutrality. Accusations have been made after the war about the 'silence' of Pius XII in failing to condemn the Nazi extermination of the Jews. There is no easy answer to the controversial matter of this 'silence'. The Pope's critics hold that what ranks as the largest genocide campaign of the twentieth century ought certainly to have been condemned by the leader of the largest Christian church. The Pope's supporters suggest that he was not fully aware of what was being done to the Jews and that, in any case, an

Pope Pius XII gives his blessing to the crowds of Rome as he is carried in the papal throne across St Peter's Square. The centuries-old ceremonial of the Roman Catholic church was still in use during his reign, but much of it was gradually abandoned by later popes.

open condemnation of Nazi Germany at that time may have caused widespread persecution of the many millions of Roman Catholics who were then under Nazi rule. It has also been pointed out that Pius XII gave much assistance to Jews in Italy, allowing many to hide in Italian monasteries and in the Vatican. Somewhat less controversial was the Pope's full support of Christian Democracy in Italy after the war. He had encouraged the development of this party during the closing stages of the war and at elections had urged Italy's Roman Catholic population to vote for Christian Democracy. In the Cold War atmosphere of the late 1940s and the 1950s, Pius XII proved the sternest of Communism's opponents, both in Italy and elsewhere.

Quite apart from his close involvement in diplomacy and in politics, Pius XII was a pope much concerned with maintaining spiritual values in a world of change. The Roman Catholic church in his time still held to its centuries-old liturgy and under Pius XII's leadership there was little prospect that this, or anything else, would change. His emphasis upon the importance of church doctrine led him in the Holy Year of 1950 to proclaim the doctrine of the Virgin Mary's bodily assumption into Heaven as a matter of faith to be believed by all Roman Catholics. But it was apparent during the closing years of his long pontificate, when Pius XII became a virtual recluse, that the Roman Catholic church would be subject to substantial change after his death.

Few expected the election to the papacy of the elderly Cardinal Roncalli in the 1958 conclave. During his comparatively brief five-year pontificate as Pope John XXIII, he developed a new style for the papacy and led his church towards a re-thinking of its role in the world. Shortly after becoming pope, he summoned the bishops of the Roman Catholic church to meet in Rome for a general council, the first such council to be held for more than ninety years. It was known as the Second Vatican Council and it was in session from 1962 to 1965, continuing into the time of Pope Paul VI. Many changes and reforms were made as a result of the decisions of the council and the work of the Pope. Church services were simplified and priests were to use in them the language of the people and not just the traditional Latin. There was a relaxation of the prohibition against the reading of books and the viewing of films considered dangerous to Roman Catholic belief. The Roman Catholic church no longer maintained its remoteness from the other churches: warmer relations, seen as early steps towards the reunion of all the Christian churches, were encouraged by the Pope. In Italian and in world politics, the condemnation of Communism was less forceful than before.

But the Second Vatican Council and the pontificate of Pope John XXIII were not easy legacies for the former Cardinal Montini during his fifteen-year pontificate as Pope Paul VI (1963–78). Though wanting in many respects to follow the policies of his predecessor, he became anxious at demands from progressives for even more extensive changes, and from reactionaries for a return to the old ways. The demands of the progressives were for permission for priests to marry, change in the church's attitude towards birth control, swifter reunion with the other churches and closer involvement of the church in the struggle of those seeking to free themselves from colonialism and of those oppressed by right-wing regimes, especially in Latin America, where the church had massive support. Reactionary elements vigorously opposed changes in these directions and urged a return to the old authority and discipline of the church in the time of Pius XII and earlier; in Cardinal Ottaviani, himself a close candidate for the papacy in 1958 and in 1963, the reactionaries had a powerful leader, and one with continuing influence at the Vatican. In the 1970s desire on the part of many for a return to the old Latin services led to a threatened break-away of a traditionalist section of the church under the lead of a former French colonial Bishop, Monseigneur Lefebvre, whose followers, in open defiance of the Pope, continued to use the old Latin services.

In the face of these conflicting pressures, Paul VI endeavoured to steer a middle course. His decision, given in the 1968 encyclical, *Humanae Vitae* (Human life), to continue the church's teaching on birth control was greeted with much disappointment among the progressives, as was his refusal to move in some other progressive directions. The reactionaries were disappointed by his refusal to permit the old Latin services. Paul VI travelled extensively in the early years of his pontificate to different parts of the world such as India, Latin America, Israel and to New York to address the General Assembly of the United Nations. He continued his predecessor's policy of seeking to involve the church more closely in the world in which it found itself and passed to his successor a church that was more self-enquiring than at any time in its long history.

The death of Paul VI in August 1978 was followed by the brief 'September Papacy' of John-Paul I, formerly Cardinal Luciani. But the new Pope died suddenly after a pontificate of only thirty-four days. He was therefore never able to realize the genial promise that he showed. The election of his successor broke the centuries-long hold of the Italians on the papacy, as for the first time since 1522, a non-Italian was elected to it. He was the Polish Cardinal Wojtyla, who took the title of John-Paul II. The warm response he secured from people of all nationalities, not least from the Italians, and the keen response to his election even of the Polish Communist government gave evidence of a worldwide interest in the papacy. The strong-minded new Pope, who had known at first hand the difficulties that Roman Catholicism encountered in a Communist country, appeared capable of providing his troubled church with the firm leadership that it needed.

Spain under Franco

Traditional Spain re-asserted itself under the military dictatorship which Franco established in 1939. No concessions were made to the defeated and no attempt was made to unite the country on a compromise basis. In the years immediately after the end of the civil war those who had prominently supported the republic became the victims of cruel persecution: many were shot, others were sentenced to lengthy imprisonment in harsh conditions.

One saving feature for Spain was Franco's maintenance of neutrality throughout the Second World War. In view of the earlier benefits of Italian and German assistance during the civil war, this decision appeared to Mussolini and Hitler as a surprising gesture of ingratitude. The temptation to intervene on the Axis side must have been strong after the German conquest of France in 1940: Hitler made a special journey to the Spanish border town of Hendaye in October of that year to meet Franco but, to his fury, his attempts to persuade Franco to bring Spain into the war came to nothing. Franco's policy towards the Second World War was shifty. His sympathies were more with the Axis powers than with the Allied powers: but he had a keen eye for the way in which events were moving. During the successful stages of Hitler's invasion of the Soviet Union, Spanish 'volunteers' fought alongside the German forces. Later, when it became clear that Germany would be defeated, Franco adopted a more conciliatory attitude towards the Allies, allowing Jewish refugees to escape through Spain to Portugal and, in 1944, bringing to an end his programmes of mass execution of political opponents.

This policy of neutrality ensured Spain's freedom from war and Franco's survival as leader. But in the postwar years Spain, which with Portugal was the only European right-wing dictatorship to survive the events of 1939–45, was treated as an outcast nation. Spain was refused admittance to the United Nations and the question of imposing sanctions on Spain was a matter of United Nations discussion for some years.

In spite of both external and internal hostility towards his régime, Franco maintained his dictatorial hold over Spain for thirty years after the end of the Second World War, until his death in November 1975. The system he established was no more than an extension of his civil war leadership, given constitutional clothing by law in March 1947. Franco was Head of State, known as *El Caudillo* (the Leader) and a monarch in all but name, possessing extensive powers. His rule was based upon the support of the army and the church and of political parties of the right such as the Falange and the Catholic Association. The Cortes continued but had no real significance, consisting merely of appointed Franco supporters. The whole dictatorial structure was supported by a powerful police organization and the semi-military civil guards.

How was it that such a totalitarian, outmoded system survived for so long? Apart from the strong measures outlined above, the main reason lies in the real fear which gripped most Spaniards that if the political system collapsed, there would be a renewal of civil war, with all its known horrors. Franco was the price that had to be paid for internal peace. From the 1950s, changes in the Spanish economy tended to remove some prewar sources of discontent: the spread of industry and Spain's marked popularity among foreign tourists meant that agriculture was no longer the key element in the Spanish economy. Consequently the prewar agitation for land reform and hostility towards landowners no longer aroused such widespread concern. Franco's government took steps to ensure that the peasantry in the countryside and the workers in the towns shared some of the benefits of Spain's economic advance, though the standard of living of most Spaniards still compared very unfavourably with that in most other European countries. Some of the economic improvement was motivated by centralized direction such as the Stabilization Plan of 1959, and it could be suggested that only a leader who had Franco's strength would have been able to put these improvements into effect.

By the mid-1950s Spain was no longer regarded as the 'outcast' nation she had been in 1945. Whilst many Western governments continued to disapprove of Franco's system of government, it seemed important not to isolate a country which would share the West's attitudes to the Cold War. Equally, Spain was anxious to seek good relations with the rest of the world. Though never a member of NATO, Spain nevertheless accommodated some American military bases, thus showing sympathy with the West. Relations with de Gaulle's France were a marked improvement on the hostility between these two neighbours in the immediate postwar years. Conscious of the value to Spain of external trade, Franco sought

entry into the EEC, but as Spain did not fulfil the democratic obligations of the treaty of Rome, and as Franco was not prepared to compromise on this issue, the bid for EEC entry failed. There was friction with Britain over the future of Gibraltar, a British possession in the south of Spain since the eighteenth century. In the 1960s the Spanish government put forward the claim that Gibraltar should revert to Spanish control, but a referendum in Gibraltar in 1967 showed that a large majority of the inhabitants of Gibraltar favoured retaining their links with Britain.

Spain in the 1970s

By the mid-1960s Spain had experienced a quarter of a century of Franco's rule and was less docile than earlier. The Spanish church was influenced by the liberal spirit of the Second Vatican Council (1962–65), considered earlier in this chapter. The church's support was no longer so firm as it had been in the 1930s and younger priests were often critical of the régime, becoming actively involved in movements of opposition. Demands for regional autonomy, especially from Catalonia and the Basque provinces, became more vocal, expressed particularly in strikes and militant activities of the Communist-inspired Basque Separatists.

In spite of some modest concessions, Franco's government was increasingly challenged in the 1970s. Some sections of the church were by now distinctly opposed to the government. Forceful criticism was made of the régime's disregard of human rights. At a Spanish church assembly in September 1971 criticism came clearly from bishops as well as from younger priests, and Pope Paul VI gave full support to their opposition. Terrorist attacks by the Basque Separatists and other active groups increased. Carrero Blanco, Franco's Prime Minister, was assassinated in December 1973. Franco, by now old and ill, refused to bring about any further changes in his system of government, despite the advice of a number of his ministers that only by making such changes could the régime survive.

When Franco died in November 1975, Juan Carlos, the grandson of Alfonso XIII, became King of Spain. He began by releasing a number of political prisoners and by promising reforms, but he was at once subjected to demands for more concessions and swifter changes. In the early months of his reign the economic situation worsened: Spain shared in the inflation and unemployment which affected all West European countries in the mid-1970s. Strikes became more frequent, and workers demanded greater liberty as well as improved pay.

The government was divided between the supporters and the opponents of change. But the new King's position was, however, strong, and in tours throughout Spain his popularity among the people was much in evidence; he was also well liked by the army. In July 1976 he appointed Adolfo Suárez as Prime Minister, who earlier had a reputation for strict loyalty to Franco but who surprised everyone by initiating far-reaching changes. Greater political freedom was allowed and more political prisoners were released. In October 1976, a wide-ranging reform bill was put forward by Suárez, passed by a large

In June 1977 Prime Minister Suárez casts his vote in Spain's first general election since the end of Franco's dictatorship. During the late 1970s there was much hope that Spain would return to a full and stable democracy.

majority in the Cortes and approved in a referendum by a large majority of the Spanish people. It provided for a two-chamber Cortes elected by universal suffrage, to which the government would be responsible. The reform bill effectively ended the system of Franco's dictatorship.

Elections for the new Cortes, the first free elections in Spain for forty-one years, were held in June 1977. In the elections extremist parties fared badly. Alliances were formed between sympathetic parties, and the Democratic Centre Union received the majority of the votes. Suárez was confirmed in office as Prime Minister, having secured in these elections a mandate from the population to continue along the path of moderate reform. He was further confirmed in power by a later general election in March 1979.

Greece

Greece experienced warfare of one sort or another throughout the 1940s: they were engaged until 1944 in struggle against the Germans and after 1944 in struggle amongst themselves. The roots of this civil war are to be found in the two resistance movements against the German occupation: the Communist-dominated National Liberation Front and the National Greek Democratic Union, which was opposed to the Communists. Even while the Germans were present in the country there were clashes between these rival movements. With the eventual defeat of the Germans in the autumn of 1944, there was a struggle by both forces to secure control of their liberated country. British forces, largely responsible for the defeat of the Germans at that time, joined in the fighting against the Greek Communists, who by the end of the year had been forced into retreat in the northern mountains of the country.

With British and American support, a new right-wing government was formed and the Greek monarchy was restored. Britain was particularly concerned that the Greek government should be friendly towards Britain, as a hostile government in Greece could endanger Britain's Mediterranean trade routes. The United States and Britain considered that there was a strong chance of Greece becoming another Communist state: the Greek Communist forces were not completely defeated, while the neighbouring countries of Albania, Yugoslavia and Bulgaria had all become Communist. Financial aid was given by the United Nations and by Britain to the new Greek government. It appears, however, that the Greek government did not use the aid it received in these years for the purposeful, constructive work which the country desperately needed. Many Greeks were therefore willing to give support to the Communists when they made a further bid for power in 1946, and the country was plunged once again into civil war.

This second civil war lasted from 1946 to 1949. Though the Greek Communists were few, they were well disciplined and well supplied with arms and equipment by neighbouring Communist states. The Greek countryside was highly suitable for the guerrilla warfare which they employed. In the early stages it appeared likely that the Communists would be victorious. Their eventual defeat is explained largely by two events outside Greece. Yugoslavia's quarrel with the Soviet Union and her expulsion from the Cominform in 1948 led to the cutting off of valuable Yugoslavian aid to the Greek Communists, who were loyal to the Soviet Union. In the meantime their opponents were receiving increased outside help from Marshall Aid, after 1948. This assistance led to a marked improvement in the equipment and in the morale of the Greek army, which by 1949 had completely defeated its Communist enemies.

Thereafter Greece was firmly committed against the Soviet Union and sought to ally itself with other West European powers. It joined early moves for European unity such as OEEC and the Council of Europe; in 1952 it made a stronger commitment by joining NATO. It became involved in the events in Cyprus during the 1950s and the 1960s. But the comparatively poor economy of the country meant that Greece inevitably played only a small part in world affairs.

On 21 April 1967 an army coup overthrew the government and established what became known as the *Colonels' government*. A situation of political confusion had been the excuse taken by the military for intervention in this way. From then until July 1974 Greece was under the control of a military dictatorship. Though the Greeks gained some advantages from the land redistribution schemes and the more efficient administration of government, they lost their civil and political liberties which had existed for a longer period in Greece than in any other country. The government was more fully committed to the cause of the Greek Cypriots. It was this policy which led to the downfall of the military régime in July 1974, the circumstances of which are explained in the following section.

The elderly Karamanlis, one of the most successful of the prime ministers in the years before the Colonels' government, formed a temporary administration. Elections followed within a few months and revealed the lack of enthusiasm by the Greek people for the type of government which had been imposed upon them between 1967 and 1974. The monarchy was rejected in a referendum, and Greece became a republic. Karamanlis was leader of a moderately right-wing party, the New Democracy party, which secured a majority in the 1974 election and gave attention to restoring the country after its misfortunes of recent years.

Cyprus

The roots of the troubled situation in Cyprus during the mid-twentieth century are closely linked with the island's long history. Predominantly Greek in population, the island contains a Turkish minority, whose descendants came to the island when it was a possession of the Ottoman Empire. For centuries there has been rivalry between Greeks and Turks, based partly on the religious differences between the Christian Greeks and the Muslim Turks and partly on the long-held dominance of the Turks over the Greeks. In the comparatively small island of Cyprus, these differences became particularly acute. Another difficulty for the people of Cyprus was the continuing control of their island by Britain which, in the face of increasing Cypriot demands for independence during the 1950s, firmly maintained that Cyprus must remain under British control. Britain's determined stand for its possession of Cyprus during the Cold War years is explained by the island's strategic position in the eastern Mediterranean, making it Britain's closest possession to the Soviet Union and the Middle East. With the end of British influence in Egypt after the 1956 Suez crisis, Cyprus became even more important for Britain's overseas strategy.

In the early 1950s Archbishop Makarios of Cyprus became the accepted leader of the Greek Cypriots in their struggle for independence from the British and for union of their island with Greece, a union that was referred to as *enosis*. In the mid-1950s a campaign was conducted in Cyprus by terrorists known as the *Eoka* under the direction of another Greek Cypriot leader, Grivas. Makarios did not fully approve of the methods of Eoka, though his critics suggest that he found Eoka useful in putting pressure on the British to withdraw, and that he did not condemn the movement with much vigour. Greek Cypriot pressure for *enosis* alarmed the Turkish Cypriots who preferred British control to Greek control. As opposition within Cyprus increased, Britain realized by the late 1950s that there was little alternative to granting Cyprus her independence. The governments of neighbouring Greece and Turkey now showed increased concern for the interests of their fellow-nationals in the island. The warfare in Cyprus between the British soldiers and the Eoka terrorists began to develop into a civil war between Greek Cypriots and Turkish Cypriots.

In the negotiations leading to independence, the British government sought to prevent the outbreak of civil war of this kind. Progress was made easier by Makarios' abandonment of *enosis*. In 1960 the independent republic of Cyprus came into being with Makarios as President. Two important concessions were made by the new Cyprus government. The British were allowed to keep possession of military bases on the island and the Turkish Cypriot minority were given guarantees of their rights, including a proportion of government posts and the appointment of their leader as Vice President.

Sadly, these safeguards in the Cyprus constitution of 1960 did not work effectively. In 1964 and again in 1974 serious fighting broke out in the island, leading to the involvement of other powers. One of the 1960 safeguards for the Turkish Cypriots had been the right of the Turkish Cypriot Vice President to veto legislation which might be considered against the interests of those whom he represented. Makarios held that the Vice President used his powers of veto too readily, and hence the government of the island was becoming ineffective. In November 1963 Makarios proposed to abolish the veto and to reduce the other guarantees for the Turkish Cypriots. His action sparked off disorders within the island and there was a strong possibility that Greece and Turkey might intervene in the island on behalf of their own nationals. The Turkish Cypriot representatives withdrew completely from the Makarios government and the Turkish Cypriot people isolated themselves in their

The division of Cyprus, 1974

own parts of the island. In March 1964, after a request from the Cypriot government, the United Nations Security Council voted to send an international peace-keeping force to Cyprus. Originally authorized for three months, the United Nations forces in Cyprus (UNFICYP) remained there throughout the 1960s and the 1970s. UNFICYP preserved a strictly neutral role and their presence on the island dissuaded Greece and Turkey from interfering in the island's affairs. One of the reasons for the continued presence of UNFICYP was the renewed activities of Grivas and his guerrilla forces, known as Eoka B, pledged to oppose Makarios on account of the President's abandonment of enosis. In Greece, after 1967, the Colonels' government supported enosis and assisted the

Eoka B forces in their guerrilla campaign against Makarios.

In July 1974 Makarios demanded that the Colonels' government should remove Greek officers serving in Cyprus, as he was concerned by the links existing between these Greek officers and the Eoka B terrorists. His demand led to a coup by the Greek officers against the government of Makarios, who left the country. A military régime, virtually a puppet of the Colonels' government in Greece, took control of the island. The emergence of this new régime signalled a massive increase in the importance of Greece in Cyprus; enosis would undoubtedly follow. UNFICYP appeared incapable of preventing the violence that swiftly engulfed the island. The coup had placed the Turkish

Turkish Cypriots greet enthusiastically the soldiers from Turkey during their invasion of Cyprus in August 1974. The violent events of that year gave particular emphasis to the deeply-felt divisions that have plagued Cyprus for centuries.

Cypriots in a threatened position and the government of Turkey decided to come to their aid by launching their long-threatened invasion of the island. For a month extensive fighting took place. The United Nations Security Council met and made the following declaration:

> The Security Council having considered the report of the Secretary-General about the recent developments in Cyprus, having heard the statements made by the President of the Republic of Cyprus and the statements by the representatives of Cyprus, Turkey, Greece and other member countries:
>
> Demands an immediate end to foreign military intervention in the Republic of Cyprus.
>
> Calls on Greece, Turkey and the United Kingdom to enter into negotiations without delay for the restoration of peace in the area and constitutional government in Cyprus.
>
> Calls on all parties to cooperate fully with UNFICYP to enable it to carry out its work.

When a cease-fire was agreed in mid-August, the Turkish forces were in occupation of substantial northern parts of the island. The military régime in Cyprus fell, as did its sponsor in Greece, and later in 1974 Makarios returned as President.

By then Makarios was able to rule only a part of the island, as the Turkish forces had effectively created a partition between the Greek Cypriot and the Turkish Cypriot areas. The partition led to a disruption of the island's economy and to difficulties for many Cypriots who found their property and possessions in the enemy zone. The situation continued with little change after Kyprianou succeeded to the presidency on the death of Makarios in 1976.

Questions

49. Study the United Nations declaration on page 184 and then answer questions (a) to (e) which follow.

(a) Explain the reasons why *each* of the countries named in the third paragraph had a general concern in the course of events in Cyprus during the 1960s and the 1970s.

(3)

(b) (i) Give the full title of the organization whose initials are given in the fourth paragraph, and

(ii) describe the circumstances which brought this organization to Cyprus ten years before this document was published.

(iii) How successfully had the organization carried out the *work* referred to in the last paragraph during those ten years?

(1+3+2)

(c) (i) Name the *President of the Republic of Cyprus*, referred to in the first paragraph, and

(ii) describe the work of this man in helping to bring about the island's independence.

(1+3)

(d) Describe the events leading to the *foreign military intervention* referred to in the second paragraph.

(3)

(e) Outline the history of Cyprus from the time of this document to the present day.

(4)

50. Show how and with what success democratic forms of government have been re-established in (a) Italy since the mid-1940s and (b) Spain since the mid-1970s.

51. Outline the history of the Papacy since 1939, showing the extent to which the popes have sought to involve the Roman Catholic church in the affairs of the world.

18
Britain since 1945

The Second World War marks a dividing point in British history. Linked with the sense of national elation at the victory over Germany was a desire to reconstruct Britain along lines that would create better social justice and improved economic efficiency. During the postwar decades progress along these lines was inevitably mixed with achievements and disappointments. Less immediate concern was felt about Britain's relationship with the world and with her Empire, though these relationships became matters of importance for Britain as her great power status declined and her large Empire crumbled. But throughout these decades, and contrasting with the experience of some countries in Europe and elsewhere, the British two-party system provided a stable framework for the country's development.

Political changes

The chart below summarizes the major political changes of these years. The earliest was one of the most important: the general election of July 1945. Churchill's coalition government broke up as soon as the war ended and competition between the political parties recommenced. It was widely felt that Churchill would return to power in the post-war election. But the result was a major landslide victory for the Labour party which, for the first time in its history, was able to form a government that did not depend on the support of other parties in the House of Commons. What caused this surprising result? There was a distinct feeling against the Conservative party which had dominated the prewar National government, whose

Governments in Britain since 1945		
General Election	*Government*	*Prime Minister*
July 1945	Labour	Clement Attlee
February 1950	Labour	Clement Attlee
October 1951	Conservative	Winston Churchill
		(Anthony Eden from April 1955)
May 1955	Conservative	Anthony Eden
		(Harold Macmillan from January 1957)
October 1959	Conservative	Harold Macmillan
		(Alec Douglas-Home from October 1963)
October 1964	Labour	Harold Wilson
March 1966	Labour	Harold Wilson
June 1970	Conservative	Edward Heath
February 1974	Labour	Harold Wilson
October 1974	Labour	Harold Wilson
		(James Callaghan from March 1976)
May 1979	Conservative	Margaret Thatcher

domestic policies had only partially solved the problem of the depression and whose foreign policies had failed to prevent the outbreak of war. Many doubted whether Churchill, whose wartime leadership was widely respected, was the right man to lead the nation in time of peace: in prewar years he had been on the right of the Conservative party and his statements in the election campaign suggested that Conservative plans for the country's future were not well thought out. The Labour party, under the leadership of Clement Attlee, presented an image which successfully caught the desire held by many for a complete change in the people who governed, and the policies they employed. Labour's election manifesto, *Let us Face the Future*, promised a wholehearted commitment to the welfare state, to nationalization, and to rehousing. The vote of returning soldiers was an important factor in the success of the Labour party. As the last general election had been held in 1935, soldiers in their twenties were voting for the first time in 1945 and they were persuaded that under Labour they could be assured of a more prosperous and a more stable future.

Its large overall majority assured the Attlee government of a full five-year term, but they were years in which severe economic problems made difficult the full achievement of all that Labour had promised. In the general election of February 1950 Labour held on to power, but with such a seriously-reduced majority that a further general election was bound to follow shortly. When the election came in October 1951, the defeat of the Labour party was no surprise.

The Conservatives won three successive general elections in the 1950s: in 1951 under Churchill; in 1955 under Eden and in 1959 under Macmillan. Altogether the Conservatives remained in power for thirteen years, until their defeat in 1964. The years were not without difficulty for the Conservative party. Churchill's poor health meant that in the early 1950s the government was not always well coordinated. Churchill retired at the age of eighty in April 1955. Anthony Eden's policies in the Suez crisis of 1956 caused serious division within the Conserva-

Clement Attlee at Labour party headquarters after the general election of July 1945. The new Prime Minister and his wife show their delight at the landslide victory which their party had just scored.

tive party as well as within the country at large: his policies during the crisis were a major factor in his decision to resign in January 1957. His successor, Harold Macmillan, experienced serious problems in the country's economy in the early 1960s. Ill health caused Macmillan's retirement in October 1963, when he was succeeded by Douglas-Home, who used recent legislation to abandon his peerage and enter the Commons after a successfully-contested by-election. In spite of these difficulties, the Conservatives won each election with an increased overall majority. The Conservatives showed a degree of moderation in not seeking purposefully to destroy the Labour legislation. Thus a situation of greater harmony existed within the country. The main explanation for their success lies in the widespread affluence in these years, which contrasted significantly with conditions under Labour. After its defeat in the 1955 general election, the Labour party was subject to much internal debate between those who stressed pure Socialist ideals and those who urged fuller support to the popular affluence of the time. Attlee was succeeded as party leader by Hugh Gaitskell in 1955 and, after Gaitskell's premature death in 1963, Harold Wilson led the party into the 1964 general election.

Labour's victory in that election was very slender. The new administration was highly critical of the Conservatives' handling of the economy yet it was Britain's economy that continued to present the Labour government with its most serious problems. In March 1966 in a further election, the Labour party won with a substantially increased majority, assuring Labour of continuing power for the rest of the 1960s.

New elements entered into the practice of politics in Britain in the 1950s and 1960s. The television, which was now found in most households, became a vital medium of communication between the politicians and the electorate; political meetings, which still held as much appeal in the interwar years as they had in the previous century, were no longer significant. Opinion polls represented another new element. Random members of the public were asked their opinion on political issues and from these results analyses were made of the popularity of the political par-

ties. Though there were many controversial aspects in the use of the polls, the information they provided could be helpful to the Prime Minister of the day, whose task it is to decide when an election should take place.

Favourable polls were the major factor persuading Wilson to call a general election in June 1970. But those polls misled Wilson, for the election brought him defeat. A new Conservative government was formed under Edward Heath, who had succeeded Douglas-Home as leader of the Conservative party in 1965. Heath lacked the privileged background of many of his immediate predecessors as leaders of the Conservative party: his appointment suggested a changed image of the party and a stronger appeal for the vote of working-class people. When his firm stand on pay restraint was challenged by the miners in the winter of 1973–74, Heath called a general election for February 1974. That election produced a confusing political result.

For the first time since the war, parties other than Conservative and Labour played a really significant role in the election: the Liberals gained substantially increased support, as did the new Welsh and Scottish Nationalist parties. The Conservatives were able to form a government only if they formed a coalition with the Liberals. When a coalition proposal, made by the Prime Minister, was rejected by the Liberals, Heath had no alternative but to resign and Wilson then formed a government. Labour lacked an overall majority and called another general election in October 1974 in which Labour managed to secure an overall majority. Heath's loss of two successive general elections was the major factor that led to his replacement as leader of the Conservative party by Margaret Thatcher in February 1975, as a result of a vote among Conservative MPs. Wilson resigned, somewhat unexpectedly and for no apparent reason, in March 1976 and was succeeded as Prime Minister by Callaghan, who allowed the government to continue for almost the whole five-year term, calling an election only in May 1979. In this election, the Conservative party, led by Margaret Thatcher, won

The 1974 Elections		
	February	October
Conservatives	296	276
Ulster Unionists (allied to the Conservatives)	11	10
Labour	301	319
Liberal	14	13
Scottish Nationalists	7	11
Welsh Nationalists	2	3
Others	3	3

an overall majority in parliament. The Labour party's downfall had been brought about by its failure to gain support for devolution for Wales and Scotland. But other issues, such as the Labour party's approach to inflation, the trade union movement and immigration moved the country farther to the right.

The nationalized industries

The policy of the Labour government which received most publicity was nationalization. It was not an entirely new policy in the later 1940s: during the interwar years the BBC, the Central Electricity Generating Board and London Transport had all been created as state-owned organizations, while during both world wars essential industries had been temporarily taken over by the state. The Labour party was strongly committed to nationalization, as state ownership of essential industries eliminated private profits and competition and, they believed, was a fairer form of ownership and a more effective method of industrial organization. Its large majority after 1945 enabled the Labour government to put their policy into practice on an extensive scale. Nationalization was undertaken in a thoroughly legal and orderly way: those who owned the industries to be nationalized were compensated and the public corporations which ran the nationalized industries were democratically based. In these respects nationalization in Britain stands in marked contrast to the seizure of private industry in, for example, the Soviet Union during the time of Lenin and Stalin.

Some of the nationalization moves were uncontroversial. The nationalization of the Bank of England was an inevitable move by which the Bank was to be organized and administered as were the national banks of most other countries of the world. The nationalization of electricity in 1947 and of gas in 1948 led to an improvement in the technical efficiency of both industries. Electricity came under full state control and its distribution was more effectively organized.

The gas industry, which had been poorly and chaotically organized before nationalization, profited from nationalization and from later legislation in 1964, which ensured that the newly-discovered North Sea gas should be used only by the nationalized gas industry.

Greater controversy surrounded the nationalization of coal, transport and the iron and steel industry. The bitterness in the coal industry persisted during the interwar years, and the Labour party was determined to get a better deal for the miners now that it was in a position to do so. The Coal Industry Nationalization Act of 1946 was similar to the rest of the nationalization legislation: with effect from January 1947 the nationalized mines would come under the direction of the National Coal Board, the mine owners having received compensation. Immediate difficulties were encountered as the exceptionally cold weather in the early months of 1947 caused an unprecedented demand for coal, which the newly-nationalized industries could not meet. But thereafter, coal production continually improved and industrial relations developed peacefully, even when, during the 1960s, the competition for new forms of energy caused a reduction in coal output and the closure of smaller pits. Only in the winter of 1973–74 were these relations broken when the miners went on strike in support of a wage demand that broke the limits of the wage restraint imposed by the Heath government. Heath's defeat in the general election of February 1974 is partly attributable to public sympathy for the miners and a feeling that the conditions of their work underground made them a case deserving special treatment.

The Transport Act of 1946 was wide in its application: railway tracks and rolling stock, road haulage, canal transport and the docks were all nationalized and came under the overall authority of the British Transport Commission. In view of the increasing competition from the roads, the railways were in much need of assistance. By uniting rail and road together at the time of nationalization it was hoped that the latter would subsidize the former. But competition from the roads became an even more serious problem for the railways, which continued to show financial loss and to be the subject of public criticism. In 1963 the Beeching report recommended the closure of unprofitable tracks and the development of inter-city services. Over the next decade the implementation of the report led to the closure of many small country lines. Much debate followed on the issue of whether a nationalized industry's first priority should be profit making or public service. The implementation of the Beeching report suggested that the government took the former view.

The proposed nationalization of iron and steel was more controversial. Though there was, in socialist theory, as much justification for the nationalization of this as of any other leading industry, its good shape in the late 1940s robbed the government of a claim, which had much weight in the other industries, that nationalization would improve its efficiency. Nationalization was proposed in 1948 and was vigorously opposed by the owners and by the Conservatives. The expected opposition from the Conservative-dominated House of Lords had led the government to reduce the Lords' delaying power for passing legislation from two years to one year, by the Parliament Act of 1949. After much controversy and some amendments, the bill was finally passed in November 1949, but the refusal of the owners to cooperate in the implementation of the new Act meant that it was ineffective. The nationalization of iron and steel production was now a major point of political difference between the Labour party and the Conservative party. Once returned to power, the Conservatives de-nationalized iron and steel in 1953. Once Labour was returned to power again in 1964, they were intent on re-nationalizing the industry, which they did partially by an Act of 1967, which nationalized the major steel companies.

The Beveridge report and the welfare state

In a *welfare state* the government actively involves itself to assist any member of society during times of sickness, unemployment and old age, when people cannot support themselves adequately. The Labour governments of 1945–51 made the most significant contribution towards the development of the welfare state in Britain: but earlier governments had already laid its foundations, and later governments were to bring further adjustments and developments.

During the Second World War, Sir William Beveridge was given the task of enquiring into the running of Britain's welfare services and to make proposals for their future development. His report, published in December 1942, recommended a universal national insurance scheme, so that in return for regular and compulsory contributions, there would be free medical treatment for the sick, financial assistance for the unemployed, pensions for the elderly and allowances for large families. Some of these benefits were already available, but Beveridge wanted to see improved rates and fairer distribution of them, without the need for the hated, degrading means test. All parties pledged their support for the Beveridge report, but Churchill's wartime coalition maintained that victory in the war must be achieved before action could be taken on the report. In any case, Churchill had little real interest in the Beveridge report or in the development of the welfare state, though one of the report's recommendations, family allowances, was begun by Churchill's coalition government in February 1945, just as the war was ending. It was inevitable that the Labour party, with its emphasis upon social justice, would show a stronger commitment to the Beveridge report. Once in power, it acted fully upon this commitment, the crucial areas of the report being implemented by two acts of 1946: the National Insurance Act and the National Health Act.

The National Insurance Act of 1946 was the work of James Griffiths. As recommended by Beveridge, it introduced the uniform, compulsory contribution to cover all the different times when aid may be needed. Initially most advantage was taken of the Act's provisions relating to pensions for the elderly and the widowed and benefits for

Sir William Beveridge points the way out of the difficulties of this bus. Although the road towards his solution has not been as smooth as is suggested here, his wartime report has dominated thinking on Britain's social services ever since.

the sick and for expectant mothers, all of which were paid on a uniform scale. Two acts made further provision for national insurance. The 1946 Industrial Injuries Act allowed for improved and more easily obtained benefits for those injured at work. The 1948 National Assistance Act made the central government responsible for the granting of further aid to those who still remained needy: local government was given the responsibility of providing homes for the aged

and destitute. A further National Insurance Act, of 1966, introduced the principle of *earnings-related payments* which permitted contributions above the uniform rate in order to secure increased pensions and benefits. By this last act, national assistance benefits were renamed *supplementary benefits*, though applicants were still subject to careful scrutiny. The principle of earnings-related payments was taken further by the Social Security Act of 1974 which required both contributions and benefits to be related to a person's normal income.

The National Health Act of 1946 was the work of an ardent left-winger in Attlee's government, Aneurin Bevan, the Minister of Health. All hospitals under voluntary or local government control were nationalized and reorganized, a process from which a number of small and ill-equipped hospitals benefited considerably. All doctors were to be employed by the state, which paid them a salary according to the number of patients for whom they had responsibility. Medical fees for consultation and medicine were abolished, apart from those paid by patients who wished to consult a doctor as a fee-paying private patient. The initial strong opposition of the medical profession declined and most doctors agreed to serve as national health doctors. Some critics suggested that the availability of medicine led many patients to make unreasonable demands on the new services, but it is possible that the upsurge in demand merely showed that patients were now able to obtain medicine which they genuinely needed but which previously they had been unable to afford.

Although the creation of the national health service was one of the most important social advances in twentieth-century Britain, its subsequent history has been a troubled one. The continual expansion of the service has been encouraged by both political parties, so that by the late 1970s it accounted for a major part of national expenditure. The service has become a point of some sharp political exchanges. In 1951 the Labour government's introduction of prescription charges led to the resignation of Bevan and Wilson. During the thirteen years of Conservative rule, prescription charges remained, but were removed when Wilson became Prime Minister in 1964. Subsequently they were re-imposed, but their re-imposition no longer aroused such acute conflict as it once did. In the mid-1970s the status of private patients in national health hospitals came under attack, as by making payment for their hospital treatment private patients were delaying treatment for national health patients. In the mid-1970s many doctors were concerned at the Labour government's threat to their right to treat patients privately.

Government economic policies and the trade unions: 1945 to 1964

One of the earliest moves by Attlee's government was the repeal in 1946 of the hated Trade Disputes Act of 1927, thus reverting to the system of 'contracting out' of the political levy, removing the definition of a general strike as illegal and permitting civil servants to belong to trade unions. The repeal, long promised by the Labour party in opposition, was a great moral victory for the Labour party and also for the trade union movement. The spirit of cooperation which existed between government and unions was much needed by the Attlee government as it faced severe postwar economic difficulties.

The rebuilding of bombed areas and the development of British industry all demanded the immediate attention of the new Chancellor of the Exchequer, Hugh Dalton. The United States gave assistance: in 1945 a substantial loan was obtained from them, and after 1947 Britain obtained the further benefits of Marshall Aid, considered in chapter 20. The old spectre of unemployment seemed to be banished as the economy quickly returned to peacetime conditions. But other economic problems developed. The war had caused a massive dislocation of the country's economy, which could be healed only with time. Further, during the bitterly cold early months of 1947, the country suffered severe shortages in domestic and industrial supplies. Later in 1947 a new Chancellor, Stafford Cripps, initiated a policy of severe austerity: wage increases were prohibited, taxation levels were raised, hire purchase agreements were restricted. Though his policies were unpopular, they produced results. The trade unions cooperated fully, prices remained stable and, most important of all, exports increased. As part of that export drive, Cripps devalued the pound in relation to the world's major currency, the dollar, thus making cheaper the price of British goods which were sold abroad. Gaitskell as Chancellor of the Exchequer for the final year of Attlee's government, faced the financial difficulties brought about by the Korean War and the Iranian oil embargo. He was anxious not to increase government expenditure as this would raise the already high taxation to impossible levels.

In opposition the Conservatives had been critical of the high taxation, which they associated with the expenditure on the welfare commitments of the postwar Labour governments. Once in power, they were determined to reduce taxation and were assisted in doing so by the general improvement in world finances during the 1950s. Butler (1951–55) and Macmillan (1955–57) were chancellors during years of successful economic development, years which saw the emergence of what was often called the affluent society. Income tax rates dropped, hire purchase restrictions eased, home and overseas investments increased, rationing came to an end. As Minister for Housing, Macmillan had fulfilled the earlier Conservative promise to increase the number of houses constructed. As Chancellor, he continued to further the affluent society by increasing interest paid on government investments and introducing premium bonds, in which interest was given as prizes to bond holders selected by a computer. Macmillan took pride in the affluence of these years, later stating that sections of society had 'never had it so good'. It is true that many problems of the past such as unemployment and excessively low wages had largely disappeared, and the Conservative government had maintained generally harmonious relations with the trade unions.

But affluence cloaked a number of problems. It was generally the middle classes who benefited most: the wages of working class people failed to match increasing prices. The good economic conditions were unlikely to last long and during the premiership of Macmillan and of Douglas-Home, successive Chancellors of the Exchequer attempted to resolve the serious difficulties which the economy now faced. There was little effort made by the government to modernize British industry during these years of affluence.

But the main difficulty arose from the *balance of payments*, which is the difference between the value of a country's imports and the value of its exports. In these years the imports had a higher value: the country was therefore losing money, and action needed to be taken to correct this situation. The government attempted to discourage purchase at home, hoping thereby to encourage a rise in exports. In the late 1950s there were a series of 'credit squeezes' which, by restricting hire purchase agreements and other domestic loans, helped to slacken home demand for purchases. In July 1961 an unpopular 'pay pause' was imposed for a year, during which pay and company dividends were to remain fixed.

The Conservatives therefore restricted the economy from time to time, but were ready to relax the restrictions when the balance of payments showed an improvement for Britain. The Labour opposition was critical of what it called a policy of 'stop-go' and suggested that more expert thought needed to be given to the overall economic strategy of the country: the need for *economic planning* was now strongly advocated by the Labour party. Towards the end of their thirteen-year hold of power, the Conservatives established the National Economic Development Council, a body representative of employers, employees and the government, and assisted by economic experts. It was to encourage the planned growth of the economy.

Government economic policies and the trade unions: from 1964

When the Labour party again secured power they loudly condemned the Conservatives for leaving the legacy of an unfavourable balance of payments. George Brown, the Minister for Economic Affairs, worked with employers and with the trade unions to produce a much-publicized *National Plan*, which envisaged a four per cent growth rate and a substantial improvement in the country's economy by the 1970s. But it was never clear how much authority the National Plan was to have, and George Brown's hopes that it would at last put Britain's economy on the road to stability and success remained unfulfilled. The government resorted to traditional methods. In July 1966 there was a severe credit squeeze, accompanied by another pay pause. In November 1967 the pound was devalued for a second time since the war. As was to be expected, devaluation certainly encouraged exports.

In the late 1960s the economy began to suffer seriously from two problems: a rapid rise in the inflation rate and an increasing militancy among the trade unions. Inflation had existed in the British economy through-out the twentieth century, but in the late 1960s it became a really serious problem. After its success in the general election of March 1966, the Wilson government was strong enough to pass the Prices and Incomes Act, by which the government was authorized to freeze increases in wages and dividends. The TUC was strongly opposed to any extension of the 1966 Act beyond the six months of the imposed freeze. Among trade unionists there was general concern at this extension of government power into the task of wage bargaining between the employers and the unions.

The five dockers, imprisoned in 1972 under the Industrial Relations Act, are carried shoulder high by a jubilant crowd after their release. The rôle of the trade unions in British society became a much-debated issue during the 1970s.

The breaking point of these relations came during the Heath government. As wage settlements in the early 1970s were becoming dangerously inflationary, the government used legislation to limit wage settlements and to curb the power of the trade unions. Discussion with the TUC and with the Confederation of British Industry, the organization which represents the employers, preceded this government legislation. The Industrial Relations Act of 1971 created the Industrial Relations Court, presided over by a high court judge, to decide controversial issues in industrial relations. Though the Act contained some concessions to the trade unions, the creation of this powerful court was bitterly opposed by them. In July 1972 the imprisonment of five dockers was ordered by the Industrial Relations Court for their refusal to end the 'blacking' of a cold storage depot. This action resulted in widespread strikes and protests, which very nearly developed into a general strike and which was only ended by the court's release of the men later in the same month. Relations between the Conservative government and the trade unions continued to be poor, and the fall of Heath's government was brought about by a successful miners' strike early in 1974.

In 1974 the new Labour government also aimed to end the bitterness in industrial relations, yet it shared with its predecessor an awareness that inflation must not be allowed to get beyond control. The Industrial Relations Act was clearly unworkable and was abolished. Consultations began with the TUC, resulting in the *Social Contract* by which the trade unions agreed to hold down the level of wage demands to percentages agreed annually by the TUC and the government. Relations between government and the trade unions improved and wage settlements were reasonable. Inflation appeared to be much less of a problem in the late 1970s than it had been in the early 1970s. But in 1978 the TUC refused to renew the Social Contract, which had always been disliked by some of its members and deplored by many rank and file members of trade unions.

Constitutional changes

The great struggle to secure the vote for all adults belongs to an earlier period of British history. By 1945 Britain had been a democratically run country for some decades and there was no need for fundamental constitutional changes. What has occurred in the postwar years has been a determination by successive governments to ensure that knowledge of democratic rights has become fully available, and that the workings of democracy in Britain have taken account of changing circumstances. But there has been one significant extension of voting rights in recent years: the lowering of the voting age from 21 to 18 in 1970.

The House of Lords has received detailed reform, in order to emphasize its role as a second, reviewing chamber and to diminish its role as a preserve of the hereditary peerage. The Conservative majority in the House of Lords was usually cautious and constructive in its opposition to the measures of Attlee's government, but the Lords' opposition to iron and steel nationalization prompted the Labour government to introduce an amendment to the 1911 Parliament Act, by which the House of Lords could in future delay legislation by only one year instead of the previous two years. In 1958 the Life Peerages Act allowed the nomination to the peerage for their own lifetime of persons who had made important contributions to the nation's life, but who were not necessarily involved in party politics. This was a positive step towards making debate in the House of Lords more useful and better informed. Later development along these lines was less successful. The proposals made by the Labour government in 1969 for an extensive reform of the House of Lords, involving the abolition of the use of the delaying power and the representation of the hereditary peerage, stirred up much political controversy. Meanwhile, by the Peerage Act of 1963, a peer who wished to do so was permitted to resign his peerage and seek election to the House of Commons. Later in the same year, Lord Home took advantage of this act in order to join the House of Commons, membership of which was considered necessary for a Prime Minister.

In the 1970s, Britain's membership of the EEC led to some constitutional innovations. One of these was the holding of a referendum. Out of office, Wilson opposed the terms agreed by the Heath government for Britain's membership of EEC and promised that a Labour government would renegotiate these terms and then present the issue to the British people for them to vote on in a referendum. After February 1974 Wilson put this promise into effect, and in June 1975 the British people voted 'yes' by a large majority for acceptance of Britain's continued membership of EEC. As a referendum had been held on one vital political issue, should the use of a referendum form a part of British constitutional practice? Another EEC issue was the 1979 election for direct British representation at the European Parliament.

During the 1970s there were significant changes in the support of the Scottish and Welsh electorate for the two major parties. With this change came demands for altering the constitution to provide for some kind of parliament for Scotland and Wales. The figures for the two elections of 1974, given on page 187, show the increasing strength of the Scottish Nationalist party and, to a lesser extent, of the Welsh Nationalist party. Though the historic roots of nationalist feeling in both countries are deep, Scottish nationalism was given positive encouragement in the early 1970s by the discovery of North Sea oil, most of which was drilled from rigs off Scotland's eastern shores. It was impossible for the government at Westminster to overlook the fact that there was demand for *devolution* in these parts of the United Kingdom. In 1975 proposals were made for the establishment of Scottish and Welsh assemblies, to be elected for a period of four years, each with control of much of its own internal administration and development. But devolution was not a recipe for independence. The Secretary of State for each country would still represent the interests of the United Kingdom government and was empowered to over-rule decisions of the assemblies if he thought it right to do so.

In the late 1970s devolution became a highly controversial issue, especially in Scotland and Wales. The machinery for setting up the assemblies was worked out, and in order to establish whether Scotland and Wales could accept the proposals, it was decided to use the precedent of the referendum on EEC membership. A referendum in March 1979 resulted in a substantial defeat of the proposals for Wales, and a narrow defeat of the proposals for Scotland.

Education

The only major piece of legislation during the Second World War was concerned with education: the Butler Education Act of 1944. It provided the framework for secondary education within Britain for the next twenty years. By it there were to be three types of secondary school: grammar, technical and secondary modern. At the age of eleven selection would be made to determine a pupil's suitability for one of these types. Fees, which had formerly been paid at grammar schools, were abolished. The local education authorities were to control state education. But the 1944 Act came increasingly under criticism. Opponents doubted whether it was right to make decisions on a child's future by means of the 'eleven plus' examination and whether it was right to separate children into different categories. Supporters pointed to the value of the academic work of the grammar schools and at the manner in which the other schools were tackling work suitable for their pupils. The comparative freedom allowed to local authorities in the development and control of education under the 1944 Act meant that it was possible for alternative systems to be used, subject to the approval of the Minister of Education. Some Labour-controlled authorities created comprehensive schools, attended by all pupils in their area, irrespective of academic ability. In 1965 the Labour government required local authorities throughout Britain to change to a system of comprehensive education and gradually to phase out the three-fold division of education as earlier stipulated.

By the 1960s the issue of comprehensive schools was one of sharp political controversy, as the Conservatives were opposed to the request for all schools to become comprehensive. During Heath's premiership the request was dropped. Strong opposition from Conservative-controlled authorities meant that even by the late 1970s a fully comprehensive system was still not established, in spite of an Act in 1976 which compelled authorities to adopt the comprehensive system. The Conservative government elected in 1979 pledged its support for those schools wishing to remain selective.

Meanwhile, raising of the school leaving age to fifteen in 1947 and to sixteen in 1973 had resulted in a substantial increase in the school population. With the increasing emphasis laid on qualifications, the new Certificate of Secondary Education (CSE) was introduced in 1965. It was intended to cater for pupils who did not enter for the longer-established General Certificate of Education (GCE). The two forms existed in somewhat uneasy partnership and though in 1978 long-discussed proposals for the amalgamation of the two systems were accepted by the government little progress was made towards implementing this decision.

Considerable expansion took place in higher education during the late 1950s and early 1960s, twelve new universities being founded in Britain during these years. The 1963 Robbins report into higher education suggested even further expansion of universities and polytechnics and a substantial increase in the amount of money spent on higher education. The economic uncertainties of the 1960s was the major factor preventing the application of many of the Robbins proposals. One new and very successful form of higher education did emerge in that decade: the Open University. Its students worked at home, tuition being given by television, radio and correspondence. A particular hope was that the Open University would cater for older students who earlier in life had been denied the chance of a university education.

The expansion of the education system occurred at a time of considerable social change: inevitably it produced problems. It was widely suggested that the generally more liberal attitude of teachers had undermined order in schools and that new teaching methods, instead of improving students' achievements, had resulted in a decline. In the mid-1970s both major political parties showed concern at the widespread criticisms of this kind. In October 1976 Callaghan, as Prime Minister, suggested that the government might in the future adopt a firmer control of the content of the school curriculum in order to ensure that essential subjects were properly taught.

Immigration

As the British Empire had expanded during the nineteenth century, the British government had given full British citizenship to all inhabitants of the newly-acquired overseas territories. The right to travel anywhere within the British Empire and to settle anywhere within the British Empire was an essential part of that citizenship. When given, it had the appearance of a generous gesture and it was not expected that the inhabitants of the colonies which Britain had acquired would ever employ the technical rights which British citizenship gave to them. But in 1948 some West Indians did take advantage of this right. The ship *HMS Windrush* arrived in Britain carrying some hundreds of West Indian immigrants. This was the beginning of immigration from the West Indies, and from India and Pakistan, throughout the 1950s. Not only had the immigrants a legal right to settle in Britain but, especially in those years when there was no unemployment problem in Britain, they were much needed in the development of the British economy.

Although by the end of the 1950s black and coloured immigrants accounted for less than one per cent of the population of Britain, their concentration in certain areas led to some social conflict with the white inhabitants, who found a contrast between the lifestyles of the immigrants and their own, which some did not accept. Events in 1958 suggested that there was serious tension in some of the areas of immigrant settlement. In London's Notting Hill, in the summer of that year, rioting occurred on racial issues. For the first time, attention was concentrated on immigration and suggestions were made that it should be curbed. Exceptionally high immigration in the early 1960s prompted partly by anxiety to enter Britain before any controls were imposed, increased the intensity of the demand for immigration control. The Conservative government, though strongly opposed by Labour, decided to introduce restrictions. By the Commonwealth Immigration Act of 1962, the right of entry by any Commonwealth citizen was removed: only those who had relatives within Britain or who had a definite job in Britain were now permitted to enter. Despite Labour opposition, once the Labour party was in power, it maintained the Act, and in 1965 and in 1968 reduced further the number of immigrants.

Government action to assist immigrants once they were within the country had been slight during the early years of immigration. In 1965 a major piece of legislation was designed to rectify a number of the humiliations suffered by immigrants, and to assist in their better integration into British society. This was the Race Relations Act, which made racial discrimination illegal: it was reinforced by a later Act of 1968. Instances of discrimination were to be referred to the Race Relations Board which had legal powers to enquire into the justice of the claims. These Race Relations Acts have made some contribution to solving some of the problems in this sensitive area, where progress has too often been hindered by extremist politicians and racial prejudice.

Questions

52. Study the cartoon on page 190 and then answer questions (a) to (c) which follow.
    (a) (i) Outline the main proposals of the report suggested by the new *way*,
        (ii) name the Prime Minister during whose government the report was published, and
        (iii) name the Prime Minister during whose government the report was largely put into practice.

        $(3+1+1)$
    (b) (i) With what justification does the cartoonist show this particular bus as stuck and its passengers confused at the time of the report's publication?
        (ii) Explain the significance of the institution represented by the bus driver in getting this bus on to the clear road.

        $(3+2)$
    (c) With reference to any *two* of the proposals of the report, show how they were put into practice and developed
        (i) during the prime ministership of the man named in (a) (iii), and
        (ii) subsequently.

        (10)

53. Show how successive British governments have attempted to deal with the problems confronting them in their management of the British economy and their relations with British trade unions *either* between 1945 and 1964 *or* since 1964.

54. Examine the significance for Britain of (a) the immigration of people from the West Indies and the Indian sub-continent and (b) the devolution of power for the people of Scotland and Wales.

19
Ireland

The English presence in Ireland dates back over many centuries. Towards the end of the nineteenth century the Irish had begun to make demands for home rule, for control of their own internal affairs under the overall control of the British government at Westminster. Though immense efforts were made by politicians to secure home rule, it was in fact never achieved. The major stumbling block was the strongly-held Protestantism of Ireland's northern counties, who felt that home rule would create a Roman Catholic-dominated Ireland in which their own interests would be overlooked. These differences in religion were sharpened by differences in the economy of the two parts of Ireland, the richer north being based largely on industry and the poorer south, largely on agriculture. This division has remained the fundamental problem in Ireland's history.

The 'troubles' and the achievement of independence

In 1912 a third home rule bill had passed the House of Commons but had been rejected by the Conservative-dominated House of Lords. According to practice at that time, the bill would nevertheless become law two years later in spite of the opposition of the House of Lords. But by then the First World War had broken out and wartime circumstances made it impossible to implement home rule. Although most Irish supported Britain's war efforts, the further delay of home rule encouraged a demand pressed by members of the increasingly strong *Sinn Fein* (ourselves alone) party: complete independence for Ireland. The war, according to the Sinn Fein leaders, presented a fine oppor-

tunity for the achievement of Ireland's independence. They prepared for a rising in southern Ireland at Easter 1916, aiming to overthrow the British rule and establish an independent republic for the whole of Ireland, in spite of the known opposition from the northern counties. In the Easter rising at Dublin the rebels took control of the city post office, where they proclaimed their country's independence and where they held out until their defeat a few days later by troops loyal to Britain. The rising therefore appeared to have been a failure. But its real importance lies in the treatment of those who had taken part in it, many of whom were executed by the British military authorities. Those executed at once became martyrs to the cause of Irish independence, which consequently became an accepted objective for an increased number of Irish people. Under the leadership of Eamon de Valera and Michael Collins, the Sinn Fein party became the party to which the majority of southern Irish gave their support.

The 'coupon' election of December 1918 revealed the full extent of Sinn Fein support. In the north, the Unionist party, pledged to maintain the links with Britain, was expectedly successful. But in the rest of Ireland the formerly dominant Irish Nationalist party was almost totally replaced by Sinn Fein which previously had only a small representation. Sinn Fein naturally interpreted this success as a sign of Irish support for independence. They now refused to attend the Westminster parliament. Instead they met together at Dublin in January 1919, forming the Irish *dail* (assembly), and unanimously confirmed the 1916 proclamation of independence. Their action could only be interpreted by the British government as one of rebellion against which they felt justified in taking military action. Over the next few years Ireland was the scene of much disorder and violence, in which three major issues were involved. One was the rebellion of the Dublin dail against British control, the second was the conflict between the independent south and the unionist north, and the third issue, at a later stage, was the internal conflict within the south on the acceptability of the 1921 treaty. Inevitably there was overlap between these three issues, which made the postwar years in Ireland ones of confusion as well as violence.

Armed support was given to the dail's stand for independence by the Irish Republican Army (IRA), formed in 1919 from early irregular groups. It was a secret, highly disciplined army which operated against British supporters in Ireland by raids, ambushes and assassinations. Its members did not wear uniforms and consequently formed a highly elusive enemy for the British authorities. Many Irish gave their support to the IRA as the only means of restoring their country's independence and the movement was not short of funds from Irish sympathisers in the United States. The British government relied initially on the Royal Irish Constabulary, the police force of Ireland, to deal with the rebellion and the IRA activity. But the task proved to be beyond their strength and as violence continued into 1920, the government decided to recruit ex-soldiers in England to assist in its work. Two groups sailed for Ireland: the 'Black and Tans' (so-called because, due to a shortage of uniforms, they were decked out in the odd combination of black belts and khaki battle dresses), and the 'Auxis', or the auxiliary division of the Royal Irish Constabulary, a group made up largely of officers. In Ireland both groups employed tough measures against the Irish in general, as it proved very difficult for

IRA suspects are searched by British troops during Ireland's bitter 'troubles' of the postwar years.

them to locate the IRA which, they rightly believed, had much support among the people of southern Ireland.

The factor that persuaded the British government of the justice of their policy of suppression was concern at the dail's claim of authority over the unwilling north. In order to strengthen the relationship between England and Northern Ireland, a home rule bill for the six northern counties, which were collectively known as Ulster, was passed early in 1920. By its terms a parliament was to be established at Stormont, near the northern capital of Belfast, to have control of the administration of Ulster. The people of Ulster would in future select two sets of MPs: those for their own parliament at Stormont and those for the United Kingdom parliament at Westminster. The creation of this parliament for the north was a further cause of anger to the dail, which continued to assert that its authority extended throughout the whole of Ireland. IRA activity in the north emphasized the rift that now existed between the two parts, and the north produced its own military defence, the Ulster Volunteers, who aimed to defeat IRA activity in Ulster and keep their province separate from the rest of Ireland. Both the British government and the Dublin dail were anxious to bring an end to the continuing violence, which became even more pronounced in the early months of 1921. In the summer of 1921 a truce was arranged and negotiations began on a settlement for the south. The negotiations were lengthy and difficult and only in December 1921 was final agreement reached. The treaty signed was an agreement on the creation of the Irish Free State, with dominion status within the British Commonwealth, having therefore a relationship with Britain identical to that held by Canada, Australia, New Zealand and (at that time) South Africa. Britain was to retain control of three 'treaty ports' along the Irish coast, for purposes of defence. The treaty certainly provided much that the Irish had wanted during decades of struggle, but it did not provide for all their demands. Dominion status was not the same as complete independence, and Ulster was in any

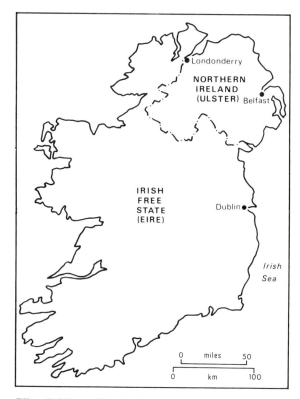

The division of Ireland

case excluded from control by the south. Some members of the dail were not prepared to accept the treaty's terms. Among them was the dail's President, Eamon de Valera, who had himself not been among the representatives at the negotiations. Those who had acted as negotiators argued that even though the treaty did not contain everything that they wished for, it was nevertheless a significant step towards complete independence.

The dail voted narrowly to accept the treaty. Ireland was thrown once more into chaos. This time the struggle was one among the people of the south, between those who favoured the treaty and those who opposed it. De Valera resigned and his place was taken by Michael Collins, one of the leading treaty negotiators. The division of the south was deepened when dail elections were held in the summer of 1922. The IRA was as divided as the politicians and for the rest of the year the violence that had typified the struggle against English control was repeated among the Irish themselves. Only in 1923, when de Valera decided to make the struggle against the treaty a constitutional one rather than a military one, did peace return. Though the upheavals during the five years after the end of the First World War had resulted in the partial achievement of Irish demands, the Irish Free State and the province of Ulster faced each other in an atmosphere of mutual suspicion.

Ireland after the treaty

Under the premiership of William Cosgrave during most of the 1920s, the Irish Free State settled to a more peaceful existence. De Valera obstinately refused to abandon full independence for Ireland. To press for this more vigorously, without the aid of violence, he formed in 1926 the *Fianna Fail* (soldiers of destiny) party, which quickly secured widespread support. In the early 1930s, with unemployment as much a problem in the cities of the Irish Free State as in Britain and elsewhere, the Cosgrave government became distinctly unpopular and thus an opportunity was presented to Fianna Fail. In an election early in 1932, the party secured a majority, de Valera became Prime Minister and the ten-year premiership of Cosgrave came to an end.

Gradually, and by the constitutional means he had promised, de Valera separated the Irish Free State further from Britain. The oath of allegiance to the Crown was abolished immediately. Appeals to the Privy Council in Britain were no longer to be made. The abdication of Edward VIII was used as an excuse for deeper changes: the Irish name of *Eire* was adopted in place of the treaty title of the *Irish Free State*, and internal changes were made which provided more fully for Irish control of Eire. In 1938 the treaty ports were taken fully into Irish possession. Why did de Valera not take matters to their logical conclusion by declaring a republic? The reason at that time was his hope that the province of Ulster might be incorporated in Eire before the final break with Britain came.

But de Valera's success in further separating Eire from Britain was not matched by his government's management of Eire's economy. His deputy Prime Minister, Sean Lemass had the difficult responsibility of directing Eire's economic affairs. As in England, the importance of economic protection became an especially noticeable feature of economic policy in the 1930s. In Eire's case the policy was pursued not only to protect Irish industry from foreign competition, but also to build up Irish self-sufficiency as a matter of pride in the newly independent country. It was also a form of retaliation on Britain, which had shown its opposition towards de Valera's policies in the 1930s by imposing special taxes on imports from Ireland. But in spite of the efforts of Lemass to improve Eire's economy in these years of depression, and in spite of some increase in the country's industrialization, the overall economy of Ireland was still weak, and many of its inhabitants in town and country were desperately poor. Furthermore, these years saw little social improvement: provision for education and medical care both received little encouragement from the government. To many Irish, the best solution to their problems in these years appeared to lie in emigration from their country, and most of the emigrants chose neighbouring Britain as the land most likely to provide reward for work, and a better standard of living.

The weakness of Eire's links with Britain during the time of de Valera was most strongly illustrated by Eire's determined bid for neutrality during the Second World War. Churchill's plea to de Valera for Ireland to join Britain in the struggle against Germany went totally unheeded. By 1949 any hope of British agreement to the incorporation of Ulster into Eire was abandoned, and under Prime Minister Costello, Eire declared itself a republic, left the Commonwealth and severed all its connections with Britain.

At the time of Eire's declaration of the republic, the British government gave a guarantee, upheld strongly by all later British governments, that it would defend union between Britain and Ulster until such time as the Stormont parliament should vote to end it. There was little likelihood that any such vote would ever be passed at Stormont. Since the early 1920s, the majority of Ulster's MPs at Westminster had been Unionist, closely linked with the Conservative party. The Stormont government had continued to represent the Protestant majority in Ulster, whose interests were staunchly upheld by Sir James Craig, Ulster's Prime Minister throughout the 1920s and the 1930s. As in these years relations between Britain and Eire became more distant, so relations between Britain and Ulster became closer. Protestant unity in Ulster was demonstrated by the continuing influence of the Protestant Orange Order in the political and social life of Ulster, and in annual marches and celebrations designed to commemorate the seventeenth-century victories of Protestantism over Roman Catholicism in Ireland, and Ulster's loyalty to the Crown. That loyalty was shown especially during the Second World War when Ulster, as a part of the United Kingdom, became fully involved on the British side, the Ulster ports providing an invaluable link between Britain and the United States during the war years.

Nevertheless, approximately a quarter of the population of Ulster were Roman Catholics, among whom there was a feeling that their interests were not properly represented at Stormont and that within Ulster they existed as second-class citizens. A number of these Roman Catholics hoped for the incorporation of Ulster into Eire, and gave support to the IRA which, though less active than in the time of the 'troubles' was still a significant body in Irish political affairs.

The problem of Ulster

There were two root causes of the violent disorder which developed in Ulster in the late 1960s and 1970s: discrimination against Ulster's minority group, Roman Catholics, and the partition between Ulster and Eire. Both the Eire government and the Ulster Roman Catholics looked for a fully united Ireland. But by the 1960s the partition had hardened considerably and change from the

Unionism of the Protestant majority in Ulster was unthinkable. In the meantime, the discrimination against Ulster's Roman Catholic population was an injustice about which some positive action could be taken.

In the late 1960s as a result of carefully conducted surveys, the Northern Ireland Civil Rights Association publicized the forms that discrimination was taking in Northern Ireland. Many Roman Catholics were unable to vote in local government elections as voting in these elections was confined to ratepayers, a category to which the majority of Roman Catholics did not belong; this virtual denial of representation had particularly serious effects in the city of Londonderry, where Roman Catholics formed a majority of the city's population. Apart from this denial of the basic right to vote, there was evidence of widespread discrimination against Roman Catholics in obtaining employment and housing. Areas of some Ulster cities were virtually designated by the Protestants as Roman Catholic zones, and steps were taken to ensure that Roman Catholics were housed within them. Discrimination in these different ways had become a traditional feature of Ulster life. The Protestant supporters of the Ulster government justified this attitude towards Roman Catholics by pointing out that the province's Roman Catholics were enemies of Ulster, as they looked for the eventual incorporation of Ulster into Eire. The suggestion was also made that IRA violence, which had erupted in Ulster during the late 1950s, was often based on Roman Catholic support. In the late 1960s the Northern Ireland Civil Rights Association organized marches and demonstrations, which often led to violence between Roman Catholics and Protestants. The issue of discrimination was now given much wider publicity both in Ulster and in the United Kingdom as a whole.

Whatever justification there might or might not have been for the discriminatory policies of the Ulster government, the Westminster government insisted that Stormont should remove these injustices. In 1968 and 1969 the Ulster government of O'Neill responded to these demands by making some

An open air march in Northern Ireland. Notice the various religious and political emblems that are being used. Such marches, though traditional in the province, often aroused opposition in the late 1960s and the 1970s.

moves towards ending discrimination in local government, education, housing and employment. His policy of moderate reform met opposition within his own government and from extreme Protestants, such as the Reverend Ian Paisley, who spread fears that accommodating the Roman Catholic minority in this way would lead to Ulster's destruction. Such extremist opinion was particularly inflamed when in April 1969 the O'Neill government gave voting rights to all inhabitants of Ulster in local government elections and redrew local government boundaries to provide for fairer representation. His opponents interpreted these moves as an early stage in the abandonment of Ulster and its incorporation in Eire. In the contro-

versy which followed, O'Neill resigned, though his successor, Chichester-Clark, continued along the main lines of O'Neill's policy of moderate reform.

In August 1969 severe rioting occurred in Ulster, altering the situation substantially. During the course of the traditional Protestant marches, clashes took place between Roman Catholics and Protestants, especially in Londonderry and Belfast. As the police were unable to restore order, the Stormont government asked the Westminster government for military help, and British troops were immediately sent. The arrival of the British troops established a new pattern for the conflict in Ulster.

Ulster in the 1970s

The early 1970s were years of increasing disorder and violence in Ulster, which the efforts of the Westminster government and the Stormont government seemed powerless to prevent. Whilst the Civil Rights Association continued to press for further reform, the power of the IRA developed as a more military form of opposition. It was concerned not only with the achievement of civil rights, but also with the ending of partition. The 'provisional' wing of the IRA believed that revolutionary militancy was the only solution to Ulster's problems and throughout the early 1970s they conducted campaigns against the supporters of the Stormont government and against the British troops in Ulster. The destruction of many towns, such as Belfast, was similar to that experienced in wartime. Both Chichester-Clark and Faulkner, who succeeded Chichester-Clark in March 1971, continued the policy of moderate reform, despite this violent opposition from the provisional IRA, the demand for fuller reforms by the Civil Rights Association, and the clear misgivings of many Protestants that the policy was undermining Ulster's foundations.

Britain's role in these events was a difficult and thankless one, satisfying neither side. Many Protestant opponents of the reforms considered that it had been pressure from Wilson's Labour government in the late 1960s which had begun the moderate reform which they so much disliked. The presence of the British army appeared seriously to undermine the independence of action of the Stormont government which had been provided for in the terms of the 1920 Home Rule Act. But in March 1972, the mounting chaos in Northern Ireland caused the Westminster government to go further, and take over direct rule of Ulster, suspending the Stormont parliament. Ulster politicians protested vigorously. At much the same time, the masked and uniformed men of the Ulster Defence Association appeared, pledged to take physical action to protect Protestant interests in Ulster. In these different ways the policies of the British government had, by 1972, alienated Ulster Protestants. Similarly in these years they had alienated Ulster Roman Catholics. Although in 1969 Roman Catholics welcomed the British army as affording them protection against Protestant extremists, by the early 1970s the army was regarded as an instrument of British repression. The introduction in August 1971 of internment of those suspected of IRA membership deepened Britain's unpopularity among Roman Catholics. Numerous clashes between the British troops and the Roman Catholic population occurred. On 30 January 1972, a day that became known as 'Bloody Sunday', the killing of 13 people by the British army in the Roman Catholic Bogside area of Londonderry, inflamed anti-British feeling still further. Events in the early 1970s thus presented to the outside world the image of Britain as a repressive and dictatorial force in Ulster. Neighbouring Eire, whilst condemning the IRA violence in Ulster, was still firmly committed to the union of all Ireland as the ultimate solution for the land's problems.

In the spring of 1973 the British government made new proposals for a settlement to Ulster's problems. The most important of these was the creation of an Ulster assembly to be elected on a system of proportional representation, which would allow greater Roman Catholic participation in government. The scheme provided for what was termed *power sharing*. Preparations were made for the summoning of this assembly at the start of 1974. Before then, in December 1973, at meetings held at Sunningdale in England, representatives of the governments of the United Kingdom, Ulster and Eire met together and agreed on the formation of a Council of Ireland to produce better relations between the two parts of the land. When the new assembly came into being in January 1974 its Protestant and Roman Catholic members worked together in promising harmony, but it became clear that the whole idea of power sharing was unpopular. Opposition came from a new source in May 1974: the Ulster Works Council. This body, representing the Protestant workers of Northern

Ireland, organized a general strike which had such widespread support that it paralysed the whole of Ulster and brought an end to the assembly, the Sunningdale proposals and the whole idea of power sharing. Protestant opinion showed that it would make no further concessions to Roman Catholics. There was a return to the earlier situation, and Ulster once again came under direct rule from Westminster.

A further attempt at a solution was made. In 1975 a convention for Ulster was to be elected to work out a formula for the province, but the Unionist dominance in the convention, and their now firm opposition to power sharing, made it inevitable that it would make little progress. The British government increasingly took the view that there was little more that it could do to solve the problem. In the meantime, the years of the mid-1970s saw continuing acts of violence, though on a somewhat less widespread scale than before. Many in Ulster were by now desperate at the confusion and violence into which their province was plunged, and the apparent impossibility of finding a satisfactory solution. A symptom of the despair of the people of Ulster, and their wish for an end to the violence, was the Peace Movement started by a group of women after the death of three children in August 1976. Though the movement gathered substantial support from both Roman Catholics and Protestants and though it might have had some influence in curbing violence, it was not by itself a solution to Ulster's problems. Nevertheless by the late 1970s, Ulster was showing signs of accepting direct rule as the best solution for the foreseeable future. There was a significant decline in the incidence of violence: in 1977 some units of the Ulster Defence Association disbanded and IRA activity slackened. Much of this improved situation was attributable to the sensible administration of Ulster by the British Secretary of State for Northern Ireland, Roy Mason, as well as to a sense among many in Ulster that to maintain the existing situation was perhaps the best solution for the immediate future.

Questions

55. Study the photograph on page 203 and then answer questions (a) to (d) which follow.
    (a) (i) Are those taking part in this march *Protestants* or *Roman Catholics*?
        (ii) What evidence from the photograph supports the answer you have given in (a) (i)?
        (1+2)
    (b) (i) Name the government in Ireland to which, until the early 1970s, the people in this march would most probably have given their support.
        (ii) Outline the circumstances leading to the establishment of this government during the years just after the First World War.
        (1+3)
    (c) With reference to events in this part of Ireland between the early 1920s and the late 1960s, explain
        (i) why the political and religious opponents of the people shown marching in this photograph felt dissatisfied, and
        (ii) why the people shown in the photograph felt justified in pursuing their policies against their political and religious opponents.
        (3+2)
    (d) Outline the history of this part of Ireland from the late 1960s to the present day, explaining why religious differences have continued to be so important.
        (8)

56. Describe and account for the violence that took place in Ireland between 1918 and 1922. Why was the treaty of December 1921 only partially successful in bringing peace to Ireland?

57. Why had Northern Ireland become an area of so much conflict by the late 1960s? Examine the attempts made by the British government since that time to deal with the problem of Ulster.

20
West European unity

The long-held military and technological superiority of the nations of Western Europe, and their direct control of many colonial lands made them the dominant powers in world affairs during the interwar years. The United States and the Soviet Union were still not equal to them in power or prestige. The former had taken steps to ensure its virtual isolation, and the latter was too much concerned with putting Communism into practice within their country to involve itself in events elsewhere. The Second World War changed this situation totally. After 1945 both countries found it impossible to retreat into their former isolationism and their increased role in world affairs had considerable effects on Western Europe.

The foundations of West European cooperation

The maintenance of American troops in Western Europe, and the American commitment to world affairs was significantly strengthened in 1947 by the Truman doctrine and Marshall Aid, and by the policy of containment. For its part, the Soviet Union had influence in many states of Eastern Europe, where the establishment of Communist governments owed much to Soviet activities. The increased world importance of these two countries made the nations of Western Europe realize the need for cooperation and unity if they were to survive collectively, and still have some say in world affairs.

The colonial power of different West European countries was challenged as soon as the war ended: in particular, British power was challenged in India, and French power was challenged in Indochina. In the 1950s and the 1960s independence was granted to many colonial lands of Africa and south-east Asia, lands which at the time of the Second World War had been regarded as likely to remain under colonial control for many decades. The European retreat from imperial possessions is considered later. As a result of this retreat, the European powers gradually realized that they must look for a future not among their former overseas possessions but among their immediate European neighbours who were experiencing similar problems, and with whom they shared many political and cultural similarities.

One fundamental form of unity which the West European countries already possessed was in religion: all were Christian countries and in most of them the Roman Catholic church, with its then highly centralized form of administration and control from Rome, was the largest Christian denomination. Political life in the different countries also had many similarities: new parties of the right, such as the Christian Democrats of West Germany and Italy, and the MRP of France, shared many ideals and attitudes, whilst the different Socialist parties of the left gave loyalty to the common Socialist ideal which itself tended to make little of national divisions. The development of television and travel led Europeans to be more aware of their immediate neighbours. Though this fuller awareness sometimes led to a reinforcement of prejudices against fellow-Europeans, it nevertheless led also to a closer knowledge of them.

Cooperation between the countries of Western Europe can be seen on three different levels: military, economic and political. In all respects the cooperation and the unity of Western Europe was undertaken with the approval, support and aid of the United States which saw in these processes the strengthening of those countries which, like itself, were opposed to Communism.

Military cooperation in Western Europe

In the late 1940s the gains of the Communist parties in countries such as France and Italy added to the tension between the states of Western Europe and the Soviet-dominated states of Eastern Europe. The governments of Western Europe therefore began to feel that cooperation between their armies was advisable. The successful Communist coup in Czechoslovakia in 1948 showed that this cooperation could no longer be delayed. Already, in March 1947 a rather vague treaty of mutual assistance between Britain and France, known as the Dunkirk treaty of alliance, had been signed. A year later, in March 1948, just after the Czechoslovak coup, the Brussels treaty was signed by Britain, France and the three Benelux countries of Belgium, the Netherlands and Luxembourg. These countries pledged themselves to mutual defence in the event of attack; and it was certainly the Soviet Union that the signatories had in mind as a possible aggressor.

The Brussels treaty was only a start: it was insufficiently comprehensive both in its terms and its membership to provide an adequately united military command in Western Europe. The Berlin blockade of 1948–49 gave further warning of possible Soviet aggression and the need for a more effective united defence by the West. The assistance by the United States in the Berlin airlift illustrated well American determination to pursue the policy of *containment*, of preventing any further expansion of Communist power. In the summer of 1948 the United States and Canada entered into discussions with the signatories of the Brussels treaty and were joined later in the year by Denmark, Iceland, Italy, Norway and Portugal. Their discussions led to the signature by all twelve powers of the North Atlantic treaty in April 1949. The most important article in the treaty was Article 5:

The parties agree that an armed attack against one or more of them in Europe or North America shall be considered an attack against them all; and consequently they agree that, if such an armed attack occurs, each of them in exercise of the right of individual or collective self-defence recognized by Article 52 of the Charter of the United Nations will assist the party or parties so attacked by taking forthwith, individually and in concert with the other parties, such action as it deems necessary, including the use of armed force, to restore and maintain the security of the North Atlantic area.

Whilst the North Atlantic Treaty Organization (NATO) was preparing for firm action when necessary, it should be noted from this extract that such action was always to be under the general oversight of the United Nations. The overall authority in NATO was its council, which contained representatives of all member countries, though it tended to be dominated by the United States. Forces of member countries were placed under the direction of the council and were to work together in close partnership. NATO was enlarged in 1952 by the inclusion of Greece and Turkey and in 1955 by West Germany. The organization can rightly claim to have achieved its aim for Europe, as no West European country has become Communist since its foundation. But its presence may also have contributed to the permanency of the *Iron Curtain*, a political and ideological division between Communist and non-Communist countries. Some European countries have been far from happy at the American influence asserted in Europe through NATO: in 1965 President de Gaulle withdrew French forces from NATO on account of this strong American influence. Though most of the members of NATO were European, it was not a specifically European institution.

An attempt to create a specifically European army in the early 1950s caused much controversy and eventually came to nothing. The attempted creation by West European governments of a European Defence Community (EDC) led to particular opposition from France and West Germany, which were expected to be its most important members. The EDC treaty was eventually ratified by the West German parliament in March 1954, though many in West Germany feared that the creation of EDC would ally West Germany too closely with Western Europe and thus delay progress towards their country's reunification with East Germany. France had stronger reservations and it was the French refusal to ratify the EDC treaty that caused its collapse. The combined political weight of the Communist party and de Gaulle's RPF was strong enough to bring the rejection: the Communist party was naturally suspicious of an organization that might be used against the Communists of Eastern Europe, whilst the RPF disliked the prospect of French forces being limited in their independence of action. Britain, though favourable to the EDC project, failed to take positive steps to help it into being.

Economic and political cooperation: the early stages

The United States was responsible for the early stages of economic cooperation between the West European powers. The American offer of Marshall Aid in June 1947 was seized upon eagerly by most European states suffering, as they still were, from the destruction and the shortages brought about by war. In order both to help distribution of Marshall Aid and to strive towards improvement in the economy of Europe, the Organization for European Economic Cooperation (OEEC) was formed in 1947 by the European states receiving Marshall Aid. OEEC had a wide membership and functioned through inter-governmental meetings. Though it was a useful start in European economic unity, it was limited to a practical task, and the degree of European unity which it created was slight in comparison with later developments. The Organization for European Economic Cooperation continued to function until the Organization for Economic Cooperation and Development (OECD) was created from it in 1960.

The Council of Europe, established in May 1949, was a very different type of organization. Its roots were more positively European and it was concerned more with cultural, social and political matters than with economic matters: it had an air of idealism,

which it has never really lost. Its origins lay in a meeting held at the Hague in the previous year, a meeting attended by supporters of European unity such as Winston Churchill, Alcide de Gasperi, Jean Monnet and Paul Henri Spaak. The Council of Europe was established at Strasbourg. This city not only formed a convenient geographical centre-point for the member-countries but also had been the subject of earlier Franco-German conflict. It had therefore both a practical and an emotive significance.

Two organizations of the Council of Europe worked at Strasbourg: a Committee of Ministers and a European Assembly. The former was attended by ministers of the governments of the member-countries and the latter by members of the parliaments of the member-countries. The collective authority of the Committee and the Assembly within the Council of Europe was, however, limited: they had a purely advisory role and enthusiasts for fuller unity were disappointed at the modest nature of the authority which the new Council of Europe adopted. Despite the exclusion of many defence and economic matters from its scope, the Council of Europe nevertheless made important contributions in a number of other matters of common European interest. Much practical work was undertaken in securing common European approaches to many different concerns, legal, medical and environmental. In 1951 it produced a European Convention on Human Rights which ensures that human rights in Europe are not ignored to the extent they were by the totalitarian European powers in the 1930s. The convention showed its value particularly in 1969 when the then military government of Greece was found to have broken the convention. In 1971 a European Social Charter was produced making a similar contribution towards human welfare in Europe. The Council's practical work is therefore of far-reaching importance, even though it may appear dull and not particularly newsworthy. In spite of all its limitations, it was an important step along the road to European unity.

OEEC and the Council of Europe worked on an international basis. Both relied on close consultation between members, and decisions could only be taken if there was collective agreement. Member-countries did not give authority to any overriding administrative body, and they thus preserved fully their individual identity. With the foundation of the European Coal and Steel Community (ECSC), an organization had been created that worked on a *supra–national* basis, which not only involved close consultation between the member-countries but which also gave authority to a powerful overriding body.

The idea of the European Coal and Steel Community was first put forward by Robert Schuman, the French Foreign Minister, but it was really the product of the ideas of one of the warmest enthusiasts for full European unity, Jean Monnet. He had already had considerable impact on the economy of France through the postwar plan for revitalizing the archaic and war-devastated French industry. When the ECSC came into being in July 1952, Monnet was appointed its President.

The basic purpose served by the ECSC was to cooperate in the exploitation of the resources of the coal and steel industries of six member countries: France, West Germany, Italy, Belgium, the Netherlands and Luxembourg. The supra-national body which administered the Community was known as the High Authority and in the administration of the Community the members of the High Authority were expected to shed their national identity and entirely serve the interests of the Community. To remove any element of dictation, the High Authority was responsible to a parliament, composed of those representatives of the parliaments of the member countries who were already represented on the assembly of the Council of Europe. The ECSC was further guided by a Council of Ministers of the member-countries.

The Community's practical economic aims were for the eventual end of the import taxes and import quotas applied by member-countries on coal and steel from other member-countries. The import taxes, usually referred to as *tariffs*, were a long-established means of protecting the home-produced goods by increasing the price of the foreign-produced goods. The *quota system*, again in order to protect home-produced goods, limits the amount of imported foreign-produced goods. In the early 1950s successful progress was made towards the achievement of these aims and increased output was encouraged by the gradual elimination of these nationally-imposed restrictions on the movement of coal and steel.

But the Community had a wider, political aim as well as this practical, economic aim. In the interwar years, coal and steel had often been a cause of international conflict: German reparations, the French occupation of the Ruhr, the conflicts about the ownership of the Saar are all important instances of such conflicts, and they had contributed to the earlier hostile relations between the two most important members of the new Community, France and West Germany. Practical cooperation over coal and steel would, so it was hoped, pave the way for cooperation in other matters.

Economic and political cooperation: the European Economic Community

The early 1950s had thus seen a successful venture into economic cooperation (ECSC) and failure in military cooperation (EDC). The example of the former and the warning of the latter spurred on enthusiasts for European unity to further achievement. Monnet resigned his presidency of the ECSC High Authority in order to work wholeheartedly for fuller European unity.

In June 1955 at the city of Messina in eastern Sicily, a meeting was held of the foreign ministers of the six members of the ECSC. Here the collective decision was taken to work towards closer unity in wider economic and political matters. Extensive, collective work by civil servants of the Six led to the signature of the two treaties of Rome in March 1957. One of the treaties established the European Economic Community (EEC), often termed the *Common Market*, and the other established the European Atomic Energy Community, often

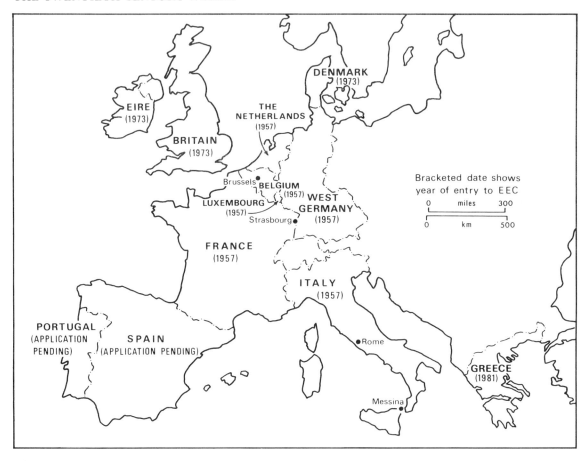

The European Economic Community

termed *Euratom*. Though in 1957 much hope was placed in this latter organization, its actual development over the next decade was unsuccessful: those member countries such as France and West Germany which were developing nuclear power showed in practice a marked preference for developing it along national rather than community lines; it was further handicapped by the absence of Britain, which was a leading power in the development of atomic energy. By the later 1960s it was clear that Euratom had failed.

The progress of EEC was a very different story. Its organizational structure, based mainly at Brussels, was a development of the structure of the ECSC and as such it had a supra-national basis. The *European Commission* is the main supra-national body, staffed by European international civil servants whose loyalties lie exclusively with the Community. The Commission is responsible for forming and carrying through Community policies. In the *European Council* each member country is represented here by one of its ministers, and the Council's function is to approve or disapprove the policies of the Commission. Inevitably there had been some conflict between the Commission and the Council. During the 1960s the Council increasingly asserted its importance by agreeing that only if all the ministers of the Council were in agreement on any issue would they give formal approval to the policies proposed by the Commission. Members of the *European Parliament* of the EEC were to be chosen by the parliaments of the member countries.

The signing of the treaty of Rome by the six created the EEC. Though the value of the organization is still much debated, there is no doubt of its importance in the history of Europe since the signing of this treaty in March 1957.

In composition, this body was to overlap with the assembly of the Council of Europe and the assembly of the ECSC: its meetings were therefore held at Strasbourg. The Parliament provided a forum for the views of the parliaments in the different countries, but in the early years of the Community's existence its importance was comparatively slight: only after the enlargement of Community membership in 1973 did it take on a more important role. The *European Community Court of Justice* at Luxembourg has the delicate task of interpreting community law and practice.

The 248 articles of the treaty of Rome were concerned with the aims of the EEC as well as with its organizational structure. Progress towards the different aims was expected to be gradual. An early basic aim was the reduction of tariffs and quotas between member countries and also the establishment of a common external tariff for all EEC countries. Former overseas possessions of member countries were to be associated with the EEC. There was also to be progress towards common policies in agriculture and transport and there was to be free movement of people and capital between the member countries. A longer term objective was the complete integration of the economies of the member countries, involving a common monetary policy. Seen as an even longer-term policy was the complete political unity of the member countries, so that the EEC would eventually take on the work and the responsibilities of the national governments.

At the time of the treaty of Rome, the EEC set itself the goal of achieving its basic objectives during a twelve-year transitional period. So far as tariffs and quotas were concerned, these were eliminated between member countries by 1968. Goods moved freely within the Community, whose general economy consequently improved. Assistance was given by the EEC to the development of its poorer regions; parts of southern Italy benefited in this respect. At Yaoundé, in Cameroon, conventions were signed in 1963 and again in 1969 to provide direct aid from the EEC to former African possessions of member countries, of whom France was the most significant. The amount of aid given was considered, however, to be too low.

The Six become the Nine

During the 1970s a number of European countries showed interest in joining the EEC. In January 1973 Britain, Ireland and Denmark were formally admitted as members; later in the 1970s negotiations took place for the entry of Greece, Portugal and Spain.

It took more than a decade for the British entry to be agreed. In the early 1960s the British government's decision to seek entry was not only caused by the economic success that the EEC was by then proving to be. The government was aware that as the Commonwealth became less important for Britain, and as the colonies gradually secured their independence, so it was essential for Britain to find a new world role. There was also an awareness that Britain was no longer a major world power and could no longer afford to stand alone. The reduced customs duties within the EEC were a further practical incentive for entry, as it was hoped that the British economy, like the economies of the Six, would reap economic benefits.

But on two occasions in the 1960s Britain failed to gain entry to the EEC. The Conservative government was rebuffed in 1963 and the Labour government in 1967. Though on both occasions the negotiations with the EEC concerning Britain's continuing links with the Commonwealth were intricate and difficult, the reasons for Britain's double rejection in the 1960s lay with the French President. In de Gaulle's view, Britain was not 'ready' for entry into the EEC as she did not show a full willingness to abandon her links with both the Commonwealth countries and what was often termed her *special relationship* with the United States, based on the historic links across the Atlantic and the use of the English language by both countries. But de Gaulle had a more fundamental reason for wishing Britain outside the EEC. De Gaulle had done so much to build up the dominant position of France within Europe and within the EEC that he did not want to see Britain rob France of the results of his work. Although the other members of the EEC were generally favourable towards British entry, each member state had the right to veto the entry of a new member and de Gaulle therefore used this right to keep Britain out.

By the time a third British application was made in the early 1970s, de Gaulle was no longer President of France and British entry was therefore easier. Britain entered the new negotiations with a fuller intention of merging her economy with that of Europe. The negotiations centred very largely on the relationship between the EEC and British agriculture and fishing; the British commitment to purchasing Commonwealth produce (especially New Zealand dairy products and West Indian sugar) and British tariffs and monetary policy. In all areas allowance was made for a gradual change, lasting until the late 1970s. The British entry was a particular achievement for Prime Minister Heath, who had long been committed to the idea of Britain as a member of the EEC.

The enlarged Community made progress with new policies in the 1970s. The Common Agricultural Policy, under the direction of Sicco Mansholt, aimed to remove the differences between the agricultural policies of the member countries. This was a difficult aim

"I suspect you of driving under the influence of America."

De Gaulle seizes an opportunity of using his authority to prevent the British entry into the EEC. Only when de Gaulle had left politics did British entry stand any chance of success.

to achieve, as in almost all countries the farmers benefited from government protection and government subsidies. Mansholt's plan would bring about the end of both these national-orientated policies, and would boost agricultural development within the EEC by excluding agricultural products from outside. He also wanted to see the more efficient use of land resources by the movement of population from the countryside to the towns. But the Common Agricultural Policy continued to receive opposition from farmers who disliked its interference, and from those throughout the Community who attributed the rising cost of food partly to this policy. Another new policy was the European monetary system, which was an attempt to check the sharp changes that occurred in the rates of exchange of the various European currencies and to pave the way for full economic union between the member countries at a future stage.

Questions

58. Study the cartoon on page 213 and then answer questions (a) to (d) which follow.
    (a) (i) State the year of this attempted journey, shown on the car's number plate.
        (ii) Name the country and the Prime Minister represented by the man in the car.
        (iii) Name the country and the President represented by the policeman.
        (iv) Name the five other countries which at that time had close economic links with the country represented by the policeman. (1+1+1+1)
    (b) Explain the reasons that led to this attempted journey. (4)
    (c) (i) Explain what the policeman means by his words of rebuke to the man in the car.
        (ii) Explain other reasons why the policeman might wish to stop the journey being made by the man in the car.
        (iii) What powers did the policeman possess to enable him to stop this journey? (2+4+2)
    (d) (i) Name the different driver who successfully completed this journey six years later.
        (ii) Explain the reasons that led to this different driver's later success. (4)

59. Examine the attempts that were made during the 15 years after the end of the Second World War to create closer economic, political and military union among the countries of Western Europe.

60. Trace the events leading to the creation of the EEC in 1957. Describe how the community is organized and how it has developed since the time of its foundation.

21

The Indian sub-continent

Together with lands in Africa, South America and Asia, India is still developing in economic terms, and thus forms part of what is often termed the *Third World*. The Indian subcontinent is divided today between India, Pakistan and Bangladesh. At the beginning of the twentieth century this enormous area was united under British control. A special pride was taken in this British possession, partly because it contained one fifth of the world's population and partly because of its rich history and culture. But during the interwar years in India, alone of the British overseas possessions, a movement for independence gathered sufficient strength to compel the British to promise eventual self-government.

British India: early opposition

At the end of the First World War sixty per cent of India was administered directly by the British and the remaining forty per cent was administered by the Indian princes. It was a convenient way of controlling such a large population and it gave the appearance of involving Indians in the government of their country. The princes were allowed much independence of action, though ultimate control remained with the British government and with the Viceroy, the King's direct representative in India. Within the areas held directly by the British, the Viceroy's authority was extensive. He usually acted jointly with the Secretary of State for India, who remained in Britain. The Indian civil service undertook the practical work of administration. It was open, technically, to Indians themselves, provided they could reach the high educational standards

demanded for entry. But in practice, the upper ranks of the Indian civil service were composed almost entirely of British people. There was a similar British predominance in the upper ranks of the Indian army. But in the army's lower ranks and at the local level of the civil service, Indians were in the majority. Increasingly, Indians felt that they were being discriminated against precisely because they were Indian.

The sub-continent provided well for the British, who held responsible positions and settled prosperously, having a life-style of considerable prestige, vividly portrayed in the pre-1914 years by Rudyard Kipling in his Indian stories. It is, however, doubtful whether the Indian economy benefited from the British presence. The subcontinent was regarded as a useful source of raw material for British industry, especially the cotton industry, and as a profitable area for the sale of British manufactured products. Britain did not want to encourage within India industries that would compete with her own. Thus India remained essentially an agricultural nation, heavily dependent on Britain economically.

By the time of the First World War, the British in India already faced opposition from the Indian National Congress movement, which received its support from the Hindu population. This movement became the focal point of the campaign for independence. The smaller Muslim League chiefly represented the interests of the Muslims, but was allied with the Congress in opposing the British presence.

During the interwar years, the policies of the British government and the actions of the British administration encouraged the development of these opposition movements.

The ceremonial entrance into Delhi of a new Viceroy and Vicereine was always an event of importance. In this photograph, Lord and Lady Curzon make their entrance, in 1903.

In the First World War, Indian troops fought alongside British ones. Yet the war had little to do with India's interests, a fact of which many Indians were well aware: the 'European civil war' was the contemptuous and not entirely inaccurate way in which the Indians referred to the fighting between 1914 and 1918. In the immediate postwar years disturbances were common throughout India. The cruel suppression of rioting in the Punjab city of Amritsar in 1919 sharpened the grievances of the Indians against the British. The military commander at Amritsar, General Dyer, had aroused much resentment against the British by his instruction that all Indians were to crawl on hands and knees along a street of the city where a white woman had been attacked. When rioting

occurred in protest against this 'humiliating order, Dyer took the drastic decision of instructing his troops to fire into the crowd of rioters. Nearly four hundred Indians were killed as a result. All India was gripped by bitter anger against the British, even though the Amritsar atrocity had been no part of British government policy and Dyer was dismissed by the government because of his actions.

The British government's response to this developing opposition was weak. In 1919 as a result of proposals made by Secretary Montagu and Viceroy Chelmsford, a Government of India Act was passed. The major concession granted by this Act was the establishment of an Indian parliament, in which elected Indians would be in a majority. This appeared a generous concession, but the electorate was limited to comparatively few Indians and the authority of the new parliament could in any case be over-ruled by the Viceroy. Though many Indians were angered at the limitations contained in the 1919 Act, it nevertheless gave some of them opportunities of experience in the administration of their country. Increasingly, however, a fuller control was demanded.

Mahatma Gandhi and British concessions to India

Mahatma Gandhi took advantage of the disturbed circumstances of these years to become the acknowledged leader of Indian nationalism. Gandhi, a well-educated Hindu, had involved himself earlier in his life in organizing Indian immigrants in South Africa. During the First World War Gandhi developed within India the distinctive features for which his opposition became renowned. He abandoned his Western style of dress and, adopting simple peasant dress, travelled around India, attracting much support among the Hindu people. His message to them was simple and effective. To combat the British they should adopt passive resistance: they should refuse all cooperation with the British, but they should not involve themselves in any violence, even if they themselves were violently treated by the authorities. To sustain the non-violent character of what soon developed as a mass movement was no easy achievement, yet Gandhi's leadership was so inspiring and forceful that very few acts of violence took place. In the mid-1920s he encouraged Indians to take up the hand-spinning of cotton, a simple and peaceful occupation which further united Indians in his campaign. In the early 1930s, the boycott of the government salt tax maintained the non-violent character of his movement, whilst receiving mass support from Indians. Gandhi himself and many of his followers were imprisoned at different times throughout the 1920s and 1930s: passive resistance was practised even in the British gaols, where overcrowding caused by Gandhi's campaign became a

further complicating factor for the British who, it seemed, just could not win against these techniques.

Gandhi secured control of the Congress movement. Under his leadership it changed from being a middle-class movement to one with mass support. Two leading Indian politicians, Motilal Nehru and his son Jawaharlal Nehru, were persuaded by Gandhi to abandon their pro-Western attitudes and, like Gandhi, adopted a distinctive Indian approach to India's problems. The Nehrus were among the most important and the most devoted of Gandhi's political supporters.

Only in 1931 did Britain recognize the Congress movement, in spite of its widespread support from Indians long before then. In 1931 and 1932 Gandhi attended London-based round table conferences on the future of India. His continued use of peasant dress, even in England's rainy weather, attracted among the English a good deal of popular interest in Gandhi and the movement he represented: throughout the inter-war years no other national leader opposed to Britain's overseas control made anything remotely like the progress Gandhi did.

By the early 1930s, beset by its own economic problems, and with no hope of crushing the Indian demand for self-rule, the British government realized that it could not control India for ever. In 1931 the Statute of Westminster pointed the way to eventual self-government throughout all Britain's overseas possessions and to a change from the idea of the Empire to that of the Commonwealth. In this future change of status, India came first and the round table conferences were one of a number of ways in which Britain sought to make concessions to India in these years. Further discussions led to the passing of an act which the British hoped would provide stability in India for the foreseeable future.

The Government of India Act of 1935 went a long way towards the Indian demands, but it kept ultimate control by Britain. The Act provided for a federal state of India with a federal parliament of two houses. This new form of the parliament was to have greater responsibility for Indian affairs than had been allowed for under the 1919 Act, though crucial matters such as foreign affairs were still to be controlled by the Viceroy. Greater gains were made by the Indians in local government, which now became almost entirely under their control. Gandhi felt that the Act should be given a chance of working and he cooperated with it; the passive resistance campaign, which had declined in the mid-1930s, was not renewed. Not all Congress members agreed with Gandhi about the Act – Jawaharlal Nehru, for example, was strongly opposed to it – but nevertheless the Congress movement as a result of the new elections secured a majority in the parliament. The Muslim League gained little representation under the Act and they began to fear they would be at a disadvantage in a future independent India dominated by the Hindu Congress movement. But the Act was never fully implemented. The viceroys of the late 1930s were slow in putting it fully into operation and the outbreak of the Second World War took British attention away from India.

Independence and partition

During the Second World War complete independence was demanded more strongly. Winston Churchill, while out of office in the 1930s, had been vigorously opposed to the government's concessions to India. It was therefore unlikely that India's independence would make much progress while Churchill was Britain's Prime Minister. Events compelled Churchill to moderate his attitude. In the phenomenal advance of their power during the winter of 1941–42, the Japanese reached Burma, India's neighbour to the east. There was a possibility that the Japanese would go further and conquer India, an event which some Indians would have welcomed as a means of ridding their country of the British. It was important for Britain to persuade Indians that loyalty to Britain was more worthwhile than loyalty to Britain's enemy. The British government therefore proposed concessions that went

beyond the 1935 Act, and Stafford Cripps, a member of the Labour party and a man sympathetic to the aims of the Congress movement, was sent to India to put these proposals to the Indian leaders. But Congress would no longer agree to concessions or compromise. Gandhi rejected the proposals which Cripps brought and began another widespread campaign of passive resistance under the abrupt slogan, 'Quit India'. Though the Cripps mission failed, the wartime circumstances made it essential for the British to suppress opposition and maintain their presence in India: a soldier, Field-Marshal Wavell, was appointed Viceroy, with the task of holding India for at least the war's duration.

Meanwhile the issue of partition had increased in importance. Muslims within the subcontinent were not as numerous as Hindus, and their organization, the Muslim League, had never been as important as Congress in the interwar years. In 1940 the Muslim League, under the leadership of Ali Jinnah, pledged itself to the creation of the state of Pakistan for the Muslims of the Indian subcontinent. Earlier, the Muslim League and Congress had worked together against the British, but their relationship had never been easy, and the 1940 commitment by the Muslim League for the creation of Pakistan caused a permanent rift between them. Congress kept to the ideal of a united India, which would have ensured dominance of the Hindus over the Muslims.

With the ending of the war, change in the subcontinent was inevitable. To Attlee's postwar Labour government, the problem was not whether India would secure independence, but whether Hindu-Muslim violence could be averted when independence came. Attempts were made to produce a settlement. The Simla conference in the summer of 1945 merely highlighted the differences between Congress and the League. In 1946 another commission under Lord Pethick-Lawrence produced a scheme for an independent but united government, allowing such extensive powers to local government that the Muslim areas would be self-governing in practice. But Jinnah, who was confident that if he

Mahatma Gandhi wore his peasant clothes whether he was in India or in England. His successful campaign of opposition had a significance far beyond his own country.

persevered long enough independent Pakistan would be achieved, opposed the Pethick-Lawrence scheme and the last months of 1946 were marked by extensive Muslim rioting and some thousands of deaths, which even Gandhi's appeals could do little to avert. Attlee judged that only a bold policy would work: in the spring of 1947 he announced that Britain would withdraw in June 1948 and that the Hindus and the Muslims must therefore resolve their differences before then. The last Viceroy was to be Lord Mountbatten, whose qualities of leadership and general sympathy with the aims of the Attlee government fitted him well for this responsible task.

On arrival in India in March 1947,

Mountbatten became convinced that the British withdrawal should take place in August of that year, substantially earlier than Attlee had originally planned. He also became convinced that partition was the best solution, and he persuaded Nehru, already Prime Minister in the parliament established by the 1935 Act, to accept this solution. At independence the land of the Indian princes would be incorporated into either India or Pakistan and though technically the princes were to retain control of their territories, it was unlikely that such control would last long. More important was the drawing of the partition boundaries. As finally agreed, Pakistan was to consist of two areas, one in the subcontinent's north-west region, generally in the area of the Punjab, and a second in the subcontinent's north-east region, generally in the area of Bengal. The two areas were separated by about a thousand miles of Indian territory. The location of the Muslim population coincided only approximately with the areas allotted to Pakistan: many Muslims were outside these areas and many Hindus were within them. Uncertain of the security of their future as a minority, many Muslims sought to enter the new Pakistan boundaries and many Hindus sought to enter the new Indian boundaries before the partition took legal effect. In the summer months of 1947 the movement of millions of people in circumstances of chaos, fear and resentment led to fighting and the death of hundreds of thousands of refugees.

Nevertheless, in August 1947 the independent states of India and Pakistan came formally into existence. Both continued as members of the British Commonwealth and had the status of dominions, comparable, therefore, with the other British dominions of Canada, Australia, New Zealand and (at that time) South Africa. In India, Nehru became Prime Minister; Mountbatten, necessarily abandoning the position of Viceroy, became Governor-General. In Pakistan, Jinnah became both Prime Minister and Governor-General. In mid-August ceremonies at the Indian capital of New Delhi and the Pakistan capital of Karachi, effected the formal transfer of power. Partly as a result of the influence of these events, two smaller neighbouring members of the British Empire achieved independence under much less troubled circumstances in the following year: Burma, which decided that it did not wish to remain a Commonwealth member, and Ceylon, which remained a member, changing its name to Sri Lanka in 1972.

The bloodshed surrounding the achievement of Indian independence saddened the elderly Gandhi. His appeals for non-violence had met with little response, though in Bengal, where his influence was still strong, the bloodshed was less than elsewhere. Gandhi never sought the political office of Prime Minister and until his death in January 1948, at the hands of a fanatical Hindu who was critical of Gandhi's attempts to modify the traditional caste system of the Hindu religion, he maintained his simple life-style and his doctrine of passive resistance. In many respects, though he had not played a crucial role in the final stages, Gandhi was the real creator of Indian independence. He was important also in another way: the passive resistance which he had so skilfully used in India's cause was adopted by others in attempting to further independence for their countries or to demonstrate opposition to government policies, though no group adopting passive resistance tactics in later decades was able to match the achievement of Gandhi in India.

India since independence: Nehru

Jawaharlal Nehru was Prime Minister of India from the time of independence until his death in 1964. Concerned that India should not abandon the cultural heritage of the past, he nevertheless wanted the new country to develop its political and economic life along modern lines. Despite his opposition to Britain during the struggle for independence, Nehru sought to establish many features of British political life in the new India. The new constitution, effective from 1950, owed much to British examples. The parliament consisted of two houses, elected for the first time by universal suffrage. But the head of state was to be an elected President and not the British monarch, as it had been since 1947: India therefore became a republic. In the election that followed, the Congress party secured a majority and therefore Nehru was confirmed in power.

The newly independent country faced immense social and economic problems. As a result of the caste system of the Hindu religion, society was rigidly divided and formed an inadequate social basis for the economic development which the country needed. The population was growing rapidly and was fast outrunning India's meagre mineral and agricultural resources. In his attempts to develop the Indian economy, Nehru adopted Socialist techniques. Inspired by the example of the effect of the five-year plan on the underdeveloped economy of the Soviet Union in prewar years, he developed a similar planned economy for India. As part of this planned economic development, many industries were nationalized. Though the Indian economy showed improvement during Nehru's premiership, with some important developments – for example, the production of fertilizers, steel and motor manufactures – the advances in India were less impressive than they had been in the Soviet Union. In spite of these industrial advances, agriculture remained the occupation of the majority of Indians. Attempts were made to improve on the very simple methods of the Indian peasantry, but India's agriculture made only modest improvement in output. In agriculture, no plans were made for collectivization on the Socialist pattern, as the peasants, who used traditional methods, would have opposed the government strongly.

In seeking the improvement of India's economy Nehru, like many third world leaders, was prepared to obtain overseas aid from any source. The United Nations countries gave aid collectively through the International Monetary Fund. Commonwealth countries contributed through the Colombo Plan, a system of Commonwealth aid established in 1950 in Colombo, Ceylon. Aid was also received from the Soviet Union.

The education of Indians was as much a problem as the improvement of India's economy. Here also Nehru's success was only limited. At the time of independence the mass of the population were illiterate. Priority was given to the teaching of adults and children to read and write. Efforts were also made to reduce deep-seated social prejudices associated with the Hindu caste system, and in this Nehru was continuing Gandhi's work. Throughout the 1950s, Nehru legislated against the injustices suffered by women and by the *untouchables*, the lowest level in the Hindu caste system: both were no longer to be discriminated against. He also attempted to begin a programme of birth control for India. These attempts to alter the traditional social structure of India encountered their strongest opposition from Hindus.

India since independence: Indira Gandhi

Nehru was succeeded in 1964 by Shastri, whose brief premiership was dominated by hostilities between India and Pakistan which are considered later. Early in 1966, after Shastri's sudden death, Nehru's daughter, Mrs Indira Gandhi, became Prime Minister. She followed the policies of her father but her political problems were greater. In 1969 the Congress party became seriously disunited, as Mrs Gandhi's policies were opposed by a splinter group representing business interests and known as the *Syndicate*. Members of this group criticized Mrs Gandhi's policies, in particular her policy of nationalization of the banks, as being too left-wing. Mrs Gandhi's justification for these policies was that they were necessary both for India's economy and for preventing the further development of Communism in India, which would otherwise gain support by advocating the changes she intended to make. The split within the Congress party meant that Mrs Gandhi's group, now known as the Ruling Congress party, had increasingly to rely on support from left-wing parties. Nevertheless, a general election early in 1971 confirmed Mrs Gandhi in power.

To these political difficulties were added economic problems that troubled many parts of the world in the early 1970s: inflation and unemployment. The planned economy, still vigorously pursued, appeared incapable of finding a solution to these problems: the fifth five-year plan, due to commence in 1974, was doomed to failure as the unprecedented rate of inflation made nonsense of the planned targets. The testing of a nuclear bomb by India in 1974 appeared a highly unnecessary achievement in view of the country's acute economic problems. Cyclones and the failure of harvests were by no means new to India, but these disasters nevertheless contributed to the serious economic problems of these years.

In the mid-1970s there was a serious threat to the parliamentary system of government which had appeared to be firmly established at the time of independence. In June 1975, after Mrs Gandhi had been legally condemned for irregularities in the 1971 general election, she declared a state of emergency, arrested leading members of the opposition, censored the press and took on dictatorial powers. In a message to the nation she justified her action as necessary in order to preserve national unity and continue her 'progressive' measures. Mrs Gandhi's action was followed by the announcement of an economic programme, designed to rally the country to her support in a common endeavour.

India was under the control of this dictatorship until February 1977, when Mrs Gandhi permitted elections to be held. She and her government were heavily criticized, once press censorship was relaxed, and the Congress party suffered a devastating electoral defeat. The new Janata party, formed from a number of parties opposed to Mrs Gandhi, held control of the Indian parliament. Its elderly leader, Morarji Desai, became Prime Minister and gradually dismantled Mrs Gandhi's dictatorship.

The defeat of the Congress party in February 1977 signalled the end of an era for India. The Janata party adopted a different approach to India's economy. The fifth five-year plan was replaced by a less ambitious annual plan; emphasis would be placed in future on the more modest development of small-scale industry rather than the ambitious programmes of the planned economy. By the late 1970s, India's population had risen to over six hundred million. A policy of birth control had been discredited under Mrs Gandhi's government when some people had been forcibly sterilized, so the Desai government was unwilling to continue a similar policy. The prospect of a further increase in the population was in many respects a more serious problem for India than the political disturbances that had attracted so much attention.

Independent Pakistan

The death of Jinnah in September 1948, only a year after Pakistan came into existence, robbed the new country of a man capable of providing sound leadership. For a decade after Jinnah's death, political life in Pakistan was confused, with numerous

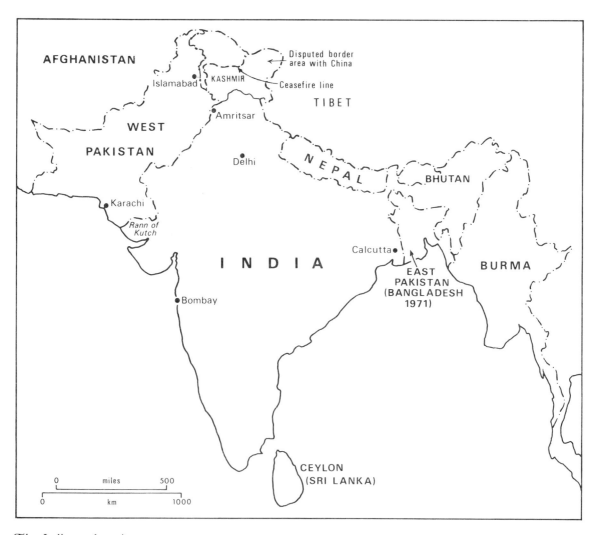

The Indian subcontinent

changes of government. The efforts made in the early 1950s to give the country a new constitution encountered many problems. There was dispute over the extent to which the Muslim religion should be linked to the state: some felt that it was an essential element in the government of Pakistan, while others wanted to lessen its importance. The Muslim League itself became divided into factions: but most important of all were the linguistic, cultural and economic differences between the two parts of the country. There developed in East Pakistan a sense of inferiority and subjection to a government which was based in West Pakistan and which generally advanced West Pakistan's interests.

In February 1956 agreement was reached on a constitution for what was now termed the *Islamic Republic of Pakistan*, but it was suspended in October 1958 when the President abolished all political parties and established martial law under the direction of the Commander-in-Chief of the army, Colonel Ayub Khan. The new leader sought a rebirth of his country and he believed that only a dictatorial policy could bring this about. Though the position of President, which Ayub Khan took on, was to be considerably strengthened, it was intended to have links with popular feelings throughout the country by a series of *basic democracies*, small local councils which were to have much responsibility for local administration and which at the same time were to advise the President on matters of national policy. By this new device, Ayub Khan aimed to rid Pakistan of the political corruption which had featured so strongly in the previous decade.

Pakistan profited from Ayub Khan's economic policies, which followed the planned economy then being adopted in India. Industry was boosted by five-year plans, a device earlier rejected. Agriculture was assisted by attempts to introduce more scientific methods, and by land redistribution, a policy which earned Ayub Khan much support from the peasants and much opposition from the landowners. Like Nehru, Ayub Khan secured foreign aid for his country, though in his case none from the Soviet Un-

ion, as he maintained Pakistan's pro-Western alignment. The construction of a new capital, Islamabad, became a symbol of the country's rebirth under Ayub Khan.

In the presidential election of 1965, Ayub Khan was returned to power, having promised gradual movement towards greater democracy. His opponents had pressed for swifter movement in that direction and had claimed that the election result had been rigged. During the late 1960s his dictatorial rule became increasingly criticized. The main leader of the opposition in West Pakistan was a former minister in Ayub Khan's government, Ali Bhutto, who now formed a left-wing People's party which secured a widespread following, especially among students. Disorders and strikes in the early part of 1969 led to Ayub Khan's resignation. Those who at that time were agitating for greater freedom were to be disappointed, as once again a military ruler, General Yahya Khan, secured control. Meanwhile in East Pakistan, under the leadership of Sheikh Mujibur Rahman, opposition was developing not only to Ayub Khan, but also to the continued union of East Pakistan with West Pakistan which, in spite of Ayub Khan's economic programmes, appeared to bring little improvement to the country's eastern area.

Yahya Khan differed from his predecessor in promising a speedy return to democracy and the abandonment of the by now discredited system of basic democracies. In 1970 he introduced a new constitution which provided for genuine political freedom. Among the large number of parties which contended for power in the general election of December 1970, two emerged clearly victorious: Bhutto's People's party won in West Pakistan and Mujibur's Awami League won in East Pakistan. Nonetheless, martial law under Yahya Khan was to continue for a while.

Indo-Pakistan relations

The 1947 partition having been accompanied by so much violence, it was inevitable that relations between the two new dominions would be poor. Conflict focused

strongly on the troubles of the state of Kashmir. This northern state was attached to
neither India nor Pakistan at the time of
partition. Its internal situation was confusing,
as it was ruled by a Hindu Maharajah, though
the bulk of its population was Muslim. In
the autumn of 1947, infiltration by Pakistan
caused the Maharajah to make an appeal
to India for help, an appeal to which India
responded by the despatch of troops to Kashmir. The fighting that then occurred was
only ended in December 1948 after intervention by the United Nations. The situation
thereafter was uneasy. Indian troops occupied one part of Kashmir and Pakistan troops
the other: the cease-fire line between them
was often violated. Meanwhile India's influence grew, with the adoption by the Kashmir government of a constitution modelled
on that of India, and going so far as to
declare Kashmir a part of India.

Another source of conflict concerned the
use of the waters of the Indus basin. India
controlled the head waters of the rivers of
this basin and Pakistan made allegations that
waters essential for Pakistan agriculture were
being diverted. The dispute continued
throughout the 1950s until the Indus Waters
Treaty of September 1959. Only in a land
with such a hot climate, low water resources
and so meagre an agricultural economy can
the importance of this matter be fully appre-
ciated.

In 1965 Indo-Pakistan relations reached
a crisis point. The Indo-Pakistan border in
the Rann (desert) of Kutch had been disputed since partition and in the spring of
1965 serious fighting occurred and continued
into the summer, when a British proposed
cease-fire agreement was accepted. More serious was a further outbreak of violence in
Kashmir. The cease-fire line of 1949 had
never been well observed by either side and
in August 1965 in spite of the recently agreed
settlement in the Rann of Kutch, there were
serious breaches of the Kashmir cease-fire
line by both sides, followed by a declaration
of war on India by Pakistan. An offer by
the neighbouring Soviet Union to act as
mediator in the dispute led to a meeting
between Prime Minister Shastri of India,

President Ayub Khan and Prime Minister
Kosygin of the Soviet Union at Tashkent
in the Soviet Union in January 1966. As
a result of Kosygin's successful work of
mediation, a declaration was signed at Tashkent in which both sides accepted a cease-fire
line. Though the problems surrounding
Kashmir were not automatically solved at
Tashkent and though Pakistan continued to
object to India's view of Kashmir as a part
of India, relations between India and Pakistan developed relatively smoothly in the late
1960s, until the Bangladesh war in 1971.

The policies of these two new, neighbouring countries towards foreign powers showed
marked differences. India's foreign policy
was *non-aligned*: she did not want to take
sides in the Cold War but wished to benefit
by both Western and Soviet assistance. India
viewed herself as one of the leading voices
of the third world. She had participated as
a leading member of the 1955 Afro-Asian
summit at Bandung, considered more fully
in chapter 25, had voiced its opposition to
Britain's action in the Suez crisis, to the
fighting by the United States in Vietnam
and to the white régimes in Rhodesia and
South Africa.

The smaller, less secure country of Pakistan
felt its interests best served by alignment with
the West. Pakistan was a member of the
American-inspired South-East Asia Treaty
Organization (SEATO), though it withdrew
in 1972. Pakistan also belonged to the Central Treaty Organization (CENTO), a pact
similarly opposed to Communism. Relations
between Pakistan and the Soviet Union were
poor. Though Pakistan did maintain increasingly friendly relations with China, this was
in any case a policy pursued by leading
Western powers in the 1970s.

The creation of Bangladesh

Though at the time of independence East
Pakistan was economically the more
advanced of the two parts, the policies of
the Pakistan government and a series of
flooding disasters in the Ganges delta had
led to a substantial decline in the East's
economy. Sheikh Mujibur used the resent-

Three Mukti Bahini fighters (left) and two Indian soldiers (right) during the war for an independent Bangladesh in 1971. Indian military assistance in the closing stages of the war was the decisive factor in the success of the Mukti Bahini.

ment at the government's lack of attention to the East's problems to develop the Awami League from the mid-1960s. The basic demand of the Awami League was regional self-government for East Pakistan. When in 1970 the Awami League secured a majority among the representatives of the East in the Pakistan parliament, they increased their pressure for independence. Political conflict between Bhutto and Mujibur intensified, the former claiming that autonomy for East Pakistan could only be achieved with the approval of the whole of Pakistan.

Attempts at mediation between the two on the part of President Yahya Khan came to nothing. He therefore decided that in order to prevent further political hostilities, the newly elected parliament would not meet and martial law would once again be streng-

thened. Instead of producing a calming effect, this dictatorial action led to strikes and violence in East Pakistan and with the failure of further talks between Yahya Khan, Bhutto and Mujibur, the East prepared to fight for its independence.

At the end of March 1971 Mujibur proclaimed the creation of the independent state of Bangladesh in place of the former East Pakistan. Conflict occurred in the East between Mujibur's Mukti Bahini forces and the Pakistan army. In April 1971 ferocious fighting took place on land and in the air, the East's capital of Dacca being particularly badly hit by aerial attack. But in spite of the Pakistan determination to ensure control of the East, Mujibur's newly established government gradually asserted control of the recently proclaimed state.

Given the unsatisfactory history of Indo-Pakistan relations, it was inevitable that Mrs Gandhi should support the East's struggle. But a particular problem for India was the arrival of millions of East Pakistan refugees, fleeing from the Pakistan army. As the number of refugees steadily increased throughout the summer and autumn of 1971, relations became strained. At the start of December 1971 serious border clashes occurred between India and West Pakistan: in response to an air attack on India from West Pakistan, Indian troops entered East Pakistan and linked with the Mukti Bahini in a united attack on the Pakistan army. The Indian forces provided the necessary strength to bring the campaign of the Mukti Bahini to a successful conclusion. Spectacular advances were made and late in December 1971 Pakistan agreed a truce in the fighting and acknowledged the independence of Bangladesh.

Bangladesh and Pakistan in the 1970s

In January 1972 Sheikh Mujibur, who for most of the war had been imprisoned in West Pakistan, returned to become his country's first Prime Minister. The devastation of the war, the return of the refugees, the high population and the lack of resources all contributed to the difficulties of his task as Prime Minister. Substantial foreign aid, channelled through the United Nations, was of immense value in helping the reconstruction of the area, while Mujibur's government revived the country's export of jute, improved its agricultural output and began to develop the country along socialist lines. But improvement in the early 1970s was slow and uncertain. Flooding of land, corruption among politicians and the problem of inflation all impeded progress. In December 1974, to combat these difficulties, Mujibur declared a state of emergency and became President with dictatorial powers. He expected that his popular following would enable this bold move to be successful, but in August 1975 he was overthrown and mur-

dered in an army coup. Major General Ziaur Rahman then established military control of the country. Assisted by a strong government, by better weather and by continuing overseas aid, the country's economy made significant improvement over the next few years.

Pakistan, defeated in war and now reduced in territory, suffered similar problems in these years. In view of the previous value of East Pakistan as a source of raw materials for the industry of the West, its loss was a serious blow to Pakistan's economy. Immediately after the defeat, Yahya Khan resigned and Bhutto became President. After long military rule, Pakistan under Bhutto's lead returned to democracy, the new constitution receiving the support of the leading opposition parties. The economy demanded and received speedy attention from Bhutto: some essential industries were nationalized, land reform was undertaken and the traditional export of cotton was increased.

The 1971 war interrupted Pakistan's pro-Western policy. The British government's comparatively swift recognition of Bangladesh led Pakistan to withdraw in protest from the Commonwealth. Relations with India and with Bangladesh took time to heal. A meeting at Simla between Bhutto and Mrs Gandhi in June 1972 signalled the beginning of considerably improved relations between the two countries.

> The government of India and the government of Pakistan are resolved that the two countries put an end to the conflict and confrontation that have hitherto marred their relations, and work for the promotion of a friendly and harmonious relationship and the establishment of durable peace in the sub-continent, so that both countries may henceforth devote their resources and energies to the pressing task of advancing the welfare of their people.

In the mid-1970s, Pakistan's recognition of Bangladesh was followed by resumption of trade between the two areas, to their mutual advantage.

In March 1977 Bhutto felt that his government was in a sufficiently strong political and economic position to call a general election. But the opposition parties combined as the National Alliance to contest the power of Bhutto's People's party. Though Bhutto was victorious in the election, there was widespread criticism of official interference in the election results. Disorders followed, in the course of which the army intervened and declared a state of martial law. Bhutto and many of his followers were imprisoned and in 1979 Bhutto was sentenced to death. The country had still not found the political stability that it so much needed.

Questions

61. Study the photograph on page 216 and the photograph on page 219 and then answer questions (a) to (c) which follow.
    (a) With reference to the photograph on page 216, taken in the early twentieth century,
       (i) identify the foreign power whose authority is shown in this photograph,
       (ii) describe the ways in which the authority of this foreign power is shown, and
       (iii) describe the methods used by this foreign power in controlling the Indian sub-continent at this time.

$$(1+2+3)$$

(b) With reference to the photograph on page 219, taken in the early 1930s,
   (i) name the Indian leader shown in the photograph,
   (ii) explain why he was dressed in this way,
   (iii) explain the main demands he put to the authority represented by the photograph on page 216, and
   (iv) describe the methods he employed to secure those demands.

$$(1+1+2+2)$$

(c) Show to what extent, during the years 1935–47, the demands of the Indian in the photograph on page 219 met with success.

$$(8)$$

62. Examine the problems which have confronted India during the years since independence and show to what extent the governments of India have succeeded in solving these problems.

63. Explain the circumstances leading to the creation of (a) Pakistan in 1947 and (b) Bangladesh in 1971. Outline the relations between these two countries during the 1970s.

22
The Middle East

In the early years of the twentieth century the area of the present-day state of Israel, then known as Palestine or the Holy Land, formed only a small part of the vast Ottoman (Turkish) Empire, whose rule sprawled across most of the Middle East and a substantial part of south-eastern Europe. The poverty of the land and the corruption of the Palestine government were typical of other areas of the Ottoman Empire, and this small province had little to distinguish it other than its wealth of historical heritage: even the way of life of many of its inhabitants was still based almost entirely on agriculture, the methods of which were scarcely different to those practised in biblical times. To the Jewish people dispersed throughout the world, Palestine had a deeply felt attraction, as it was the land in which the Jewish faith had originated and thus was the land to which many wished to return. But a Jewish migration to Palestine in large numbers would bring conflict with the Arab population that already lived there. The clash between the interests of Jews and Arabs, in relation to the area of Palestine, is the fundamental cause of twentieth-century conflict in the Middle East and it came into sharp focus at the time of the First World War.

The creation of the mandate of Palestine

Ever since the time of the *diaspora* (dispersion) of the Jewish people under the Roman Empire, there had always been a minority of Jewish inhabitants in Palestine. Though the religion of these Jews kept them distinct from the Palestinian Arabs, practising their own religion of Islam, there was little else that was different in their way of life. For centuries, relations in Palestine between the majority Arabs and the minority Jews had been comparatively harmonious. But in the late nineteenth century, under the inspiration of Theodore Herzl, an Austrian Jew, a worldwide movement known as *Zionism* had been established and in the years before the First World War its influence among Jews in different lands grew steadily. The main objective of Zionism was to re-establish a Jewish homeland in the area of Palestine, to be called by the ancient Jewish name of *Israel*. The movement sought the approval of the governments of major world powers. It received encouragement within the United States, though more effective encouragement in the early years came from the British government which, through its Foreign Secretary, A. J. Balfour, gave support to Zionism in the Balfour declaration of November 1917:

> His Majesty's government view with favour the establishment in Palestine of a national home for the Jewish people and will use their best endeavours to facilitate the achievement of this object, it being clearly understood that nothing shall be done which may prejudice the civil and religious rights of existing non-Jewish communities in Palestine, or the rights and political status enjoyed by Jews in any other country.

Why did the British government issue this declaration? A pure, disinterested wish to assist Zionist aims may have been one motive. But Jewish gratitude for the declaration would lead to the establishment of British influence in any new Jewish homeland in Palestine; British influence in such an area would advance the imperial power of Britain as the imperial power of Turkey continued to decline, hastened by military failures in the closing stages of the First World War.

Palestine's position close to the Suez canal would enable Britain to protect the canal, the essential artery connecting the British Isles with British India. Whatever the full motives of the British government, the issuing of the Balfour declaration was the most significant step that enmeshed successive British governments in the affairs of Palestine for the next thirty years. The declaration, coming as it did from a great power such as Britain, also gave immense encouragement to Zionist hopes.

The prospect of fulfilment of these Zionist hopes was viewed with alarm by the Arab majority in Palestine, as the consequence for them would be exclusion from land they had held for centuries. Further, they had reason to feel that the Balfour declaration represented a deceitful approach by the British government. To assist in the defeat of the Ottoman Empire during the First World War, Britain had encouraged rebellion by the Arab subjects of the Turks. Wartime negotiations between Sir Henry McMahon, the British high commissioner in Egypt, and the Sharif Husain of Mecca, the most prominent of the Arab leaders, suggested that the reward for Arab assistance against the Turks would be British support of Arab demands for independence, including Arab control of the area of Palestine. There was a series of letters between McMahon and Husain. One of the most important in October 1915, made the following promises to the Arabs:

> As for the regions lying within the proposed frontiers, in which Great Britain is free to act without detriment to the interests of her ally, France, I am authorized to give you the following pledges on behalf of the government of Great Britain, and to reply as follows to their note: That, subject to the modifications stated above, Great Britain is prepared to recognize and uphold the independence of the Arabs in all the regions lying within the frontiers proposed by the Sharif of Mecca.

Thus the opportunity of Ottoman collapse was seized upon by Jews and by Arabs for the furthering of their own aims and by the British government for the advance of its imperial control. France also had imperial ambitions in the Middle East. A British–French agreement known as the Sykes-Picot plan, was made during the summer of 1916 and provided for the partition of the Ottoman Empire, with France securing influence in the northern areas and Britain in the southern areas. Although the Sykes-Picot plan made some concessions to Arab ambitions, it made rather more to Jewish ambitions and it was a blatant example of two major powers intent upon advancing their imperial control. As the war drew to a close, three issues therefore contended with each other in the Middle East: Jewish nationalism, Arab nationalism and Western imperialism.

Given these conflicting aims, negotiations on the future of the Middle East were lengthy. Part of the treaty of Sèvres, October 1920, put into effect the general outline of the Sykes-Picot plan: France secured the northern areas of Lebanon and Syria as mandates and Britain secured the southern areas of Palestine, Transjordan and Iraq as mandates. The purpose of the mandate system has been explained in chapter 3. So far as the former territories of the Ottoman Empire were concerned, these were regarded as being nearer to independence than were the former German territories in Africa and the Pacific. The mandates of Lebanon, Syria and Transjordan were of this pattern, but the mandate of Palestine was somewhat different, for in the exercise of the mandate, Britain was given the specific task of encouraging the establishment of a Jewish national home within the mandate, at the same time ensuring fair treatment to the Arabs. But to fulfil this responsibility with justice to both sides proved impossible.

Palestine under the mandate

A mandate framed along these lines naturally encouraged settlement in Palestine by Jewish immigrants. These new settlers gave particular attention to the improvement of the Palestinian economy. They cultivated land formerly considered barren and developed modern industry in place of traditional crafts. Their impact upon the economy was so marked that even Arabs in neighbouring mandates, in this respect at least, felt envious of Arabs living within Palestine. Jewish immigration figures increased modestly throughout most of the 1920s and more substantially throughout the 1930s as Nazi hostility towards German Jews became more pronounced. German Jewish immigrants in the mid and late 1930s made especial contribution towards the economic success of the mandate.

The essential point of conflict between Arabs and Jews in these years was land purchase. Jewish immigrants found little difficulty in purchasing land from the less wealthy Arabs. Once purchased, this land remained in Jewish hands and was never resold to Arabs. On this newly acquired land, Arab labour was boycotted. Thus distinct areas of Palestine passed exclusively into Jewish hands. This was especially true of northwestern Palestine: in this area, the city of Tel Aviv became almost entirely populated by Jews. On the eve of the Second World War about one third of the population of Palestine was Jewish; the Arabs were fearful that they would be swamped by increasing numbers of Jewish immigrants.

The Arab population expressed their fears in a series of rebellions. The most serious developed from a general strike in April 1936 and Arab rebellion continued periodically throughout the late 1930s. As a response to this worsening situation, Britain appointed a royal commission under the chairmanship of Lord Peel, to advise on future policy in Palestine. The most important conclusion of the Peel commission was that Palestine should be partitioned between Jews and Arabs, generally along the lines of the then existing settlements, with continuing British control of the highly controversial city of Jerusalem. Zionists felt little enthusiasm for partition, but the Arabs objected far more vigorously, as partition to them meant that a part of what they considered to be their own land would pass completely under Jewish control. Renewed violence occurred, necessitating the sending of extra British troops to Palestine merely in order to secure the maintenance of law and order. Mean-

while war in Europe between Britain and Germany was about to break out; the Jews would naturally support Britain in a struggle against Germany, but the Arab support for Britain was uncertain because of the belief that British promises to them had been broken. The Arabs might even be tempted to see an alliance with Germany as a means of preventing Britain from advancing further Zionist interests in Palestine. Britain was also more aware at this time than earlier of the value of oil supplies in Arab hands throughout the Middle East: a policy of conciliation to the Arabs might ensure the survival of these oil supplies for Britain. Consequently the British government attempted to placate the Arabs by abandoning the idea of partition. In a white paper in May 1939 restrictions were placed on both the purchase of land by Jews and on the number of Jewish immigrants, who were restricted to 75,000 over the following five years.

But the 1939 white paper failed to secure Arab support. When war came, and when Germany was so successful during the early stages of fighting, the Palestinian Arabs sought an understanding with Nazi Germany as a means of ending the possibility of a Jewish national home on their territory. To the Jews, the restrictions of the white paper were naturally unwelcome and particularly so at a time when Jewish need to find refuge outside Nazi-dominated Europe could not have been more desperate. Nevertheless in the early stages of the war, when the prospect of eventual German victory appeared strong, the Jews gave wholehearted support to Britain in their struggle against the common enemy. Jewish attitudes to the war changed after the British victory at El Alamein in October 1942. No longer was there real fear of eventual German victory: thereafter the struggle was directed against Britain and the policies of the 1939 white paper.

The last years of the mandate in Palestine

Midway through the Second World War various different factors show that Zionism was intent upon a more concerted and more effective drive to secure its aims. David Ben Gurion, a Polish-born Jew who was the Zionist leader at this time, adopted a more forceful policy than his predecessor, Chaim Weizman. In May 1942, a conference of American Zionists was held at the Biltmore Hotel in New York. There the 1939 white paper was roundly condemned as unjust and the American Zionists pledged themselves anew to strive towards the creation of a Jewish national home in Palestine. The Biltmore conference suggested that Zionist opinion in the United States was becoming a factor of increasing importance and reflected itself particularly in a strong Zionist element in the support of the then dominant Democrat party. Through Harry Truman, President of the United States after April 1945, much pressure was asserted on the British government to bring about a solution to the problem that would be favourable to the Zionist cause.

This American pressure came at a time when the Western powers needed solidarity among themselves in the developing Cold

Illegal Jewish immigrants at sea near Palestine in 1947 make a desperate appeal to the consciences of the British authorities. Notice the British troops in the foreground, whose duty of turning back such would-be immigrants caused much world opinion to turn against Britain on the Palestine issue.

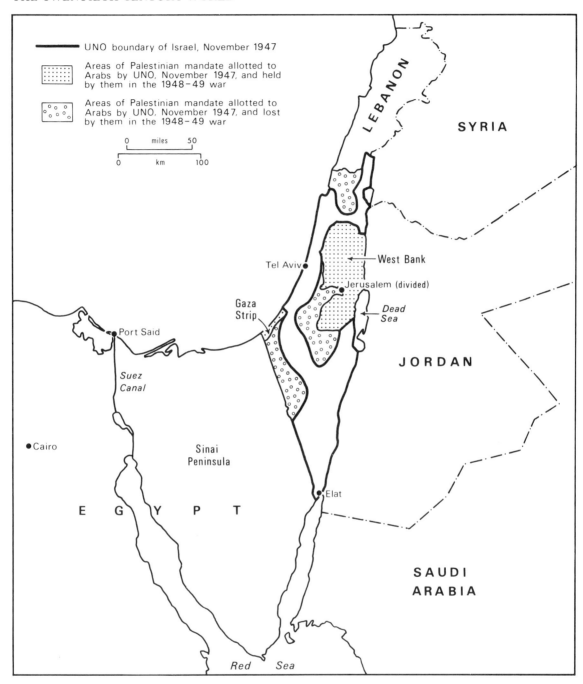

Legend:
- UNO boundary of Israel, November 1947
- Areas of Palestinian mandate allotted to Arabs by UNO, November 1947, and held by them in the 1948–49 war
- Areas of Palestinian mandate allotted to Arabs by UNO, November 1947, and lost by them in the 1948–49 war

Israel and neighbouring states at the time of the wars of 1948–49 and 1956

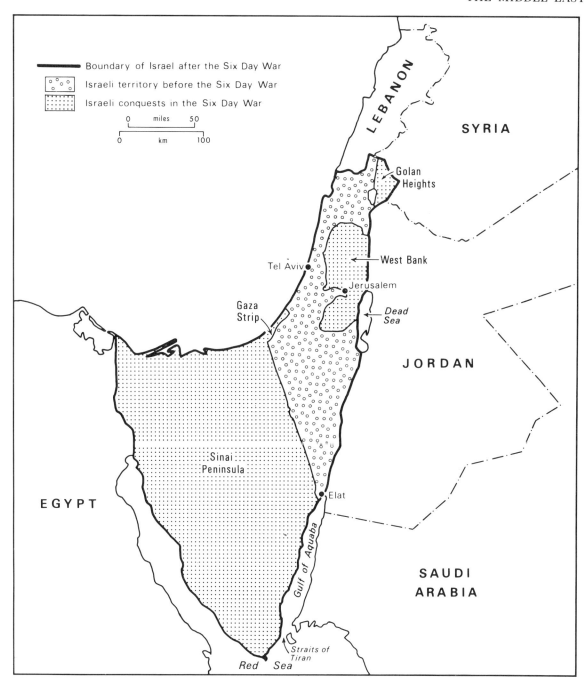

Israel and neighbouring states at the time of the Six Days War, 1967

War struggles with the Soviet Union. Yet, in spite of American pressure at such a time of East-West tension, the British government persisted in maintaining a strict limit on Jewish immigrants. British policy appeared especially heartless after the end of the Second World War, as the extent and nature of the Nazi extermination programmes was by then known throughout the world, and those Jews who had survived those extermination programmes desperately needed a home where they could attempt to rebuild their shattered lives. In order to evade British immigration controls in Palestine, many illegal attempts were made to smuggle Jews in. Conditions were appalling on these crowded ships, which often sailed for many weeks on high seas in order to avoid detection. Most of these tragic journeys ended in failure, the illegal immigrants being then placed in transit camps on Cyprus or Mauritius. The publicity given to these attempts to enter Palestine and to the British refusal to adopt a more generous policy towards Jewish entry led to worldwide hostility towards Britain.

Meanwhile within Palestine, terrorism had reached new proportions. Two Jewish terrorist groups known as the Stern gang and the Irgun gang received substantial, though not wholehearted, Jewish support for terrorism against the British authorities. Their aim was to drive out the British and open Palestine to unrestricted Jewish immigration. Terrorist attacks became daily occurrences within Palestine, their most effective single action being the blowing up of the King David Hotel in Jerusalem, the hotel serving as the headquarters of the British administration. The attack resulted in the loss of nearly a hundred lives and a considerable disruption to British control.

Thus in the immediate postwar years, Britain's policy on Palestine faced the opposition of the government of the United States because of American Zionist influence, the opposition of world opinion on account of the plight of the would-be Jewish immigrants and opposition from terrorist groups within Palestine itself. The mandate had been granted only for a limited period and it was due to expire in May 1948. But the problems facing the British government were so intense that they decided to abandon the mandate rather earlier. In February 1947, Ernest Bevin, the British Foreign Secretary, who had become somewhat embittered by the difficulties of the situation, announced that the British government would abandon the Palestinian mandate and requested the United Nations to take on the responsibility of seeking a solution.

The United Nations and the emergence of Israel

The issue of Palestine was a difficult test of the peacekeeping work of the infant United Nations. In May 1947, the United Nations Special Committee on Palestine (UNSCOP) was created to gather information on the problem and to recommend solutions. The Jews cooperated with UNSCOP and sought to impress it with the economic improvements they had made in the Jewish-settled areas; the Arabs were suspicious of UNSCOP and refused to cooperate with it. UNSCOP's eventual report proposed partition, and was the subject of one of the most important debates ever held at the New York headquarters of the United Nations, in November 1947. As a result the United Nations accepted the partition proposals. This meant that in the areas where Jewish population predominated, the state of Israel would come into existence; the city of Jerusalem was to be under international control.

Zionist opinion, though concerned at not being allocated more territory, was prepared to accept the decision. Arab opinion, both in Palestine and elsewhere in the Middle East, was outraged at what it considered to be the robbery of their own land. Violence at once resulted, the Palestinian Arabs being assured of support from neighbouring Arab states, such as Lebanon, Syria, Jordan and Egypt. In December 1947 the Haganah, the Jewish underground army in Palestine, became active against Arab attacks and in defence of Jewish settlements. The early months of 1948 were the final months of the British presence in Palestine, during which a gradual withdrawal of British troops was taking place. There was comparatively little attempt made by the British in these months to stem the increasing violence and bloodshed in Palestine.

14 May 1948 was the date of the final British withdrawal. At once the state of Israel was proclaimed, with Weizman as President and Ben Gurion as Prime Minister. The United States led world opinion in giving recognition to the new country. The neighbouring Arab states of Lebanon, Syria, Jordan and Egypt at once invaded, viewing Israel as an alien presence and intent on its complete destruction. But military coordination between these Arab states was poor and they were hampered by much bickering between their governments. The Israelis fought back vigorously, conscious that the very continuance of their new country depended on their ability to repel the invasion. This first major war between Israel and the neighbouring Arab states came to an end nine months later in February 1949. By then Israeli forces had defended the territory allocated to them and had secured substantial territory from their Arab enemies. They had also taken over the administration of half the city of Jerusalem.

From the Israeli point of view the major postwar problem was to make their frontiers secure. But in spite of discussion fostered by the United Nations, no solution could be found and the armistice arrangements of February 1949 remained as an uneasy settlement. Though no major war broke out until the Suez War of October-November 1956, there were numerous border clashes in which attacks by Arabs were met by vigorous Israeli counter-attack against the Jordanians at Quibya in October 1953 and against the Egyptians at the Gaza strip in February 1955.

In order to diminish tensions, a tripartite pact was signed in May 1950 by Britain, France and the United States, by which the signatories pledged themselves to supply arms to both Arabs and Jews in strict proportion, so that neither side became more powerful that the other. This policy failed to survive for long. France became angered at Egyptian aid to the Algerian rebels against French

rule and, in retaliation, secretly began to supply Israel with arms. In September 1955 an arms deal was made between Egypt and Czechoslovakia, signalling an involvement of the Soviet Union on the side of the Arabs. These factors destroyed the balance of arms which the tripartite pact of 1950 had aimed to achieve. From September 1955 the arms race in the Middle East quickened considerably. Few were left in doubt that this would eventually result in the outbreak of a further war.

The most practical human problem resulting from the upheavals of the late 1940s was the problem of refugees. Some three-quarters of a million Arab refugees left their homes in the territories occupied by the Israelis during the war waged in 1948–1949. They were housed in refugee camps in Arab states. Here again the work of the United Nations was of importance, as the refugee camps were organized by one of their special agencies, the United Nations Relief and Works Agency (UNRWA). The Arab states refused to give a permanent home to these refugees, as to do so would be to recognize the permanency of the Israeli frontier and the permanency of the refugees exiled from their Israeli-held lands. Israel, for its part, refused to take steps to re-accommodate the refugees, as it claimed that such action could take place only after a general peace had been established in the area. The refugee problem was the most tragic reminder of the human suffering that the Arab-Israeli conflict had created. For the future, it was also the most dangerous.

The revival of Egypt

Though at the time of the First World War there was an Egyptian Royal Family and some self-government, the country had for decades been under British control. Britain regarded the Suez canal, which it had acquired in the late nineteenth century, as essential for the maintenance of connections with India: as the canal ran through Egypt, it seemed important to maintain control of that country as well. Though the

Egyptian economy had benefited from the work of some dedicated British administrators, there developed after the First World War a movement for national independence. During the war the Egyptians had been conscious that their fellow-Arabs under Ottoman rule were likely to throw off that rule when the war ended and they, in turn, sought to throw off British rule. Wilson's Fourteen Points, with their promise of self-determination, were a further encouragement to them. The movement for national independence, spear-headed by the Wafd party under the leadership of Saad Zaghlul, became strong in the years just after the war. In the face of increasing violence and disorder the British government conceded a form of independence in November 1922. Britain still held responsibility for the defence of Egypt, for the protection of foreign interests, for minorities within the country and for the full control of the area of the Sudan to the south. Britain also continued to control the Suez canal. The new government was itself still very much under the despotic rule of the Egyptian monarchy in the person of King Faud, supported by the British government, which still refused Zaghlul the prime ministership.

Nationalist opposition was dissatisfied by these half measures. Another compromise, this time more acceptable to the Egyptians was reached in 1936. Nationalist opposition had led the British to realize that a more acceptable compromise was needed, whilst Mussolini's invasion of nearby Abyssinia during 1935–36 had led the Egyptians to realize that they also must make concessions to the British if they were to expect British protection if Egypt was invaded by the Italians. The Anglo-Egyptian treaty of 1936 provided for a fuller Egyptian control of their own affairs under the nominal rule of the new sixteen-year-old King Farouk, whilst the British troops were in future to be stationed only in the canal zone, where continued British control was guaranteed. Although Egypt remained neutral during the Second World War, the Italian Fascist control of Libya to the west and Abyssinia to the south was sufficiently menacing to encourage Egypt to welcome British troops in Egypt during the war and to ensure no difficulties existed in the smooth supply of these troops via the Red Sea. Egypt was to prove its value as a base from which the battle of El Alamein could be launched in October 1942.

Chaotic conditions prevailed inside Egypt during the years after the Second World War. Though British troops eventually withdrew from all areas, with the exception of the canal zone, there was still much foreign influence in the country. King Farouk's luxurious and decadent life-style was also the subject of much criticism. He presided inefficiently over a series of corrupt and slow-moving governments. By this time the Wafd party had lost its original fire as a forceful nationalist movement. The leading opposition to the monarchy came this time from the army, whose younger officers were appalled by the totally inadequate government of their country, especially when they could see other Arab countries at least beginning to adjust themselves to the twentieth century. Much rioting occurred during the first six months of 1952, and in July, the army successfully unseated Farouk's government, proclaimed Egypt a republic and established its own military government under General Neguib. Farouk went into a comfortably-financed exile, spent mainly in expensive European resorts.

In 1954 a 36-year-old colonel in the Egyptian army took control from Neguib. From then until his premature death in 1970, General Abdul Nasser was the leader of Egypt and in many respects the most significant leader in the Middle East. He had been a key figure in the successful army coup of July 1952. He had essentially two aims for his country after the defeat of the monarchy. He wanted an internal transformation of Egypt, based upon Socialist principles. He also wanted a reassertion of a sense of Egyptian nationality and he looked to a future in which Egypt would be the leading Arab power in the Middle East. His work for the modernization of his country gained much admiration. His vigorous nationalist policy became something of a model for other third world nations, but it also elicited sharp

Western suspicion, leading eventually to the conflict over Suez in 1956.

The Suez crisis: origins and motives

The military hostilities of the Suez crisis in the autumn of 1956 occurred solely in the Middle East, but the crisis itself had worldwide origin, and a worldwide significance. Just after Nasser secured power, friendly relations developed between Egypt and the Western powers. In 1954, agreement was reached for the withdrawal of the remaining British troops from the canal zone. In 1955, Britain and the United States, in conjunction with the World Bank, promised financial assistance to Nasser in his ambitious project to construct the Aswan dam, in order to harness the waters of the river Nile for the provision of much-needed irrigation and electricity. For Nasser and the Egyptians the Aswan dam became a symbol of their country's regeneration.

Nasser was not satisfied with the amount of British and American aid for the Aswan dam. Already he had established relations with the Soviet Union: following the Czech arms deal of 1955, Soviet arms and aid had been sent to Egypt. Nasser considered that Egypt's desperate economy made it reasonable for him to get as much help as he could from any source. In any case, such an approach was typical of the non-aligned policy which he intended to pursue. In the early months of 1956, Nasser attempted to secure more aid from Britain and the United States by suggesting that lack of financial cooperation from them would make him turn more to the Soviet Union. American Secretary of State Dulles was vigorously opposed to Communism and was highly angered at this approach by Nasser. In mid-July 1956, in retaliation, Dulles cancelled the American assistance to Egypt. At the end of the same month, Nasser, infuriated at the suddenness of this action, declared the nationalization of the company which operated the Suez canal. Though Nasser did this hastily and in anger, there was nevertheless good financial sense in his actions from an Egyptian

Prime Minister Eden's intense dislike of the Egyptian President was shared by many people in Britain, as this cartoon suggests. But Nasser's main objective throughout was to improve the condition of his down-trodden country.

point of view, as the dues from ships passing through the canal would go directly to Egypt and would be used to finance the Aswan dam project. Furthermore, the Egyptian government was entitled to nationalize any asset that was within the country.

Though it was action by the United States which had precipitated the nationalization of the Suez canal company, it was Britain and France which felt the consequences, as it was these countries which held the majority of shares in the company. Moreover, British and French ships used the canal much more than did American ships. An important aspect of this use was carrying oil to Europe. Both the British and French governments

237

reacted bitterly, and over the next few months set in chain a series of events which led to the Suez invasion in late October. In the meantime, there were attempts to reduce the impact of the nationalization. The most notable of these was Dulles' suggestion of a Suez Canal Users Association to ensure that ships would continue to be able to use the canal. But this did not satisfy the British and French governments. Within Britain, Prime Minister Anthony Eden and Foreign Secretary Selwyn Lloyd, and within France Prime Minister Guy Mollet and Foreign Secretary Christian Pineau, wished to pursue stronger policies.

Apart from the ill-feeling over the treatment of the Suez canal company, what other reasons had Britain and France for feeling aggrieved at Nasser's action? After all, for Britain, the Suez canal was no longer an essential artery of the Empire, as it had been when Britain held India. Yet many still considered British control of the canal to be essential: 'The Egyptian has his thumb on our windpipe' commented Eden, somewhat emotively, when he heard news of the nationalization. The British government, supported by much British public opinion, developed an irrational hatred for Nasser, picturing him as a tyrannical upstart whose policies in the Middle East in the mid-1950s were as dangerous as those of Hitler in Europe in the late 1930s. This hatred of Nasser was felt in particular by Eden, whose poor health may have contributed to his highly temperamental behaviour throughout the crisis. Britain was still considered a great world power and the government felt that a stand should be made against this 'disrespectful' treatment of British overseas interests.

France had other reasons for hostility to Nasser. Throughout the 1950s, France was fighting a losing battle to retain control of her extensive overseas Empire. Indochina had already been lost. Now in the mid-1950s, Algeria was troubling France, and Algerian rebels were known to be receiving aid and encouragement from Nasser. France had also developed close relations with Israel throughout the early 1950s, to the extent of giving military aid, and from 1952 neglecting the restraints of the tripartite declaration of 1950. France was therefore strongly committed to the aid of Israel, the major enemy of Egypt.

But the enmity of Israel for Egypt was stronger, more immediate and of longer duration than the enmity Egypt received from either Britain or France. The defeat of Egypt and the other Arab states in the Arab-Israeli war 1948–49 had embittered Egyptian attitudes towards Israel. The borders of Israel were still unconfirmed by Egypt. After the Israeli reprisal raid against Egypt in the Gaza strip in February 1955, Egypt gave direct encouragement to a set of guerrilla fighters, the Fedayeen, to conduct border raids into Israel and thus to prove that under its new leadership Egypt would continue to pursue the Arab policy, seeking the destruction of Israel. For its part, by the time of the Gaza raid of February 1955, Israel was convinced of the necessity of a further war with Egypt.

Suez crisis: events and significance

Desire to defeat Nasser was therefore a common objective of Britain, France and Israel. Towards the end of October 1956 a secret meeting took place at a villa in the fashionable Parisian suburb of Sèvres. There, representatives of Israel and France, including Ben Gurion, Mollet and Pineau were joined briefly by the British Foreign Secretary, Selwyn Lloyd. Agreement was reached that Israel should launch an attack on Egypt across the Sinai desert and the resulting conflict between the Egyptians and the Israelis would provide Britain and France with a reason to launch their own invasion of Egypt under the excuse, acceptable, so it was hoped, to international opinion, that they were intervening to protect shipping in the Suez canal, and to prevent warfare. At the time, and for some years after, varying attempts were made by the three governments to deny that this *collusion* between them had taken place.

On 29 October 1956 the Israeli land and air forces swiftly and successfully attacked Egypt in the Sinai desert. The Sèvres arrangements were then put into effect. The British and the French governments made formal requests to the Israeli and Egyptian governments to give assurances that shipping would pass freely through the canal. To do this, troops should withdraw their forces ten miles from either side of the canal. As this request would involve an Egyptian withdrawal within their own country, Egypt's refusal was inevitable. British and French military action, carefully planned during the previous three months, then followed. Military installations in Egypt were bombed to prepare the way for a joint Anglo-French paratroop landing in the area of Port Said on 5 November. As the Anglo-French forces advanced southwards the Egyptian death toll mounted to about 1,000. But the entire canal was never taken over fully: abruptly, on 6 November, Britain and France accepted a cease-fire proposal put forward by the United Nations.

Many different factors led to the abandonment of the Suez invasion. World opinion was markedly hostile: the episode even brought the United States and the Soviet Union together in the United Nations, condemning Britain, France and Israel. Strong opposition also existed within Britain and France. The British Labour party gave vigorous opposition under the slogan 'Law not War', and some Labour MPs already voiced their suspicions of collusion. The Conservative party was disunited and some Conservative ministers resigned. There were also adverse financial effects on Britain, as the crisis caused the value of sterling on the international market to fall drastically. Later in November, as the British, French and Israeli troops left, a United Nations peacekeeping mission moved in between the Israeli and Egyptian forces and successfully preserved peace until the time of the next major war in 1967.

While in its Middle-Eastern context, the Suez War is one of a sad series of Arab-Israeli engagements, for the Western powers it had a wider significance. Britain and France had made a last, dramatic bid to impose their will, as great powers, on the affairs of what was regarded as a colonial power. In the nineteenth century such policies worked, but by the mid-1950s they were woefully out of date. Both countries were thrown into internal disarray. In Britain, Eden's government had become seriously divided and in January 1957, for reasons of ill-health, he resigned the premiership. In France, Suez was a further sign of the incompetence of the Fourth Republic, which collapsed totally two years later. The *special relationship* between England and the United States was seriously harmed: Britain blamed America for bringing about the crisis and for then refusing to support Britain in attempting to resolve it. The fact that the Western world was preoccupied, in one way or another, with the Suez crisis, meant that there was no unified Western approach to the Russian invasion of Hungary, which occurred at the same time. The role of the United Nations appeared in a favourable light however. Throughout, the United Nations had advocated moderation and it had condemned aggression. Moreover, the United Nations forces remained in Egypt for rather more than ten years in a successful peacekeeping role. Finally, the departure of the invading countries from Egypt gave considerable encouragement to Arab nationalism, not only in Egypt, but also elsewhere in the Middle East and north Africa.

Nasser and the Arab world after the Suez crisis

To the Arab world, Nasser's policies and actions in 1956 were seen as the successful opposition of Arab nationalism to Western imperialism. Nasser emerged from the events of that year as the virtual leader of the Arab world. In February 1958, the United Arab Republic came into being as a union of Egypt and Syria. Though this union was seen as the beginning of a wider union of Arab states, the Arab world never responded wholeheartedly to this initial step on the way to Arab unity. The United Arab Republic collapsed in 1961, though Syria continued to have some links with Egypt.

Other issues encouraged further Arab

differences. The Soviet Union had shown itself favourably inclined to the Arab world and after Suez gave increased military and economic aid to Arab countries. Concerned by these developments, President Eisenhower issued in January 1957 what became known as the *Eisenhower doctrine*, to the effect that the United States would adopt military intervention in the affairs of the Middle East if increased Soviet involvement made such intervention necessary: the Eisenhower doctrine was in practice the application of the Truman doctrine to the situation of the Middle East.

In July 1958, the monarchy in Iraq was overthrown in a bloody revolution and a republic was established under Kassem. Though he wished for no association with Nasser, neither did he wish for links with the West. There was danger that a similar revolution might unseat the pro-Western government of the Lebanon. The United States became alarmed and the Eisenhower doctrine was implemented. American marines were landed on the beaches of the Lebanon: they met little resistance, but their presence maintained the status quo in Lebanon and its alliance with the West. The sympathies of the government of Jordan under its young monarch, King Hussein, rarely wavered from loyalty to the West. Lebanon and Jordan were therefore opposed to Nasser. In the Arabian peninsula, the government of Saudi Arabia, under King Feisal, was rigidly monarchist and based firmly on the principles of Islam: effective links between Nasser's Egypt and such a traditional country were unthinkable. Only in the remote south-west corner of the Arabian peninsula did Nasser have much hope of securing further Arab support. In 1962, on the death of the tyrannical Imam, rebellion broke out in the Yemen and a republic was proclaimed. Followers of the new Imam fled to the hills and resisted the new republic, which throughout the 1960s was given strong military support by Nasser, support which eventually led to the triumph of the republic over the Imam's followers.

Within Egypt, Nasser maintained a firm control throughout his years of power. His country's lack of progress before 1952 had made him suspicious of a freely developing political life for Egypt, so he forbade party politics and concentrated on the economic and social development of Egypt on Socialist principles, under his firm control. Fundamental to this development was the Aswan dam, for which he received substantial Soviet assistance and which was eventually completed in 1969. His policies of land reform, by which he hoped to reduce the amount of land held by wealthy landowners by the payment of compensation, were put into effect in the mid-1950s. At the same time, encouragement was given to the development of trade unions, to the reduction of working hours and to the improvement of workers' wages. Due to the bitter hostility created by the Suez crisis, British and French companies in Egypt were nationalized. In 1962 the *National Charter* proposed increased emphasis on the development of fully nationalized industry and the continuing application of land reform. It was a carefully defined programme for the development throughout the 1960s of what Nasser termed *Arab Socialism*.

The Six Days War

Renewed conflict between Israel and the Arab states occurred in 1963 on the issue of the river Jordan: Israel declared her intention of using these waters for the purpose of irrigating the Negev desert, taken from the Arabs in 1948. As most of the water of the river Jordan came from Arab lands, and would now be used to irrigate land taken from the Arabs, Israel's plans aroused sharp hostility. Throughout these years Palestinian refugees, still housed in refugee camps in neighbouring Arab countries, were frustrated at what they considered to be the inaction of these Arab countries against Israel, so in 1964 the *Palestine Liberation Organization* (PLO) came into being. This gave to the Palestinians their own organization for 'liberating' their homeland and thus their hostility towards Israel could be better coordinated. Palestinian Arabs were now prepared to participate fully in the struggle against Israel.

The Arab countries held a series of summit meetings in 1964 and 1965, though not all of these had useful results. Political differences still sharply separated the Arab countries: countries such as Saudi Arabia and Jordan still adopted pro-Western attitudes which conflicted with the Socialist, anticolonial attitudes of countries like Egypt and Syria. In November 1966, their common attitudes brought Egypt and Syria together once more and they signed a defence pact.

Despite the presence of the United Nations peacekeeping forces, many clashes occurred along the Israeli border in the mid-1960s, sparked off by guerrilla attacks, often organized by the new PLO, based in and encouraged by Syria. Tension increased sharply when the PLO attacked Israel in April 1967. The initiative was then seized by Nasser and events moved quickly. Egypt requested the withdrawal of the United Nations peacekeeping forces and blockaded the straits of Tiran, thus stifling Israel's trade communications via the Gulf of Aquaba. In May 1967 Jordan, in spite of political differences, signed a defence agreement with Egypt. In this way Nasser had secured military links between Syria, Jordan and Egypt, all three countries bordering and surrounding Israel. Under these circumstances, war was inevitable.

Israel decided to strike first. On Monday 6 June Israel's forces simultaneously attacked the three enemy countries, making the destruction of the air force bases the prime target. After this had been swiftly and successfully achieved, land forces invaded so that by the end of the week the Israeli forces had made substantial advances. From Egypt they had secured the whole of the Sinai desert, from Jordan the west bank of the river Jordan and the Jordanian part of Jerusalem, and from Syria the area of the Golan heights. The war was one of the swiftest and most successful that the world had seen since 1945.

The territory gained by Israel in 1967 was larger in area and in population than in the earlier wars. The refugee problem now became worse: many original refugees in the newly-conquered areas now moved further into the neighbouring Arab states and others joined them. But most of the Arabs in the conquered areas remained where they were and Israel had to face the problem of administering a Jewish state with a very substantial conquered Arab population, many of whom would be ready to cooperate with guerrilla fighters when opportunity arose. Egypt, Syria and Jordan were all grossly humiliated by their rapid defeat: Nasser's reputation in particular was in decline and, for a time, in the face of internal Egyptian opposition, he resigned from the presidency. Israel claimed that the earlier threatening attitudes of the Arab states made it essential that Israel continue to hold the newly gained areas as a buffer against future Arab aggression. Attempts at seeking reconciliation after the 1967 War made very little progress. The United Nations attempted to resolve the issue and a special envoy, Gunnar Jarring, was sent to the Middle East to work for reconciliation between the two sides, but progress was virtually nil. Quite apart from the issue of the occupied territories, the Arab refusal either to recognize Israel or to negotiate directly with Israel was a fundamental stumbling block.

The PLO and the Yom Kippur War

In the years since 1967 the importance of the Arab fighting organizations increased considerably. They represented the interests of the Palestinian refugees and drew their membership from among them. By the early 1970s there were a number of these organizations, though the PLO was by far the most significant. The fulfilment of the basic aim of 'liberating' Palestine and establishing a multi-racial state in place of Israel would be inevitably resisted by Israel. The bases of the PLO were in the neighbouring Arab states, though not all of these states viewed the PLO with entire sympathy: Lebanon and Jordan, which had suffered effective Israeli reprisal raids prompted by PLO activity against Israel, themselves attempted to take action against the PLO in the early 1970s. Egypt and Syria adopted a more favourable policy towards the PLO, but were not entirely in support of their methods. The only Arab state to give them whole-hearted support was Libya.

Arab attacks became world-wide. One of the most dramatic events was the attack by Arab terrorists on the Israeli participants at the Munich Olympic games in 1972, in the course of which all Israel's competitors were killed. Another tactic that became widespread was the hi-jacking of aircraft. Their method was to hold the aircraft passengers to ransom in return for agreement to Arab demands, such as the release of Arab prisoners. Many different governments found that such activity involved them quite unwillingly in the affairs of the Middle East, and they responded very differently to these unwelcome challenges. In an age of rapid communication, the Arabs were assured of worldwide publicity for their actions. This was one of the main reasons for their use of these tactics.

All these different issues: the continued Israeli presence in the 1967 conquests, the repeated failure of peace negotiations, the increased importance of Arab fighting tactics made it likely that another major conflict would occur in the Middle East. Meanwhile there was a considerable build-up of arms in the area, the Soviet Union supplying the Arab countries and the United States supplying Israel.

In October 1973 the fourth major Arab-Israeli war took place. It began on an important Jewish festival, Yom Kippur (day of Atonement) and it is usually known as the *Yom Kippur War*. Egypt and Syria jointly struck at Israel and in the first few days were able to make advances in the Sinai desert and in the Golan heights. The other Arab states gave them general support and military assistance, though no other Arab state actively joined in the war. At the start of the war Israel had been taken off guard, but she soon managed to resecure the newly invaded areas and to make some slight further advances. A cease-fire proposed by the United Nations at the end of the month was accepted. Later in 1973 and in the early part of 1974, Henry Kissinger, the American

Secretary of State, in spite of the fact that his country had given support to Israel during the war, became accepted by both sides as an impartial mediator. In the early months of 1974, by means of frequent visits between Egypt and Israel and between Syria and Israel, he was able to secure Israeli withdrawal from the additional areas conquered in 1973 and the presence of a United Nations peace keeping force in the Golan heights.

Arab attacks on specific targets throughout the world, spear-headed by the PLO, continued throughout the 1970s. Attacks on Israel continued, as did swift and destructive Israeli counter-attack on what were believed to be PLO bases elsewhere. The most spectacular Israeli action in these years took place some three thousand miles away, in Uganda. In July 1976 Israeli air-borne forces rescued more than a hundred Israelis from the airport at the town of Entebbe, after they had been taken there by Arab hijackers and then detained there with the connivance of Idi Amin, the Ugandan dictator. Nevertheless the PLO tended to discourage activities such as aircraft hijacking in parts of the world other than the Middle East. Partly as a consequence of this discouragement and partly as a consequence of improved security by the major world airlines, such hijacking was less common in the late 1970s.

The PLO also attempted to make itself more popular with the rest of the world. This was particularly the policy of its leader, Yassir Arafat, who in November 1974 led a PLO delegation which was formally received at the headquarters of the United Nations, where Arafat was allowed to address the General Assembly. Whatever criticisms may be made of some of the PLO tactics, the new organization, the PLO, proved itself to be an effective voice of Palestinian discontent.

Oil and the Arab world

When Middle Eastern oil was first exploited by the West, in the years before the Second World War, the oil companies were dominated by the interests of the Western powers, and prices were fixed to provide the West with cheap resources of fuel. In these prewar years the despotic and backward sultanates of the Persian Gulf area were patronized and supported by the Western powers, especially by Britain, in return for oil concessions. This state of affairs proved to be particularly helpful for the British and American military effort during the Second World War, but it did not represent adequate reward for the Arab oil producers.

In the early 1950s the situation received its first serious challenge in Iran. When the nationalist politician Mossadeq became Prime Minister in 1951 he embarked at once on the nationalization of the Abadan oil refinery, built by the large and influential Anglo-Iranian oil company (today known as British Petroleum). By a series of carefully and dramatically staged television appearances, he won much world sympathy for his cause and he created much world criticism of what was presented as the bullying imperialism of Britain. Much controversy between Iran, Britain, and the international oil companies followed. Eventually, in 1954, a compromise was reached. But Mossadeq's action had pointed the way to a future in which the Arab states would be unwilling to sell their essential commodity merely for the advantage of Western powers.

Throughout the 1950s and the 1960s more oil was discovered and exploited in the Middle East. Earlier Iran, Iraq and Kuwait were the main producers; now north Africa and the Arabian peninsula joined them. The international companies, largely American-dominated, alone had the technical expertise needed for the drilling of oil. As the oil-producing countries of the Middle East became better aware of the international value of their oil they joined forces in order to press for a higher financial return: in 1960 the Organization of Petroleum Exporting Countries (OPEC) was founded in the Middle East and expanded throughout the 1970s to include almost all the Middle East oil-producing states, and some elsewhere.

During the Yom Kippur War of October 1973 members of OPEC decided to assert their united strength in a number of different ways. Following the lead of Saudi Arabia, Arab oil-producing states made the supply of oil to Western powers dependent upon the attitude of those powers towards the Arab cause in the Middle East and especially towards the Palestinian cause. Inevitably, the favourable attitudes of the United States towards Israel resulted in a cut in their Arab oil supplies. Gradually the OPEC countries adopted an easier policy towards exports. However, a more significant effect of the Yom Kippur War was the trebling of the price of oil from the Middle East during the following winter of 1973–74. This resulted in enormous financial gains by OPEC countries and worsened still further the shaky economies of many Western countries, which had little alternative but to purchase oil at the new prices, their dependency upon oil being so great. Thereafter oil prices continued to rise, though less dramatically than in that winter. The comparatively modest nature of the later increases was assisted by a series of meetings between representatives of the OPEC powers and the Western powers. In some respects, by then the wheel had turned full circle, giving the real benefit of oil production to the Arab states and also giving them far more weight in the continuing world friction surrounding Israel.

The Middle East in the late 1970s

In the uncertainty and violence that continued to plague the Middle East during the late 1970s, the one constant factor was the increasing power of the Arabs. This was illustrated particularly by events in the Lebanon and in Iran. In April 1975 civil war broke out in the Lebanon. Though this former French mandate had been comparatively quiet since the French had left in 1946, below the surface there had been much friction between the country's wealthy Christian and poorer Muslim populations for many years. Since the time of the first Arab-Israeli War of 1948–49 an increasing number of Palestinian refugees had settled in the Lebanon and by the 1970s the PLO had a strong influence among them, especially in the south of the country. Though the civil war has continued throughout the late 1970s, its intensity slackened after Syria attempted to bring peace to the area towards the end of 1976, on terms satisfactory to the Arabs of the Lebanon. Israel, aware that a number of PLO attacks against her had been launched from PLO bases in southern Lebanon, has made periodic attacks against the country.

Of much greater significance for the Middle East and for the world were the changes that took place in Iran during the early months of 1979. The Shah of Iran had attempted to 'modernize' his country throughout the postwar years, basing his work on the country's exceptionally rich oil resources. But his policies and methods aroused opposition both from Muslims who considered the Shah's policies to be anti-religious and from many Iranians who considered that his methods were too dictatorial. Throughout the closing months of 1978 there was widespread rioting throughout Iran, especially in the capital, Teheran. Concessions by the Shah appeared to make very little difference and early in 1979, he went into exile. The moderately progressive and reforming government which then took power encountered bitter hostility from those Iranians who wanted to see Iran become an Islamic republic, under the rule of the Ayatollah Khomeini, the religious leader whom the Shah had exiled. So widespread was the Muslim rioting that the government was compelled to resign, the Ayatollah returned and the Islamic republic was proclaimed.

These events had significance far beyond Iran itself. The new Islamic republic established friendly relations with the PLO and with the other Arab states with whom, under the Shah, relations had been poor. In view of her oil resources, Iran's new alignment added substantially to the importance of the Arabs in world affairs.

One useful achievement in the Middle East was the signing of a peace treaty between Israel and Egypt in March 1979, ending more than thirty years of conflict. President Carter of the United States had been closely

President Sadat (left) and Prime Minister Begin shake hands while President Carter looks on approvingly. This photograph was taken during the discussions at Camp David in August 1978 which led to the signature of an Israeli-Egyptian treaty early in the following year.

involved in bringing about this treaty. The first step towards an Israeli-Egyptian understanding had been a visit by Egypt's President Sadat to Israel in November 1977, where he was warmly welcomed by Israel's Prime Minister Begin. This was the first time in which the leaders of Israel and Egypt had met on terms of friendship. Negotiations were long and difficult. In August 1978 the two leaders met with President Carter at the presidential retreat at Camp David in the United States. Carter himself made a visit to the Middle East in March 1979 to finalize the settlement at a time when negotiations appeared to be in danger of breaking down. The treaty's main provision was the progressive withdrawal of Israeli forces from the Egyptian territory that Israel had held since 1967, over the next three years. The treaty was rightly greeted as a significant step towards peace in the Middle East. But perhaps more significant for the future of the Middle East was the total opposition to it of the other Arab states.

Questions

64. Study the cartoon of 1956 on page 237 and then answer questions (a) to (d) which follow.
    (a) (i) Name the leader who is shown in the cartoon,
         (ii) show how he secured power in his country and
         (iii) describe the main policies he pursued to improve the conditions of the people in his country.

         $(1+2+2)$

    (b) With reference to the torn treaty in the centre right of the cartoon,
         (i) name the waterway referred to on this torn treaty,
         (ii) account for the torn condition of this treaty during this year, and
         (iii) name the two world powers most immediately affected by the destruction of this treaty.

         $(1+2+1)$

    (c) Apart from the torn treaty, explain other suggestions made by the cartoon of forceful action on the part of this leader.

         (4)

    (d) Show how and with what results a policy of *collusion* was pursued by the enemies of this leader in the autumn of 1956.

         (7)

65. Outline and explain the events leading to (a) the granting of Palestine as a British mandate and (b) the creation of Israel as an independent country.

66. Why did war break out between Israel and her neighbours in 1956, 1967 and 1973? Show the importance of *each* of these wars in the history of the Middle East.

23

The United States since 1945

Harry Truman: the Fair Deal

Few American presidents came to their task in more difficult circumstances than did former Vice President Harry Truman in April 1945 on Franklin Roosevelt's death during his fourth term of office. Though the war against Germany was drawing to a close, there was still much fighting to be done in the Pacific before Japan would be defeated. Added to these military problems, were the inevitable postwar problems of readjustment in foreign relations and in the internal development of the country. The jaunty, unassuming and comparatively unknown Harry Truman brought to the presidency the much needed qualities of decisiveness and tough-ness, typified by the slogan he placed on his desk at the White House (still kept there by his successors) 'the buck stops here'.

The importance of Roosevelt's New Deal for the American economy showed most successfully during the war years and Truman was in no doubt that he should continue with the policies of his predecessor. In September 1945 he put forward a 21-point development programme that later became known as the *Fair Deal*. This was to be a continuation of the New Deal and it promised in particular increased attention to slum clearance and social security.

Economic and political factors during his first term prevented Truman from carrying out all of his programme. There was con-

Presidents of the United States since 1945			
Dates	*Name*	*Party*	
1945–53	Harry Truman	Democrat	As Vice President succeeded on Roosevelt's death, April 1945. Elected November 1948.
1953–61	Dwight Eisenhower	Republican	Elected November 1952 and November 1956.
1961–63	John Kennedy	Democrat	Elected November 1960.
1963–69	Lyndon Johnson	Democrat	As Vice President succeeded on Kennedy's assassination, November 1963. Elected November 1964.
1969–74	Richard Nixon	Republican	Elected November 1968 and November 1972.
1974–77	Gerald Ford	Republican	As Vice President succeeded on Nixon's resignation, August 1974.
1977–	Jimmy Carter	Democrat	Elected November 1976.

tinued demand for goods both from the government, now committed to fuller involvement abroad, and from the people deprived of goods during wartime. While the economy therefore continued to progress and while unemployment was low, the problem of inflation arose more acutely then before. The trade unions consequently demanded higher wages and Truman received much trade union hostility for his firm policy resisting their demands. In 1946, with increasing problems of inflation, Truman took the drastic step of taking control of the coal mines and threatening to draft striking railway workers into the army. These tough policies weakened his relations with the trade unions and did little to slow down the extent of inflation. His popularity fell and in the mid-term elections of 1946, the Republicans gained a majority in the Congress. Thus he was faced with severe political difficulties, as his policies could now be effectively opposed by Congress. The Republicans used their majority to put through Congress some right-wing legislation. The most important was the 1947 Taft-Hartley Act designed to curb the trade unions by limiting their right to strike and preventing trade unionists from contributing to political parties. Truman resecured popularity among the trade unions by using his constitutional powers to veto this Act, but Congress then used its constitutional powers to re-enact it.

At the same time, Truman did not shrink from tackling the problem of the neglect of the civil rights of American blacks. No previous twentieth-century American president had given more than minimal attention to the ways in which American blacks were denied equality in such matters as education, work, housing and voting. Widespread *segregation* kept blacks apart from whites. The situation affected the whole of the United States, though in the southern states there was more injustice than elsewhere. The ideals for which the United States had fought in the Second World War, as expressed in the Atlantic Charter, made it unacceptable for the United States to neglect their own racial problems any longer. These problems were highlighted in the postwar years by some

grisly examples of racial murder and racial lynching in the southern states. In February 1948 Truman attempted to put into effect a ten-point programme based on extensive study of the civil rights issue which had been undertaken in the previous year. But Congress opposed these plans: the opposition Republicans were joined on this issue by southern Democrats, who regarded the proposed package as dangerous to the economic and social status of whites in the south. Truman nevertheless put into effect, by presidential decree, orders for desegregation in the American army and in the civil service.

Truman's chances of success in the presidential election of 1948 were poor. The southern Democrats were opposed to him on the civil rights issue, and other members of his own party were opposed to his forceful Cold War tactics. The Republicans, even under the colourless presidential candidate, Thomas Dewey, were judged to be certain of success. Truman adopted a particularly effective strategy during the election campaign: he summoned the Republican Congress to a special session in which he requested them to undertake reforms. Congress did virtually nothing. Meanwhile Truman embarked on a 'whistle stop' rail tour, a traditional feature of presidential campaigns at that time, during which he condemned Congress thoroughly for its lack of action. The results were very favourable for Truman: not only was he returned with a majority of over two million votes, but a majority for the Democrats was also obtained in Congress.

Truman was therefore in a much stronger political position in his second, full term of office. Social security measures were extended, minimum wage levels were increased, subsidies and aid for rural areas became more widely available. The 1949 Housing Act by a series of subsidies boosted the construction of low-cost houses. All this was important and solid work, but it was unspectacular. Because of continuing concerted opposition from the southern Democrats and the Republicans, he was again prevented from putting into effect legislation that was really intended to cut new ground:

plans for a national health scheme and for educational aid thus came to nothing.

McCarthyism

It was during the early 1950s that Senator Joseph McCarthy stirred up quite unjustified fears about the presence of Communism in American government circles. This obscure Republican Senator from Wisconsin appears to have started his crusade against Communism in the early part of 1950 as an issue that might help him to success in the elections later that year. The increasing intensity of the Cold War explains the readiness with which many Americans were prepared to support McCarthy's campaigns. China's adoption of Communism in 1949 suggested that the position of the United States was not strong enough in international affairs. In a well-publicized law suit, a prominent civil servant, Alger Hiss, was condemned in January 1950 for the sale of documents which had been passed to Communist agents in the late 1930s. The following month, McCarthy launched his campaign with the wild assertion that he had the names of 205 Communists then working in the State Department. An accusation of this type, coming from a member of the United States Senate, was a sufficiently serious matter for an official enquiry to be made by the Senate. But later in the year, when the enquiry reported that the accusation was totally without foundation, McCarthy refused to believe its findings and suggested that Communist infiltration was even wider than he had originally said.

By now McCarthy had achieved widespread popularity among many Americans who were persuaded by the accusations that he made. Against this background, the Senate passed the Internal Security Act in 1950, providing for strong measures against Communists. McCarthy took the issue further during the closing years of Truman's administration and the opening years of Eisenhower's administration by staging a series of Senate enquiries in which, due to

his position as a Senator, he was able to summon suspects before him. At these special hearings, often televised, many Americans who were giving valuable service to their country, were humiliated by McCarthy's insinuations that some early association of theirs with left-wing politics was positive proof that they were now working to further Communist interests in the United States. The proceedings were staged in a manner which made it difficult for the accused to defend themselves convincingly. Truman and the Democrats were much opposed to McCarthy, but could do little to curb his activities. Eisenhower and the Republicans showed rather more sympathy. Whilst Eisenhower's government was not directly involved in the McCarthy hearings of 1953–54, it was re-

Senator Joseph McCarthy covers the microphone during a Senate investigating committee in order to listen confidentially to one of his assistant investigators.

sponsible for the dismissal of large numbers of government employees as 'security risks'.

McCarthy's downfall came in 1954. He was unsuccessful in persuading the army to allow preferential treatment for one of his wealthy young assistants, when he was called up for national service. McCarthy was highly angered and launched a series of further accusations against the army. This time he went too far in his arrogant cross-examination of distinguished military men: he lost public sympathy and later in the year his fellow-senators passed a vote of censure on him. McCarthyism fizzled out, having been a cause of unnecessary alarm among the American people and real distress among its immediate victims.

Dwight Eisenhower: Dynamic Conservatism

Dwight Eisenhower, the Commander-in-Chief of the American forces in the closing stages of the Second World War, was adopted as the Republican presidential candidate in 1952. By the time of the November election the popularity of the Democratic party, which had held presidential power for twenty years, was in decline. Eisenhower promised to curb inflation, restrict government spending and promote prosperity. He received much support by his promise to visit Korea and to take positive steps towards ending the war which was well into its third year by the time of the election campaign.

Presidential candidate Eisenhower (right) and vice-presidential candidate Nixon (left), during the 1952 election campaign. Under the Dynamic Conservatism of the 1950s many Americans enjoyed a higher standard of living and a sense of confidence in their world position rarely matched at any other time in the history of the United States.

Eisenhower's popularity gave him a successful majority in the presidential election of 1952 and again, in spite of his ill-health, in the election of 1956. In both terms of office his Vice President was Richard Nixon, a young politician who had entered the Senate only in 1950, after a campaign in which he had strongly underlined the idea of alleged Communist infiltration, then popularized by McCarthy. During Eisenhower's second term of office, with the President in poor health, Nixon took on many of the presidential functions. In Congress, Republican fortunes were less successful: their majority was only slight in the 1952 election and after the 1954 mid-term elections they lost control of Congress to the Democrats. During the last six years of Eisenhower's presidency, he was faced with the problem that had taxed Truman and other presidents: how to get policies through a Congress that was politically unsympathetic. Inevitably the situation limited the scope of government action.

Eisenhower adopted 'Dynamic Conservatism' as a political description of his policies. He formed an administration consisting predominantly of wealthy business men, who felt their practical administrative experience in the business world fitted them well for the administrative work of government. There was to be no unthinking return to the values of the previous Republican administrations of the 1920s, and there was to be no back-tracking on the New Deal and Fair Deal policies of the 1930s and the 1940s. But in both home and foreign policies, the new administration adopted conservative attitudes, fostering loyalty, encouraging economic expansion and seeking to advance the interests of the middle classes on whose support the Republicans relied. Though not unaware of social problems, these did not receive his main attentions.

In his economic policies Eisenhower encouraged private enterprise, lowered taxation and generally avoided confrontation with the trade unions. After a slight recession in 1953, the American economy flourished throughout the mid-1950s, until danger signs again appeared in 1959. At no time in the history of the United States had there been such a widely experienced boom in the country's economy. In the mid-1950s, the United States was producing approximately half the world's goods: on average, incomes had increased substantially, while hours of work had been reduced. At that time no country in the world could rival the high standard of living which many Americans enjoyed. The improved economy was due partly to the fact that the American economy had been less disrupted by the war than had the economies of most other countries. It was also due to improving economic conditions throughout the world. But many Americans, not unnaturally, gave credit to the Eisenhower administration. The apparently successful achievement of the American ideal of prosperity for all encouraged a deeper sense of loyalty both to the successful business enterprises and to the United States in general.

But not all sectors of society benefited. There was still a sizeable group whose low incomes denied them decent housing. Farming communities also failed to share in the prosperity: Eisenhower was concerned at the cost of farm subsidies but his alternative, more flexible support, failed to bring improvement for the farmers. Eisenhower's fundamental conservatism is shown by this policy towards farming subsidies. Like the Republican governments three decades earlier, he envisaged minimal federal involvement in the economy. Federal organizations such as the TVA found their aid diminished and plans for the development of similar schemes elsewhere were scrapped. Private enterprise was to secure control of the new development of atomic energy. In a similar way, individual states were allowed to develop their own economic resources and had no need to feel bound to any federal control.

Though he favoured states' rights on some economic issues, Eisenhower became much tougher when the issues concerned civil liberties. The particular area of civil liberties with which Eisenhower became closely concerned was the right of black children to equality of educational opportunities. Until the 1950s, schooling could be 'separate' provided it was also 'equal': in practice, the southern states used this legal formula to provide distinctly inferior schools for black children. A case brought before the Chief Justice, Earl Warren, led to the abandonment of the 'separate but equal' formula and, in May 1955, required the desegregation of all schools in the United States. This legal requirement aroused a storm of furious protest from the governors of many southern states. Education was the basis on which the southern tradition of segregation was constructed: educational desegregation would lead to social desegregation and the end of the traditional white hold in the governments of the southern states.

Opposition developed from both the white governments and the white people within many southern states: progress in fulfilling the federal desegregation order was slow. Much violence developed on the issue at Little Rock, in the state of Arkansas. Under the instructions of the state governor, the state guards forcibly prevented desegregation from taking place. The issue now became one of state defiance of the federal government, and Eisenhower, who never appears to have felt very strongly on the civil rights issue, took action specifically on this issue of defiance. He ordered federal troops to Little Rock in September 1957 to overcome this blatant state resistance to desegregation.

Though the Little Rock incident impressed the southern states with the federal determination to impose its decision of desegregation, progress continued to be made only

Troops escort black students to school at the town of Little Rock in 1957. The government was determined that its ruling on desegregation of schools should be obeyed.

slowly. Desegregation was far from complete by the end of Eisenhower's presidency. One other important step forward in civil rights was an achievement of Congress rather than of the President: the Civil Rights Law, August 1957. This law was concerned with ensuring that black people in the southern states were not prevented from casting their votes in elections.

Although the desegregation campaign did not result in many immediate benefits for blacks, it was important in another way: it marked the start of the civil rights movement that was to grow in importance during the 1960s and the 1970s. Their often bitter experiences during the desegregation events of the 1950s brought blacks together in a way never achieved before. They now began to campaign for their legal and social rights.

The United States and the Cold War: containment and liberation

The government of the United States was the leading Western power opposed to the expansion of Communism during the postwar years. America's concern at the Soviet advance in the closing stages of the Second World War had already been shown at the end of chapter 13. In March 1947, as Britain was unable to continue her financial assistance to Greece and Turkey, two areas of the world particularly faced with the approach of Communism, Congress accepted the President's policy, which became known as the *Truman doctrine*, of giving American support instead.

> I believe that it must be the policy of the United States to support free people who are resisting attempted subjugation by armed minorities or by outside pressures. I believe that we must assist free peoples to work out their own destinies in their own way. I believe that our help should be primarily through economic and financial aid which is essential to economic stability and orderly political progress.

In June of the same year an extension of this policy was financial assistance known as *Marshall Aid*, given to those countries who wished to receive it. Though substantial benefit was gained by many countries through Marshall Aid, it also strengthened the division between the non-Communist states which received it and the Communist ones which refused it. It was particularly important in Europe, as is shown in chapter 20.

The approach that the Truman administration generally adopted towards Communism was that of *containment*: not disturbing those countries which were already Communist, but taking steps to prevent other countries from becoming Communist. The role of America in the creation of NATO, considered in chapter 20, and in the Korean War, considered in chapter 26, illustrate the practice of containment during Truman's presidency.

Secretary of State John Foster Dulles dominated the foreign relations of the United States during most of the Eisenhower years. No postwar holder of the office was such a convinced and determined opponent of Communism as Dulles. During his early months in office he put forward the policy of *liberation* of the countries which were already Communist and the policy of *massive retaliation* by means of nuclear weapons against the Communist bloc in the event of Communist aggression in any part of the world. These were exceptionally dangerous extensions of the policy of containment. Though in practice Dulles modified his approach towards the Communist bloc, he was nevertheless determined to prevent Communist expansion. Taiwan and West Berlin, dangerous areas of possible conflict during these years, were given full military support, as shown in chapters 16 and 25. At the Geneva conference on Indochina in 1954 he took all possible steps to ensure that the Indochinese Communists were placed at a disadvantage, as shown in chapter 26. As a result of the conference, he built up SEATO and CENTO, as security pacts directed against Communism in South-east Asia and the Middle East. The Dulles years were ones during which American forces were based in many parts of the globe, on the alert for Communist aggression. This extensive military commitment overseas was one of the most important ways in which American self-confidence, based on a flourishing economy, showed itself during the 1950s.

John Kennedy: the New Frontier

In November 1960 the Democrat candidate, John Kennedy, in the closest presidential victory in the twentieth century, defeated his Republican rival, Richard Nixon. Eisenhower had been the oldest president the United States had ever had – he was in his late sixties in his final years of office – and Kennedy, 43 at the time of his election, was the youngest. The new President made much of the youthful image that he wanted his administration to project. The 'New Frontier' theme dominated his election campaign and his later policies. He stressed the theme especially in his highly effective inaugural address, given at the outdoor ceremony in a bitterly cold Washington in January 1961:

> Let the word go forth from this time and place, to friend and foe alike, that the torch has been passed to a new generation of Americans – born in this century, tempered by war, disciplined by a hard and bitter peace, proud of our ancient heritage, and unwilling to witness or permit the slow undoing of those human rights to which this nation has always been committed.

Kennedy came from a wealthy American family and was a man with many attractive qualities, who previously had represented Massachusetts in the American Senate. His membership of the Roman Catholic church was considered a disadvantage in his presidential bid, as he had to overcome some anti-Roman Catholic feeling that was still widespread in the United States at that time. Nevertheless he benefited from a reaction against the Republican party: its lack of definite economic policies had become more widely criticized as affluence had declined towards the end of the 1950s.

Kennedy's administration had a style totally different from that of Eisenhower. Idealism was more deeply a part of it. The 'New Frontier' consisted of goals comparatively neglected by the previous administration: social awareness, civil liberties, intellectual endeavour. Certainly Kennedy and Eisenhower shared a common will to contain Communism, but they had few other objectives in common. The members of Kennedy's administration were a marked contrast with those of Eisenhower: young, idealistic intellectuals were to be found in the place of the practical, wealthy businessmen.

An important early task was to resecure the American economy from the depression that had overtaken it in 1959. Kennedy stimulated the economy by encouraging public spending and by making it easier to obtain credit. He followed these moves by a policy designed to prevent price rises and by taking strong action against companies, notably against the national steel works, which attempted to undermine this policy. Tax reductions were also started by Kennedy as a further means of stimulating the economy.

Opposition in Congress, often the result, as before, of a combination of southern Democrats and Republicans, prevented Kennedy from achieving some other objectives. Nevertheless useful extensions were made to existing social legislation: social security benefits were increased, minimum wages were raised, attention was given to the treatment of the mentally retarded and some limited steps were taken to prevent water pollution.

But it was in the matter of civil rights, that the Kennedy administration made the most significant advances, in spite of Congressional opposition. Firm action was taken by John Kennedy's brother, Robert, in his capacity as Attorney General over breaches of the 1957 Civil Rights Law. Ground was thus consolidated. Further progress was made in cutting down segregation in transport. As in the 1950s, the most serious clashes were aroused by instances of discrimination in education. Discrimination in university education was weakened when in September 1962 Kennedy despatched federal troops to the University of Mississippi to secure the admission of a black student, James Meredith, whom the state authorities were attempting to refuse. In spite of the 1957 Little Rock incident, segregation in schools still existed for some years, though by 1963 only the state of Alabama still maintained school segregation. In June the state governor, George Wallace, later to become an extreme right-wing presidential candidate, personally prevented two black pupils from entering a white school. But opposition to desegregation was now less strong, and the state guards responded to Kennedy's instructions that they were to secure the admission of these students.

By 1963, prompted by the events in Mississippi and Alabama and influenced by the views of the increasingly vocal civil rights movement, Kennedy decided the time had come when a fully comprehensive bill on racial equality should be enacted. But Congress rejected this bill at the start of November 1963, the month in which Kennedy was assassinated.

Kennedy's assassination shocked and moved the people of the United States and of the world in a way that perhaps no other single event has done in the years since 1945. On 22 November 1963, during an open motorcade tour of the Texan town of Dallas, Kennedy was shot by an assassin and died in hospital less than an hour later; Vice President Lyndon Johnson was at once sworn in as President by a local magistrate. The fatal shots were said to have been fired from a nearby building by a young man, Lee Harvey Oswald, who was himself killed very soon after, at the hands of a Dallas night club owner, while being held in police custody. A year after the event, a special commission headed by Chief Justice Earl Warren concluded that Oswald alone was guilty of the deed. But speculation continued to surround those dramatic and tragic events in Dallas: further enquiries of highly varied worth were made, including a further government-sponsored enquiry in 1978, into the murder of John Kennedy and the later

President John Kennedy (left) and his wife in the back of the official car taking them through Dallas on 22 November 1963. A few minutes later the President was assassinated.

murder in 1968 of the civil rights leader, Martin Luther King. Despite the fact that Kennedy had not been particularly popular with many Americans during his lifetime, he became for many a cult figure after his death. His legacy to the United States needs to be seen not just in his own presidency, but also in the early years of his successor's.

Lyndon Johnson: the Great Society

The new President, successfully elected by a large majority in his own right in November 1964, was a Texan who had fuller political experience than Kennedy and who brought to the presidency a contrasting southern style of his own. Ambitious in the early years of his presidency, he sought to create in the United States a 'Great Society', a society with high living standards and with a sense of community. Congress was less obstructive towards Johnson than it had been towards Kennedy and the early years of Johnson's administration saw some impressive achievements in domestic affairs. In some respects the most important new laws might be considered a part of Kennedy's achievement, as they had originated under his earlier guidance and were enacted by a Congress for a long while stunned by the events at Dallas.

Kennedy's Civil Rights Bill, proposed shortly before his assassination, was passed with minimal opposition from Congress in 1964. Its comprehensive terms outlawed discrimination in the securing of jobs, provision of housing, use of public places, opportunity in education and in the casting of votes. It consolidated the ground won by earlier legislation and created firmer safeguards to prevent avoidance of the Act's terms by die-hard southerners. Among the safeguards created by the act was the Equal Opportunities Commission, to ensure that discrimination in jobs did not take place.

In dealing with the economy, Johnson also trod in Kennedy's footsteps in persuading Congress to approve substantial tax cuts, a controversial matter which Kennedy had earlier proposed as a means of stimulating the economy. These cuts worked effectively and industrial output, which had already been increasing during Kennedy's time, took a further upward turn. Johnson himself became much concerned with the issue of poverty: beginning in 1964 he sought, by means of a series of laws, to wage what he called 'war on poverty'. Efforts were made to assist school leavers from poor homes to get jobs or to further their education; a Jobs Corps provided help for unemployed young people; poverty-stricken areas, particularly the Appalachian area, were given special aid. In Johnson's second term, improvements were made in the social services. Perhaps the most important of these was the establishment of Medicare, providing free medical treatment for the elderly, and Medicaid, providing free medical treatment for the poor. The creation of a Department of Housing and Urban Development and the granting of increased federal funds for school development were further important contributions towards social improvement. Civil rights continued to demand a vigilant eye. The 1965 Public Voting Act gave authority to the federal government to investigate those states where only half of the voting population were registered to vote, and there was evidence that a number of southern blacks were still frightened to register. Over the next few years the number of registered black voters in southern states was substantially increased as a direct result of this Act. Increasingly also, black people were being appointed even in the southern states to positions of responsibility which they would never have occupied earlier.

Not since the early days of the New Deal had a president been able to get so much legislation passed. Johnson's ambitious nature led him to hope that he might achieve more than even Roosevelt himself, the President for whom he had great admiration and by whom his earlier political career had been encouraged. Vietnam prevented him from achieving this ambition. The manner in which Johnson allowed the United States to become increasingly and hopelessly involved in Vietnam is shown in chapter 26. The cost of the Vietnam War was so high that any money available for further advance of the Great Society at home was minimal. Johnson in any case was preoccupied by this foreign entanglement. When he retired to his Texan ranch in January 1969, after refusing to seek re-election, Johnson did so with a sense of ambition unfulfilled but also a sense of mighty relief that the oppressive responsibility of Vietnam had passed to another president.

Richard Nixon

Violence and disorder marked the election year of 1968. Opposition to the American involvement in Vietnam was now widespread; racial strife continued to be a source of violence in many towns; at the Democrat party convention at Chicago in the summer, ugly conflict took place between the police and demonstrators. Confusion and instability within the United States were reflected by the presence of three presidential candidates: Richard Nixon for the Republicans, Hubert Humphrey for the Democrats and Governor George Wallace of Alabama standing as an Independent opposed to the extension of civil rights to blacks. Nixon won by a narrow majority, having made much in the election campaign of the previous government's failure to preserve internal law and order or to secure an acceptable way out of the Vietnam involvement. Such were the misfortunes of the Democrats in 1968 that their loss of the presidency was scarcely surprising.

It was only in the early stages of Nixon's second term, in January 1973, that a Vietnam peace agreement was signed. During his first term there was a gradual withdrawal of American troops, as part of a policy known as Vietnamization. As shown in Chapter 26 the withdrawal was not consistent, as in 1970 there was a brief invasion of Cambodia. The unpopularity of the Vietnam War was deepened by the publication in the summer of 1971 of what became known as the *Pentagon Papers*, confidential government documents relating to the origins of the war and to the aim of the American government in it. The anti-war movement became larger in

size and more varied in composition: in October 1969 and in April 1971 massive demonstrations, of a size not seen before in the history of the United States, took place in Washington.

Within the country, the pace of reform slackened. Both Nixon and his Vice President, Spiro Agnew, sought to reassert the established American values which had been challenged during the 1960s. Nixon's appeal was to 'middle America' or 'the silent majority', to those who were less interested in reform and who wanted a return to stability. His approach to many issues was puritanical and reactionary. To enforce this general approach, Nixon appointed judges whose outlook was distinctly conservative. Congress at times frustrated these attempts, which never achieved more than partial success. The civil rights legislation was not reversed, though not a great deal was done to give it the continuing support that it needed if it were to develop effectively. Nothing was done to extend the scope of the 1965 Public Voting Act.

Such new legislation as was produced during these years usually originated from Congress, in which the Democrats had a majority. Expenditure on social security, education and health increased, though this was partly the result of inflation. Steps were taken in the comparatively uncontroversial area of environmental pollution: dangers of this kind could be checked by the Environmental Protection Agency, established in 1970.

The economic situation inherited by Nixon in 1969 was shaky, mainly as a consequence of the increased expenditure demanded by the Vietnam War. By 1971 the situation had worsened. Increasing inflation, mounting unemployment and a declining international value of the dollar had made the economy the major problem facing the government. In August 1971, though it went against earlier commitments, freezes on wages and prices were announced and the dollar was devalued. In the short-term these measures produced promising results, but in the long-term they had little significance.

Nixon's domestic achievements were thin. His years saw some spectacular journeys into space by the American astronauts, including in July 1969 the first landing of men on the moon, by the Armstrong-Collins-Aldrin team, but these were the results of the initiative of earlier governments and in any case had only very slight importance in the history of the United States, or of the world in general. The immense cost of such ventures weighed against the country's declining economy and led to their abandonment in the middle and late 1970s.

Nixon achieved more notable success in the realm of foreign affairs, where he was well served throughout by Secretary of State Henry Kissinger. The ending of the war in Vietnam in January 1973 was greeted with relief mixed with despair that it had lasted for so long and had been the cause of so much loss of life. In February 1972 a more surprising event was a visit by Nixon to Peking and conversations with the Chinese Communist leadership. The visit brought together two countries between which there had earlier been much friction. The positive results were rather limited. Nixon's promise of reducing American military support for Taiwan created further disillusion among the Chinese Nationalists who had recently been compelled to give their seat at the United Nations to Communist China. The week's visit was a useful and sensible step of limited impact, scarcely matching Nixon's description of it as 'the week that changed the world', but nevertheless an important landmark in China's relations with the West.

The Watergate scandals and the resignation of Nixon

During Nixon's second term of office he became so preoccupied in attempting to defend himself from the mounting accusations stemming from the Watergate affair that the government of the United States appeared very seriously to lack direction. In June 1972, during the presidential election campaign, intruders were discovered in the room used by the Democrat party national committee at the 'Watergate' premises in Washington. It was discovered that these

men were employed by the Committee to re-elect the President, unattractively styled CREEP. Close, detailed work by some Washington journalists revealed that the interference at the Watergate premises was not the only crime of which CREEP had been guilty: a 'slush fund' existed to pay unscrupulous agents to commit 'dirty tricks' against the President's political opponents. Its activities ranged from the bugging of rooms used by political opponents to attempts at defamation of the characters of others by securing confidential information about them. Wealthy business men who saw their interests advanced by the Nixon administration were willing contributors to the 'slush fund'.

These revelations were sufficiently serious for a Senate enquiry to be established, under the forthright chairmanship of Senator Sam Ervin. A number of Nixon's White House assistants were summoned before this enquiry, which concluded that they had knowledge of the operation to 'cover-up' White House involvement in the Watergate break-in: many of these assistants were charged and later imprisoned and fined. For Nixon, the most damaging revelation at the Ervin Committee was that he made a practice, for reasons best known to himself, of tape-recording conversations in his office. To ascertain the extent of his responsibility for the Watergate break-in, the tapes would have to be examined. For some months Nixon successfully resisted handing over these tapes and in April 1974 published his own edited versions of them. The vindictive remarks and the crude language in this edited version gave a most unfavourable impression of the way in which the United States government functioned at the highest level: furthermore, it was not a complete version. Later legal pressure brought to light the missing tapes and these left little doubt that Nixon had full knowledge of the Watergate 'cover-up' and of the illegal activities of CREEP. Close supporters advised Nixon that he was unlikely to escape impeachment, involving condemnation by the Senate and expulsion from office. Under the circumstances, though still protesting his innocence, Nixon resigned the presidency in early August 1974, being the only president to do so in the history of the United States. He retired into privacy for some years at his home in California, though he began to take a more active and critical interest in American politics in the late 1970s

Gerald Ford and Jimmy Carter

Vice President Gerald Ford, who succeeded automatically to the presidency on Nixon's resignation, held the office until his defeat in the presidential election of 1976. As President, he worked to restore the nation's self-confidence after what he called the 'long national nightmare' of Watergate. In a controversial decision later in 1974, he granted a free pardon to ex-President Nixon. But most Americans were prepared to follow the lead of their new President and put Watergate behind them.

Ford's narrow loss of the 1976 election was due mainly to his failure to present a sufficiently forward-looking image. During the early 1970s the confidence of the American people had been badly shaken by the experience of defeat in the Vietnam War and by the preoccupation with the Watergate scandals. Most of them now sought a government that would strike out in a new direction. The comparatively unknown candidate of the Democrat party, Jimmy Carter, successfully promised a new, more straightforward, more open style of government that would promote the interests and hopes of ordinary Americans. His inaugural speech in January 1977 struck a modest note.

> We have learnt that 'more' is not necessarily 'better', that even our great nation has its recognized limits, and that we can neither answer all questions nor solve all problems. We cannot afford to do everything, nor can we afford to lack boldness as we meet the future. So together, in a spirit of individual sacrifice for the common good, we must simply do our best.

In office, Carter failed to fulfil completely the hopes that many had placed in him. He began his promised overhaul of welfare in America, intending to make its distribution fairer throughout society. He also took steps to stimulate the economy by reducing taxation and increasing the amount of government aid to industry. The most serious issue confronting him within the United States was the *energy crisis*, which had been a difficulty that Ford also had faced. This crisis was caused by the heavy American dependence on oil supplies from abroad, mainly from the Middle East. Two factors had made this dependence a serious problem by the mid-1970s: the vast increase in oil prices was draining America's financial resources, while there was a growing awareness that within a few years the world's oil resources would be severely diminished. To curb the nation's heavy dependence on oil Carter put to Congress an Energy Bill, which proposed a fuller use of natural gas and coal and which encouraged Americans to reduce their consumption of oil. The bill proved unpopular in Congress and in spite of Carter's studied and sensible appeals to the American people, he still failed to persuade Congress to pass what he considered to be a vital piece of legislation for the future of the United States.

Under Ford and under Carter there were no further involvements of American forces abroad. Vietnam had ended that. There was, however, a continuing interest by the government of the United States in maintaining world peace. Henry Kissinger, Secretary of State under Nixon and Ford, had taken a leading role in seeking a peaceful settlement of the problems of the Middle East and Rhodesia; his successor in the Carter administration, Cyrus Vance, continued this work in both areas. Carter himself took a particular interest in working for a Middle East settlement, and the conclusion of the peace treaty between Egypt and Israel in March 1979 owed much to his determined efforts.

Questions

67. Study the photograph on page 251, taken in 1957, and then answer questions (a) to (c) which follow.

THE UNITED STATES SINCE 1945

(a) (i) What type of people are shown being escorted by troops?

(ii) In what part of the United States was this photograph taken?

(iii) Describe the ways in which people of the type named in (a) (i) were treated in this part of the United States during the years before this photograph was taken.

$(1+1+3)$

(b) (i) Who was the President of the United States at the time of this photograph?

(ii) What is the function of the building into which the people are being escorted?

(iii) Are the troops in this photograph responsible to the *federal government* or to the *state government*?

(iv) Outline the events which led to the situation shown in this photograph.

(v) Show how the policies of the President at the time were eventually successful on this issue.

$(1+1+1+2+2)$

(c) Examine the difficulties which confronted the next two presidents of the United States in continuing these policies and show to what extent they succeeded in overcoming these difficulties.

(8)

68. Outline the main achievements of President Truman in both domestic and foreign affairs. What problems did he pass on to his successor?

69. Show with what success the various presidents of the United States in the 1960s and the 1970s have attempted to deal with the problems of (a) civil rights, (b) poor Americans, (c) student unrest and (d) energy conservation.

24

Latin America

Almost all the Latin American republics were established in the nineteenth century as the rule of Spain and Portugal was overthrown. In the early twentieth century they still held many features in common: absence of real democracy, dominance by the Roman Catholic church, influence of big business interests, grinding poverty for the mass of the people in town and country. By the late twentieth century many of these features remained. But events in the larger, more significant republics have developed in very different ways.

Argentina

Since the overthrow of Spanish control, Argentina had developed a prosperous economy under predominantly conservative governments. This economy was based on meat exports. In 1916, in the first really free elections to be held in Argentina, Hipolito Irigoyen, leader of the Radical party, secured a narrow victory. Until 1930, he dominated the affairs of the country, ruling as a virtual dictator. Some limited reforms were made, especially in education, but Irigoyen failed to live up to the hopes of many who had earlier supported his Radical party when in opposition. His rule was made easier by the prosperity enjoyed by many sections of society, as during these years the Argentinian economy was closely linked to the prosperous economy of the United States. But this connection proved less fortunate after the Wall Street crash. Taking advantage of the consequent decline in the economy, the army staged a coup in September 1930, in which Irigoyen was removed from power. Throughout the 1930s governments sla-

vishly copied Italian Fascism and the presidents of the period relied on the army to maintain them in power. The most important achievement of the decade was President Justo's stabilization of the country's economy and the encouragement this gave to industry

Latin America

enabled Argentina to emerge as the leading Latin American country during the decade. Justo was strongly criticized for ignoring the conditions of the working classes and for binding Argentina too firmly to the British market: an Anglo-Argentinian agreement of 1933, which allowed preferential terms for British goods, was highly unpopular. Another coup in 1943 created a military government, in which the army had the support of the poorer workers. Though neutral, the government favoured the Nazi cause in the Second World War and joined the Allied side only a few weeks before the war ended.

General Juan Peron was a member of this military government and chose for himself the comparatively unimportant post of Minister of Labour. He had the foresight to see the importance of the rôle that the industrial workers and their representatives in the trade union movement were to play in Argentina. He also adopted a new approach to political affairs in his bid for power. He was friendly with the actress Eva Duarte, whom he married in 1945, and he associated himself with sportsmen and sportswomen who were popular throughout Argentina. As Minister of Labour he increased further his personal popularity among workers by supporting trade union activity, by organizing schemes for working-class housing and paid holidays. Many of Peron's military colleagues were alarmed at some of these moves, and they arranged his arrest in 1945, but he was released as a result of working-class protests in Buenos Aires and thereafter he virtually controlled the government. He successfully won the presidential election of February 1946, with the support of the newly formed Labour party.

Peron's rule from then until his fall in 1955 was based upon the support he had built up among the poor in town and country, the 'shirtless ones' as they were called. His political ideas were a curious mixture of Socialism and Fascism, linked to a belief in the value of his own strong leadership for Argentina. In the absence of well organized parties of the left, the 'shirtless ones' were a ready prey for a skilful politician such as Peron. Argentina's neutrality for most

of the Second World War had allowed the country's economy to remain healthy, while the economies of those countries which had been fully involved in the war were weakened. Argentina's industry was therefore in a position to supply the needs of many of these war-stricken countries, thus creating boom conditions for the Argentinian economy during the postwar years. Such circumstances naturally assisted Peron's successful rule in the early years of his presidency and he ensured that his government fully participated through buying products and acting as an agent in their sale overseas. His government was thus able to finance his policies for developing public works, nationalization, social services and compliant trade unions: all of which illustrated his curious blend of Fascism and Socialism. As in these years there was full employment, increasing prosperity and an absence of inflation and foreign entanglements, opposition to Peron was slight. What opposition did exist was subtly suppressed, by censorship of the press and by limiting opposition representation in parliament. Those who persisted in opposing the régime were imprisoned, and if occasional strike action got out of hand it was vigorously put down by the army.

In 1952 Peron's wife, Eva, died. She had been a very popular figure throughout the country and after her death his support declined seriously. By that time many countries throughout the world had recovered from the war and no longer traded so much with Argentina. As the country's economy declined, Peron lost his earlier support among the workers. Increasingly his government relied upon the support of the United States, and the country's business interests. Within the government and the civil service, corruption existed on a massive scale. But the issue on which he fell from power was his relationship with the Roman Catholic church, whose development of its own Christian Democrat party was interpreted by Peron as showing little gratitude for his earlier protection and encouragement of the church's interests. In September 1955 an army coup removed him from power: he was exiled, but continued to assert an influence within

Argentina and, after an absence of many years, was to make a remarkable return.

The military government that had seized power gave way to civilian rule again three years later, in 1958. In the election of that year, however, Peronist candidates were not allowed to stand. Frondizi became President and gave much attention to improving the economy of the country, one of his greatest achievements being the expansion of oil-drilling by granting concessions to foreign oil companies. His relaxation of restrictions on Peronist supporters and some limited moves in a left-wing direction, caused the army to become suspicious of him and he was removed in a military coup in 1962. A year later civilian rule was again restored under the presidency of Illia, a doctor who was

unable to deal adequately with the increasing inflation and who was always regarded with suspicion by the army. He too fell as the result of an army coup in 1966. Under its new military President, Organia, some curb was placed on the rate of inflation, though only as a result of unpopular, austere measures which perhaps only a military government could have imposed. This and the government's insistence on puritanical standards in the arts and in morality led to widespread and increasing student disturbances. In June 1970 Organia went the way of his predecessors.

In the early 1970s an easier attitude was adopted towards Peronist supporters. In November 1972 the government placed no obstacles in the way of the return of the

President Peron's wife, Eva, in discussion with Argentinian businessmen in the early 1950s. Eva Peron was a powerful and popular woman: her husband's rule became less secure after her death in 1952.

now elderly Peron, exiled in Spain to his country. He was to make one of the most successful political come-backs of the twentieth century, winning the presidential election of September 1973 with a large majority. But at the time of his election he was an ill man and in July 1974 he died. His presidency between 1973 and 1974 was not without achievement. As a result of a policy of austerity he kept inflation in check and as a result of firm action he curbed some of the extreme violence found throughout Argentina in the 1970s. After his death, his new wife succeeded to the presidency. Early in 1976 she was overthrown and Argentinian history continued a chaotic and unhappy course.

Brazil

Originally a Portuguese colony, Brazil is the largest of the Latin American states in both area and population and ranks, with Argentina and Chile, as one of the most important. In the early part of the century its successful exploitation of rubber and coffee encouraged stability in the country's economic and political life. The disturbances of the Wall Street crash had their effects in Brazil, as in Argentina. In 1930 Vargas, from the country's southern provinces, established himself as dictator, intent upon creating a strong centralized government in place of the previous loose federation. Vargas retained control between 1930 and 1945 and was able to achieve a significant revival in Brazil's prosperity. Like Peron, the political model on which he based his rule was Italian Fascism. His control of the country bore many close resemblances to that found in Fascist Italy. Although some of his methods were drastic, and he was capable of ruthless suppression of rebellion, he did create a well-organized and thoroughly planned economy in which major industrial concerns were nationalized and the control of the economy was placed very definitely in government hands. Hours of work were reduced, wages increased, advances made in working-class housing, and reforms introduced in the

education and health services. After 1941 the United States gave increased financial aid to Brazil, partly in an attempt to ensure Brazil's support in the event of a war. As a result, industrial advance was accelerated, one of the very important developments being the Volta Redonda steel works. Despite the Fascist features of his rule, Vargas brought his country into the Second World War at an early stage on the Allied side. In 1945 discontentment with the dictatorial attitude of Vargas caused his retirement from politics, but he returned as a result of an election in 1950 and continued in power, though not so successfully as before, until forced by the army to resign in 1954.

Kubitschek was President from 1956 to 1961, during which time Brazil enjoyed some of the benefits of affluence. A reflection of this was the development of the new capital of Brasilia, in the climatically more attractive interior of the country. It was an ambitious and optimistic scheme, which had been dormant for many years, and the inception of Brasilia in 1960 formed a fitting close to a successful presidency. Nevertheless Kubitschek's period contained the seeds of economic ills, as inflation increased markedly, and became especially serious in the presidency of Goulart (1961–64), who succeeded after a brief tenure of power in 1961 by Quadros, whose somewhat left-wing programme for reform of the economy met with opposition.

Goulart was overthrown in 1964 by an army coup. The military government, by a policy of integrity and austerity, attempted to restore stability in the country's economy. In 1967 civilian rule was restored under a new President, Costa e Silva, who, at the end of the following year, mindful perhaps of the example of Vargas, took on dictatorial power. Congress was suppressed, the press was censored and Costa e Silva governed by decree. The President suffered a serious stroke in 1969 and power passed once more to the military authorities. In the 1970s, the government of Brazil was exceptionally totalitarian, governed by the military who had wide powers of arrest and detention and who employed tactics for which they were widely criticized by varying bodies such as the United Nations and the Papacy. Nevertheless much economic progress was made under the government's firm direction and the new Brazilian Democratic movement was still able to assert its opposition in the Congress. Brazil continued to be a major power in Latin America, many of its neighbours being particularly concerned at the increasing power and size of the army under its military government.

Cuba in the first half of the twentieth century

Cuba was the first area of the American continent to be settled by the Spanish explorers and it was kept under the control of Spain for the next four hundred years. During the last decades of the nineteenth century the Cuban countryside was the scene of extensive guerrilla warfare by Cubans against the Spanish authorities. But it was only with the aid of the United States in 1898 that the Cubans eventually succeeded in overthrowing the Spanish. Cuba was seen as an island in which American influence should continue: the island was the largest in the Caribbean and was situated close to the United States and to the vital shipping routes of the Panama canal. In hostile hands, the island of Cuba could be highly dangerous to the United States. American capital financed much of the vital Cuban sugar industry, American forces continued to occupy the base at Guantanamo in the east of the island and the American ambassador at the capital, Havana, was regarded virtually as the Deputy President of the island.

During the first half of the twentieth century Cuban politicians generally failed to provide competent and effective government: some of them became, in reality unashamedly dictatorial and this was certainly so within the government of Batista whom Fidel Castro overthrew in January 1959. Batista's dictatorship, established by illegal means in 1952, though at times vindictive and cruel, was characterized mainly by inefficiency and laziness: the army and the

civil service, on which Batista relied for the maintenance of his rule, were generally incompetent and inactive. Cuban society contained the extremes of poverty and wealth: evidence of the former could be seen throughout the countryside and among the town workers and of the latter in the luxuriously appointed villas and apartments of Havana. But even the wealth of Cuba was challenged during Batista's rule, as the government failed to maintain its investment in the all-important sugar industry, which declined significantly in output, thus further weakening the dictatorship.

Fidel Castro, a young Cuban lawyer, first achieved prominence in an assault on an army barracks at Santiago in July 1953. The attack failed in its immediate objective; Castro and many of his followers were sentenced to imprisonment and subsequent exile. But a movement of opposition had been started, known as the *26 July Movement,* from the date of the attack at Santiago, and this movement was to struggle relentlessly against the dictatorship. Towards the end of 1956, from his exile in Mexico, Castro launched an invasion of Cuba and for the next two and a half years conducted guerrilla warfare against Batista's régime. His immediate followers were surprisingly few but remarkably effective: at most they were three hundred fighters. But they were assured of general support among the peasantry, while Batista's weak army was little match to the skill and determination of Castro's men and women. At this stage in his career, Castro was not a Communist and his guerrilla campaigns were neither inspired by Communist ideology nor supported by Communist money: he was a Cuban patriot, inspired by the example of similar guerrilla campaigns against the Spanish more than half a century previously. In 1957 the United States government withdrew aid from Batista, considering that their interests in Cuba may well be better represented by Castro. In the latter part of 1958, after a totally unsuccessful counter-offensive by Batista's army, Castro's forces became more and more successful, and he became increasingly popular in many of the rural areas. By January 1959 Batista's defeat was inevitable. On New Year's day he fled the country and a week later Havana gave a rapturous reception to Fidel Castro, whose leadership of the country was now uncontested.

It became increasingly clear that Castro intended to create a Marxist-based society within Cuba, even though he did not declare himself a Communist until December 1961. Though he promised elections, he never fulfilled this promise and instead created a Communist dictatorship, owing allegiance, although not unqualified allegiance, to the Soviet Union. Cubans whose politics were contrary to those of the new government were imprisoned or shot; the more fortunate fled the country. The direction of the economy was inspired by Marxism. In 1959 large farms and large factories were taken over by the state; in 1968 even smaller factories and shops were nationalized. Production of consumer goods was cut so that attention could be given to industrial and agricultural progress.

The United States became alarmed at this development of a Communist régime in a neighbouring country that had been regarded for so long as a preserve of American influence. Many American businessmen were angered at Castro's nationalization of American firms in Cuba and many of the Cuban exiles sought refuge in the United States. In January 1961, as one of his last acts as President of the United States, Eisenhower severed relations between the two countries.

President Kennedy continued these hostile policies. In April 1961 he gave his support to an invasion of Cuba by Cuban refugees who felt that Castro's regime could be defeated. The refugees landed in an area on the south of the island known as the Bay of Pigs and were decisively defeated by Castro's forces. Kennedy was humiliated by this failure; Castro was more convinced than ever of the hostility of the United States and sought closer understanding with the Soviet Union to protect his country from any similar invasion in the future.

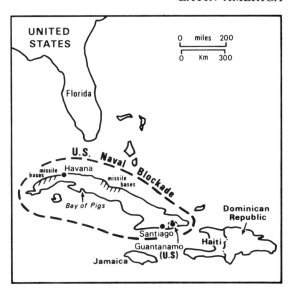

The Cuban missiles crisis, 1962

The Cuban missiles crisis

The crisis that developed as a consequence of sending Soviet missiles to Cuba in the autumn of 1962 marked the nearest point the world has yet come to the outbreak of a nuclear war. By 1962 links between Cuba and the Soviet Union were strong. In the summer of that year Cuban ministers had visited Moscow and had agreed to let the Russians station their nuclear missiles on Cuba. Though early in the autumn the United States government heard rumours of this build-up of missiles, it was not until mid-October that a U2 high-flying espionage plane took photographs above Cuba that gave undeniable proof of what was happening. Kennedy regarded this build-up as a direct threat to the United States and was appalled by the Soviet Union's denial of it when he protested to them. Kennedy decided on firm but restrained action to bring about the removal of these missiles. Procedure through the United Nations would be too slow: it was important that the missiles should be dismantled speedily before there was any chance of them being used. Invasion of the island of Cuba would be too provocative and could quickly develop into a wider conflict. The action he decided upon was to impose a naval blockade around the island of Cuba, denying access to the island by any ship bringing missiles and insisting on the removal of those missiles which were already there. This course of action was announced in a nationwide television broadcast on the evening of Monday 22 October, at the beginning of a week of acute crisis.

The blockade itself certainly appeared to prevent further missiles from reaching Cuba, as Soviet ships bearing further missiles turned back before reaching the blockade. Soviet ships that were not bearing missiles were permitted through. But by the middle of the week no progress had been made in the removal of the missiles which were already there, while further U2 photographs showed that work on the construction of the missiles sites was in fact continuing. The decision was then reached to invade Cuba on Monday 29 October, if no guarantee of the dismantling of the missiles was received by then.

On 27 October the Soviet Union made a compromise suggestion of removing the missiles from Cuba if the United States would remove its missiles from Turkey. This was a reasonable suggestion, but Kennedy felt unable to accept it as by doing so the United States would appear to abandon Turkey, which was a loyal ally of the United States. The Soviet suggestion also tended to increase the tension, as any attack by the United States on Cuba might be met by a Soviet attack on Turkey. Because of Turkey's connection with NATO, that could lead to war in Europe. Further discussion then took place

Bound for the Soviet Union from Cuba, this vessel carries eight of the controversial missiles on its deck. The return of these missiles marked the end of one of the most dangerous threats to world peace.

directly between Kennedy and Khrushchev on the telephone. Early the next day Khrushchev issued a statement in which he promised to remove the missiles, and the proposed invasion of Cuba was therefore cancelled.

In many respects the Cuban missiles crisis was more important for the rest of the world than it was for the island of Cuba. Negotiations in the crisis had been made entirely between heads of government of the United States and the Soviet Union; other major world powers and the United Nations had no significant part to play in a crisis of this importance. Kennedy had effectively demonstrated the determination of the Western powers to resist Communist pressure: no such direct threat was again made and the Soviet Union adopted a more conciliatory attitude towards the Western powers over Berlin, the other major point of friction at that time. Tension in the Cold War slackened and both sides appeared ready, for the sake of the peace of the world, to accept the boundaries of their power. There were some practical expressions of this slackening of tension. A 'hot line' of telecommunication between Moscow and Washington was established and in 1963 the Test Ban treaty was signed, by which the major powers agreed to end the practice of testing nuclear devices in the atmosphere.

Cuba after the missiles crisis

In the years since the Cuban missiles crisis Castro's continued hold on power has received little challenge within the island. In the American hemisphere, Cuba has remained somewhat isolated. During the twenty years since Castro came to power only one other Latin American country, Chile, followed Cuba's adoption of Marxism. Though Chile only had a Communist government for a few brief years in the early 1970s, the experiment there received the fullest support from the Cuban government. From the other countries of Latin America and from the powerful United States, Cuba remained totally isolated. Nor were relations with the Soviet Union entirely harmonious. The absence of serious consultation by Khrushchev with Castro during the missiles crisis angered the Cuban leader, as did the removal of the missiles as the Soviet Union's solution to the crisis. This removal, so Castro argued, left Cuba defenceless against a possible attack from the United States. There were also differences between Cuba and the Soviet Union over how best to spread Communism in other parts of Latin America: Castro looked to revolutionary activity as the best means of bringing this about, whereas the Soviet Union wanted to use the already established Communist parties. Nevertheless the connection with the Soviet Union was maintained, as the Soviet Union continued to provide aid for Cuba and a market for Cuban exports.

Economic progress within Cuba has been mixed. Castro's early hope of reducing the island's reliance on its long-established exportation of sugar remained unrealized. Nor was he able fully to break down traditional resistance to new methods of organizing industry within Cuba. At the start of the 1970s it was estimated that the island's annual output had fallen by a quarter since Castro had taken control. Correction of this trend became the main objective of the government. To fulfil it, tough action was taken. The Vagrancy Law of 1970 imposed forced labour on people who evaded work. In 1975 Castro's first five-year plan was launched as an attempt to direct the country's nationalized industries and agriculture in a more purposeful way.

Whilst attempting to tackle the country's economic problems, in the mid-1970s Castro's government began to show a renewed interest in the spread of Communism by sending Cuban troops in 1975 to assist the MPLA organization in Angola. Increasingly in the late 1970s, Castro showed a willingness to commit Cuban troops and assert Cuban influence for the spread of Communism. These moves were attempted partly to secure better relations with Caribbean neighbours. Cuba was beginning to break out of the isolation that had surrounded it since the time of the missiles crisis.

Chile

Before the First World War the economy of Chile was based upon its export of nitrates, but the introduction of synthetic substitutes for nitrates after the war meant that the demand for one of Chile's main commodities declined. Despite the importance of Chile's other chief export, copper, the economy of this country slumped in the postwar years. Moreover, the 1920s brought serious political instability within Chile, as the growing population in the industrialized towns felt an increasing distrust of the landowners, who dominated the feudal style of government.

Political instability was reduced after the creation of a military dictatorship under Carlos Ibanez in 1927, who provided definite leadership for the country, improved working conditions and prevented further disorders. In endeavouring to combat the economic dangers, Ibanez nationalized the nitrate industry, but this failed to restore prosperity and he was overthrown. Political confusion lasted from 1931 to 1932, when Arturo Alessandri was elected President and governed Chile by despotic means for the rest of the thirties. The press was censored, strikes suppressed, and opponents of the régime exiled. But there was some improvement in the economy. In 1938 the more radical Aguirre Cerda was elected President, and though the creation of valuable trading links with the United States was a positive achievement, his rule was marked by bitter political strife which he was unable to solve.

In the years since the Second World War, Chilean politics have been dominated by two groups: the Popular Front, consisting of Socialists and Communists, and a group consisting of Conservatives, Liberals and Radicals. The strong class divisions in the country were reflected in politics: the working class supporting the Popular Front, and the middle and upper classes the other parties. In the 1950s and early 1960s, these rigid class divisions within the country continued. The most pressing problem, inflation, was not solved by successive rulers. In 1964 Edward Frei was elected President. He came from the Christian Democrat party. This was a new Chilean party which, like Christian Democracy elsewhere, attempted to pursue policies of moderate reforms. Frei met some of his most serious opposition within his own party and within the Chilean Congress, but he nevertheless persevered with policies designed to bring reform, such as the land reform programme, general increases in the social services, and some moves towards nationalization. Towards the end of the 1960s there were signs that in spite of valuable achievements by Frei's government, his policies had created much division within the country between those who felt his reforms went too far and those who felt they did not go far enough. Towards the end of 1969 some measure of the country's turmoil was shown when an unsuccessful army coup took place.

The Chilean presidential election of October 1970 was one of the most significant in the recent history of Latin America. By a narrow majority the Popular Front candidate, Salvador Allende, a Socialist with distinct Marxist leanings, was elected President. His securing of power was unique: the longstanding tradition of Latin American governments whose policies were politically to the right or the centre, was broken, and it was broken by the orderly means of an election rather than a revolution or a coup. Many people in Chile were concerned that Allende's policies might result in a Communist dictatorship. Equally concerned were the countries in the American hemisphere, not least the United States, where President Nixon refused to send the customary telegram of congratulation to the new Latin American President. This internal and external opposition to his rule was a difficulty which Allende faced throughout his three years of power.

Allende's government contained Socialist and Independent members as well as Communists: he did not intend it to be entirely Communist-dominated and he himself was not a member of the Communist party. Though his creation of a mixed government of the left was an attempt to persuade his fellow countrymen that they had nothing to fear from his government, many Chilean

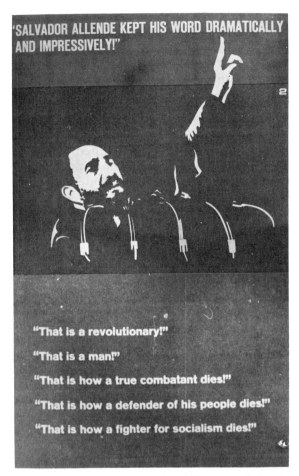

"SALVADOR ALLENDE KEPT HIS WORD DRAMATICALLY AND IMPRESSIVELY!"

"That is a revolutionary!"

"That is a man!"

"That is how a true combatant dies!"

"That is how a defender of his people dies!"

"That is how a fighter for socialism dies!"

Fidel Castro pays generous tribute to Salvador Allende and his short-lived Marxist government during the early 1970s. After Allende's downfall, Castro's government was again the only Marxist government in the American hemisphere.

ment. The Chilean Congress continued to function and within it opposition groups, especially the Christian Democrats, were able to continue to criticize the government and to oppose a number of its moves.

For many, especially the large number of poorer inhabitants throughout Chile, the Allende government brought benefits such as social security, education and medical facilities, which no previous government had encouraged so wholeheartedly. But all Chileans were caught up in inflation. This had already existed in Chile, but under Allende it reached a rate of 300 per cent each year. It has been suggested that the American CIA was partly responsible for encouraging this atrocious rate of inflation and for the eventual overthrow of Allende. It is impossible to be sure about this. Certainly relations between Nixon and Allende were poor throughout, and made worse by Allende's action in taking control of a number of American companies operating within Chile. The government of the United States had every reason to wish this government out of the way.

In September 1973 Allende's government was overthrown in violent circumstances by an army coup. Allende died in the course of the fighting. A military régime was then established under General Pinochet. In subsequent months, close supporters of the Allende government were executed or imprisoned. Activity on the part of the left was subject to severe restrictions and General Pinochet made it clear that there would be no return to civilian rule for some considerable time. Though Pinochet had got rid of Allende, he had not got rid of inflation, which continued in the mid-1970s at substantially above the 300 per cent it stood at when Allende fell.

The few policies that the new military government had were directed at undoing Allende's work in Chile and re-establishing links with other right-wing governments in Latin America. Though in the late 1970s the rate of inflation eased significantly, the military government showed no sign of preparing for civilian rule. Criticism of its methods of government and its continued

businessmen left the country as soon as he came to power. From the start, and in spite of opposition, Allende pursued Marxist policies. Key industries such as those dealing with nitrate and copper, insurance companies and private banks were all nationalized. A land reform corporation was set up to take over the large farms and organize them on a collective basis. To help augment many of these policies and to overcome the withdrawal of Western aid, Allende secured aid from many countries which were anxious to give every encouragement to his govern-

dominance of the country produced some modest concessions, such as the release of political prisoners, but little else was modified and the Chilean people continue to be ruled under dictatorship.

Latin America and the United States

The influence of their powerful neighbour to the north has affected the course of Latin American history throughout the twentieth century. For its part, the United States has consistently regarded the Latin American states as an area where the influence of any other world power should be discouraged. At times determination to maintain their influence has taken the form of military involvement or threat; at other times mutual trading and aid. The Spanish-American War of 1898 was the most dramatic involvement of the United States in Latin America. President Wilson also later intervened on a number of occasions, with military occupation of the Dominican republic and Haiti when American interests appeared threatened. Under the Republican presidents of the 1920s there was less emphasis on a direct involvement, though troops were sent temporarily to Nicaragua in 1925 to suppress a rebellion. The approach was now that of *dollar diplomacy*, of asserting influence through favourable trade agreements by which both sides would benefit. This policy was particularly put into effect by Hoover.

Roosevelt developed his *good neighbour* policy towards Latin America on the basis of the dollar diplomacy of the previous presidents. He abandoned direct intervention altogether. America's technical right to intervene in Cuba was renounced in 1934 and troops were withdrawn from Haiti, where they had been stationed since the early part of the century. More important were the financial aspects of the good neighbour policy. Dollar diplomacy had inevitably declined since the Wall Street crash and as American industry revived during the New Deal, Roosevelt began schemes from providing credit to Latin American countries to help them overcome the problem that the

Depression had caused. The good neighbour policy also encouraged holding conferences between different republics, under the chairmanship of the United States, but nothing very practical came from these moves.

During the war and the postwar years Latin American attitudes towards the United States were mixed. While some Latin American states, especially in the Caribbean area, entered the war with the United States in December 1941, others remained neutral until a few weeks before the end. After the war the Organization of American States (OAS) was formed; though intended to bring together the different Latin American states, it was dominated by the United States.

Under the formidable Secretary of State, Dulles, there was a reversal to the earlier American policy of direct intervention. The United States became concerned when in 1954 the repressive dictatorship in Guatemala was replaced by a left-wing administration under Jacobo Arbenz. His policies of reform and his obtaining of arms from Communist countries was interpreted, as was Castro's similar activity in Cuba a few years later, as a threat to the United States. Through the CIA, Dulles engineered the overthrow of Arbenz in a violent coup, led by rebels from neighbouring Honduras. Communist influence was repelled, but at the price of actual intervention and the overthrow of a duly elected government. Events in Guatemala, though providing an extreme example, show the value that Dulles placed on supporting reactionary governments in Latin America as the best bulwark against the spread of Communist influence near to the borders of the United States. During these Cold War years there was criticism from some Latin American republics that Latin America received a less than generous share in the distribution of American overseas aid under the Marshall Plan. The unpopularity of the United States on this account was shown in 1958 when Vice President Nixon was abused in a number of Latin American republics which he was visiting. Increased American aid was then given as the best means of solving this apparent hostility. President Kennedy developed the policy of aid in his *Alliance for Progress*. This policy reflected a changed view of Latin American dictatorship, as aid was to be granted under this scheme only to those countries which had democratic governments.

It can be suggested that the United States has continued to show, by episodes such as the Bay of Pigs (1961) and the overthrow of Allende (1973) the traditional features of intervention, even if the intervention has not been quite so strong as it had been in the early years of the century. Nevertheless, since then the general approach has been to discourage dictatorship, as under such systems of government Communism seems to develop strongly as a force of opposition. Financial aid to moderate governments has been considered more likely to advance the interests of the United States in these turbulent and changing lands.

Questions

70. Study the poster on page 269 and then answer questions (a) to (e) which follow.
    - (a) (i) Name the country governed by the man named at the top of the poster, and
      - (ii) give the years during which he was President of his country.

        (2)
    - (b) Show to what extent the first description of this man in the list at the lower part of the poster applied to

    - (i) his securing of power in his country, and
    - (ii) his policies while in power.

        (3+3)
    - (c) Examine the circumstances in which the rule of this President came to an end. To what extent does he deserve the tribute paid him in the last three sentences of this poster?

        (4)
    - (d) (i) Name the other Latin American leader shown here praising this President and name the country which he governed.
      - (ii) How do you account for the lavish praise which he is giving?

        (1+2)
    - (e) Outline the history since the time of this poster of *either* the country whose leader is named in the poster *or* the country whose leader is portrayed in the poster.

        (5)

71. Explain the circumstances leading to the securing of power in Cuba by Fidel Castro. Describe the main features of his rule in Cuba. Show the importance of Cuba's relations in Castro's time with (a) Communist states and (b) non-Communist states.

72. In the case of *either* Argentina *or* Brazil, explain the problems which it has had to face in the years since 1919 and the extent to which its governments have solved these problems.

25
Japan and China since 1945

The American occupation of Japan

General Douglas MacArthur, who received the surrender of the Japanese in early September 1945, became the Allied Supreme Commander of the Occupation Forces in Japan for the next seven years. For the Japanese, never defeated in any earlier war, military occupation was a novel experience which proved a useful transition from wartime defeat to peacetime prosperity. MacArthur was in some respects well suited to his task: already famed for his leading role in the war in the Pacific, he remained throughout the occupation a remote figure, removed from the mass of the Japanese people, who tended to view authority in this way. Nevertheless a period of American military occupation under so remote a figure, following as it did a period of Japanese military dominance under the equally remote Emperor, did little to encourage the development of Japanese democracy during the occupation years.

The occupying forces intended to bring about a clear break with Japan's military past. Though Emperor Hirohito remained Head of State, he accepted considerable limitations on his power and no longer claimed a semi-divine status. The Japanese politicians responsible for the war and the Japanese soldiers responsible for cruelty to prisoners-of-war were put on trial in Tokyo and elsewhere: about 5,000 were condemned and about 1,000 of those condemned were executed. In place of the zaibatsu and the traditional economy of Japan, the occupying powers attempted to implement the New Deal policies that had helped revive the American economy in the previous decade. These attempts often conflicted with the strong traditionalism in Japanese society. The new constitution, put into practice in 1946, combined features of the American constitution with those of the earlier Japanese constitution and provided for a developing political life under American supervision.

The Communist triumph in China in 1949 and the outbreak of war in Korea in 1950 increased the importance of the occupation. It seemed more than ever necessary to the United States to ensure that Japan would not become a Communist country also. The occupying authorities were relieved when some moderate right-wing politicians came to power in Japan in the late 1940s and MacArthur tended to encourage politicians of this kind, even if some who had served Japan in prewar days were among them. Substantial financial assistance to Japan also helped to hold the loyalty of the Japanese to the Americans during these years of Cold War pressure in the Far East. By the time the American forces withdrew, they left the occupied country with a political system which was stable and an economy which had recovered remarkably from the devastation of the war.

The Treaty of San Francisco and Japan's revival

Peace terms were finally agreed between Japan and her wartime enemies by the treaty of San Francisco in September 1951. Its terms were framed largely by the government of the United States, which viewed it as a formal expression of all that the occupation had striven to achieve. Its most important feature was the Japanese renunciation of her conquests during and before the Second

World War. Even so, neighbouring countries pressed for, and obtained, a series of mutual defence treaties with the United States to afford them protection in the event of renewed Japanese aggression: the Australia–New Zealand–United States (ANZUS) Pact and the Philippines–United States Mutual Security Pact both originated at this time. A defence pact was also signed between the United States and Japan providing for a continued though limited American presence to guard against another fear, the fear of Communist aggression. When the occupation came to an end in April 1952, an American presence therefore remained in Japan on the island of Okinawa.

The continued American presence became a constant source of controversy within Japan. Immediately after the occupation serious left-wing riots took place on this issue. In 1954 a number of Japanese fishermen in the Bikini area of the Pacific were affected by radioactive fallout from an American nuclear test: the episode, though of course an accident, became associated with the nuclear destruction of Hiroshima and Nagasaki and fanned further anti-American feeling. In 1969 rioting occurred on the island of Okinawa, directed against the American military base. But in spite of pressure to abandon the American alliance, the Japanese government have maintained it throughout.

Japanese political life has developed along relatively stable lines: the conservative ascendancy during the occupation has been maintained with little serious challenge from the left. Japan's impressive economic revival persuaded many Japanese to support the conservative politicians who appeared to have produced such a marked improvement. The roots of this economic revival had been established during the postwar years by American aid, and a willingness to acquire technological knowledge and skills. Loyalty to their country has been a continuing feature of the history of the Japanese: the prewar loyalty to Japan's military régime was now transferred to Japan's economic progress. The export of Japanese products was essential if the country, with its sharply increasing population, was to reap the fullest benefit.

Their search for overseas markets brought good results, as the high quality of many Japanese products won them a ready place in many countries. Only in the 1970s, however, did Japan re-establish relations with her former enemy and near neighbour, China, whose history in the immediate postwar years followed a totally different course.

Renewed civil war in China

The Japanese defeat in 1945 removed the basic reason which had brought the Communist party and the Nationalist party together in an uneasy alliance against their common enemy. After more than a decade of struggle against the Japanese, the Chinese were now plunged anew into a bitter civil war between the Communists, led by Mao Tse-tung, and the Nationalists, led by Chiang Kai-shek. This took place as the tensions of the Cold War were mounting. Both sides had the active support of the opposing great powers. The United States, anxious to prevent a Communist success in so large a country as China, gave military and financial aid to the Nationalists, even though the American government had serious reservations about Chiang Kai-shek's military rule. Though the Soviet Union had entered the war against Japan only after the first atomic bomb had been dropped, their forces had nevertheless swiftly overrun Manchuria and linked up with the Chinese Communists, whom they supplied with military aid.

In the early stages of the renewed civil war the Nationalists were victorious. In 1946 they attacked the enemy in Manchuria and brought much of it under their control. In early 1947 the Communist-held central areas fell to them and for a time they captured the Communist capital of Yenan. By the summer of 1947 the Communist forces were more effective. They had the advantage of obtaining former Japanese weapons which the Russians allowed the Communists to secure. The numbers in the Red Army rose as peasant recruitment increased. The Nationalists now realized that the extension of their power between 1946–47 had increased the problem of defence.

The Nationalists were also troubled by an alarming rate of desertion from their forces to the other side. In view of the appalling conditions created by the Chiang Kai-shek government in China during these years, desertion and disillusion was only to be expected. Their reckless policy of printing too much money had led to inflation at the rate of 30 per cent each month and attempts at curbing this inflation brought little improvement. As a result, the means of livelihood of millions of Chinese were destroyed. The social policies of Chiang Kai-shek were similarly unlikely to attract the support of the Chinese: in areas which they took over from the Japanese, the population was treated as if it were under the control of a hostile occupying power, while Chiang's secret police were active in seeking out those who did not support his régime. Many opponents were indiscriminately shot. Such circumstances inevitably repelled the Chinese from the Nationalists, and assisted the Communist cause.

In the closing stages of the civil war there were a number of massive encounters between the two sides. In the autumn of 1948 some important victories accompanied by further Nationalist desertions secured Manchuria for the Communists. At the beginning of 1949 a vital Communist success took place at Hsuchow, where about a mil-

Communist China and her neighbours

lion soldiers were linked in furious combat, fighting in conditions of snow and sleet. Shortly afterwards, a similar battle raged around Peking, resulting in a further Communist advance. By now such Nationalist strength as still existed in China was concentrated on the southern part of the country. Mao's forces gave no respite to the enemy. In April they crossed the Yangtse river; shortly afterwards the Nationalist-held towns of Nanking and Shanghai fell. Even though in October 1949 the entire Chinese mainland was not under his complete control, Mao felt sufficiently strong to proclaim the Chinese People's Republic, with its capital at Peking.

The remaining support for the Nationalist cause withered rapidly and by December 1949 all of the mainland was under Communist control. Chiang Kai-shek and those Chinese who were still loyal to him fled to the island of Taiwan (sometimes called Formosa) where a Nationalist government has since continued. Communist China neither then nor later made any serious attempt to bring down the Taiwan government. Control of the vast land mass of China was the real objective. This the Communists had: it was now necessary to consolidate their control of it.

The consolidation of Communist power

The success of the Communists in China had been based upon the peasantry. It was therefore to be expected that, unlike the industrial-based Communism of the Soviet Union, their own brand of Communism would be based upon the improvement of conditions for agriculture. The Agrarian Reform Law of June 1950 provided for taking over the land and livestock of the Chinese landowners by the state, and the distribution of these possessions among the peasantry. After 1953 the government encouraged the formation of collective farms, though this policy led to some opposition from the peasantry, who generally showed a preference for individual holdings rather than a collective system.

Though by the end of the 1950s most of the farms in China were collectivized, the agricultural methods employed by the peasants remained traditional and primitive.

The improvement of the position of the peasantry was only one of the aims of the Agrarian Reform Law. The other was rooting out the opponents of Communism. In the villages of China people's tribunals were set up to supervize the enforcement of the new law. These tribunals also organized the *Speak Bitterness* campaign, in which the Chinese were encouraged to denounce former landowners and those suspected of being opposed to the new Communist government. Some hundreds of thousands of victims of this campaign were executed. But by these violent means the new rulers of China were able, with substantial support, to eliminate potential opposition and to assert their control of the country more firmly. The Agrarian Reform Law was therefore not just an early step in the development of a Communist economy, but also a means by which the Communist control of China was to be strengthened.

The basic element of the constitution established by the Communists was a series of People's Congresses, the members of each being elected for a local area by all its inhabitants, with the exception of so-called 'public enemies', a category applied to millions of Chinese. No opposition parties were to be allowed and only Communists were able to stand for election. Though the constitution gave an appearance of democracy, it in practice prevented those who were not loyal to the Communist party from holding any office of significance in China, and it thus consolidated the dominance of the Chinese Communist party.

Some liberalization of the constitution appeared likely when in 1957 in the *Hundred Flowers Movement* the Chinese were invited by Mao to put forward their own views on the policies of the government. It was an attempt at a greater degree of democracy. But many of the views that the Chinese put forward were so critical that the government felt threatened, and the movement was therefore brought to an end. Critics were then imprisoned, some of them remaining in captivity more than twenty years later. The suggestion has been made that the Hundred Flowers Movement was designed by Mao to enable him to identify and eliminate those who were opposed to him.

Economic progress in Communist China

Though in the early years particular attention was given by the Communist government to the changes in the organization of agriculture, improvements in industry were not entirely neglected. The length and severity of the warfare in China before 1949 had naturally prevented any serious industrial development. The new government was aware that even with the emphasis they gave to agriculture, in order to construct a new Communist society, attention must also be given to industrial development. By 1952 industry had recovered much of its lost ground and the government was ready to begin a five-year plan modelled on the experience of the Soviet Union and assisted by Soviet technical and financial aid. The first five year plan in the years 1953–57 concentrated on the development of heavy industry, though attention was also given to the improvement in transport, agricultural machinery and facilities for education and health: though it got off to a slow start, the first five year plan eventually overfulfilled its targets.

The second five year plan in the years 1958–62 built on the success of the first and aimed to fulfil even higher objectives: an overall increase of 75 per cent in both agricultural and industrial output was promised and particular emphasis was placed on increasing the number and expertise of Chinese scientists and technicians. A similar scheme to promote industrial expansion was also launched in 1958: the *Great Leap Forward*. Inspired by the success of the first plan and by the objectives of the second, the Great Leap Forward aimed at even higher production in heavy industry. For the next three years production quotas were increased as frequently as once every few months, tending therefore to reach unrealistic levels.

Like the Agrarian Reform Law of 1950, the Great Leap Forward of 1958 was intended to bring change to both the economy and the society. All Chinese took part in their country's industrial upsurge. The production of steel in small backyard furnaces was encouraged. Even though output from this primitive method of steel production was both limited in amount and unsatisfactory in quality, the involvement of millions of people of widely varying occupations in the same work, and aiming at the same objective, brought a sense of common involvement in China's progress under Communism.

More significant was the development of the commune movement which flourished in the early years of the Great Leap Forward. Communes came into existence in both town and country districts: all private property was taken over by the local commune, which took on responsibility for the administration of the area's economy and for government services. Family life was not destroyed by the commune movement: it did not involve, as is sometimes suggested, splitting up families in communal dwellings and houses. The only people who lived in communal houses were single or widowed people, for whom such a system of living had some obvious advantages. But the system led inevitably to an involvement of all Chinese in the Communist state: escape from such involvement was almost impossible.

By the late 1950s, after a decade of Communism, China was in an exuberant mood: the Communist system was firmly established, the country's economic life had made impressive advances and the creation of the communes suggested that in China a really authentic form of Communism had been created. But the exuberance hid a number of real problems, which eventually caused a modification of the policies of these years. Though substantial economic advances had been made, it was acknowledged that output figures for both industry and agriculture had been exaggerated. A more modest set of objectives was therefore set for the later five-year plans of the 1960s and 1970s, decades during which progress was less spectacular, less publicized but nevertheless solid and useful in spite of a number of harvest failures. The commune experiment was shown to have been unsuccessful and, though communes continued, their importance declined.

China's foreign policy: the early years

The Chinese have always maintained that the creation of peace is the principle on which their foreign policy is based. But Chinese actions against neighbouring states have caused Western countries to doubt China's sincerity. The apparently hostile attitude adopted by China may be explained in two ways. One is that the Chinese campaigns were often directed towards securing of territories which were formerly Chinese, but to which the Chinese claims had lapsed. The other is the general hostility with which the world greeted Communist China: just as Imperial China and Nationalist China had faced hostility, so did Communist China, at least during the first two decades of its existence. The Chinese build-up of armaments, and production of an atomic weapon in 1964 were developments only to be expected.

The favourable attitude initially adopted by the United States towards the Nationalist régime on Taiwan sharpened the hostility that existed between Communist China and the exiled Nationalists. This was shown particularly by the consistent opposition with which the United States and other Western powers greeted attempts by the Soviet Union to have Nationalist China replaced by Communist China on the Security Council of the United Nations, over a period of more than twenty years. After the Communist victory on the mainland in 1949, it was widely expected that before very long Taiwan would also fall. The United States gave strong support to Taiwan, showing particular concern when the small off-shore islands of Quemoy and Matsu, possessions of Taiwan which were located only a few miles off the mainland coast, came under attack by Communist fire from the mainland. But during these years

of tension, neither side felt it wise to launch a major attack on the other.

Other centres of nearby hostility were on the mainland shore itself: at British-held Hong Kong and Portuguese-held Macao, both legacies of the 'unequal treaties' of the previous century. Macao would probably have been absorbed by Communist China long since had it not been for its nearness to the larger and more significant Hong Kong. As the lease on the mainland territory of Hong Kong expires in 1998, the British presence there is unlikely to continue beyond the present century. In the meantime, Hong Kong provides an immediate link with the world outside China, and a convenient place where exchange of money can take place. But as it is also a convenient objective of refugees from Communist China, relations are inevitably strained.

In Tibet and along parts of the Sino-Indian border, China has exerted military pressure. The remote area of Tibet, which was still under the feudal rule of its religious leader, the Dalai Lama, had earlier been a part of the Chinese Empire and had taken the opportunity of the 1911 revolution in China to establish its independence. In October 1950 Chinese Communist forces marched into Tibet and incorporated it once more within China: a historic claim had been fulfilled and an archaic system of government brought down. The new authorities set about the task of readjusting Tibetan society along Communist lines, though their methods encouraged opposition from the conquered population. In the spring of 1959 some thousands of Tibetans rose in rebellion: by the use of strong tactics, the Chinese won the struggle while many thousands of Tibetans, including the Dalai Lama, fled as refugees to India. The United Nations condemned the methods used by the Chinese in suppressing the rebellion and in governing the country. Though Tibet was now ruled by the imposed system of Communism, the social system which had been replaced was one of the most archaic, cruel and unjust societies to have survived into the middle of the twentieth century.

India's provision of a base for the Dalai

Lama's government-in-exile tended to prejudice its previously good relations with Communist China. In the early 1960s border disputes arose between the two countries. In both cases the Chinese had a historic claim to territory which India held. In the desert area of the Aksai Chin, bordering on the area of Ladakh, the Chinese planned to construct a vital highway to link Tibet more closely to China. To strengthen their hold of this area the Chinese occupied Ladakh. In the autumn of 1962 the Indians took the offensive against the Chinese in both Ladakh and in another less important area of dispute along India's north-eastern boundary. In both areas the Indian forces were driven back, China secured control of the disputed areas but, though in a position to do so, took no further action against India.

In its approach to the rest of the world, Communist China has not been totally pre-occupied with the problems of Taiwan and disputed neighbouring territories. Conscious of the size of their country and eager for the spread of Communism, the Chinese have sought a position of leadership in the affairs of the third world. An early instance of this was the first large-scale meeting, in 1955, of the leaders of Afro-Asian nations at Bandung, a meeting to which the great powers were not invited. At Bandung, the Chinese Prime Minister, Chou En-lai, became the acknowledged leader of the conference. Many countries of Asia and Africa were now prepared to look to China for guidance and support, especially in the struggle against colonialism, in which many of them were actively engaged. Since then, China has responded in different ways to the Afro-Asian countries. Aid has been given to Communist parties seeking to establish their power, and to the governments of third world countries seeking to improve their backward economies. Aid of this latter kind has been especially valuable for Tanzania in east Africa and for parts of Latin America.

The Sino-Soviet quarrel

Even before 1949, the relations between the Chinese Communists and the Soviet Union had been uneasy. In the 1920s and the 1930s Stalin had openly disagreed with Mao's emphasis on the important role of the peasantry in a Communist society and had sought, without success, to replace Mao as the Communist leader. In the 1940s, there were still points of conflict. The Russians seized many of the resources of Manchuria for their own purposes and even after 1949 were slow to return them. Another early source of Chinese dissatisfaction was the so-called treaty of friendship signed by the Soviet Union and Communist China in February 1950. Though this provided much-needed Soviet aid to the new government in China, it also permitted the Soviet Union to exploit the resources of some Chinese territories, and it was an attempt to reduce the status of China to that of a satellite, similar to the new Communist states of eastern Europe.

Nevertheless, during the big industrial drive in the 1950s, increased Soviet aid to Communist China was of invaluable assistance in helping the Chinese achieve their industrial objectives. Especially valuable for a backward country emerging from a prolonged civil war was the help of Russian scientists and technicians. In international affairs also, by its support of the Chinese Communist application for United Nations membership, the Soviet Union showed itself a warm friend.

But from the late 1950s tension between the Soviet Union and Communist China increased markedly. This tension was focused on differing interpretations of Communist theory and on disputed territorial boundaries. Khrushchev's de-Stalinization speech of 1956 caused much concern to the leaders of Communist China. His condemnation of Stalin's personality cult seemed dangerous to them, as it could be interpreted also as a criticism of Mao's personality cult in Communist China. Further, his suggestion that Communism might spread by more subtle means than war and revolution was regarded as weak and inadequate. The difference between the Communist Revolution in Russia and the one in China was that in China it had been achieved only after prolonged civil war: the Chinese Communists believed that their success was due to military endeavour, and that this would be necessary for the continuing spread of Communism. *Revisionism* was the term used by the Chinese Communists in their condemnation of the new Soviet interpretations of Marxist-Leninism.

The disturbances in eastern Europe in 1956 appeared to confirm the Chinese fear that the Soviet Union's revisionism was leading to a weakening of Communism as a world force. In the spring of 1960 open Chinese criticism of the Soviet Union caused a breakdown in relations, resulting later that year in the withdrawal of Soviet technicians. The ideological split was not healed during the 1960s. As Khrushchev had been a source of the difficulty, it was hoped that his fall from power in 1964 would help, but Sino-Soviet relations were little affected by this change in the Soviet government's leadership. Meanwhile the ideological split had its effects in other parts of the world, as Communist parties in different countries became divided on allegiance to Moscow's views or Peking's views. In Albania the entire Communist party gave its loyalty to Peking and many of the newly developing Communist parties in Latin America and Africa felt that, as non-Europeans, the Communist Chinese had greater sympathy with their struggle than had the Russians. Communists in countries with peasant-based economies were likely to give their support to a Communist country which had brought about its revolution with the support of the peasant class.

Controversy over the Sino-Soviet boundaries actually brought the two countries into military conflict. Along the 4,000 mile Sino-Soviet frontier numerous areas of dispute existed, most of which dated back to the bullying attitudes of tsarist Russia towards Imperial China in pre-revolutionary times. The Soviet government of Russia refused to return the disputed areas to China and in fact advanced Soviet power even further at China's expense by securing virtual control of the Mongolian People's Republic in 1950. This territory was almost equal in size to Europe. A war of words became one of action

in March 1969 when fighting broke out between Chinese and Soviet troops along the border area in the region of the Amur river: this was shortly followed by fighting along other parts of the border, further inland. Despite negotiations, the situation thereafter was tense: both sides massed troops and equipment to protect their positions, and there was even a possibility that the Soviet Union might use nuclear force against China. The Sino-Soviet split had reached so intense a peak that in the early 1970s China sought understanding with the West as a means of combatting Soviet hostility.

The Cultural Revolution

The failure of the Great Leap Forward and the development of the Sino-Soviet split led to some internal Chinese criticism of Mao Tse-tung's leadership: the view was put forward that economic advance should be planned more modestly and that real efforts should be made to resolve differences with the Soviet Union. After a decade of Communism, more and more Chinese were beginning to look for some improvement in their standard of living. Many Chinese felt that their government should moderate its approach to China's foreign relations and domestic affairs. Mao Tse-tung was completely opposed to any such moderation and was alarmed at what he saw as evidence of a lack of revolutionary fervour. For Mao, Communist revolution was something which did not only happen during the struggle for power: it was a continuing process, which was just as important after power had been secured as it was before.

The *Cultural Revolution* was an attempt by Mao to lead the Chinese people in the 1960s to a re-living of the revolutionary struggles of the 1930s and the 1940s. In the summer of 1965 attacks were made by Mao on Chinese politicians who appeared to lack revolutionary enthusiasm and who favoured revisionism along Soviet lines. Assured of the support of the army, Mao embarked on what became known as the Cultural Revolution by purging those party members whose loyalty to his ideals was doubtful. The Cultural Revolution then began to have effects amongst all the Chinese people, who were encouraged to study and practise the *Thoughts of Mao Tse-tung*, or Mao's philosophies. Mao Tse-tung's personality cult rose considerably during these years. Young Red Guards paraded with apparent spontaneity and enjoyment to demonstrate their loyalty to Mao and his *Thoughts*. They became the shock troops of the Cultural Revolution, often becoming involved in violence in their demonstration of loyalty to Mao: foreign journalists and diplomats, Chinese who had adopted Western clothes or who were known to be out of sympathy with the Cultural Revolution were attacked and humiliated by the Red Guards. As their numbers grew, their activities got out of hand. In June 1967 the army was commanded to re-establish order throughout China, though activity by the Red Guards continued for a while. From the late 1960s, the Cultural Revolution developed less strongly.

One of the most important effects of the Cultural Revolution was the confirmed

The Cultural Revolution of the mid-1960s developed as a widespread personality cult of the founder of Chinese Communism. Notice in this photograph the disciplined loyalty and apparent happiness of his supporters.

supremacy of Mao and his political views. Thereafter, until his death in 1976, China deviated little from Maoism. It had also been an exceptionally thorough means of ensuring that the Communist revolution was thoroughly planted among all the Chinese. But quite apart from the acknowledged excesses of the Red Guards, it had also trampled further upon the liberties of the Chinese, especially those accustomed to city life, who had been forcibly compelled to work in the countryside. Though internally China was comparatively stable for the rest of Mao's life, his successors in the late 1970s inherited some of the problems which the Cultural Revolution had created.

China's foreign policy: relations with the West

China had retained the remoteness which had been associated with her imperial past during the first two decades of Communist rule. As has been seen, her remoteness was also associated with the hostility of leading world powers. The United States had vigorously opposed Chinese Communism by support of Taiwan, intervention in Korea and Vietnam, opposition to a Communist Chinese presence in the United Nations and the creation of SEATO, an organization largely directed against China. Yet in the 1970s it was with the United States that China made some limited progress in mutual understanding. This provided her with a possible ally against the increased hostility of the Soviet Union.

When America stopped opposing the Communist Chinese presence on the Security Council of the United Nations, it was an early sign that the United States was prepared to modify its earlier hostility. An exchange of table-tennis teams signalled a further willingness on both sides for cooperation. Then in February 1972 President Nixon made a formal visit to China, engaging in conversations with Prime Minister Chou En-lai and Chairman Mao Tse-tung. The keynote of the visit was struck by Nixon at the welcoming banquet arranged for him by his hosts:

Let us, in the next five days, start a long march together, not in locked step, but on different roads leading to the same goal – the goal of building a world structure of peace and justice in which all may stand together with equal dignity and in which each nation, large or small, has a right to determine its own form of government free of outside interference or domination. There is no reason for us to be enemies. Neither of us seeks domination of the other. Neither of us wants to dominate the other.

The visit was well publicized and Nixon proved an appreciative guest. The major achievement of the visit was the fact that so remarkable a meeting had taken place at all. Its practical results were limited, though provision was made for closer contact between Communist China and the United States, so far as exchange of diplomats and trading relations were concerned. The visit did nothing specific to bring to an end the war in neighbouring Vietnam. But a friendly relationship with the West, often referred to as *détente*, had been definitely established by this visit. Other visits by other Western leaders followed and achieved comparable results.

Détente with the United States contributed significantly to improved relations with neighbouring Japan. Relations with the conquering enemy of the 1930s had been virtually non-existent since the end of the war, but Nixon's visit to China prompted interest on both sides for a renewal of Sino-Japanese contact to their mutual advantage. In September 1972 Prime Minister Tanaka of Japan paid a visit to China. At another welcoming banquet Tanaka referred to the bitterness of past relations:

It is regrettable that for several decades in the past the relations between Japan and China had unfortunate experiences. During that time our country gave great troubles to the Chinese people, for which I once again make profound self-examination. After World War Two, the relations between Japan and China remained in an abnormal and unnatural state. We cannot but frankly admit this historical fact.

Richard Nixon and Mao Tse-tung meet during the American President's visit to Communist China in 1972. The later development of closer relations between the United States and Communist China dates from this visit.

Like Nixon, Tanaka found the problem of Japanese recognition of Taiwan an awkward matter in his discussions, but as with Nixon, the Chinese attempted to make little of this problem. Japan now recognized the Communist government of China and the way was open for improved relations and fuller trading contacts between the two most powerful nations in the Far East.

Viewed together with the continuing Chinese penetration of parts of Africa and Latin America, the détente of the 1970s was a significant new step in Chinese foreign policy. China's isolation at the start of the 1970s, made more serious by the hostility of the Soviet Union, had changed by the end of the 1970s to involvement with a number of leading world powers. This change in policy was a remarkable Chinese achievement and one which greatly strengthened the country's standing in world affairs.

The April Fifth Movement

Two great Chinese leaders died in 1976: Prime Minister Chou En-lai in January and Chairman Mao Tse-tung in October. Both had controlled the destinies of China for more than a quarter of a century and it was inevitable that the following years would bring changes. The fifth of April is the day on which, by tradition still maintained in Communist times, the Chinese honour their ancestors. Under the inspiration of Deng Xiaoping, who had been condemned at the time of the Cultural Revolution and had been out of office for some years, 5 April 1976 developed into a demonstration against the rule of what had become known as the 'Gang of Four', an inner group of politicians who, it was alleged, had dominated the affairs of China in Mao's last years. The demonstration also emphasized the growing desire to break with many of the rigid features of Mao's rule and to grant a greater degree of liberty to the Chinese. The demonstrations were suppressed, Deng was removed from office and it appeared at the time that the

Wall posters, a traditional Chinese method of spreading new ideas, began to contain criticisms of established Chinese attitudes in the late 1970s. These particular ones were critical of the thinking of the ancient Chinese philosopher, Confucius; others criticized the more recent government of China under Mao Tse-tung.

events of 5 April 1976 were of little significance.

After Mao's death in October 1976, Hua Guofeng, who earlier in the year had emerged from comparative obscurity to succeed Chou En-lai as Prime Minister, now succeeded Mao Tse-tung as Party Chairman. The 'Gang of Four' gradually declined in political importance, though the fundamental direction of the Chinese government changed little. But in the autumn of 1978 wall posters in the major cities of China contained criticisms of Mao Tse-tung, one poster going so far as to describe Mao's government from the Cultural Revolution in 1966 to his death in 1976 as a decade of 'fascist dictatorship'. Other posters now made appreciative reference to the *April Fifth Movement* of two years previously as pointing the way ahead for China: while not seeking any change from Communism, it was hoped that elections could take place and that the administration could be more firmly separated from the party. The policy of seeking closer understanding with the West was to be continued, outside trading contacts were to be given particular attention. Deng Xiaoping had again inspired the revival of the views he had encouraged two years previously. Increasingly the April Fifth Movement was hailed as a new direction for Chinese Communism, linking with the new approach already given to Chinese foreign policy, building upon the earlier work of Mao Tse-tung, but liberating the country from the dictatorship which the Chinese appeared to have accepted without question in the years before 5 April 1976.

Questions

73. Study the photograph on page 280 and then answer questions (a) to (c) which follow.

(a) (i) What is the book which the people in the photograph are holding?
    (ii) How would you describe the age range of the majority of these people?
(2)
(b) (i) Name the Chinese leader to whom these people are showing their loyalty.
    (ii) Describe the stages by which this leader had
        a. secured his power in the 1940s, and
        b. consolidated his power in the 1950s.
    (iii) Why and in what ways did this leader encourage people in the age range referred to in (a) (ii) to give him their loyalty at the time this photograph was taken?
(1 + 4 + 4 + 3)
(c) (i) Why would it not have been possible to take a photograph such as this in the later 1970s?
    (ii) Explain other ways in which internal conditions in China in the late 1970s differed from those in the mid-1960s.
(6)

74. Describe the methods used by Mao Tse-tung in governing the Chinese people and improving the Chinese economy in the years since his triumph in 1949. What changes have occurred within China since Mao's death?

75. Show the importance of *each* of the following in the history of Japan: (a) the use of the atomic bomb at Hiroshima, (b) the occupation by the Americans, (c) the development of the Japanese economy and (d) Japan's relations with the rest of the world.

26
East and South-east Asia

The Korean War: origins

The Korean peninsula was annexed by Japan in 1910, having been under the fairly loose control of China earlier. Throughout the interwar years, Japan had little difficulty in maintaining control of this neighbouring area, which proved useful as a base for the Japanese invasions of China in the 1930s. Though Korea was a comparatively untroubled area during the Second World War, Japan's declining fortunes towards the end of the war led the Koreans to hope that the eventual withdrawal of the Japanese would result in the achievement of Korean independence.

But the actual circumstances of Japan's collapse in August 1945 resulted in the division of the Korean peninsula along the 38th northern parallel and the emergence of two very different régimes in the North and South As has been shown at the end of Chapter 13, in August 1945 Soviet troops invaded Japanese-held areas that bordered on the Far-Eastern frontier of the Soviet Union, resulting in Soviet occupation of Manchuria and Korea north of the 38th parallel. In North Korea, as in other countries occupied at that time by Soviet troops, a Communist government was created under the lead of Kim Il Sung, whose much needed policies of land reform won him the support of many Koreans. The United States was also anxious to maintain a presence in eastern Asia and therefore occupied former Japanese possessions: as well as Japan itself, American forces entered the Philippines and Korea, south of the 38th parallel. In South Korea a Western-style government was encouraged under the leadership of Synghman Rhee, an elderly man who had spent most of his life in the United States and who was a vigorous opponent of Communism. Both the Soviet Union and the United States gave aid to the governments of the areas they occupied, though Soviet assistance towards the development of an effective military force in the North was fuller than American assistance in the South. The North also possessed most of the peninsula's limited industry. When in the late 1940s the great powers left Korea, it was the North that was in the stronger position. While there was a hardening of the division of the peninsula at that time, many Koreans were conscious that only if Korea was fully united could their country achieve its full potential.

In June 1950, North Korea, relying on its superior military strength, launched an invasion across the 38th parallel, with the aim of bringing the whole of Korea under its control. Circumstances appeared to favour this action. They were assured of a friendly neighbouring great power, as only nine months previously Communism had finally triumphed in China. A further temptation for the North may have been public statements made by the government of the United States that it no longer felt that it was responsible for the defence of South Korea.

The Korean War: changing aims

The invasion was at once referred to the United Nations at New York. There, the Security Council accepted an American resolution condemning the invasion, demanding the withdrawal of the North to the 38th parallel and calling all United Nations members to send armed forces to assist South Korea in its struggle. As the Soviet Union had temporarily withdrawn from the Security Council, out of anger at the continued

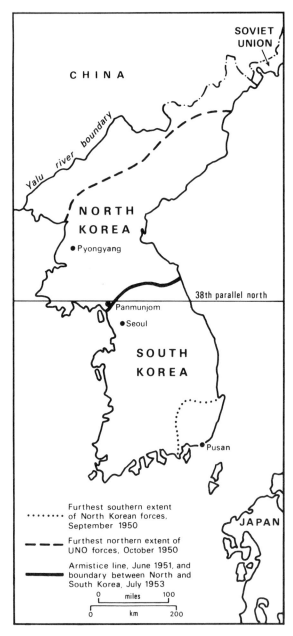

The Korean War

representation of China by the Nationalists, the Soviet Union was unable to employ its veto powers against this resolution, something which it would certainly have done otherwise.

The war that was fought in defence of South Korea was therefore fought by countries belonging to the United Nations, though the country which participated most fully in the South's defence was the United States. General Douglas MacArthur took overall command. His leadership of American forces in the Pacific during the Second World War and his subsequent command of the American occupation forces in Japan gave him a unique position of respect among the American people. But his hatred of Communism was so strong that, as a Commander, he became a dangerous liability.

The North Korean army had by mid-September 1950 conquered the whole of the South, with the exception of the area around the city of Pusan in the south-east. The United Nations counter-attack then began to have effect, the North Korean army suffered reverses in the South and by the end of the month the United Nations forces had reached the 38th parallel: the initial objective of the war had therefore been achieved.

At this stage the United States persuaded the United Nations to adopt a further and more aggressive aim: the pursuit of the North Korean forces into their own territory, with the intention of creating a fully united Korea. The aim was now offensive rather than defensive. MacArthur's military skill was as successfully employed north of the 38th parallel as it had been to the south of it. By late October, United Nations forces had reached almost as far as the Yalu river, which separates North Korea from Communist China. It was known to be MacArthur's own objective, though not that of the United Nations, to invade China and bring down its recently established Communist government. Conscious of this possibility and of the need to support their Communist allies in North Korea, Communist China sent troops over the border to assist the North Koreans in expelling the United Nations forces. This extra help turned the tide. By the beginning of 1951 the United Nations troops had been forced to retreat to a position south of the 38th parallel: the South Korean capital of Seoul came under Northern control. In the wake of the defeat of their offen-

During the fighting in Korea of the early 1950s, tired American troops rest by a roadside. Notice the Korean peasants, with heavy packs, walking along the road.

sive against North Korea, the United Nations reverted in December 1950 to its original aim of defending the South.

MacArthur saw the war on a wider scale. In his view only a more forceful policy against Communist China could prevent the continuing reverses of the winter of 1950–51. In the long term, so he held, only by the defeat of Communist China could further Communist aggression in south-east Asia at a later stage be prevented. His military proposals were forceful: bombing of

China and active support of the Chinese Nationalists on Taiwan. Differences developed between MacArthur and President Truman, whose policy was to limit the war strictly to the defence of South Korea. But MacArthur made public his disagreement with the President and thus created a situation that was both dangerous and delicate: dangerous, as a military Commander is expected to obey his political superior; delicate, as MacArthur had an immense popular following within the United States. Truman judged that in spite of MacArthur's popularity, his presidential duty was to dismiss him, and this he did in April 1951.

The United Nations forces had managed by June 1951 to return to the 38th parallel: so a year's intensive fighting had resulted in both sides being once again in their original positions. Armistice negotiations then began and were continued for two years, taking place mainly at Panmunjom. Fighting continued during this time, though it was less intense than in the first year of the war. In the early months of 1953, the new American President, Eisenhower, adopted a firmer attitude towards North Korea and the armistice was agreed in July 1953, providing basically for a division of Korea along a line very close to the 38th parallel.

Korea since the war

Those countries which had contributed to the United Nations forces in Korea, the United States in particular, felt that the final result had justified their action, as the North Korean forces had been compelled to retreat to the North. *Containment* of Communism had therefore worked. But their invasion of the North in the autumn of 1950 had not led to the projected unity of the peninsula under a Western-style government. *Liberation* from Communism had therefore failed.

Though the agreement in July 1953 was merely a short truce, it has nevertheless proved to be long-lasting, and the Korean peninsula appears to be permanently divided, with little communication between either side. In 1972 negotiations between North and South were started, in an attempt to bring about a more satisfactory relationship, especially in economic matters. But though the talks continued for some years, they made no real progress. The 1974 discovery of a mile-long tunnel dug by North Koreans across the border and in 1976 the outbreak of some ugly border incidents accompanied by loss of life showed that even a quarter of a century after the end of the Korean War, the issues on which it was fought are by no means fully resolved.

Both North and South Korea have developed dictatorial-style governments, both of which are bad advertisements for the systems they are meant to represent. North Korea has tended to isolate itself from the rest of the world and reliable information about it is not easy to obtain. Its leader, Kim Il Sung, has continued in power since the Korean War and he and his family have become the centre of a personality cult. Lacking the better natural resources of the South, the standard of living in the North appears to be lower, though much effort has been put into the development of basic industry. In the South, Synghman Rhee continued in power until overthrown in the spring of 1960 by an internal coup, the result of his intolerant, police-style government. General Park, who eventually succeeded him, has maintained a similarly strong rule: an opposition party, created in 1972, failed to develop purposefully. By contrast with the North, the economy of the South is reasonably successful and the standard of living is reasonably high: hence many Southerners have been willing to support Park's government in spite of his intolerance.

Though in the postwar years there have been many differences between the situation in Korea and the situation in Indochina, they are both countries bordering on to China and both have been divided into Communist areas in the north and non-Communist areas in the south. The eventual success of Communism in Indochina in 1975 acted as warning to South Korea to maintain its vigilance, and to the United States to continue its aid, in spite of reservations which the American government had in the 1970s about the nature of Park's administration. Though the division appears permanent, few Koreans can be satisfied with the present situation.

French military involvement in Indochina

In 1940 Japan was prepared to seize every opportunity afforded by the defeat in

Europe of powers holding colonial lands in south-east Asia and the Pacific. Immediately after the surrender of France in the summer of 1940, the Japanese Army launched an invasion of French Indochina, and rapidly incorporated the French colony as a part of the Japanese Co-prosperity Sphere. The inhabitants of Indochina thus exchanged a European ruling power for an Asiatic one, though their opposition to this new presence was of increasing significance throughout the war. By 1944, the strength of the opposition to the Japanese was encouraged by two views of the future of Indochina. Roosevelt made his opinion known that in the postwar years there would be no acceptable place for colonial empires and the Indochinese people ought therefore to be permitted the right of self-determination: this view from the President of the United States at a time when the American position in world affairs was so strong, gave welcome encouragement to the Indochinese to continue their struggles. But a quite different view was put forward by de Gaulle and other French leaders who said that the new France, emerging strengthened from the wartime chaos, would continue to rule the country's former colonies: the Indochinese leaders were therefore aware that the achievement of independence would result only from continued resistance to reimposed French rule.

In the event, freedom from the Japanese came suddenly with the total defeat of Japan after the atomic destruction of August 1945. The opportunities afforded by this dramatic collapse were seized by the most able of the resistance leaders within Indochina, Ho Chi Minh, who had studied Marxist-Leninist theories of revolution during extensive stays in Paris and Moscow before the war and who, as leader of the Vietminh, was now in a position to put these theories into practice within his own country. In September 1945 Ho Chi Minh established an independent republican government based on the north of Indochina, where his influence was more firmly established. During the following years his rule met opposition both from the returning French and from the American government, whose earlier encouragement of colonial self-determination was abandoned as it recognized Indochina as an area of potential Communist development. Towards the end of 1946 violent clashes occurred between French forces and the Vietminh, leading to the overthrow of Ho Chi Minh's government in 1946 and the beginning of an eight-year period of guerrilla warfare.

During these eight years, in spite of numerous economic and political problems inside France and the need for constant vigilance in other colonies, France fought with determination against the Vietminh. The French offensive was based on their hold on the South, where they fostered a government under the rule of the Vietnamese Emperor, Bao Dai, and where they recruited substantial numbers of Vietnamese opposed to the Vietminh. A French offer of strictly-limited independence was made in 1949 and accepted by Bao Dai, but it was rejected outright by the Vietminh. After the outbreak of the Korean War in the summer of 1950 the French also received military aid and financial support from the United States, whose government after that time was extremely concerned about the dangers of the spread of Communism in south-east Asia.

Eventually this vast expenditure of men and money proved worthless. The French were engaged against an elusive enemy, fighting on their home territory, plentifully supplied with men and equipment and employing guerrilla tactics to which the French were incapable of making effective response. Though most of the opposition was from the Vietminh in the area of Vietnam, there was also opposition, though less intense, from the Khmer Rouge in Cambodia and the Pathet Lao in Laos. On their side, the Vietminh received outside support after 1950 from the Soviet Union, and the new Communist government in China. Above all the Vietminh were united in their loyalty to Ho Chi Minh, whose position as leader in the struggle was unchallenged and who inspired his followers in their pursuit both of national independence for their country and a Communist revolution within it.

In the spring of 1954, the French decided to offer a bold and dangerous military challenge to the Vietminh. Large numbers of French troops fortified themselves in the remote northern town of Dien Bien Phu, flanked on the west by an extensive mountain arc and surrounded by jungle territory. The French were planning to draw out the Vietminh from their hiding places and engage them in open combat, a type of engagement with which the French were more familiar and which they believed would lead to a substantial defeat of the Vietminh. The plan failed totally. Between March and May 1954 the Vietnamese General Giap organized a massive, sustained assault on Dien Bien Phu, leading to the eventual fall of the city to the Vietminh and the death and imprisonment of many thousands of French soldiers. The fall of Dien Bien Phu was not a militarily decisive factor in the withdrawal of the French from the Indochinese struggle: they could continue to fight, even though the odds against them were strong. But it was a psychologically decisive factor: the French government, the French army and French public opinion no longer had any desire to continue to fight in a cause that seemed so hopeless.

The Geneva agreement on Indochina

Between April and July 1954 representatives of the major world powers and of the different areas of Indochina met at Geneva to resolve the problems of the country's future. France had pressed strongly for the holding of this conference, which took place during the bitter fighting and eventual defeat at Dien Bien Phu. An armistice was arranged for the whole of Indochina, which was to be divided into the four countries of Laos, Cambodia, North Vietnam and South Vietnam: the boundary between North and South Vietnam was along the demilitarized zone of the 17th parallel, the North coming under the control of the Communist government of Ho Chi Minh and the South under the control of the government of the former Emperor, Bao Dai. Elections were to be held throughout the whole of Vietnam in two years time, with the intention of creating a united Vietnam.

Alone among the major powers, the United States refused to support the agreements reached at Geneva. Secretary of State Dulles had hoped to create a security pact among major Western powers to act as a strong deterrent to further expansion of Communism in south-east Asia, but Britain and France had refused to participate in the creation of such a pact. Thereafter the United States came to play an increasingly important role in South Vietnam, which it viewed as a vital area to be protected from Communist advance. American influence in South Vietnam was responsible for the abdication of the ineffective government of Bao Dai and for the rise to power in his place of Ngo Dinh Diem, who remained as Presi-

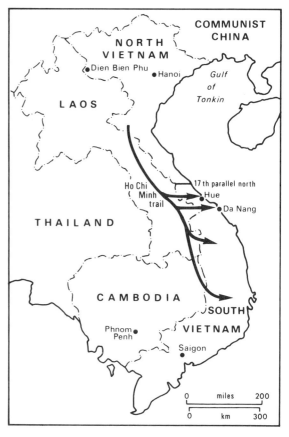

Indochina at the time of the Geneva Conference, 1954

dent of South Vietnam until 1963. This very able Vietnamese leader came from a wealthy family and had earlier been implacably opposed both to the French presence in Indochina and to the attempts made by the Communists to secure control there. For the remainder of the 1950s there was comparative calm in Vietnam.

The Vietnam War: 1960–73

During the 1960s and the 1970s Vietnam became the scene of some of the most horrific warfare that the twentieth century has witnessed. The National Front for the Liberation of South Vietnam, whose members were usually called the Vietcong, was an effective Communist guerrilla organization, loyal to Ho Chi Minh. It aimed at the creation of a Communist state throughout the whole of Indochina, and from 1960 it became increasingly active. In South Vietnam the high-handed Diem government, virtually consisting of members of his own wealthy family, had failed to secure the allegiance of the peasant Vietnamese, many of whom were subject to the brutality and corruption of Diem's own security forces. They turned to the Vietcong in the hope that success for the Vietcong would lead, as they promised, to a more prosperous future and to a fairer society.

The Vietcong also benefited by events in the neighbouring states of Laos and Cambodia. In the early 1960s there was much conflict in Laos between the Communist Pathet Lao forces and anti-Communist forces. By an international agreement in July 1962 Laos was declared a neutral state. But throughout the 1960s, in spite of this agreement, Laos was sympathetic to the Communist cause. As can be seen from the map, the eastern boundary of Laos bordered on to both North and South Vietnam: Laos therefore afforded a highly valuable supply route, popularly known as the Ho Chi Minh trail, by means of which the Vietcong were able to infiltrate South Vietnam. Though Cambodia was not subject to any similar neutralization agreement, it also inclined to favour the Vietcong

and the Ho Chi Minh trail extended into Cambodia, thus affording further supply points for the Vietcong in South Vietnam.

The Vietcong presence in South Vietnam was thus assured of local peasant support and efficient external supply. Meanwhile, the policies of the Diem government had virtually no effect on bringing about the much needed land reforms or in stemming penetration by the Vietcong. The United States now became disillusioned with the Diem government, which appeared helpless in preventing further Communist expansion. When internal political unrest led, in November 1963, to the downfall and assassination of Diem, the United States in fact assisted in his overthrow.

The United States had sent a number of military advisers to South Vietnam in the early 1960s, but by now the American government was much concerned at the apparent disintegration of South Vietnam. Diem's removal was followed by a period of political chaos in South Vietnam. Such circumstances gave even better opportunity for Vietcong advance. The new American President, Lyndon Johnson, decided that his ideal of the *Great Society* was applicable to foreign as well as to domestic policies, and he wanted fuller economic and military support for South Vietnam. In economic matters, lavish aid was given to South Vietnam for the improvement of agriculture and transport. In military matters, increased numbers of American soldiers and supplies were sent: a process that had begun under Johnson's predecessor, Kennedy, was considerably increased.

Until 1964 American involvement had been confined solely to the defence of South Vietnam. But the American military command in South Vietnam held the view that this defensive task could not be adequately fulfilled unless there was also attack against North Vietnam. Johnson's difficulty was that American public opinion was not interested in the war and to order an attack on North Vietnam could have unfortunate political effects in the presidential elections later in 1964. Johnson's political opportunity came when, in August 1964, in the Gulf of Tonkin,

North Vietnamese ships attacked American espionage vessels: this, at any rate, was what the American government said, though there are conflicting accounts of what actually happened. The President at once appealed to Congress to permit him to take action against North Vietnam and it did so by a substantial majority. Johnson used this support early in 1965 when he authorized a policy of aerial strikes against North Vietnam and when he further increased the number of American troops to a maximum figure somewhat in excess of half a million by the late 1960s.

It was in the late 1960s that the warfare in Vietnam was at its most intense. The life-styles and fighting methods of each side could scarcely have made a stronger contrast. The Vietcong intermingled with the peasants of South Vietnam: they dressed like the peasantry and sympathized with peasant dissatisfaction. In this way they laid an extensive, popular foundation for their success. They were able to launch their various guerrilla attacks on the Americans and on the South Vietnamese forces in the secure knowledge that they would be housed and hidden by many peasant villagers of the South and also continue to receive aid from the North via the Ho Chi Minh trail. Though their guerrilla fighting methods were brutal and the tactics used to gain influence in some villages often violent rather than persuasive, their ultimate success in the mid-1970s illustrates the value of their disciplined dedication to their cause in South Vietnam.

The American troops were confronted with an unfamiliar military situation. Unlike Korea, a decade earlier, Vietcong methods made it impossible to see clearly where the enemy was or where the front line of the fighting ran. To perform effectively their work of defence against a particularly slippery opponent, the Americans needed substantial resources in men and equipment. In the United States, vast sums of money were being diverted to the Vietnam War and more and more young men were being drafted for fighting, which created much American hostility towards the war. General Westmoreland, Commander of the American forces in Vietnam from 1964 to 1968, symbolized the fuller American commitment to

Vietnam and he put maximum effort into the aim now given to his troops to *search and destroy*. American infantry were provided lavishly with the most up-to-date equipment, and air strikes against supposed Vietcong areas were launched from well-supplied aircraft carriers or bases within South Vietnam and neighbouring Thailand, whose government at this time saw the best way of preserving its independence from Communism by giving wholehearted cooperation to the American forces.

In attempting to fulfil their defensive role, the American army resorted to some horrific fighting techniques. Napalm, a highly inflammable jelly, adhered to human beings after the explosion of the bombs which contained it: a protracted and painful death usually resulted. Toxic sprays and non-poisonous gases were also used. A particularly murderous incident occurred in March 1968 at My Lai, when over one hundred Vietnamese were wantonly massacred at the hands of some disillusioned American soldiers. Though the soldiers responsible were put on trial and punished, it was known that My Lai was not a totally isolated incident and it was widely felt that the real condemnation should be of the American government which had, by its policies, created the situation in which the massacre could occur.

In the spring of 1968 the Vietcong escalated the war by launching the Tet offensive, which advanced the Vietcong position further in the South. The city of Hue fell for a time into Vietcong hands, resulting in a massacre of about a thousand of the city's inhabitants. Vietcong penetration also occurred in Saigon itself. Though the Tet offensive did not achieve the full success that the Vietcong had anticipated, it unnerved the American troops in South Vietnam and also the American government in Washington. In spite of the substantial American military involvement in Vietnam, no progress at all was being made towards the achievement of American objectives and the war appeared to be dragging on indefinitely. Meanwhile there was an increasing number of demonstrations within the United States for an end to the war.

This New York demonstration in 1967 against American involvement in Vietnam was typical of the internal American opposition to the war from the mid-1960s. Notice how the slogans suggest that the war is not the only point of criticism among these demonstrators.

The gradual ending of the Vietnam War

In May 1968 peace negotiations began in Paris. Initially only North Vietnam and the United States were represented: the Vietcong and South Vietnam joined later in the year. The peace talks were exceptionally slow-moving: throughout virtually five years' duration more than a hundred formal meetings were held and much of the discussion concentrated on technical and diplomatic issues, discussion of which did little to bring about an end to the war.

The United States agreement to start peace negotiations at Paris occurred in the closing months of the Johnson administration, when it was evident that the United States was getting no results from its immense military efforts in Vietnam. The new administration of Nixon, after January 1969, continued this policy of seeking a respectable means of withdrawal. In July 1969 Nixon adopted a new policy, usually termed *Vietnamization*, by which there was to be a progressive American military withdrawal from Vietnam and a shift of the responsibility for defence on to the armed forces of the South. Nixon considered that the greater stability of the government of South Vietnam by the late 1960s, under the firm lead of General Thieu, gave some hope that this would work, until an acceptable peace agreement was reached at Paris.

The withdrawal of American troops did not mean that America had abandoned the cause of South Vietnam. The United States government took steps to try to ensure that when the troops eventually left, South Vietnam would be in a strengthened military and strategic position. American involvement, including air strikes on the North, continued, though with less intensity than earlier. A limited attack on Cambodia was made during the summer of 1970 to destroy the enemy bases in the eastern part of the country, from which the Vietcong in South Vietnam were receiving valuable supplies: the attack was said to have achieved its objective, but it is doubtful whether it gave any long-term advantages to South Vietnam. In

the spring of 1971, the South Vietnamese forces, for the same reasons, made similar attacks into Laos. This invasion of Laos is an example of the extent to which Vietnamization was encouraging the government of South Vietnam to take action on its own account. As well as taking steps to combat its military enemies, Thieu's government also took steps to improve the deplorable social and economic situation of his country. In 1970 his government attempted to stabilize his country's economy and bring about reform in land-holding.

Suddenly, somewhat unexpectedly, in January 1973, the Paris peace conference on Vietnam produced what appeared to be a workable peace solution. In the final months, the negotiations had been led by Henry Kissinger, American Secretary of State, and Le Duc Tho, of North Vietnam. The final pressure that brought North Vietnam to conclude the peace was a massive aerial bombardment of North Vietnam around Christmas 1972. Thieu naturally disliked any settlement: the Nixon administration managed to get Thieu's support, though it was grudgingly given, by means of offering certain confidential assurances.

The peace agreement was a skilful compromise in which all participants in the war could feel their actions had achieved at least a part of their aims. The United States was to withdraw, and the return of American prisoners-of-war was promised; provision was made for the continuation of some American advisers to the South, a situation oddly similar to the situation before America became fully involved in the war. The government of South Vietnam was assured of its independence: to try to bring harmony within South Vietnam a Council of National Reconciliation and Concord was to be created to include Communist representatives, and was to have a significant role in the future government of South Vietnam. For the North, in addition to the advantage of seeing an end of hostilities against them, there was the promise that under the guidance of the Council of National Reconciliation and Concord, a united Vietnam would eventually be created. An internal commission was to ensure that these peace terms were held. After so much bloodshed and so long a period of war, the signature of the peace treaty in January 1973 was greeted by worldwide relief. But the peace which it established was fragile.

The Communist take-over of all Indochina

Further seriously-sustained American involvement in Vietnam, or elsewhere throughout the world, was unthinkable by the mid-1970s. The American economy passed through a period of crisis during these years that caused severe cut-backs in foreign aid: the American Congress was against further military adventures overseas and by the War Powers Act of 1973 had deprived the President of the freedom of action which earlier presidents had used in the conduct of the Vietnam War. Neither the government of South Vietnam nor the government of North Vietnam seriously attempted to fulfil their obligations under the 1973 peace treaty: Thieu did nothing to assist the successful working of the Council of National Reconciliation and Concord and Pham Van Dong,

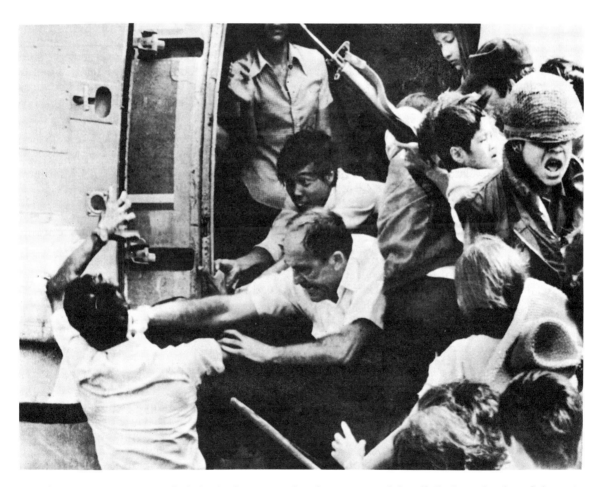

Would-be refugees are pushed back from an already over-crowded relief plane leaving Saigon in the spring of 1975. Those who had cooperated with the previous régime in South Vietnam had reason to fear the Communist success.

Prime Minister of North Vietnam, continued to send North Vietnamese troops to the South.

In the early months of 1975, with South Vietnam receiving less support from the United States, a final and successful campaign was launched by the North against the Thieu government. Substantial successes for the North Vietnamese in the central highland region of South Vietnam at this time made it clear that the country's independence was now being challenged. Morale in the South fell further when it became clear that no American help was forthcoming. At this late stage, and for the first time in the entire struggle, it was possible to see where the enemy were. Thieu ordered the evacuation of the northern provinces of his country and prepared for a last-ditch stand in the area of Saigon. Da Nang fell at the end of March. Civilian panic gripped the country, as the retreat southwards took place. Many South Vietnamese, fearful of their prospects under a Communist government, made desperate attempts to get out of the country by any means possible. Helicopters, aircraft and ships were jam-packed with these refugees, the United States giving assistance in this matter only. At the end of April, North Vietnamese troops entered Saigon in triumph, Thieu having resigned a few days earlier.

This spectacular success for the North Vietnamese forces in South Vietnam was matched at the same time by further Communist advance in neighbouring Cambodia and Laos. The ending of American air attacks in Cambodia in 1973, had assisted the Communist Khmer Rouge in making substantial territorial gains: early in 1975 their major objective was to bring down the capital, Phnom Penh, and this they achieved in April. In Laos, ever since the so-called 'neutralization' of 1962, Communist influence had always been strong. Encouraged by Communist success in neighbouring countries, the Communist Pathet Lao were able to secure complete control of the country. The events of the early months of 1975 ended a long, complicated and, in the final analysis, unsuccessful American involvement in the affairs of Indochina. As President Ford said

at the time, they 'closed a chapter in the American experience'.

It is not possible to speak with certainty about life in Vietnam after the Communist success, as united Vietnam has sought to isolate itself from the Western world. The unification has tended to favour the North. The South was disadvantaged because it no longer received outside supplies, which had previously helped the Southern economy. Many of the city-dwellers of the South were forced to leave their city life and begin work in the countryside, as the new government planned to develop agriculture in the South in order to finance industry in the North: for thousands of southern Vietnamese this brought ruthless reduction in living standards. Camps were established in which they were forcibly taught the principles and advantages of Communist society. Thus a Northern-dominated Communist government has been the price that Vietnam has paid for the eventual securing of peace.

The unification of Vietnam under its new government was not, however, the end of hostilities for the country. In 1978 the traditional hostility between Laos and Vietnam, which had been dormant for some decades, erupted in border warfare. Early in 1979 fighting also took place on Vietnam's border with China, caused partly by China's dislike of Vietnam's alignment with the Soviet Union. It appeared by the late 1970s that Vietnam might well become seriously involved in the dangerous Sino-Soviet quarrel.

Indonesia, Malaysia and confrontation

The postwar achievement of independence in the Dutch East Indies (which became Indonesia) and in Malaya (which joined with Singapore and northern Borneo to form Malaysia) was followed in the 1960s by a period of military *confrontation* that added another disturbing element to the situation in south-east Asia.

Like most of the areas of the Pacific, the Dutch East Indies had come under Japanese occupation during the Second World War.

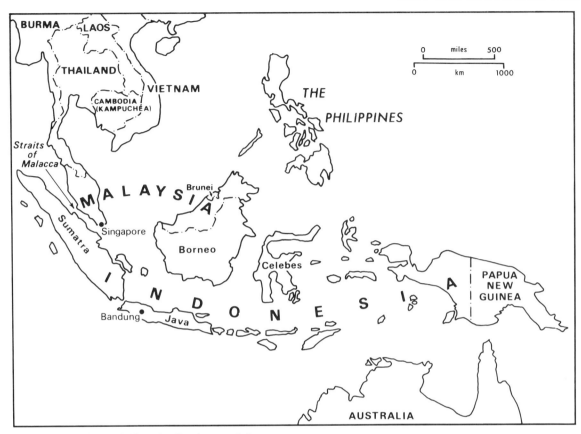

The ending of colonialism in South-east Asia

Even after their defeat in 1945, the Japanese were slow to leave the area, and they purposefully left behind large stocks of ammunition which might be used in the struggle against continued Dutch control. In the event, the Dutch were hardly in a position to reassert control very speedily, as their own country had been occupied by Nazi Germany for the previous five years and they had no adequately equipped army to send.

The prewar Indonesian Nationalist party was revived under the leadership of Sukarno, and became actively involved in securing independence while the Dutch government was in this enfeebled condition. In August 1945 Sukarno felt strong enough to declare the establishment of the republic of Indonesia. The Dutch government, powerless to offer resistance to Sukarno's action, entered into negotiations with him, proposing acceptance of his new republic provided that he would agree to maintain links between his republic and Holland. But Sukarno insisted on severing the Dutch connection completely. The Dutch government was angered at the rejection of their compromise terms, and in November 1946, sufficiently recovered from the war, they sent armed forces to the East Indies to reassert Dutch control. But they had taken on a hopeless task, and their defeat was mainly attributable to the difficulties of fighting in such a dispersed geographical area. In December 1949 they decided to withdraw their forces, though the western part of New Guinea remained under Dutch control until 1962. The new republic of Indonesia was admitted as a member of the United Nations in 1950. Under Sukarno

297

Indonesia gave a strong lead for cooperation among third world countries. This was especially noticeable by Sukarno's sponsorship of the Bandung conference of such countries in 1955.

Sukarno's dictatorial control of Indonesia became even more apparent after 1959, when an attempt was made to establish a parliamentary system of government. The strongest opposition which confronted him came from the Communist party, though the Muslim party was also opposed. In October 1965 the Communist party, with encouragement from the Chinese, carried out an unsuccessful coup against his rule. Their failure was followed by the extensive slaughter of Indonesian Communists, regardless of whether or not they had been connected with the coup. Estimates of the number killed vary, but the figure of a million is not far out. It was one of the most ruthless and extensive political purges that have occurred in the years since 1945. In this and in the execution of all his policies, Sukarno relied heavily on the army. He also relied on his own immense popularity throughout Indonesia, in spite of the dictatorial nature of his government. He was a gifted speaker and had an unerring ability in securing the support of the massed crowds whom he frequently addressed. But early in 1967, the economic decline in Indonesia and the widespread corruption of Sukarno's régime compelled him to resign. Thereafter, under the rule of General Suharto, the government of Indonesia was conducted on less dictatorial lines and relations with neighbouring states, such as Malaysia, improved.

Malaysia itself was formed in 1963 from the former British colony of Malaya and the city of Singapore. Like the Dutch in the East Indies, the British in Malaya faced opposition to their rule in the postwar years. The prosperity of the Malayan rubber industry made the British unwilling to grant immediate independence after the end of the war, but they did work out a plan for a federal union of the 11 states of the Malayan peninsula, allowing a degree of independence for each state. This plan for federal union was partly designed to prevent domination of Malaya by the descendants of the Chinese immigrants of the previous century, amongst whom Communist influence was increasingly strong. When the federation came into being in February 1948, it was immediately faced with rebellion from the Chinese Communists, who continued an extensive guerrilla campaign against the British over the next five years. By 1953, as a result of cutting off supplies for the Communist forces, the British had resecured control of the peninsula.

A succession of conferences led eventually to the granting of complete independence for the federation of Malaya in 1957. The island of Singapore, at the southern tip of the Malayan peninsula, became independent in 1959, but remained for a while separate from Malaya. In September 1963, with British and Commonwealth support, the federation of Malaya was changed into the federation of Malaysia, by linking Singapore and northern Borneo to the original federation. The Prime Minister from 1957 until his retirement in 1970 was Abdul Rahman, who succeeded in improving the prosperity of the new country and maintaining the democratic features of its original constitution, in spite of problems such as Singapore's withdrawal from the federation in 1965 and the conflict with Sukarno's Indonesia between 1963 and 1966.

The differences between Malaysia and Indonesia during these years were referred to at the time as *confrontation*. The basic issue producing the confrontation was Sukarno's opposition to the proposed federation of Malaysia in 1963. He continued his active opposition after the federation's creation by infiltrating Indonesian forces into northern Borneo and by periodic attacks across the straits of Malacca. He condemned Malaysia as an example of *neo-colonialism*, suggesting by the use of this term that despite its apparent independence Malaysia was still under Western imperial control. It may be that he saw it as a threat to his own ambitions to extend Indonesian control into the area of Malaysia and the Philippines. The military confrontation itself, never systematically applied by Sukarno, came to an end during the summer of 1966.

Questions

76. Study the photographs on page 293 and page 295 and then answer questions (a) to (d) which follow.

(a) (i) In which country did the demonstration shown in the photograph on page 293 take place and against which war was it directed?

(ii) What circumstances led to the increasing involvement of the country named in (a) (i) in this war by the mid-1960s?

(iii) Describe the methods of warfare employed in this war by both sides in the struggle.

$(1+3+3)$

(b) (i) Is the political stance of the demonstrations shown in the photograph on page 293 *right wing* or *left wing*?

(ii) By reference to the placards shown in the photograph, give *two* reasons for your choice in (b) (i).

(iii) What factors, other than demonstrations such as this, contributed to the government's withdrawal of support for waging this war?

(iv) Show how there was a gradual withdrawal from this war during the first half of the 1970s.

$(1+2+2+2)$

(c) (i) What events in 1975 led to the incident shown in the photograph on page 295?

(ii) Account for the general atmosphere suggested by this photograph.

$(2+2)$

(d) With reference to the period after the photograph on page 295, identify the main features of the government of the country in which the war was waged.

(2)

77. Explain why warfare broke out in Korea in 1950. Examine the changing objectives throughout the war of the forces fighting for South Korea. Trace the history of Korea from the end of the war to the present day.

78. With reference to the years since 1945, explain the involvement in and the eventual withdrawal from Indochina of (a) the forces of France and (b) the forces of the United States.

27

Independence in British Africa

During the 1920s and the 1930s Britain held its African colonies with a sense of security. It was accepted that independence would eventually be achieved, but at such a remote, future date that those who administered the colonies during the interwar years rarely gave the matter more than fleeting attention. The Second World War changed all that, because it showed that European superiority could be effectively challenged. Though African nationalism was a comparatively small movement, its leaders were determined men. They were dissatisfied with the slow and uncertain approach to independence adopted by the British government and by the colonial governors and administrators. Some held that Africa's future lay in its acceptance of Communism and Socialism. All of them were determined to create through independence a new pride among the African people.

The British Gold Coast becomes Ghana

Of all the differing climatic conditions within Africa, those found in the west are the least suitable for European settlers. The 'white man's grave' was an expression often applied to western Africa. But the unsuitable climate did not prevent many Europeans, mainly French, British and Portuguese from settling there from the seventeenth century onwards. Names such as the Gold Coast, the Ivory Coast, the Slave Coast all suggest the fundamental reason why, in spite of the well-known dangers to health, settlement was worth while: Europeans were aware of the economic gains.

By the time of the Second World War, gold was still mined in the Gold Coast, but the colony's main source of wealth now lay in the cultivation and export of cocoa. Timber-felling, and the mining of diamonds and manganese also assisted the colony's development. Colonialism had certainly developed the economic potential which this part of Africa possessed. A feature which in prewar years distinguished the administration of the Gold Coast from that of other African colonies was the extent to which Africans, sometimes tribal chiefs, sometimes prosperous merchants, were involved in both local and central administration. It was therefore not surprising that the Gold Coast was the first of the African colonies to secure independence.

Britain's postwar Labour government took seriously the responsibilities of making provision for the early preparation of Africans for their future independence, even though the government felt that the date for self-rule was remote. Few colonies were more suitable than the Gold Coast for developments of this kind. Britain's Colonial Secretary, Arthur Creech-Jones, put forward a constitution for the Gold Coast in 1946, providing for an African-elected parliament. Only a few Africans were allowed to vote in the elections for this parliament, and its decisions could in any case be over-ruled by the Governor, who was the Monarch's direct representative in the Gold Coast. But it was a start. The United Gold Coast Convention developed in the late 1940s as a powerful African political party, willing to cooperate with the 1946 constitution, but aiming to secure independence more rapidly than the British government wished.

The United Gold Coast Convention soon came under the leadership of Kwame Nkrumah. This forceful African leader was well

The ceremony at the opening of a harbour in the Gold Coast during the late 1920s. Such occasions as this show the apparent security with which Britain held her African possessions during the interwar years.

acquainted with Europe and the United States, where he had been educated, and where he had spent the war years. He was already known as a leading figure in the Pan-African movement. Nkrumah became critical of his own party's narrow political base among the African middle class and sought to create a party that would involve the mass of the Gold Coast Africans in the movement for their independence. With the aim of broadening its base in this way, Nkrumah reorganized the party, establishing branches in the more remote parts of the Gold Coast and recruiting ex-soldiers to take the lead in stronger protest against the British. His strengthened and enlarged party was in a position to agitate more forcefully and there was extensive rioting throughout the colony in February 1948. Britain's position in the Gold Coast was weakened further by the killing of a number of Africans during

the suppression of the riots. The riots revealed a widely held dissatisfaction felt by the people of the Gold Coast against the British.

Consequently, Creech-Jones appointed a commission under a local judge called Coussey, to produce a new constitution. The Coussey commission, on which only Africans served, recommended an increase in the rights of Africans to administer the Gold Coast and to elect their parliament on the basis of universal suffrage. The British government agreed to abandon the 1946 constitution and put the new one into practice. Arrangements were made for holding an election in 1951 on the basis of universal suffrage.

Nkrumah considered that the concessions given by the British after these riots did not go far enough. He therefore founded a new party, the Convention People's party, which pursued a militant policy in order to secure immediate independence. In spite of the fact that the British imprisoned Nkrumah, his Convention People's party secured a majority in the following election. Nkrumah's leadership of the people of the Gold Coast was by now undisputed. Both sides compromised. The British released Nkrumah so that he could take his rightful place as Prime Minister. For his part, Nkrumah dropped his opposition to the new constitution, and agreed to cooperate in putting it into effect. The next six years were a period of comparative harmony between the British authorities, then headed by the Governor, Sir Charles Arden-Clarke, and the new Gold Coast parliament which was headed by Kwame Nkrumah. In these years the ground was carefully prepared for eventual independence, which was granted in March 1957. The Gold Coast was renamed *Ghana*, the name of a vast pre-colonial West African Empire, and became a dominion within the British Commonwealth. As the first African colony to secure independence, Ghana became an example for other African countries attempting to gain their own independence. As Nkrumah had been the man so largely responsible for this achievement, he became regarded throughout Africa as an important leader of African nationalism.

Ghana

Kwame Nkrumah remained a central figure in the politics of Africa until his fall in 1966. He was a loyal member of the Commonwealth, retaining membership of it even after Ghana became a republic in 1960. But Britain and other Commonwealth countries did not always approve of some of his attitudes towards world politics. His attempts to establish friendly relations with Communist powers, mainly in order to secure economic aid from them, were considered as affording an opportunity for Communism within Africa. Nkrumah played a key role in the foundation at a meeting in the Ethiopian capital of Addis Ababa in 1963 of the Organization of African Unity (OAU). This new organization's pledge to end colonialism in Africa had been largely achieved by 1963,

but it also provided a means through which the new African states could come together to demonstrate the importance of Africa in world affairs, and possibly to create a united Africa.

The Commonwealth viewed with increasing concern not only Nkrumah's international ambitions but also his developing internal dictatorship. Though Ghana possessed a parliament, through which a Western two-party system could develop, even under the British during the years before independence, Nkrumah's Convention People's party was the only party of any real strength. So when independence came, the chances of a two-party system developing successfully were not strong. Before the end of 1957 itself, Nkrumah had begun to suppress political opposition. His rule became progressively more dictatorial: the press was censored, political opponents were imprisoned without trial and Nkrumah's own personality cult was enhanced. In 1964 Ghana was declared a one-party state. A subsequent referendum showed that Nkrumah had the overwhelming support of the Ghanaian people for his rule, though the conduct of the referendum itself was not above suspicion. Such developments were not approved by the Commonwealth.

Nkrumah held that only by strong rule could Ghana's economy be exploited for the benefit of the Ghanaians. Good natural resources, earlier economic development and international aid all suggested a bright future for Ghana's economy. In keeping with his basic Socialistic principles, Nkrumah did much to develop provision for education, for health and for social services. The development of the resources of the Volta river for hydro-electricity and irrigation was a large-scale undertaking of real value, and Ghanaians also derived benefit from small-scale schemes to improve local economies in villages and towns. Other schemes were less sensible. Government buildings at the capital, Accra, were unnecessarily large and grand in their design. Much attention was given to the construction of a port at Tema and its motorway connection with Accra, but for all the lavish expenditure that went into this project, there were embarrassingly few ships entering the port, or vehicles travelling along the motorway.

This combination of political dictatorship and financial irresponsibility encouraged the growth of opposition to Nkrumah. A number of assassination attempts were made against him in the early 1960s, causing him to take extreme precautions to preserve his life. In February 1966, while he was on a visit to Communist China, a group of army officers led a military coup, declaring the deposition of Nkrumah and the creation of a temporary military régime. The new military rulers refused to allow Nkrumah to return: he established himself in neighbouring Guinea, hoping in vain that he would be able to rule his country again one day.

Ghana was under military rule for three years. In August 1969 elections were held for a new civilian government. Nkrumah's Convention People's party no longer existed. A number of new parties, which had developed during the period of military rule, entered the contest. Victory went to the Progress party of Kofi Busia, who became Prime Minister of a government which now tolerated political opposition. Ghana was ruled by Busia for just over two years. He was removed by an army coup in January 1972. His rule was less flamboyant, less dictatorial and less ambitious than that of Nkrumah. The financial debts left by the former dictator formed a serious problem which Busia attempted to overcome by a policy of economic austerity and overseas aid. But in spite of the government's efforts, unemployment grew and inflation increased. The vital cocoa industry suffered decline. Discontent led to disorders within the country in the early 1970s and the government's strong measures to suppress them only added to the government's unpopularity.

This worsening situation led to Ghana's second military coup in January 1972. Like Nkrumah in 1966, Busia was temporarily absent when the coup occurred. It was led by Colonel Acheampong, whose military régime, called the National Redemption Council, dominated Ghana until his own overthrow in 1978. Acheampong had played a part in the military rule of 1966–69 and

like a number of army officers, was angered at the military cuts which were a part of Busia's austerity measures.

In attempting to solve Ghana's continuing economic problems, Acheampong adopted the technique of a planned economy, announcing the first five-year plan in January 1974, while continuing to try to seek international aid and to attract foreign companies to invest in Ghana. *Operation Feed Yourself* was aimed to cut down food imports and it secured some success in achieving this aim. But inflation and food shortages were still much in evidence. A return to civilian rule became a steadily accepted aim in Ghana during the mid-1970s. Elections were to be held in 1978 and a new civilian government would come into being after that. Many doubted Acheampong's sincerity. In July 1978 he was removed from power in a coup led by one of his own ministers, General Akuffo. His first action was to release a number of political prisoners and to promise elections in 1979. But within a year, in May 1979, this new government was overthrown by another military coup whose leaders declared their determination to rid the country of corruption. Some former leaders, among whom were both Acheampong and Akuffo, were summarily executed.

The dreary succession of military coups and military régimes in Ghana's recent history and the continuing problems of the economy are saddening features in the history of a country which in 1957 set out on the road to independence with such promise and such high hopes. But in spite of its very real problems, Ghana had been spared the injustices caused by racial division and the ravages caused by civil war. Ghana's near neighbour in West Africa, Nigeria, has been less fortunate in this latter respect.

The independence of Nigeria

As in other parts of West Africa, the unsuitability of the climate deterred many settlers in Africa from choosing Nigeria. Europeans were never numerous in this large British colony, which was administered largely through the tribal chiefs, supervised by European district officers. The system, known as *Indirect Rule* had been developed by Lord Lugard, a Governor of Nigeria in the early part of the century. Britain did not prevent Nigerians from securing education in Europe, but on their return to Nigeria, Britain was unwilling to allow them positions of major responsibility.

Nkrumah's achievement of independence for Ghana in 1957 had direct effect on the course of events in Nigeria. If the British

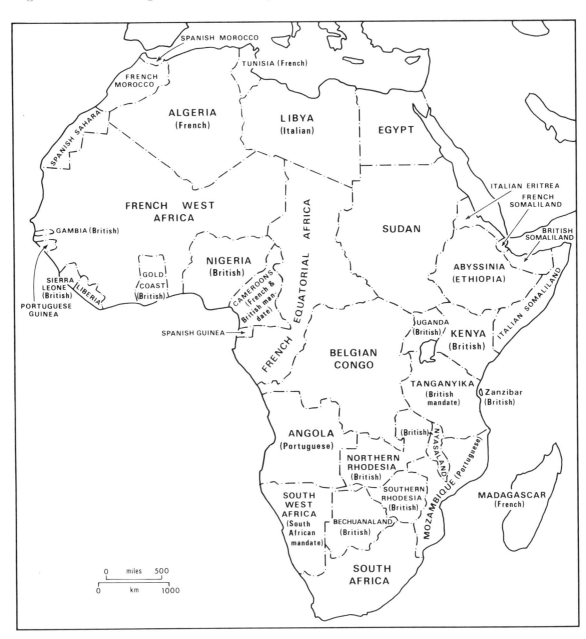

Africa during the interwar years

granted independence to Ghana, there was no reason why they should not do the same in Nigeria. Pressure was asserted by Nigerian nationalists, who secured their goal in June 1960, the very year of Macmillan's *Wind of Change* speech, considered in Chapter 29.

Independence in Britain's other West African possessions followed shortly after: in Sierra Leone in 1961 and in the Gambia in 1965.

But serious divisions existed within Nigeria, leading to civil war within a few years of independence. The roots of these

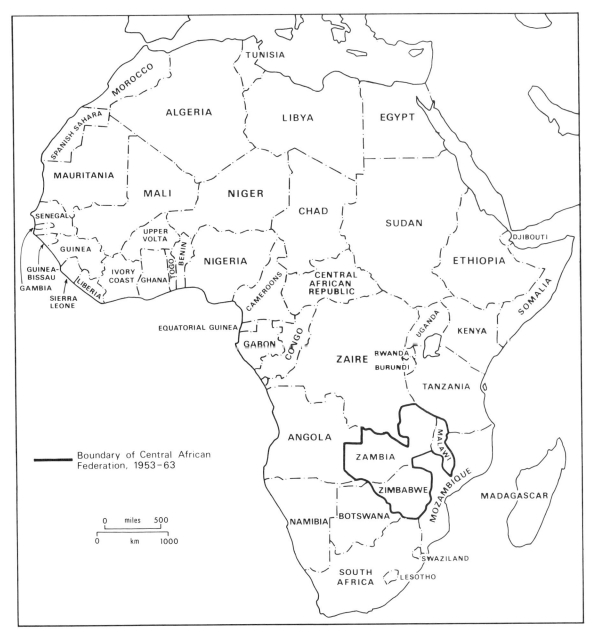

Africa in the early 1980s

divisions lay in tribalism. Within the boundaries of Nigeria established by the British there were three main tribes: the Hausa of the north, the Yoruba of the south-west and the Ibo of the south-east. These differences were not the only ones to be found in Nigeria. The country was divided in religious matters, between Christianity and Islam. The economy varied considerably in different areas, while the discovery of oil in the east added further conflict over how and by whom this new resource was to be developed.

The five years after independence were unhappy ones for Nigeria, as these internal differences became more serious. The constitution created by the British at independence provided, as did the Ghana constitution, for a two-party system which did not exist and was unlikely to develop. It did however, allow a degree of independence in the regions – North, West and East – each of which was permitted its own Prime Minister under the ultimate control of the federal Prime Minister at the capital, Lagos. Although the President, merely a ceremonial figure, was an Ibo, real political power was held by the Hausa tribe. The endeavours of the first Prime Minister, Balewa, to steer a course between the developing rivalries among the different peoples came to little. Meantime, accusations of government corruption, the developing problem of inflation and the exploitation of Nigeria's resources by business interests outside Nigeria, added to the general atmosphere of tension.

In January 1966, a coup by Ibo officers took place. It was a bloody affair, involving the murder of the Prime Ministers of the North and West regions as well as Prime Minister Balewa himself. Following these events, the government asked the Ibo General Ironsi to assume power as head of state. For the early months of 1966 it appeared that Ibo interests were dominant throughout Nigeria, in the army and in local administration. Ironsi's main policy for Nigeria was to bring an end to the conditions inherited by the country in 1960 and create in their place a *unitary state*, with no internal divisions whatsoever. But during his few months of power Ibo interests became dominant throughout Nigeria so that for those who were not Ibo, Ironsi's unitary state was interpreted as an Ibo-dominated state. By the spring of 1966, opposition to the Ibos was strongly felt and in the North led to the massacre of Ibos who over a number of years had gone there earlier to find work. In July 1966, Ironsi was himself overthrown and murdered by a coup of northern soldiers led by General Gowon, by birth not a member of any of the major peoples of the country.

The most troublesome of Gowon's early problems was the North, where strong demands were being made for secession from the rest of Nigeria. In September 1966 another and much worse massacre of Ibos in the North took place. Ibos throughout Nigeria became alarmed and all returned to their native eastern region where they found a leader in the military governor General Ojukwu. The threat of secession from the East was now stronger than the threat from the North, as Gowon attempted to preserve the country's unity. Politicians who, like himself, were not members of the major tribes, were brought in to assist him. Early in 1967, he put forward a new scheme of government. Ironsi's unitary state was abandoned. Instead there were to be twelve states administered in the foreseeable future by military power, but eventually by civilian government. For the Ibos in the eastern region, a fatal stumbling block to acceptance of this scheme was the exclusion of the eastern oil-producing regions from their control. In July 1967, in retaliation, Ojukwu declared the independence of the eastern region, which took the name of *Biafra*.

The Nigerian Civil War

Thus began a three-year civil war between the central government under Gowon and the separatist Biafran government under Ojukwu. For Nigeria, involvement in the war was costly, leading to restraint on other government expenditure and an immense increase in the size of the army. Biafra proved a determined foe. Ojukwu inspired loyalty throughout the separatist state from both

Ibos and other neighbouring peoples who felt their interests threatened by Gowon's policies. As Nigeria slowly moved towards victory against Biafra, the plight of the besieged Biafrans got worse. Starvation and disease were rampant throughout the area. These appalling conditions became known throughout the world and stimulated much outside sympathy from a number of African and European countries, and from a number of independent charity organizations, all of which supplied the food and relief which enabled Biafran resistance to continue.

Initially Biafra had some success in its plan for independence and it was not until 1968 that Gowon's forces were able to make significant advances. In the summer of that year Port Harcourt fell to Nigeria, thus robbing Biafra of its sea-outlet. At much the same time successful advances were made into northern Biafra, where the important town of Enugu was secured. Gowon's military plan was to split Biafra in two by advancing from these points in the north and on the coast. Bombing raids were also made. Nevertheless, though it was generally expected that Biafra would fall in 1968, it continued to hold out. It was in these years that external supplies brought by air via the make-shift runway at Uli were invaluable for Biafra, though those supplying aid in this way were likely to be shot down by Nigerian forces. An assault by Nigeria, launched in December 1969, brought the final surrender of Biafra in January 1970. The early months of 1970 were nevertheless ones of continuing difficulty, as many Biafrans were still starving and their lands became prey to restless soldiers of the defeated Biafran army and the victorious Nigerian army.

General Gowon made all possible attempts to conciliate his defeated fellow-countrymen. He urged that throughout Nigeria, Ibos should be given jobs on an equal basis with other Nigerians. He made generous grants from government funds for improvement of the war-devastated areas. But Gowon held that an economic revival of all Nigeria would be the best long-term solution for defeated Biafra, and would stress Biafra's identity with the rest of the country. A

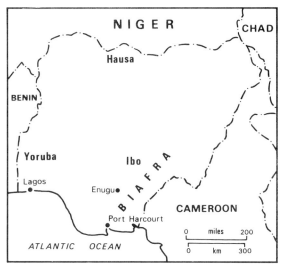

The Nigerian Civil War, 1967–70

National Development Plan was put forward to help achieve this revival, based upon the development of the country's prosperous oil industry. The government was to remain in military hands, but encouragement was to be given to the development of political parties on a Nigerian national basis, and the goal was set for an eventual return to civilian rule.

Though Biafra was quite successfully reincorporated into Nigeria during the 1970s, the political development of the country as a whole continued to reveal problems. The economy, however, made some significant advances, especially as a result of the exploitation of the country's oil resources: by the mid-1970s Nigeria was Africa's leading oil-exporting country and benefited further by the sharp rise in oil prices in the autumn of 1973. But Gowon's delay in returning to civilian rule, coupled with widespread criticism of government corruption and the emergence of friction between the country's different regions all combined to produce opposition to him. Widespread rioting occurred in 1974 and 1975. Taking advantage of Gowon's absence at an OAU meeting in Uganda, Brigadier Murtala Mohammed, an assistant of General Gowon, took over control of the government in July 1975.

Mohammed's government made the eradication of corruption its first aim. Strong measures were taken against many civil servants, police and teachers: before the end of the year some thousands had been dismissed. The new government revived plans for an eventual return to civilian rule. Closer encouragement was to be given to the development of national political parties and it was expected that civilian rule would return before the end of the 1970s.

Brigadier Mohammed held power for only slightly more than six months, as in February 1976 he was assassinated during an attempted coup, led by those who favoured the return of Gowon. His successor, General Obasanjo, continued with his predecessor's policies. The return of civilian government before the end of the 1970s was a strongly-held aim of the new government. Proposals were made for the creation of 19 instead of 12 states, in order to create areas more equal in population. This was intended to reduce the likelihood of rivalries developing. The 19 states were to be united under a federal government, whose structure was to be similar to that of the United States government: a powerful President, a two-chamber parliament and a degree of independence for each of the 19 states. Attempts were to be made to safeguard the administration from the problems of rivalry and corruption at all levels, and to create a stable political situation in which Nigeria could develop her resources. By the late 1970s, the world energy crisis enabled Nigeria to assert an increasingly significant role in African and world affairs.

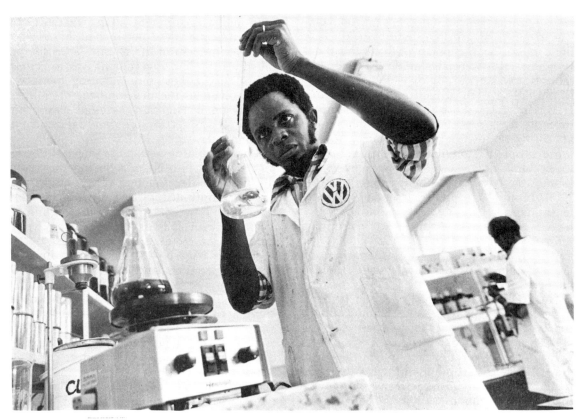

Scientific research in Nigeria during the 1970s. After the civil war the government gave full encouragement to the exploitation of the country's valuable natural resources.

Kenya

Amongst Britain's African colonies, Southern Rhodesia and Kenya had the highest number of white settlers, attracted to their colonial homes by the favourable climate generally enjoyed in these parts of Africa, which were suitable for extensive and profitable farming. Demands for self-rule challenged the interests of these large groups of settlers in both colonies. The Kenyan whites were forced to compromise eventually: a compromise that has led to the development of Kenya as a successful multiracial country within the Commonwealth. The story of Southern Rhodesia, outlined in chapter 29, has been very different.

Kenya's development towards independence was, however, far from easy. The development of Kenya's agriculture by British settlers had begun in the early years of the century and continued throughout the interwar years. Land grants were made to settlers by the British government, though the work needed to exploit these lands was often beyond the capacities of some British who came to Kenya with hopes of an easy and prosperous future. British control of the colony was disliked by many of the settlers, who considered that their interests would be far more effectively advanced if Kenya were to have a constitution similar to that granted to Southern Rhodesia in 1923, allowing the white settlers a much stronger say in the colony's administration. Nevertheless, a Kenya assembly provided for a good representation of white interests at the Kenya capital of Nairobi, though under the ultimate control of the British Governor. A limited representation was also allowed for Kenya's Asians, some of whom had settled along Kenya's coast before the British, while others had come to work on the construction of a railway which the British undertook; they played an important part in the country's commerce. Until the Second World War, no African was allowed on the assembly.

Dissatisfaction developed sooner in Kenya than elsewhere. It was even a factor of some importance during the interwar years, when Jomo Kenyatta, supported in his campaign by the Kikuyu people, began to agitate against the British. The main resentment on which Kenyatta based his opposition was the wholesale manner in which the land of the Kikuyu, and of other tribes, had been taken over by the British settlers. After having spent the 1930s in Europe, Kenyatta returned to his country and formed the Kenya African National Union (KANU) after the Second World War. Its early demands were not for independence, but for an increased representation of Africans in the assembly.

By 1952 the movement known as *Mau Mau* had become a serious and widespread problem for the settlers and the British government. Its members swore oaths to destroy those who were supporting the British in Kenya. The Mau Mau guerrillas were Kikuyu as it was mostly the land of these people which had been taken by the settlers. Attacks were made upon British settlers and upon those Africans supporting them. As a result of Mau Mau activities throughout the 1950s, far more Africans were killed than Europeans. The aims and methods of Mau Mau were bound up in African tribal tradition as well as the achievement of self determination, so it was difficult for the settlers or the British government to understand the movement properly; the authorities were alarmed at the methods of violence that the movement used and caused. In 1952, the Governor declared a state of emergency and British troops were sent to Kenya to suppress the movement. Those involved in Mau Mau were detained in camps and those convicted of offences were executed.

Whilst continuing to adopt firm tactics, the British government in 1957 offered Africans equality with Europeans in the assembly so that it would be *multi-racial*. The British also hoped by this technique to encourage a new African political group to emerge to replace KANU and their leader Kenyatta, whom the British disliked and who had been imprisoned because of his alleged involvement in Mau Mau. The Kenya African Democratic Union (KADU) was the alternative party which the British favoured. But even from prison, Kenyatta continued to

During the Mau Mau emergency of the 1950s a white police officer, with black security forces, questions a Kikuyu tribesman in a Kenya village. Notice the huts and the contrast in clothing between the men on the right and the tribesman on the left.

have influence, and the British were unable to get any cooperation from Africans in their hesitant moves towards a multi-racial assembly. The British administration was further discredited by the revelation that at a camp for Mau Mau prisoners, inmates had been beaten to death for refusing to work. The revelation of the Hola Camp atrocities and

the publication of the Devlin commission's report on the 'police state' of Nyasaland, considered in chapter 29, both came in 1959 and both were powerful influences on Macmillan's *Wind of Change* policy early in 1960.

Preparation now began for the establishment of an independent Kenya. In 1961 Kenyatta was released from prison in order to take part in elections. Though the KADU party gained some seats, Kenyatta's KANU party swept to victory and he became Prime Minister in the same year. He then headed the negotiations for independence, at the same time adopting an attitude of compromise towards the Asians and the British who were settled in Kenya. The Asians were allowed the option of retaining British citizenship or of adopting Kenyan citizenship. A number of British decided to leave Kenya before independence was declared, although many decided to stay and work within the new multi-racial state. Negotiations were completed for a hand-over of Kenya to Kenyatta's government in 1963.

Kenyatta remained in control of the country until his death in August 1978, after which his Vice President, Arap Moi, was elected to succeed him. Throughout his long years of power, Kenya was one of the most stable of the African states, and continued stability marked the first year of his successor's rule. In 1964 Kenya had followed a number of other newly independent African states by adopting a new form of government: the one-party state. This has been maintained despite the fact that Kenya's written constitution allows for more than one political party within the state. However, Kenyatta preserved unity within Kenya, despite this policy, or maybe because of it.

On the whole, relations between the whites and Kenyatta after independence were harmonious, but those with the Asians were less satisfactory. The fact that many of them had chosen to retain British citizenship and to reject Kenyan citizenship was taken by Kenyatta as an excuse for persecution of those Asians who were not Kenya citizens. As they were deprived of their jobs, many of them had little option but to leave the country.

The unpleasant consequences of conflict between different tribes were felt from time to time. The most dangerous occasion was at the time of the assassination of Tom Mboya in 1969. Mboya was widely regarded as Kenyatta's successor and was a Luo. His assassination led to some conflict between the Luo and the Kikuyu. As Kenyatta was

a Kikuyu, this conflict could have upset his previously unchallenged position. Kenyatta solved this dangerous situation by allowing a general election in 1970 which successfully confirmed him and KANU in power. Opposition to the regime reached another high point in 1975 at the time of the assassination of the populist politician J. M. Kariuki.

In furthering the economy, Kenyatta sought to bring many businesses under direct state control, and he insisted that foreign-owned companies operating in Kenya should only continue their work in the country if Kenya could benefit directly from them. But in spite of these hesitant moves in the direction of Socialism, Kenya's economy remained capitalist. Kenya benefited by economic cooperation with neighbouring states in the East African Community, and continued a loyal member of the Commonwealth. The allegiance of Kenyatta's government was to the West.

His immediate problems in foreign affairs concerned relations with neighbouring countries. Kenya's northern provinces were claimed by Somalia, angry at Britain's refusal to grant them these provinces at the time of independence. Somalia guerrillas became active in this area, but were eventually suppressed by Kenya's own forces. Somalia still claims these areas.

Kenyatta never became an enthusiast for the OAU, preferring to see the achievement of immediate goals in his own country rather than to pursue policies that would attempt to link together the differing policies of the developing states of Africa. The difficulty of an understanding with other neighbouring African states was well illustrated in the 1970s by the uneasy relations with Tanzania to the south, and the breakdown of relations with Uganda to the west. In the early 1960s, an idea for the creation of an East African Federation between Kenya, Tanzania and Uganda had been proposed by Britain. It had never been put into practice, but President Nyerere of Tanzania had been one of its supporters even though Kenyatta had opposed it. During the late 1960s and early 1970s, however, there was closer economic cooperation between Kenya, Uganda and

Tanzania even though Kenyatta did not approve of Tanzania's Socialist government. Relations with Uganda worsened after the coup of 1971, in which President Idi Amin came to power: Kenya and Uganda began to dispute the use of the Uganda–Kenya railway line, and the position of the borders between the two countries.

Uganda

The land-blocked colony of Uganda never attracted many British settlers. At the time of its colonization in the late nineteenth century, one part of the area colonized had its own Monarch, the Kabaka of Buganda. He and his successors were maintained in power by the British, who had overall control of the colony's development. In the mid-1950s the major problems confronting the British in Uganda came from the Kabaka, who demanded the separation of his own area, Buganda, which constituted about a quarter of the whole colony, from the rest. He was also concerned about Britain's plans for bringing Uganda, including Buganda, into the proposed East African Federation. When the British exiled the Kabaka to Europe, the Ugandans protested vigorously, and the British were compelled to allow him to return. Independence was granted in 1962. The special circumstances of Uganda were to an extent maintained in the agreement for independence: the Kabaka retained control of Buganda and was to become President of Uganda, but the government was to be controlled by a prime minister elected on the basis of universal suffrage. Milton Obote of the Ugandan People's Congress was elected Prime Minister. In 1966 he overthrew the authority of the Kabaka, bringing the area of Buganda fully under the control of his own government. He himself took on the position of President and established one-party rule.

Obote was determined to develop the Ugandan economy to its full potential. Extensive policies of nationalization of underdeveloped land, and of the developing cotton industry took place, while the resources of the major banks were brought more closely under state control. Obote was determined to narrow the gap between the extremities of wealth and poverty within the country. Obote's *Move to the Left*, as he himself termed his economic policies, was not universally popular within Uganda. In January 1971 an army coup took place, led by the Commander-in-Chief of the Ugandan army, Major-General Idi Amin. The army justified its removal of Obote on the grounds that his rule had become dictatorial and his policies were not working successfully. Possibly the army was concerned also at Obote's attempts to curb its own power. President Amin initially promised that the rule of the military would be only temporary: his early moves in releasing Obote's political prisoners appeared to suggest that his role would in fact be temporary and that he would remove some of the restrictions which Obote had imposed.

Throughout the 1970s Amin developed a cruel and erratic dictatorship within Uganda. The Ugandan Asians were one of his early targets. As in Kenya, these Asians had settled during colonial times and were particulary influential as traders in Uganda. Amin's excuse was that they were unwilling to integrate fully into Ugandan life. He also alleged that they took measures to prevent other Ugandans, principally Africans, from becoming involved in trade. He therefore gave orders in August 1972 that they were to be expelled. Similar measures were taken against other minority groups. Africans who were opposed to the Amin régime were even more vulnerable to the President's unpredictable anger. In 1974 the International Commission of Jurists published a careful and detailed account of the manner in which human rights were being violated in Uganda.

The country's economy did not prosper under Amin's rule. There was evidence of shortages of goods throughout the country, especially after the break with Kenya in 1976. The transportation of goods through Kenya was curbed, as Kenya had assisted the Israeli rescue assault team at Entebbe during a hijack of an aeroplane by the PLO. This incident is more fully explained in chapter 22. The opposition to Amin's régime was shown by attempts on the President's life. These were followed by ruthless purges of those suspected of involvement.

In his foreign relations there was one consistent feature of his rule: support for the importance of Africa in world affairs. This led him to be an enthusiast for the work of the OAU, of which he was elected chairman between 1975–76. Amin's relations with Britain and with the Commonwealth were unsteady. Sometimes he would express his loyalty to the Queen and the Commonwealth; at other times he would accuse British politicians of planning invasions of Uganda. His treatment of a number of British residents in Uganda led to a breakdown of relations with Britain. It was unfortunate that many in Britain, and elsewhere, viewed Amin as a figure of fun, something which he certainly was not for those who lived in Uganda.

Though able to maintain satisfactory relations with some African states, such as Zaïre and Libya, relations with others were poor. There was friction particularly between Uganda and Tanzania, where President Nyerere's Socialist outlook was not shared by Amin, who had further reason for disliking Nyerere for sheltering the exiled Obote. The border between Tanzania and Uganda was the scene of violent clashes on a number of occasions in the 1970s and this border warfare intensified considerably during the early months of 1979, when Tanzanian invasion forces linked with Ugandan rebels in a determined struggle which led to the overthrow of Amin in April 1979. Thereafter the ex-dictator's whereabouts were unknown, though it was considered likely that he had sought refuge in Libya, which had given him military assistance during the closing months of his rule. Under the new, moderate government of President Lule, attempts were made to restore political and economic stability to Uganda. But Lule fell from power two months after Amin's overthrow and in a situation of political uncertainty, the claims of former President Obote were again put forward. Though relieved of the Amin dictatorship, Uganda was still seriously beset by problems of adjustment.

This British cartoon of Idi Amin was a forthright comment, not only on the ruthlessness of his Ugandan dictatorship during the 1970s, but also on the unthinking response to it of many people outside Uganda.

Tanzania

Tanzania was created in 1964 from the former British mandate of Tanganyika, which had become independent in 1961, and the former small British colony on the island of Zanzibar, which had become independent in 1963. As a mandated territory, Tanganyika's relationship with Britain was different from that of Britain's African colonies. Initially, the League of Nations Mandates Commission gave Britain responsibility for the administration of the territory: later, it was given by the United Nations Trusteeship Council. The early moves for independence came in the 1950s, prompted by the Trusteeship Council: within Tanganyika political life was very inactive at that time. But it was during the 1950s that Julius Nyerere founded the Tanganyika African National Union (TANU) in order to campaign for self-rule. Few independent movements have been less violent or have had an easier passage to success. At all stages Nyerere received the support of the Trusteeship Council and, to a lesser extent, of the British government, which had some doubts about the speed at which independence should be secured.

Since independence the two neighbouring countries of Tanzania and Kenya have both shown, by contrast with some other new African states, a marked degree of stability. But there the similarity ends. Kenya's development has been along Western, capitalist lines. Tanzania's development has been along non-aligned, Socialist lines. The inspiration for these developments has been that of Nyerere. Nyerere had become committed to Socialism as a student in Europe and since independence has tried to put it into practice in his country. In order to be certain that his solution for Tanzania was consistently applied, Nyerere took firm control of the government after independence: he changed its status to that of a republic, with himself as President, and he established the state on a one-party basis, the party being TANU. His own life-style has been modest: he lives simply in an ordinary house and has totally rejected the grand style of life which a number of other leaders have cultivated. In this matter, ministers and civil servants have been expected to follow the example of their President, 'the Teacher' as he is often called. The entire government and administrative system has been comparatively free from corruption and intrigue. Nevertheless, the one-party system has led to the persecution of a number of political opponents.

In developing his government along these lines, Nyerere has been conscious that his country possesses the least resources of any African state and that only by a careful pursuit of Socialist principles will it be able to develop these resources adequately. In January 1967, at Arusha, he put before a group of regional commissioners a government policy statement that became known as the *Arusha Declaration*, which explained in detail the Socialist future for Tanzania's economy and society. It was followed swiftly by the nationalization of the banks and of a number of leading firms, and by the restriction of any further development in the direction of capitalism. Many of the aims of the declaration were long-term. Attention was to be given to the extension of educational facilities for both children and adults, and to the teaching of Socialism in schools. Most important of all were his plans for the development of agriculture which was to be the basis of the country's economy, being the country's main resource. In the vast rural areas, *ujamaa* (Socialist) villages were to be encouraged. These involved the regrouping of rural inhabitants in village communities that were designed to work more effectively as economic units than the traditional village structures, their organization being based on Socialist principles. In the late 1960s and early 1970s, special attention was given to the development of these ujamaa villages. But in spite of all this, by the early 1970s agricultural output was still low.

Nyerere also attempted to decentralize the administration of government in order to effect his policies, and to bring government closer to the people. Ten years later, early in 1977, Nyerere made a careful and realistic assessment of progress in a document entitled *The Arusha Declaration: Ten years after*. The substantial development of ujamaa villages was recorded as a major advance during these ten years, but the President was concerned that Tanzania was still 'neither Socialist nor self-reliant', and that poverty was 'still the experience of the majority of our citizens'. In the same year, the TANU party merged with the party to which it was allied in Zanzibar to form what was known as the Revolutionary party, under which Socialist goals would continue to be pursued.

Nyerere's Socialism has been the deciding factor in his country's foreign relations. Links with Western countries have never developed very closely. In seeking his own distinct form of development for Tanzania, he has avoided close contact with foreign enterprises which, in a different political environment, might

A Tanzanian family build their own home in a ujamaa village. Under Nyerere's Socialist rule throughout the 1960s and 1970s, every effort was made to ensure fair distribution of Tanzania's scant resources.

have been invited to involve themselves in developing Tanzania's economy. Instead he has sought assistance from those countries which share his outlook and which are willing to give aid. The Communist government of China, which had gained power through the support of the Chinese peasantry, saw a similarity in the Tanzanian situation and gave generous assistance. The construction of the Tanzam railway, linking Tanzania's coast with Zambia's copperbelt, was undertaken in the early 1970s as a joint enterprise between Zambia and Tanzania, and financed by an interest-free loan from the Chinese. It was built with the aid of Chinese technical advisers. The line was completed

in 1976 and in spite of some maintenance problems, it should eventually assist the economies of both the countries which it links.

The relations between Tanzania and Zambia have been good. The fall of Mozambique to the FRELIMO forces which Nyerere had earlier supported in their struggle against the Portuguese, led to the establishment of another friendly neighbour. He has supported the Patriotic Front's struggle against Smith's régime in Rhodesia, and was chairman of the *Front Line Presidents* of the independent countries surrounding Rhodesia. As has been shown, relations with his northern neighbours of Kenya and Uganda have been

315

less harmonious, principally because Tanzania's development is on a totally different basis to that of Kenya and, especially, that of Uganda. The idea of an East African Federation, advanced originally by the British in the early 1950s, was not entirely lost. In 1967 the three countries grouped together as the East African Community, aiming to assist each other's economies by the reduction of import duties and by a pooling of resources. The increasing frictions of the 1970s led to the scheme's collapse in 1977. But in spite of difficulties in relations with other African powers and in spite of the poverty of his country, Nyerere's bold Socialist experiment has over the years produced a more stable government and a fairer society than is to be found in many African nations.

Questions

79. Study the photograph on page 301 and then answer questions (a) to (d) which follow.
    (a) (i) Give the title of the British colonial official shown in the centre of the photograph, wearing the plumed hat.
        (ii) Give the position of the person in Britain whom he represented.
        (2)
    (b) (i) What pieces of evidence in the photograph suggest the superiority that whites felt and enacted over blacks in the Gold Coast at this time?
        (ii) Suggest reasons why white people had come to settle in the Gold Coast. What difficulties did they encounter there?
        (2+3)
    (c) (i) Name the main postwar leader for the independence of the Gold Coast,
        (ii) name the successor of the British official shown in the centre of the photograph and with whom the leader named in (c) (i) negotiated, and
        (iii) examine the importance of the work of both these men in the achievement of independence by 1957.
        (1+1+5)
    (d) Outline the history of Ghana during the ten years after independence had been achieved.
        (6)

80. Describe the events leading to (a) the achievement of independence by Nigeria and (b) the outbreak of civil war in Nigeria. To what extent has Nigeria been a more settled country during the 1970s?

81. Show the importance of *three* of the following in the history of East Africa: the Mau Mau incidents; Kenyatta's leadership; Nyerere's Socialist policies; Amin's dictatorship.

28
The Belgian Congo and Portuguese Africa

The Belgian Congo

In 1908 the Belgian government had taken over control of the Belgian Congo from an independent Belgian company under whose ruthless control it had been cruelly exploited during the late nineteenth century. They thus acquired vast territory in central Africa, about 78 times the size of Belgium itself, and an area rich in minerals and rubber.

Until three years before the granting of independence in 1960, the attitude of the Belgian government towards the Congo may be described as *paternalistic*. Government policy was geared to this attitude, and the colonial administrators, trained at a colonial university at Antwerp, in Belgium, were encouraged to work hard for the well-being of the Congolese, but on a physical level only. Substantial advances were made in medical care and Belgian doctors and Belgian medical research in the Congo did much to curb diseases such as malaria and sleeping sickness. Primary education spread, and many people became literate, but very small provision was made for the extension of education beyond the primary level, as the Belgian government considered there was no purpose in the Congolese seeking an education which might fit them for the upper levels of the colonial administration, which the Belgians intended to occupy indefinitely. The Roman Catholic church played an important part in educational and medical advance through its missionary work, though in some respects the very direct and forceful teaching of the Christian missionaries represented an assault on traditional values and the traditional religious beliefs of the Congolese peoples.

In the areas of health, education and religion, the Belgian administration attempted to protect the peoples of the Congo and, within certain limits, to provide for their welfare. But in other ways the Belgian administration tended towards exploitation of them. The mining of minerals was organized exclusively by Belgian-controlled companies such as *Union Minière*, which mined copper in the rich Katanga province. Recruitment of Africans to work in these companies was often at the expense of traditional social structures and values. The introduction of the money economy, with all its trappings, such as taxation, forced Africans to move from villages to towns in order to find work. In the villages, women and children were left on their own to cultivate the soil: in the towns and mines men lived in poor conditions and worked hard for a very low wage.

The movement for independence

Belgian influences were responsible for the early development of the movement for independence. After 1945, trade unionism developed among the Africans in the towns, and although trade unions never had many members, they gave Africans an opportunity to practise political organization. They also showed the real value of the strike-threat in order to obtain their objectives. The two major parties were the Abako party in Leopoldville, led by Joseph Kasavubu, and the Conakat party in Katanga, led by Moise Tshombe.

A political party with a wide vision of

the Congo's future was founded in October 1958. This was the Congolese National movement. It encompassed many different peoples within the country, and urged that fundamental liberties be secured. It also wanted rapid independence for a unified Congo. The party was founded by a 33-year-old post office worker from Orientale province, Patrice Lumumba, a man of forceful personality who was also a persuasive speaker, and destined to play a key role in the creation of independence.

Agitation mounted within the main towns of the Belgian Congo, particularly in Leopoldville, where poor living conditions among the migrant workers tended to encourage such activity. The Belgian government had no clear policy to meet the increasing problems in the Congo in 1958 and 1959. If they were to embark fully on an attempt to maintain control, they might well become involved in a lengthy, costly and ultimately unsuccessful military campaign: French difficulties in Indochina and Algeria demonstrated the problems that might result from such a policy. So when the African leaders

met with the Belgian government at a conference in Brussels in January 1960, they discovered that the Belgian government presented not the slightest opposition to their demands for obtaining independence by June 1960, and for holding of elections in the Congo before independence was achieved.

The elections in May 1960 resulted in no clear political lead: numerous small political parties had now developed in the Congo, but of the major parties, Lumumba's National movement received the most votes. Lumumba was to become Prime Minister, and his ally, Kasavubu, was to become President. The independence ceremony on 30 June 1960 was an unhappy event, in which King Baudouin of the Belgians made a speech containing ill-judged references to Belgium's work in the Congo, eliciting from Lumumba a colourful condemnation of Belgian rule in the Congo, and from Kasavubu an assurance that the Africans were 'no longer your monkeys'.

The disintegration of the Congo

The situation in the Congo deteriorated rapidly after independence, revealing both serious problems of conflict between different tribes and the disastrous consequences of Belgian paternalism. In Leopoldville province the military police force mutinied. Throughout the country attacks were made on Belgian residents, many of whom still played vital parts in the country's administration: the Belgian government sent troops to protect these Belgians. Most serious of all was a declaration by Tshombe, the leader of Katanga, that his province intended to secede from the newly independent Congo; without the mineral wealth of this province, the new Congo would be unable to survive.

Lumumba intended to keep the Congo united and peaceful. He appealed for practical assistance from the United Nations, whose Secretary-General, Dag Hammarskjöld, proposed sending a peacekeeping force, and requesting the withdrawal of Belgian troops. This forthright move for peace in the Congo was not welcomed by Tshombe, who refused

Civil War in the Congo

to allow entry of United Nations forces into Katanga. The Belgian government and a number of Western countries tended to support Katanga's stand for independence, as did Western businessmen who had commercial interests in Katanga. It was Hammarskjöld's diplomacy during a personal visit to Tshombe in Katanga, a visit by no means danger-free, that persuaded Tshombe to allow United Nations troops into his province.

This attempted conciliation with Katanga was denounced by Lumumba, who pressed for more vigorous military action by the United Nations against the rebel province. The problem was heightened by Soviet military support for Lumumba, and Soviet condemnation of the United Nations, which they saw as being too heavily influenced by Western opinion. In September 1960, a military coup, organized by the army chief, Joseph Mobutu, resulted in the confinement of Lumumba to his house in Leopoldville and the creation of a puppet government, consisting mainly of students, dominated by Mobutu. Though Lumumba was now powerless, his supporters rallied in his native province of Orientale, under the leadership of Gizenga.

Thus by the end of 1960, half a year after the creation of a Congo that was united and independent, there existed three governments in the Congo:

1. Mobutu's military government, dominant in the provinces of Leopoldville and Equateur, and supported by the United Nations.
2. Gizenga's Lumumbist government, dominant in the provinces of Orientale and Kivu, with Soviet support.
3. Tshombe's independent government in Katanga, with influence in Kasai province, with some Western support.

In January 1961, Mobutu sent Lumumba to Elisabethville in Katanga province. By sending him to this rebellious province, a virtual death sentence was imposed on him. During the journey to Elisabethville and on arrival there, he and his companions were beaten, and a few hours after their arrival they were shot. The murder of Lumumba

Moise Tshombe greets Secretary-General Dag Hammarskjöld in Katanga province, shortly after the Congo achieved independence. Despite Hammarskjöld's visit, Tshombe continued to pursue policies which troubled the newly-independent Congo.

had certainly rid his opponents of a threat to their power. But many in Africa and elsewhere saw Lumumba as an African national leader martyred at the hands of those acting for imperial interests. The cult of Lumumba still has a lively following in many African countries.

The United Nations' role in the Congo

Renewed initiative from the United Nations came in February 1961, when the Security Council accepted more far-reaching proposals.

The Security Council,
Having considered the situation in the Congo,
Having learnt with deep regret the announcement of the killing of the Congolese leaders, Mr Patrice Lumumba, Mr Maurice Mpolo and Mr Joseph Okito,

Patrice Lumumba bound and humiliated by his captors in January 1961, shortly before he was murdered. Earlier he had been the first Prime Minister of the independent Congo and has subsequently become a cult figure for many Africans in their search for independence.

Deeply concerned at the grave repercussions of these crimes and the danger of widespread civil war and bloodshed in the Congo and the threat to international peace and security:

1. Urges the convening of the parliament and the taking of necessary protective measures in that connection.

2. Urges that Congolese armed units and personnel should be reorganized and brought under discipline and control, and arrangements be made on impartial and equitable bases to that end and with a view to the elimination of any possibility of interference by such units and personnel in the political life of the Congo.

3. Calls upon all states to extend their full cooperation and assistance and take such measures as may be necessary on their part, for the implementation of this resolution.

Until this time the United Nations role in the Congo had been that of a peacekeeping mission. The resolution of February 1961, and particularly its third clause, showed a determination to take positive military action in the event of further civil war.

Early in 1961, President Kasavubu was able to reassert his authority and to dismiss Mobutu. Parliament again met in the summer of 1961 in Leopoldville city, thus fulfilling the first requirement of the resolution. In August 1961, a more moderate government was formed under Adoula, a trade union leader who had played comparatively little part in the earlier government. Between them, Kasavubu and Adoula were able to come to an understanding with Gizenga's government in Orientale. But in spite of the new government's attempts, little progress was made in ending Katanga's opposition, or in removing foreign mercenaries whom Tshombe had attracted to his cause, and who increasingly appeared to dominate his régime.

In August 1961, after the clear failure of attempts at conciliation, Adoula made a formal request to Tshombe for the expulsion of the mercenaries in Katanga, and to the United Nations for enforced expulsion should Tshombe still refuse. United Nations troops had been stationed in Katanga since Hammarskjöld's initiative of the previous autumn, and they now began the operation of disarming mercenaries in the province and taking over the main centres of the administration. This forceful action brought bitter condemnation from Western countries such as Belgium, France and Britain, and from the neighbouring Western-dominated Central African Federation under Roy Welensky (considered in the following chapter). Hammarskjöld attempted a further move of conciliation and flew to see Tshombe during September 1961 but his aircraft, under mysterious circumstances, crashed as it was about to land in Katanga, and Hammarskjöld was killed.

Warfare continued in the area of Katanga until an armistice was agreed in December 1961, and Katanga agreed, on paper, to end its secession.

In practice Tshombe showed himself slow in fulfilling the agreement, aware that his opponent Adoula had no very strong political backing and that the United Nations forces were unlikely to be maintained in the country indefinitely. Even after a new compromise agreement had been worked out in August 1962 by the new Secretary-General, U Thant, under which Katanga was generously allowed to retain half the mining revenues of the province, Tshombe showed little readiness to cooperate. Meanwhile he built up more mercenary forces and developed close links with Welensky's Central African Federation. Finally, in December 1962, United Nations forces again took action against Katanga, on this occasion convincingly breaking the secession threat. Tshombe fled to Europe, but continued to be a focus of political interest.

The Adoula government, though by no means strong, now had less opposition within the Congo, and was assisted by American financial aid. This was the first significant example of real American interest in African affairs, encouraged largely by their desire to counteract Soviet influence. The United Nations forces maintained a presence in the country until June 1964, when the situation appeared calm enough to allow them to withdraw. Although their presence had been controversial and, in the view of some, unnecessarily lengthy, it is true to say that it was ultimately successful: involvement by outside forces had been eradicated and the unity of the Congo had been maintained.

The rule of Mobutu

An immediate result of the withdrawal of the United Nations forces was the return of Tshombe from Europe and his appointment as Prime Minister of the Congo. Many of his earlier policies in Katanga were now put into effect throughout the whole of the country and mercenaries, many of them from South Africa, were recruited. The country under Tshombe benefited by increased American financial aid and by useful financial agreements with Belgium: with both these Western powers Tshombe maintained close and good relations. Tshombe attempted to build up a firmer political base for his rule but he lost the autumn elections in 1965, and fell from power.

General Mobutu, for the second time, intervened in the politics of the Congo and on this occasion more decisively. In November 1965 he staged a bloodless coup and took over the position of President, with power to rule by decree. His term of office was originally to be for five years, but he remained in power throughout the rest of the 1960s and 1970s.

Mobutu declared that his intention was to 'abolish politics' in the Congo. His régime developed along dictatorial lines in which the army played a vital part, as in 1966 when Tshombe's original followers in Katanga were crushed outright. Mobutu also showed himself more positively nationalistic than his predecessors. A sign of this was his replacement of the old colonial names in the country with original African names. Thus Leopoldville became Kinshasa; Stanleyville became Kisangani; Elisabethville became Lubumbashi; the name of the country was changed to Zaïre. Economic resources also came more fully under the control of the Zaïre government; *Union Minière* and other foreign companies were nationalized. In other respects Mobutu was prepared to cooperate with foreign powers, as in the development of railway communications within Zaïre by Japanese engineers.

The country's mineral products kept the economy comparatively buoyant until 1974, when the world price for copper declined. The overthrow of Portuguese control in Angola towards the end of 1975, considered in the following section, resulted in the closure of the vital rail link between the copper-producing areas in the south and the Atlantic Ocean. This had a serious effect on Zaïre's exports. In the spring of 1977 matters worsened when forces from Angola invaded the province of Shaba, as Katanga province had been renamed, and combined with forces of opposition to Mobutu's rule. But in spite of this invasion and the country's economic problems, Mobutu continued in power.

Independence in Portuguese Africa

The Portuguese were among the first Europeans to settle in Africa and they have been the last to leave. Their most important possessions within Africa were Portuguese Guinea, Angola and Mozambique. The reason for the long delay in granting independence lies in the political situation within Portugal itself. As Portugal was a small, poor country, it was felt that she could not afford to lose her colonies, which supported a large Portuguese settler population. Until his retirement, on the grounds of ill-health, in September 1968, Portugal had been governed by the dictator Salazar. Under his régime there had been no prospect of independence being granted to the Portuguese colonies. This policy was supported vigorously by the Portuguese in Africa. His successor, Caetano, ruled in a slightly more relaxed style and in the early 1970s he promised limited independence to the colonies. At the same time, in spite of heavy financial cost, the government continued to send troops to fight against the increasing activities of the guerrilla forces in their African colonies.

Nationalist movements had existed in the Portuguese colonies since the 1950s. The success of similar movements elsewhere in Africa and the apparent weakening of the government of Portugal had brought them increasing support by the early 1970s. In Mozambique there was only one nationalist movement: the Front for the Liberation of Mozambique (FRELIMO). But in Angola there were three nationalist movements: the National Front for the Liberation of Angola (FNLA) had the support of many other African states and was initially the most powerful; the Popular Movement for the Liberation of Angola (MPLA) had the support of the Soviet Union; the Union for the Total Independence of Angola (UNITA) was initially less significant than the other two.

In the early months of 1974 the increasing cost of the fighting in Portugal coupled with the current increases in world oil prices contributed to an economic decline inside Portugal. Meanwhile, a number of leading army officials, led by General Spinola, had stated that continued fighting in Africa was pointless, as the war against the guerrillas would never be won. It was the army that took the lead in Portugal during these increasingly difficult times and in April 1974 an army coup established military rule under Spinola. He at once set about dismantling what remained of the Salazar system in Portugal, and the abandonment of the Portuguese possessions in Africa.

In Mozambique, power was handed to FRELIMO whose leader, Samora Machel, became President when independence was declared in June 1975. The transfer of power was eased by the absence of any other nationalist movements within the country. Most of the Portuguese residents decided to leave the country. As they had controlled the country's services and administration and had provided most of the country's skilled manpower, their absence had serious effects throughout Mozambique, comparable to those experienced in the Congo after the departure of the Belgians. President Machel looked to Tanzania as an example of the kind of Socialist society which he hoped to develop in his own country.

The situation which the Portuguese left behind in Angola was far more troubled. Several African leaders and the OAU attempted to bring better unity among the nationalist movements, but to no effect. The nationalist forces were divided by region and by the different tribes within Angola: they were also divided by ideology. Thus, certain areas were almost entirely committed to one particular movement: the northern areas supported FNLA, the central areas supported MPLA and the southern areas supported UNITA. As the Portuguese left, a civil war developed in which foreign powers actively intervened. Cuba and the Soviet Union supplied men and arms to support the MPLA forces under the command of Neto. In the early stages of the war FNLA had secured some American aid. There was also some limited South African involvement on behalf of UNITA. Increasingly the MPLA became the dominant force and early in 1976 President Neto's government became widely accepted as the government of Angola, in spite of the fact that fighting was still continuing in parts of the country, with the movements opposed to MPLA aided by mercenary forces.

The sporadic warfare and the country's shattered economy were the major problems confronting Neto's government. He was assured of the aid of the Soviet Union and the continued presence of Cuban troops and technicians. The value to Neto's government of the Cuban troops was illustrated in May 1977 when they suppressed an attempted coup against Neto by fellow MPLA members, as well as by the other nationalist movements. As was only to be expected, the MPLA government pursued full Socialist policies, similar to those in Mozambique and Tanzania. Like those countries also, Angola was in the forefront of opposition to the white governments of South Africa and Rhodesia.

Questions

82. Study the document on pages 319–20, issued by the United Nations in February 1961, and then answer questions (a) to (d) which follow.
    (a) In the case of the first politician named in the fifth and sixth lines,
        (i) name the position held by him at the time of the independence of the Congo,
        (ii) explain the circumstances in 1960 that led to his appointment to that position, and
        (iii) explain the circumstances later in 1960 and early in 1961 that led to his death.
        (1+2+2)
    (b) What reasons are suggested by lines 7 to 11 for the continued involvement of the United Nations in the affairs of the Congo? What other reasons might there have been for such intervention?
        (4)
    (c) Show how *each* of the three resolutions adopted by the United Nations had been fulfilled by the time of the withdrawal of their forces in June 1964.
        (6)
    (d) Give an account of the further political developments in the area of the Congo between 1964 and the present day.
        (5)

83. In what respects was Belgian control of the Congo in the years between 1908 and 1960 (a) advantageous to the Africans in the Congo and (b) disadvantageous to them? Outline the events that led to the granting of independence. Why were the five years after independence so troubled for the Congolese?

84. Why did Portugal retain control of its colonies for so much longer than other European powers? Trace the events in these former colonies in the mid-1970s and explain why the achievement of independence by them was of importance for southern Africa generally.

29
Southern Africa

The Union of South Africa

The Dutch, who first settled on the southern shores of Africa, and who were referred to at that time as the *Boers*, and later as the *Afrikaners*, arrived there in the seventeenth century: later the British joined them, and were able to assert their authority over the Afrikaners. The early relations between the two settler groups were so unsatisfactory that they still influence the difficulties in Afrikaner-British relations to the present day. The Boer War (1899–1902) was the most vivid of a number of examples of the difficult relations that existed in South Africa. The Afrikaners became embittered not only by their loss of the war but also by their enemy's use of concentration camps, which the British troops found to be the most effective way of eliminating the Boer opposition in South Africa. Postwar negotiations were brought to a conclusion in 1910 when the Union of South Africa was established, bringing together uneasily the two Boer republics of the Orange Free State and the Transvaal and the two British republics of Cape Colony and Natal. South Africa was granted dominion status by Britain and so the new government at Cape Town possessed a considerable degree of independence. An example of the extent of South Africa's independence is shown by the granting of German South-west Africa, today known as Namibia, to the Union of South Africa in 1919 as a mandated territory.

During the decades after the Boer War the conditions of the Afrikaner farmers were poor. Resentment developed against the British-dominated government at Cape Town, which appeared to disregard their plight and treat them as an inferior and defeated section of South African society. Poverty compelled many Afrikaner farmers to move to the towns, where economic prospects were somewhat brighter. But their circumstances in the towns were in practice little better than they had been in the countryside. Often they were compelled to work as *poor whites* for British employers. This situation was felt to be a humiliation for the Afrikaners, who were forced to work with blacks to whom they considered themselves racially superior. Their culture, their traditions and their Afrikaans language were all discouraged by the British, who wished to force their own language and customs on the Afrikaners. The dominant political party after the creation of the union was the South Africa party. It was not entirely British-controlled. The two Prime Ministers that it produced, Botha (1910–19) and Smuts (1919–24) were both men of Afrikaner origin. But their policies were directed towards the development of South Africa as a leading and successful member of the British Commonwealth. Many Afrikaners therefore felt dissatisfied with the South Africa party, which appeared not to be advancing real Afrikaner interests, the ultimate aim of which was the creation of South Africa as an independent republic, completely separated from the Commonwealth. Afrikaner support was therefore given to the Nationalist party under the leadership of Herzog, in whom much Afrikaner hope was placed when he became Prime Minister in 1924. Herzog proved a disappointment to many of his followers. In power, the Nationalist party became more fully aware of the advantages, particularly regarding trade, of Commonwealth membership, and the idea of leaving the Commonwealth was dropped. Herzog's policies seemed therefore to be very similar in practice to those of Smuts, a fact that was given public acknowledgement in 1935 when their parties joined together to form the United party.

For many Afrikaners, this action of Herzog was a betrayal. Their interests and the ideal of independence appeared to have been forgotten by a man in whom much hope had been placed. The Afrikaners needed to look elsewhere for an organization that would represent their interests more effectively. In 1932 a secret society came into existence, the *Afrikaner Brotherhood* which aimed eventually at achieving control of the government of South Africa. By establishing banks exclusively for Afrikaners, the Brotherhood did much to encourage the economic progress of their people. It was also responsible for founding a new political party, the Afrikaner Nationalist party, to take the place of Herzog's National party with which many Afrikaners were disillusioned. Throughout the 1930s, these two organizations gave much encouragement to the development of the Afrikaner way of life. When, with Smuts again as Prime Minister, South Africa entered the Second World War on the Allied side, the Afrikaner opposition was strong. Many of them preferred neutrality. Some of them, who would have preferred entry on the Axis side, became involved in vicious sabotage attacks on South Africa's troops. Those with Nazi sympathies considered that a defeat of Britain in the war would lead to the independence of South Africa.

The blacks of South Africa

Afrikaner and British interests dominated the political situation in South Africa until the time of the Second World War. But the Afrikaners and the British formed less than a quarter of the population of South Africa. The rest of the population was considered inferior. The black inhabitants, consisting of a number of different peoples, were the most numerous group in South Africa. The Indians were descended from those who had travelled to South Africa in search of work. The term *coloured* was applied to those who were of mixed racial parentage. Though conditions varied from area to area, the general standard of living among the blacks, and especially among the Africans, was poor.

Especially unsatisfactory were the conditions of those housed in shanty towns outside the large cities.

In the first half of the twentieth century European attitudes of superiority over the blacks in South Africa were not particularly different to the attitudes adopted by Europeans towards native people in other parts of the African continent. But differences did already exist between British and Afrikaner attitudes. The 1926 Statute of Westminster, putting forward independence as the ultimate goal for the British overseas possessions, encouraged the British to advance the interests of those whom they governed, and to allow them at least some limited representation. As Prime Minister, Smuts made modest progress in this direction. Wartime circumstances led him to encourage black recruitment in the armed forces. These few concessions did little to alter the poverty and restrictions on blacks in South Africa. The Afrikaners, however, adopted an even sterner approach towards blacks. Their idea of white racial superiority was sustained both by a close awareness of their historic struggle to establish themselves in South Africa and by the teachings of the Dutch Reformed church, of which most Afrikaners were loyal members. In Afrikaner-controlled areas of South Africa, the right of blacks to vote in local elections was totally denied and in 1936, under Herzog, all rights of blacks to vote were removed throughout the country.

The Nationalist party and apartheid

The general election of May 1948 was crucial for South Africa's history. The widely respected Smuts was defeated and the Afrikaner Nationalist party came to power. Malan, under whose skilful direction the party had developed so successfully during the previous decade, now became Prime Minister. The Afrikaners in South Africa had at last fully triumphed over the British. The Nationalist party did not intend to lose the power which it had secured, neither to an opposition party nor to any form of majority rule which would include blacks. Against these internal dangers and regardless of the increasing hostility of world opinion, the Nationalist party adopted and held firmly to the policy of *apartheid*, which was introduced in order to separate blacks and whites in every sphere of life, always maintaining white dominance over blacks.

This Afrikaner policy has been put into effect by successive Nationalist Prime Ministers: Malan (1948–54), Strijdom (1954–58), Verwoerd (1958–66), Vorster (1966–78) and Botha (from 1978). All believed that demands from blacks would be made with increasing force if suppression was not undertaken. Already, India had achieved independence from Britain and in parts of Africa, including South Africa, demands from Africans for the right of eventual independence were being made. To strengthen its control of South Africa the new government embarked upon the policy, built to a considerable extent upon previous practice in South Africa initiated by the British, of separating blacks and whites. According to Prime Minister Verwoerd, this was not a policy of discrimination but a 'policy of good neighbourliness'. This view of apartheid is still held by the South African government, which suggests that they have made provision for development of blacks which is separate but not inferior to that of whites. The eventual aim of apartheid was the creation of different zones in South Africa for whites and blacks, an aim which was substantially fulfilled by the late 1970s.

The policy was implemented by Malan from the start of his Prime Ministership and its early development was continued throughout the 1950s. The most obvious feature was racial separation in all public places, the provision of separate education and separate medical facilities, the promotion of whites over blacks in the army, the civil service and industry. The policy was also carried into the personal lives of individuals by the prohibition of marriage.between black and white people. This prohibition further involved the strict classification of people into racial categories, a process which caused much distress, particularly among the coloured people. Stricter control was exercized

on the movement of black people by insisting that all blacks in South Africa should carry an identity pass. To enforce these regulations and to rout out opposition to them, the South African police were supported by the Suppression of Communism Act of 1950, which allowed them to interpret as 'Communism' virtually any form of opposition to apartheid.

This notice—in English, Afrikaans and a local dialect—clearly reserves an attractive part of South Africa's seaside for white people. In spite of hostile opinions from the outside world and from within South Africa, the Nationalist government has kept firmly to its racialist policy of apartheid.

At the time Malan came to power, black voting rights were already restricted and in some parts which had been dominated by the Afrikaners, they did not exist at all. The Nationalist government intended to abolish black voting rights completely. Their attempts to do this in the early 1950s were delayed by the opposition of the country's Supreme Court, though when Strijdom became Prime Minister he overcame this opposition by nominating known Nationalist supporters to the Upper House of the South African parliament, which was then able to over-rule the Court's opposition.

The apartheid policies of the 1950s certainly achieved their object of separating the races and also ensured that blacks were kept in an inferior position. At the end of this period, Verwoerd, while certainly intending to continue apartheid, aimed at giving the policy a more favourable image by the creation of *homelands* or *Bantustans* for black people. The Bantu self-government Act of 1959 began this phase of apartheid. The basic idea was that an increasing number of areas should be placed under the direct administration of the blacks, who would be granted their 'independence' in these areas, and who would in theory have their own elected black governments. Economically and politically, however, these homelands are still controlled by South Africa. The first homeland to be established was Transkei. Amongst others which have subsequently been established a particularly large and important one has been Bophuthatswana, consisting of many unconnected pieces of land, with no geographical unity at all. Though the idea of homelands had the appearance of a generous gesture, it was little more than a further consolidation of apartheid.

The blacks are thus further separated from the whites, while the overcrowded homelands and the presence of the country's major economic resources in the white areas maintain the low standard of living for blacks, most of whom live on, or below, the poverty line. Even more black workers are forced to leave their families and seek work in other areas because of the establishment of the homelands, which have poor job prospects for their inhabitants.

Internal opposition to apartheid

By the late 1970s, after more than 30 years of apartheid, the Nationalist government saw no reason to feel that its basic policy for South Africa was mistaken. The policy appeared to have the support of the majority of the country's white inhabitants, who continued to vote for the Nationalist party. Successful economic policies, based upon the country's valuable natural resources and cheap black labour, contributed to this massive support. The relative stability of the country when contrasted with some African republics to the north was another significant factor in this continuing support of the Nationalist government.

The main internal opposition to apartheid came, expectedly, from those who suffered most from it. But the tough approach of the South African police towards open opposition intimidated many from supporting its movement. In the mid-1950s, in imitation of Gandhi in India, a Congress movement was established in South Africa, demanding an end to apartheid and the achievement of political equality for all races in South Africa. Police action effectively suppressed the movement, though it managed to continue for some years. Further opposition was sporadic and unorganized, and was suppressed. Two instances illustrate this particularly. In March 1960 at Sharpeville, in the course of an anti-apartheid demonstration, the police opened fire and killed about 70 blacks. Further disorder was stimulated by this atrocity, but the only solid result was a considerable strengthening of police powers. No disorders took place again on such a large scale until the summer of 1976, when young people in the black township of Soweto, on the outskirts of Johannesburg, staged a series of demonstrations which were vigorously suppressed. Opposition spread to a number of other black townships throughout South Africa and, significantly, coloureds and Asians also took part in these demonstrations. Police activity was at all times expectedly severe, and it is estimated that some 500 youths and children were killed in South Africa during the 1976 demonstrations. Hundreds were arrested and many young people were imprisoned, interrogated and tortured. The death of a popular black leader, Steve Biko, while held in police captivity during the following year, further inflamed opposition and sparked off further riots. But in the face of this opposition the government made only minimal concessions and in 1978, under the new Prime Minister, P. W. Botha, an even more rigid pursuit of existing policies seemed likely.

South Africa and the world

The known opposition of the Nationalist party to the Commonwealth made it more than likely that South Africa would leave it at some time after the 1948 election. Throughout the 1950s relations were uneasy. Early in 1960 the British Prime Minister, Macmillan, undertook a lengthy, detailed tour of Britain's African possessions. His tour ended in South Africa where he delivered a historic speech in which by his reference to the *Wind of Change* in the African continent he advocated independence for Britain's colonies in Africa:

> In the twentieth century, and especially since the end of the war, the processes which gave birth to the nation-states of Europe have been repeated all over the world. We have seen the awakening of national consciousness in peoples who have lived for centuries in dependence on some other power.
>
> Fifteen years ago this movement spread through Asia. Many countries there of different races and civilizations pressed their claims for an independent national life. Today the same thing is happening in Africa. The most striking of all the impressions I have formed since I left London a month ago is of the strength of this African national consciousness. In different places it may take different forms, but it is happening everywhere.
>
> The wind of change is blowing through the continent.

The *Wind of Change* speech, delivered in South Africa, was not without particular significance for South Africa itself. Prime Minister Verwoerd expressed his concern shortly afterwards in a speech to the South African parliament.

> It appears to me that the White Nations are prepared to abandon the Whites in Africa. The White man of Africa is not going to be told that, because he is outnumbered by the Black people, he must allow his rights to be swallowed up and be prepared to lose his say. We do not accept that the White inhabitants must be satisfied as a minority in a multi-racial country to compete with the Black masses on an equal basis, which in the long run can only mean a Black government.

Towards the end of 1960, by a small majority, the white people of South Africa voted in a referendum for their country to become a republic. South Africa still wished to maintain membership of the Commonwealth, but when strong opposition to apartheid was raised by other Commonwealth countries at a meeting of Commonwealth heads of government in the spring of 1961, Verwoerd decided that the best course was to withdraw from the Commonwealth.

South Africa's relations with the United Nations were marred by continuing friction which has focused particularly on the problems of the possession of Namibia and the practice of apartheid. Namibia had been placed under South African administration as one of the mandated territories of the 1919 peace settlement. After the Second World War it was usual for these mandated territories, where they had not yet achieved independence, to remain directly administered by the former mandatory power, but also to be under the overall control of the United Nations Trusteeship Council, which replaced the League of Nations Mandates Commission. South Africa refused to accept that the Trusteeship Council had any authority in Namibia, which they continued to control virtually as a part of South Africa itself. The people of Namibia therefore have had a double grievance: their country is controlled by a foreign power, while other former African mandates have achieved independence. Within their country apartheid is fully practised, while in other former mandated territories a multi-racial society has been developed. Within Namibia, an opposition group, the South-west Africa People's Organization (SWAPO), encouraged guerrilla resistance to South Africa's presence, becoming particularly active in the 1970s. Further factors led South Africa to make concessions to the people of Namibia: in 1971 the International Court reversed its previous decision and declared South Africa's presence in Namibia illegal and in 1975 when neighbouring Angola, to the north, achieved independence from Portugal, it was clear that the SWAPO rebels were likely to achieve increased support. South Africa's own proposals for independence for Namibia were not considered by SWAPO or the United Nations to make satisfactory provision for full independence. In the late 1970s, while South Africa resisted United Nations proposals and maintained its troops in the country, the SWAPO guerrilla forces became increasingly active.

The United Nations has shown continued opposition to apartheid. Very few countries have felt able to support South Africa on this issue, though until their departure from Africa in 1975, the Portuguese government had an outlook similar to that of South Africa. In the 1960s, the Menzies government in Australia, with perhaps a nostalgic eye to the old Commonwealth, wondered whether South Africa was standing out against too rapid a movement towards a multi-racial society elsewhere in Africa. As independent African states took their place in increasing numbers in the United Nations during the 1960s and 70s, so condemnation of apartheid became more pronounced. In 1962, after a number of previous condemnations of apartheid, the General Assembly of the United Nations voted in favour of imposing economic sanctions on South Africa. Throughout the 1960s, amongst those elsewhere who felt keenly on the issue of apartheid there have been boycotts of South African goods and of South African teams in international sport. But economic sanctions have never been uniformly and effectively applied. In any case, South Africa is a land of immense natural resources and therefore is less likely to be hampered by sanctions than

countries less well provided for. Some powerful businesses, more concerned with the achievement of profits than the abandonment of apartheid, have sought means to evade sanctions.

A particularly controversial matter has been the supply of arms to South Africa, for instance by the British government in the early 1970s. Opponents of apartheid suggested that these arms might well be used against blacks if an uprising occurred. But Western governments have taken a world view of these arms supplies. The whole of Africa and of the neighbouring Indian Ocean is an area where the Soviet Union attempts to assert its influence; the South African government and the Western governments are united in wishing to prevent the possibility of Soviet expansion in this part of the world, and the arms supplies are intended to help achieve this.

Essentially it is for the continent of Africa that South Africa's policies are most dangerous. South Africa has not only provoked the hostility of the countries of the British Commonwealth and of the United Nations but also of the Organization of African Unity. The maintenance of a united opposition among OAU countries has, however, not been easy and by the 1970s was showing signs of strain. This was due partly to the subtle policy of South Africa in building up commercial relations with new African states, most of whom were far less wealthy than South Africa. If these countries were to apply economic sanctions against South Africa, in retaliation South Africa could sever trading links with them, thereby doing much harm to their developing economies. But with neighbouring Rhodesia a different, closer and, for Africa, a potentially more dangerous relationship developed during the 1960s and the 1970s.

Northern and Southern Rhodesia

The lands just north of South Africa, which in the early part of the century were known as Northern Rhodesia and Southern Rhodesia, were amongst the last to be colonized by European powers. Their colonization in the 1890s was due to Cecil Rhodes, an ambitious, determined and devoted imperialist, whose work in the establishment of Northern and Southern Rhodesia typified Britain's pride in the Empire at its peak. The capital, Salisbury, was named after the British Prime Minister of the day. The new area was grandly seen as a part of the continuous British presence from 'the Cape to Cairo'. The policy for the exploitation of this area was unique. Rhodesia's pioneering work was done under the auspices of a private company, the British South African Company, to which the British government had granted a charter empowering the company to develop the area. Though the company was controlled from London, most of the white immigrants who assisted Rhodes in establishing the economy of the country were in fact drawn from the British

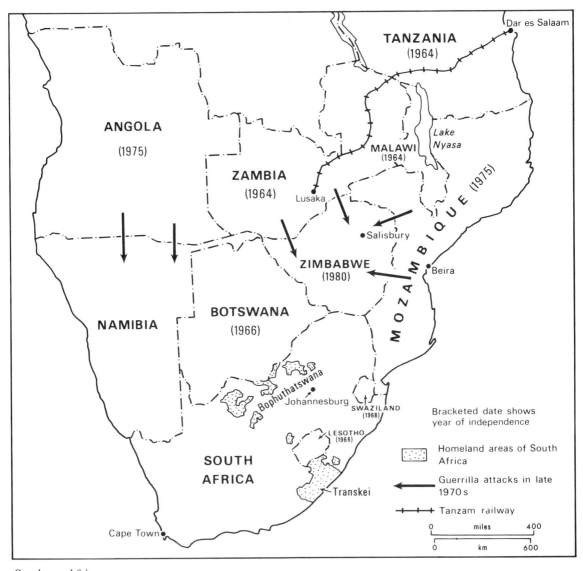

Southern Africa

in South Africa. All these immigrants felt in this pioneering work a strong sense of pride, still held among their descendants later in the century.

The company's charter expired in 1923. Northern Rhodesia, with a smaller white population than Southern Rhodesia, was then granted the status of a British colony. As Southern Rhodesia's links with South Africa were so strong, it was expected that the white settlers would prefer to become a part of South Africa. It may have been the concern of these settlers at the developing Afrikaner influence in South Africa which caused them to reject the proposed union with South Africa in a referendum. Southern Rhodesia therefore also became a British colony in 1923.

For a British African colony in the 1920s, Southern Rhodesia had a comparatively high white population, equalled in this respect only by Kenya. The settlers were not only fired with a sense of pride in their country but also a determination to continue to pursue Rhodesian development without unnecessary outside interference. In 1923 they won themselves an important victory in securing a form of constitution for Southern Rhodesia by which a government elected by the settlers was to have major control over the colony's development. The status of Southern Rhodesia was almost, but not quite, that of a dominion country. Assisted by this constitution, the next few decades saw a continuing consolidation of white power in Rhodesia. Even though the land's economic potential did not entirely live up to earlier expectations, agriculture, particularly tobacco cultivation, was successfully developed. In the 1920s, 1930s and 1940s, when issues such as a multiracial society and majority rule were scarcely even mentioned, the white inhabitants of Southern Rhodesia were loyal members of the British Empire. These were happy, stable and untroubled years for white Rhodesians, interrupted only to a limited extent by the Second World War, in which Southern Rhodesians demonstrated their loyalty to the Empire by fighting on the Allied side.

The Cèntral African Federation

By the early 1950s, Churchill's government in Britain decided that the time had come for them to take some early, limited steps towards granting independence to African colonies. The recent achievement of independence for the Indian sub-continent was proof that the British did not intend to follow the French example, in Indochina and Algeria, of fighting to the bitter end to maintain control of their colonies. The early plans of the British government for African colonies were based on the idea of *partnership* between blacks and whites. For Central Africa, as for parts of East Africa and the West Indies, their practical proposal was for *federation*. The three colonies of Northern Rhodesia, Southern Rhodesia and Nyasaland were to be grouped together in the *Central African Federation*. Each colony, so it was argued, had much to contribute: Nyasaland had a large black population as a workforce, Northern Rhodesia had the valuable mineral resources of its copperbelt and Southern Rhodesia had a well-established and stable white government. The idea of federation was pressed strongly by the British Colonial Secretary, Oliver Lyttleton, a businessman who saw federation as a tidy and profitable basis for Central African development. The Prime Minister of Southern Rhodesia, Godfrey Huggins, also strongly supported the idea, as it provided a means by which the government of Southern Rhodesia could derive benefit from the economic potential of the two other colonies and at the same time extend its authority over the whole of the proposed federation. Neither Lyttleton nor Huggins were particularly concerned about the opinion of the blacks, who were strongly opposed to the idea, as this' experiment in *partnership* seemed to them designed to maintain the blacks as a distinctly inferior partner. The blacks of Northern Rhodesia and Nyasaland feared that the discriminatory policies of Southern Rhodesia towards blacks would trickle northward, and that they would be allied more closely with South Africa.

Ignoring the opposition of the blacks of

Central Africa and of the Labour party in Britain, Churchill's Conservative government established the Central African Federation in 1953. Its constitution was elaborate. Each of the three territories of the Federation was to have its own government with control of the territory's internal administration; in the case of Northern Rhodesia and Nyasaland, Britain retained considerable control, but in the case of Southern Rhodesia the white inhabitants held most power. Over these territorial governments was set the federal government, based on the Southern Rhodesian capital of Salisbury and representing predominantly the interests of the whites in Southern Rhodesia. All white inhabitants had the right to vote, but amongst blacks, voting rights were restricted on a basis of education and wealth, so that few blacks were in practice able to vote for the Federation's government. The entire complex structure came under the overall control of the British government at Westminster.

Huggins became the first Prime Minister of the Federation, succeeded later by Welensky of Northern Rhodesia. Both men worked to ensure the success of the Federation and the maintenance of white supremacy within it. Federation brought some of the promised advantages to the economy of the area, one of its greatest achievements being the construction of the Kariba dam on the Zambezi river. The South African policy of apartheid was not applied in name but, as the blacks had suspected, they were nevertheless separated from the whites as effectively as they could be and were given only very limited opportunities to advance their position. The white population, many of whom had in fact emigrated to Southern Rhodesia quite recently during the years since the ending of the Second World War, were anxious to preserve the high standards of living they had enjoyed, and supported government policy to prevent African advance. As no real concessions were made to blacks, their opposition became an increasingly serious factor throughout the Federation.

Three opposition leaders emerged in the 1950s: Kenneth Kaunda in Northern Rhodesia, Hastings Banda in Nyasaland and Joshua Nkomo in Southern Rhodesia. The most significant of these was Kaunda, whose call for universal suffrage was regarded by the federal government as wholly irresponsible. Opposition mounted throughout the Federation. In 1959 disturbances in Nyasaland led to a declaration of a state of emergency and to the imprisonment of African leaders. The British government was by now concerned at the way in which the Federation was developing. After the disturbances, a British commission, led by Patrick Devlin, a British High Court judge, enquired into the administration of Nyasaland, and described the territory's administration as that of a 'police state'. By implication the Federal government was also strongly criticized. Shortly after the Devlin commission, came Macmillan's *Wind of Change* speech.

The British government now came to the conclusion that the Federation must be disbanded and this occurred at the end of 1963. Encouragement was given to nationalist movements in Northern Rhodesia and Nyasaland, where British control was more direct than in Southern Rhodesia. In 1964 both territories became independent, on the basis of universal suffrage: Kaunda became Prime Minister of Northern Rhodesia, which changed its name to Zambia, while Banda became Prime Minister of Nyasaland, which changed its name to Malawi.

Welensky's government in Salisbury was furious at what it considered to be betrayal of the Federation by Britain. Southern Rhodesia was now alone, and its white inhabitants were strongly opposed to abandoning their position by agreeing to the majority rule which had become the basis of independence in the two other territories. Those whites who had earlier been suspicious of the idea of Federation now seemed to have been proved correct in their judgment. In the early 1960s the Rhodesia Front party was formed. Its aim was to defend white interests, and in December 1962 it secured a majority in the elections. The new government at once left the Federation and attempted to secure independence from Britain on its own terms. In the middle of 1963,

Ian Smith became Prime Minister. Smith's personality was to dominate Rhodesian affairs throughout the 1960s and the 1970s. In the eyes of his supporters, his greatest quality was his obstinate determination to protect Rhodesia's rights as he and his followers saw them.

Rhodesia under the Smith regime

In negotiating with the Conservative government of Douglas-Home and the Labour government of Wilson in 1964–65, Smith doggedly pressed for independence without majority rule in what was now simply called *Rhodesia*. But the negotiations, partly in Salisbury and partly in London, became a deadlock. Britain firmly refused to allow Rhodesian independence unless majority rule was agreed by Smith's government. In November 1965, when no further progress seemed possible, the government of Smith made a *Unilateral* (one-sided) *Declaration of Independence* (UDI), thereby establishing itself as the sole government of Rhodesia, no longer responsible to the British and no longer concerned with what they considered to be the irrelevant issue of majority rule. Smith's action over UDI was a rebellion against Britain. It was open to the British government to take steps against it. Swift military action by Britain may possibly have undermined the rebellion and allowed for a more representative government in Rhodesia. But there was risk that such a campaign would become protracted and that many lives would be lost. Public opinion in Britain was also opposed to such a move against the white Rhodesians. The British government decided against military action and adopted economic sanctions against Rhodesia in an attempt to bring down the Smith régime. In the event, it was not until almost 11 years later, in September 1976, that Smith announced his government's acceptance of the principles of majority rule and the end of his régime. Even that announcement was followed, in the late 1970s, by considerable uncertainty on the country's future.

Though independent African states

"You're getting nowhere, man—let us try."

Wilson's use of economic sanctions to defuse the Rhodesian situation in the mid-1960s failed to produce results. The onlooker's implement for doing the same job suggests a more direct approach to one of Africa's most dangerous problems in the 1960s and the 1970s.

reacted with anger to UDI, there were few practical steps that they were able to take. Rhodesia was fortunate that those countries which did support her stand happened to be among Rhodesia's neighbours: Portuguese Angola, Portuguese Mozambique and the Republic of South Africa. This provided confidence for the régime in its continued pursuit of policies aimed at maintaining white supremacy, and it also provided some protection from the economic sanctions imposed by hostile nations, as goods could be imported through these countries.

Within Rhodesia, legislation enhancing white supremacy received substantial support from the white population. The 1969 Land Tenure Act divided the country firmly into white and black areas, and was decidedly unfavourable for blacks who received the

333

poorest land. In 1970, after the retirement of the last British governor, the country was declared a republic. Throughout, the régime applied firm action against any internal opposition. Censorship was imposed, imprisonment without trial was permitted and opponents to the régime could be placed under arrest. Rhodesia was now very like South Africa. Opposition groups, using the African name *Zimbabwe* in reference to their country, emerged: the Zimbabwe African People's Union (ZAPU) under the leadership of Nkomo and the Zimbabwe African National Union (ZANU) under the leadership of Sithole. By the 1970s, guerrilla activity became a feature of life in Rhodesia and was encouraged by the Organization of African Unity, who held that only in this way could the régime be brought down. Nkomo's ZAPU movement became the main guerrilla force within the country.

Guerrilla forces justified their activity on account of the failure of the British attempts to bring down the régime. Britain's first move had been to impose economic sanctions, prohibiting the exporting of goods from Britain and other Commonwealth countries to Rhodesia. But Rhodesia's friendly neighbours continued to provide for most of the country's needs and these early sanctions had little effect. In December 1966, Prime Minister Wilson made the first of two attempts to end UDI by negotiating with Smith on the neutral territory of the ship *Tiger* in the Mediterranean. A compromise formula was agreed by the two men but was rejected by Smith's colleagues back in Rhodesia. Britain then increased the economic pressure by requesting the United Nations to ask all its members to impose economic sanctions on Rhodesia. This action ought to have produced results. But essential goods, such as oil, were still reaching Rhodesia via Portuguese Mozambique or South Africa, and the régime was therefore able to continue in power. In the late 1970s, when the *sanctions busting* during these years became known, accusations were made that British governments at the time had been less than vigilant in preventing the arrival of the supplies that kept the régime in power. Though there may

be some justice in these accusations, the British navy had maintained an extensive blockade of the Mozambique port of Beira throughout these years to prevent oil from reaching Rhodesia.

In October 1968 the second set of Wilson-Smith talks took place on board the ship *Fearless*, again in the Mediterranean, but no solution came from these talks either. In November 1971 the Conservative Foreign Minister, Douglas-Home, visited Rhodesia and worked out a settlement proposal, which was criticized by the Labour party in Britain as not giving sufficient guarantees for majority rule. In 1972 the agreement was rejected in a referendum among the black people of Rhodesia, who were encouraged in this course by the work of a new political party, the African National Congress, under the leadership of Bishop Abel Muzorewa. Sanctions continued to be applied by Britain and the conflict continued as guerrilla activity increased markedly towards the mid-1970s.

Rhodesia in the late 1970s

The achievement of independence in Angola and Mozambique in the mid-1970s significantly affected Rhodesia. Both countries now became bases for increased guerrilla activity in the areas of Rhodesia. Many white Rhodesians felt that the struggle was now lost, and many left the country. In 1976 the United States began to take a closer interest in African affairs, concerned especially to prevent the spread of Communism in Africa. Kissinger, Secretary of State for the United States, engaged himself in discussions on Africa. His most important meetings were with Prime Minister Vorster of South Africa whom he persuaded to abandon support of the Smith régime. In September 1976, Smith, Vorster and Kissinger met in South Africa at Pretoria, where Smith agreed to begin negotiations leading to majority rule. The events in Angola and Mozambique, the increased guerrilla activity, the desertion of many whites from Rhodesia and now the abandonment of their staunchest ally left Smith with no other option. On his return to Rhodesia he made a historic broadcast to his people:

> As you are all aware, I have recently had a series of meetings in Pretoria, with Dr Kissinger and Mr Vorster.
>
> At these meetings the position of Rhodesia in relation to the rest of southern Africa, and indeed to the Western nations, was discussed in great detail. It was made abundantly clear to me, and to my colleagues who accompanied me, that as long as the present circumstances in Rhodesia prevailed we could expect no help or support of any kind from the free world . . .
>
> As soon as the necessary preliminaries have been carried out, sanctions will be lifted and there will be a cessation of terrorism. Dr Kissinger has given me a categorical assurance to this effect and my acceptance of the proposals is conditional upon the implementation of both of these conditions . . .
>
> What I have said this evening will be a cause of deep concern to you all, and understandably so. But we live in a world of rapid change and if we are to survive in such a world we must be prepared to adjust ourselves to change. We have the satisfaction of knowing that, in spite of the odds against us, we Rhodesians of all races have built up a magnificent country where the prospects are second to none in Africa. I hope and believe we shall be able to keep it so.

In the following years progress towards majority rule was still dangerously slow. Together with moderate black leaders such as Muzorewa and Sithole, Smith worked out an *internal settlement* for the new state providing for majority rule and for a black majority within the government. At the beginning of 1979, a majority of whites showed acceptance of this internal settlement. Some outside opinion suggested that the new constitution was insufficiently democratic. An Anglo-American plan provided for a swifter achievement of majority rule and less privileged position for the whites of Rhodesia. The American and British governments were generally critical of the internal settlement. So also were the guerrilla forces which in the late 1970s were united together as the *Patriotic Front*, led by Mugabe and one of the earliest Zimbabwe leaders, Nkomo. The Patriotic Front has absorbed the ZAPU and ZANU organizations and was particularly angered at their proposed exclusion from the new government. In conducting this guerrilla activity, the Popular Front had the support of the OAU and of the so-called *Front Line Presidents* of neighbouring black states.

In spite of this opposition, elections under the internal settlement were held in May 1979 and resulted in Muzorewa's appointment as Prime Minister and Smith's continued membership of the government. Opponents of this internal settlement held that the elections had not been fairly conducted and that white influence in the country was still uncomfortably strong. At the Commonwealth Conference in neighbouring Zambia in August 1979, the British government agreed to open negotiations for a settlement that would be acceptable both to the Patriotic Front and to the Front Line Presidents. Discussions at London in the autumn of 1979 involved all parties to the dispute and resulted at the end of the year in agreement for the temporary restoration of British rule in their former colony. This was to be purely for the purposes of supervising the election of a government for an independent Zimbabwe on the basis of majority rule.

In the early months of 1980 these arrangements were successfully carried out, under the control of a specially appointed British Governor, Lord Soames. As a result, Robert Mugabe was overwhelmingly elected Prime Minister of the new country, which formally received its independence in April. The statesmanlike policies of the new Prime Minister gave ground for hope that the troubles which had plagued this part of Africa for the previous fifteen years were at last over, and that a happier future awaited the new Zimbabwe.

Questions

85. Study the broadcast on this page and then answer questions (a) to (e) which follow.

(a) Give evidence which might be used
  (i) to support Smith's view of Rhodesia in the second part of the fourth paragraph, and
  (ii) to refute this view.
                                    (4)
(b) What development within Rhodesia, referred to in the third paragraph, might have been an added reason for the approach adopted by Smith at the time of this broadcast? Why had this development become .particularly serious during the 1970s?
                                    (3)
(c) What country did *Dr Kissinger* represent? Account for the interest shown by that country in Rhodesian affairs at that time.
                                    (3)
(d) What country did *Mr Vorster* represent? Account for his general agreement with Dr Kissinger on Rhodesian affairs at this time. What had been his country's earlier attitude towards Rhodesia?
                                    (3)
(e) Outline the history of this country since the time of this broadcast.
                                    (7)

86. How do you account for the electoral success of the Nationalists in South Africa in 1948? Show the importance of their policies since then for (a) the people within South Africa and (b) the foreign relations of South Africa.

87. Explain why the Central African Federation was (a) established in 1953 and (b) abandoned in 1963. Trace and explain the history of the former colony of Southern Rhodesia from 1963 to the present day.

30
The United Nations and world peace

The United Nations Organization was the most hopeful institution to come into being as a direct result of the Second World War. In the years since then, in spite of a chequered history, the organization has contributed significantly to international order and to human welfare. It has profited from the example and the mistakes of the League of Nations, and it has also proved itself far more powerful and far more purposeful than its predecessor.

The origins and organization of the United Nations

The term *United Nations* was first applied during the Second World War to those countries which were opposed to the Axis powers. The origin of the idea of a new international organization is found in the agreed principles of Winston Churchill and Franklin Roosevelt in the Atlantic Charter of August 1941. As all who fought against Germany subscribed to the principles of the Atlantic Charter, there was a wide support for the creation of the new organization. Its formation was a matter for discussion at a number of high-level wartime conferences, but practical proposals for its structure were worked out at two conferences in the United States: the Dumbarton Oaks conference in August 1944 and the San Francisco conference of April-June 1945. The *Charter*, which defined the purpose and outlined the organization of the United Nations, was signed by the 50 original members in October 1945.

In its organization, the United Nations bore many close resemblances to the League of Nations. Attempts were made in 1945 to avoid the mistakes made in the League Covenant, and subsequently to adjust the organization in the light of experience, so that it could continue to play a purposeful part in world affairs. Its declaration of equality for all human beings, its decision to locate its headquarters outside Europe in New York and the increasing representation of newly independent countries showed determination by the new body to avoid the European dominance from which the League had never freed itself. This wish to assert the worldwide nature of the new institution was also apparent in the structure of the General Assembly, the Security Council, the Secretariat, the International Court of Justice and the specialized agencies.

The General Assembly consisted of representatives of each member nation, meeting together in the autumn of each year. The assembly has a responsibility for the maintenance of world peace, for the supervision of the work of the specialized agencies and for agreeing the admission of new members of the United Nations. Any important decision must be accepted by a two-thirds majority in the General Assembly.

The Security Council originally consisted of 11 members and was increased to 15 in 1965. Five of these were permanent members: Britain, France, China, the Soviet Union and the United States. The remaining members were elected by the General Assembly for a two-year period. The members of the Security Council are in permanent readiness to take collective action to fulfil their major responsibility: the maintenance of world peace. In doing this, they have power to take action against a country which is judged to be endangering world peace. In fulfilling this responsibility they are able to impose, on behalf of the entire United Nations, both economic sanctions and military sanctions. The former usually involves cutting trade links between member-countries and the offending country; the latter could involve sending United Nations troops, drawn from member-countries, to support a decision of the Security Council.

For any action to be taken by the Security Council there must be complete agreement between all five permanent members, each of whom therefore possesses a *veto* on the actions of the United Nations. The original purpose of the veto was to ensure that importance was attached in the new organization to the views of the great powers. But in the developing situation of the Cold War in the late 1940s it often prevented actions by the United Nations, as the Soviet Union, the only Communist power represented on the Security Council, frequently employed its right of veto. In order to overcome this unforeseen weakness, the *Uniting for Peace Resolution* was passed by the General Assembly in November 1950, allowing action to be taken by the General Assembly when the work of the Security Council had collapsed as a result of the application of the veto by one of the permanent members. The representation of the permanent members was open to criticism for some years as, until replaced by Communist China in October 1971, Nationalist China continued to be a permanent member, in spite of the Communist victory in China 22 years previously.

The Security Council of the United Nations in session at New York. Despite the problem of the 'veto', it has continued to show a determination to work for world peace during the years since its creation in 1945.

The Secretariat, the organization's civil service, was fully international in composition. It was headed by the Secretary-General, who reported annually on the work of the United Nations to the General Assembly, who brought threats to peace to the immediate attention of the Security Council and who undertook much work on his own account for the preservation of peace. Some dedicated men have served the United Nations in the office of Secretary-General: Trygve Lie of Norway, Dag Hammarskjöld of Sweden, U Thant of Burma and Kurt Waldheim of Austria. In the early 1960s the Soviet Union proposed that the post of Secretary-General should be replaced by a *Troika* system, in which the office would be held by three men representing the Western powers, the Soviet powers and the non-aligned powers. The proposal, which was never put into effect, was designed to reduce what the Soviet Union held to be the strong Western influence generally associated with the office.

The United Nations International Court of Justice was almost identical in composition and function to the Permanent Court of International Justice of the League. Like its predecessor, it was located at the Hague and its judges, appointed from different member-countries, had the responsibility of giving legal rulings on international disputes sent to them by member-countries for their decision. The Court possesses no power for enforcing its decisions. It relies entirely in this matter on the voluntary implementation of its decision by the member-countries bringing the disputes to the court in the first place.

The work of the Mandates Commission

United Nations Specialized Agencies		
Initials	*Full title*	*Responsibilities*
UNICEF	United Nations Children's Emergency Fund	Health and welfare of children, especially at times of disaster.
UNESCO	United Nations Educational, Scientific and Cultural Organization	Promotion of education and curbing of illiteracy.
UNRWA	United Nations Relief and Works Agency	Relief work among political refugees. It has been especially important among the Palestinian Arabs.
ILO	International Labour Organization	Achievement of reasonable conditions for workers, especially in matters of pay, hours and job security.
FAO	Food and Agriculture Organization	Increase in the quantity and improvement in the quality of agricultural produce.
WHO	World Health Organization	Curbing of diseases by medical treatment and research.
IMF	International Monetary Fund	Distributing development loans from a fund to which all members contribute.
UNCTAD	United Nations Conference on Trade and Development	Promotion of closer trading links between developed and developing countries.

of the League was taken on by the Trustee-ship Council, which continued to supervize the administration of the earlier mandated territories, adding to their responsibilities former Axis colonies such as Libya. The main aim of the Trusteeship Council was the guidance of the *trust territories*, as the original mandates now came to be known, towards independence. The Trusteeship Council was given much fuller power than its predecessor to intervene in the administration of the trust territories and to ensure that they were properly administered, and that there was no undue delay in progress towards independence.

By the terms of the Charter, the United Nations was to give increased attention to improving the standards of living, especially of the poorer people, throughout the world. In this respect it built upon the work of the League, which had supervized the work of a number of international organizations.

HISTORY DOESN'T REPEAT ITSELF

The President of the United States gives a firm lead to the United Nations in 1950. The involvement of the new organization in many world disputes was more effective and more thorough than that of its predecessor.

Within the United Nations, the Economic and Social Council (ECOSOC) had responsibility for this work, which was largely undertaken through a series of specialized agencies. The most important of the specialized agencies are shown in the chart on page 339, together with their worldwide responsibilities.

The peacekeeping work of the United Nations

The United Nations efforts to preserve peace have been referred to on a number of occasions in the course of recent chapters. In this section, a summary of page references shows where fuller details of United Nations work can be found. The work of the United Nations in peacekeeping has taken three different forms: direct military involvement, a peacekeeping presence and economic sanctions.

crisis	pages
Korea	285–288
Congo	318–321
Middle East	234–242
Cyprus	183–184
Kashmir	224
Rhodesia	334
South Africa	328–329
Cuba	265–267

In the Korean War of the early 1950s and in the Congo War of the early 1960s United Nations troops, recruited from different countries, were sent to fight for the cause which the Security Council had considered worthy of support. This use of an international army was an innovation. Though the United Nations involvement in Korea and the Congo became a matter of sharp controversy, it did show a strong determination to act on what it judged to be the interests of world peace, even to the extent of using force to implement its decisions. By comparison, the League of Nations had no effective military support at its disposal.

On other occasions, United Nations troops were used as a type of police force in areas where there was continuing conflict between two groups of people. They did not involve themselves directly in the disputes that divided the area to which they were sent. They were to take military action only as a last resort, if under attack. A United Nations *presence* of this kind occurred in the Middle East for almost 11 years after the Suez crisis of 1956, in Cyprus after the outbreak of hostilities between Greeks and Turks in 1964, and in Kashmir after the ceasefire in the war of 1965. In all three cases, though the presence of the United Nations troops created a more stable atmosphere, it was not able to provide a long-term solution to the problems of the troubled areas: warfare has subsequently ravaged both the Middle East and Cyprus and the situation in Kashmir remains tense.

A useful but less forceful means by which the United Nations sought to influence countries which appeared to threaten world peace was the application of the method favoured earlier by the League, economic sanctions. These have been applied on the régimes in Rhodesia and South Africa. But sanctions appear to have made very little difference to the countries against which they have been applied.

The United Nations has therefore achieved only partial success in its peacekeeping work. Its inability to perform a useful role in the really serious crises that have occurred between the great powers has been a further disappointment to its supporters. Though an attempt was made by the United Nations to resolve the Cuban missiles crisis, the course of events in the autumn of 1962 was in fact dictated by the governments of the United States and the Soviet Union. Similarly in the conflicts concerning Berlin, in the lengthy war in Vietnam and in the later wars in the Middle East, the United Nations has played no crucial role. The main reason for this is the unwillingness of the countries involved to call on the help of the United Nations in seeking a solution. But the history of the United Nations is by no means one of gloom. In spite of disappointments, its continued existence shows a concern by the nations of the world for peace. More significant has been the wide scope of the work undertaken by the specialized agencies, whose contribution towards human welfare has been of vital importance in many developing countries.

Disarmament and arms limitation

In spite of immense efforts, no solid progress was made towards disarmament during the interwar years. This earlier lack of success led those who framed the United Nations Charter to take a realistic view and to emphasize instead the *regulation* of armaments. But knowledge of the destructive power of the atomic bomb, used in August 1945 just a few weeks after the Charter had been framed, inevitably produced worldwide demand for the abolition of such weapons. The United Nations set up an Atomic Energy committee in 1946, but neither it nor the Geneva Disarmament conference of 1952, with which it was later merged, was able to produce any agreement among the powers for the disarmament of their atomic weapons. In the meantime, by 1949, the Soviet Union had developed an atomic weapon, and research into the future development of such weapons in both the Soviet Union and the United States continued to produce weapons of increasingly destructive power. A balance of terror existed between the two power blocs of the Cold War by the 1950s.

Little success came from proposals by individual countries. In 1946 the American Baruch plan was an early, unsuccessful attempt to ensure that nuclear power was used solely for peaceful purposes. But to be certain that no nuclear weapons were being developed, inspection of a country's nuclear plant was needed, and no agreement could be reached on this essential issue. In 1957 the Polish Rapacki plan made proposals for a nuclear-free zone in central Europe, but this scheme also collapsed during negotiations.

Public opinion became rightly concerned in the late 1950s and early 1960s at the dangers to health created by the fallout from a series of nuclear tests conducted by the Soviet Union and the United States. The continuing intensity of the Berlin crisis in these years added to the concern that manifested itself in many protest movements urging nuclear disarmament. The development of satellites orbiting the earth added a further potential danger, by increasing the speed with which a nuclear attack could be made on an enemy country. In 1962 a new Disarmament conference met at Geneva, but though it was in session throughout the 1960s, it produced no firm results. Its discussions were inevitably weakened by the absence of two new nuclear powers. France refused to attend for reasons of prestige, believing that possession of an atomic bomb confirmed her rôle as a great power. Communist China was not permitted to attend as she still was not a member of the United Nations. Nevertheless, though there was little progress at Geneva, the conference did help to produce the Test Ban treaty in 1963, signed by the Soviet Union, the United States and Britain, all of whom agreed not to conduct nuclear tests in the atmosphere. In the same year a 'hot line' of telephone contact was established between Moscow and Washington to provide immediate telephone contact between the governments of the Soviet Union and the United States during a time of crisis.

By the late 1960s attention was directed less at disarmament itself and more at arms limitation. The 1968 Non-Proliferation treaty was designed to prevent the spread of nuclear weapons by agreement among some countries with nuclear power not to assist any other country in the development of such weapons, and, among countries without nuclear power, not to develop such weapons of their own accord. It was unfortunate that a number of non-nuclear countries, among them West Germany, Israel, Japan and South Africa, refused to sign the treaty; nor did the nuclear powers of France and China. At the end of 1969, the Soviet Union and the United States began the Strategic Arms Limitation Talks (SALT) with the aim of the mutual limitation of their own nuclear weapons. These talks continued periodically into the 1970s. In 1973 the SALT 1 agreement was signed. Further negotiations were slow-moving, but in the summer of 1979 the SALT 2 agreement was signed in Vienna by Secretary Brezhnev and President Carter. Some of Carter's American critics considered the agreements undermined the security of the United States; others in America and elsewhere felt that both SALT agreements were too limited and looked forward to a more far-reaching agreement in the 1980s.

The destructive potential of their weapons was not the only reason that brought these super-powers together in the SALT talks. In a decade of widespread economic difficulty, the vast cost of these nuclear weapons was an increasingly serious factor to these powers, whose economic difficulties would be eased if there could be a limitation on the production of nuclear weapons. Another factor was the atmosphere of détente in the 1970s, which made possible the holding of the talks in the first place. Though, therefore, some progress in arms limitation has been made, the destructive potential of nuclear weapons remains one of the most serious threats to mankind in the closing years of the twentieth century.

Questions

88. Study the cartoon on page 340 and then answer questions (a) to (c) which follow.

(a) By reference to events during the 1930s, examine the extent to which the inscription on the tomb is justified.

(6)

(b) (i) Give the name of the man shown in the cartoon,
   (ii) give the name of the country to which he was leading his companion,
   (iii) explain the reasons why he is shown hand-in-hand with his companion, and
   (iv) explain the reasons why the ghostly figure reacts as she does.

(1+1+3+2)

(c) Describe the circumstances in *two* areas of the world where the man's companion intervened less violently than is shown here. For *each* of the areas you select, show the importance of the work that she undertook.

(7)

89. Show the importance of the peacekeeping work of the United Nations since the time of its foundation, in any *three* areas of the world.

90. Describe the attempts that have been made since 1945 to disarm, and to limit weapons of warfare. Why have these attempts not met with greater success?

Glossary of terms as used in the text

autarky   A system of economic self-sufficiency for a country, designed partly to reduce imports to a minimum.

balance of payments   The difference between the value of a country's imports and the value of its exports.

capitalism   The organization of the social and economic life of a country on the basis of private enterprise and private property.

coexistence   Agreement by Communist and non-Communist powers to live in peace with each other.

constituent assembly   A body elected with the main purpose of creating a new constitution for a country.

constitution   The set of rules by which a country is governed.

containment   Preventing any further expansion of Communist power, thus 'containing' it within the limits it has already reached.

coup (d'état)   Translated literally from the French it means a *blow of state*. It refers to a sudden and illegal change of government.

détente   Improved relations between Communist and non-Communist countries. It refers in particular to the attempt to improve relations in the 1970s between the Soviet Union and the United States.

devaluation   The lowering of the value of a country's currency in relation to the currencies of other countries, thus making exports cheaper.

devolution (of power)   The granting of specific powers of government to regional administrations within a country.

federation   The grouping together of different regions, states or countries for the purpose of common government.

free trade   The absence of protective tariffs on goods entering a country.

left (-wing)   A political attitude, which generally favours reforming change.

legislature   A law-making body, usually called a parliament, chamber or assembly.

majority rule   A constitutional system in which the government is elected by a majority of the adult population, regardless of colour or belief.

mandates   Colonies of countries defeated in the First World War which, subject to the supervision of the League of Nations, were to be administered by countries victorious in the war, referred to in this respect as *mandatories*.

minority government   A government whose continuance in power depends on the parliamentary support of political parties other than its own.

neo-colonialism   Attempts by great powers to assert their influence in countries which have achieved independence.

non-aligned   A term used to describe those countries which support neither Communist nor non-Communist powers in world relations.

personality cult   The placing of excessive emphasis on the personality of a country's leader.

proletariat   People without property, who are therefore compelled to earn their living by their own labour.

proportional representation   A system of election in which the number of elected politicians is directly linked to the number of votes cast for their party in the election.

protection   The economic policy of placing tariffs on imports, in order to provide economic 'protection' for home-produced goods.

putsch   The German word for a *coup d'état*, explained above.

referendum   A vote by the people of a country on a particular issue of their country's policy. The term *plebiscite* refers to the same thing.

revisionism   An attempt to compromise the doctrines of Communism, in order to develop better relations with the West.

right (-wing)   A political attitude which generally represents property and status and which seeks to defend the country's traditions.

sino-   A reference to *China* when used together with the name of another country.

supra-national   A term used to describe a body which seeks to advance the interests of an international body, regardless of the particular, individual interests of its member-nations.

third world   The poor countries of Asia, Africa and Latin America.

veto   Power given to a country or organization to prevent, in certain circumstances, action which others have agreed to.

Index

Numbers in *italics* indicate maps.

INDEX